OTHER WORLDS

Other Worlds

Spirituality and the Search for Invisible Dimensions

CHRISTOPHER G. WHITE

HARVARD UNIVERSITY PRESS
Cambridge, Massachusetts & London, England / 2018

First Printing

Library of Congress Cataloging-in-Publication Data

Names: White, Christopher G., 1969– author.
Title: Other worlds : spirituality and the search for invisible
dimensions / Christopher G. White.
Description: Cambridge, Massachusetts : Harvard University Press,
2018. | Includes bibliographical references and index.
Identifiers: LCCN 2017041042 | ISBN 9780674984295
(hardcover : alk. paper)
Subjects: LCSH: Religion and science—United States. | Religion and
science—Great Britain. | Arts and religion—United States. | Arts and
religion—Great Britain. | Fourth dimension. | Hyperspace.
Classification: LCC BL240.3 .W485 2018 | DDC 201/.65—dc23
LC record available at https://lccn.loc.gov/2017041042

For Tracy

CONTENTS

It would seem that mythological worlds have been built up only to be shattered again, and that new worlds were built from the fragments.

—FRANZ BOAZ,
in James Teit, *Traditions of the Thompson
River Indians of British Columbia*

Introduction

Science, the Supernatural, and Higher Realms

I t is a remarkable fact that in modern Europe and America institutional religion has declined while belief in God and the supernatural has remained strong and in some settings has even increased. Recent surveys, for example, show that while a declining group of Americans regularly go to church or synagogue (20–30 percent), overwhelming majorities of Americans report believing in a God who responds to prayer (80–90 percent), in angels and demons who actively interact with the living (70 percent), or in a heavenly afterlife that welcomes the souls of the departed (70–85 percent). An astonishing 30 percent of Americans report that they have been "in touch" with someone who has died.[1] Similar data are also available for European nations, which report even lower levels of religious affiliation but an explosion of self-identified "spiritual but not religious" people. There are many reasons for the distaste for institutional religion, and these reasons have been well documented. Less understood, however, is how this cresting wave of those who refuse to affiliate with traditional religions formulate new, spiritual views of the world. The more one thinks about it, the more puzzling the issue becomes. How can people who reject the institutions that have anchored supernatural worldviews for millennia now speak confidently about the existence of unseen heavenly landscapes, guardian angels, or other supernatural realities? Out of what raw materials have they developed new ways of imagining these things?

I began thinking about these questions while researching an earlier book that examined how Americans used psychological sciences to re-imagine religious experiences, faith development, and ways of thinking about spirit and spirituality.[2] When beginning that book I assumed that the important conversations between scientists and religious people were those that took place between psychologists and theologians discussing religion and spirituality. But I discovered that scientists in a number of different fields were talking about issues such as faith, free will, miracles, consciousness, and immortality. I discovered Christians, Jews, and agnostics borrowing from the natural sciences, and from physics in particular, as they thought about the place of supernatural miracles in a natural world, as they imagined the precise geographies of the heavens, as they speculated about the possibilities of alternate dimensions and the location of a spirit realm, if one existed. The number of books, articles, and sermons about physics, faith, and philosophy in the twentieth century was astonishing—and they included books by the architects of modern physics, books such as Arthur Eddington's *The Nature of the Physical World* (1928), Niels Bohr's *Causality and Complementarity* (1950), and Werner Heisenberg's *Physics and Philosophy* (1958). It also was surprising to find nonscientists acknowledging again and again that scientific research, not literature or religion, provided the imaginative framework for modern life. "In our own day," the progressive editor Herbert Croly insisted in *The New Republic* in 1922, "experimental science furnishes the vital conception of reality."[3]

Croly's testimony and the testimony of others like him made me think that scientific ideas had taken a central role in the West's imaginative life that we had yet to appreciate adequately. Over time I became more and more interested in how scientific ideas had shaped modern western worldviews and religious or spiritual views in particular.

In this book I examine how key scientific assumptions, ideas, and even technologies have shaped religious and spiritual views in Europe and America since the nineteenth century. I do this by exploring the remarkable history and imaginative power of one scientific idea in particular, an idea that has become crucial in many settings, from modern physics to fantasy literature and science-fiction television—namely, the idea that the universe has higher, invisible dimensions. I analyze how scientists, mathematicians, writers, artists, screenwriters, theologians, televangelists, and others have used this idea to make supernatural phenomena such as ghosts and miracles seem more reasonable and make spiritual beliefs possible again for themselves and others. By showing how scientific insights were used sometimes not to attack spiritual beliefs but to buttress them in unexpected ways, this book revises the conventional way of speaking about the modern "conflict between science and religion." Scientific ideas have not just fostered secularity and religious decline but have also been used to help people believe in the existence of unseen, heavenly realms and recover an imaginative sense for the supernatural.

What is a higher dimension and how might this scientific idea be "spiritual"? Though the idea of a higher dimension might initially seem difficult to grasp, the basic concept is very simple. A dimension is just a direction in space, such as left/right or up/down. For instance, a line has one direction or dimension, length. A square has two dimensions, length and width. A cube has three dimensions, length, width and depth. Everything in our world is (or at least appears to be) three-dimensional. A higher, invisible dimension therefore is a direction or a dimension in space that is somehow beyond our familiar three dimensions. Could objects have length, width, depth—and something else? Could there be another direction or dimension in reality that we cannot see or perceive? These questions emerged during the last 150 years in part because scientists developed mathematical models of the universe that incorporated higher-dimensional spaces. (They did this in order to develop simpler, more elegant, or more encompassing mathematical models of the universe's laws and forces.) For the most part scientists developing these models thought of higher-dimensional spaces as spaces that existed wholly within nature. In other words, one could not see or perceive them, but they were nevertheless physical spaces.

But a few mathematicians and scientists, and certainly many nonscientists, embraced the idea of higher dimensions as a more scientific way of suggesting a space *beyond* physical reality. As this book will show, the idea of higher dimensions has helped many people imagine and believe in the existence of what we might call "spiritual" things—supernatural beings, layers, or levels of existence. These ways of talking about higher dimensions have sometimes irritated secular scientists and mathematicians, but they nevertheless have inspired a remarkably creative array of imaginative books, theological reflections, fantastic fictions, otherworldly TV programs, new religious convictions, and assorted manifestoes concerning paranormal phenomena, uncanny dreams, and the afterlife. In fact, one of this book's unexpected discoveries is that many people in the last century have developed new spiritual views not by relying on older religious concepts but instead by borrowing apparently secular scientific notions. Many have exchanged an older, religious way of talking about the supernatural with what I am calling here a *more scientific supernatural*. I understand a *more scientific supernatural* as a category of things that 1) are either beyond nature or at its boundary and 2) are suggested by scientific theory or empirical evidence while also at least partially eluding scientific tests, instruments, or measurements.

◡◡◡◡

This book focuses more on how scientific ideas get repurposed in popular culture than it does on the history of scientific discoveries themselves, but some attention to the history of key ideas in mathematics and physics is necessary in order to understand how these ideas have been linked to shifting popular discourses on the universe's boundaries and ultimate meaning.

Scientific ideas have shaped (and been shaped by) religious views since the scientific revolution, but in the nineteenth century scientific ideas became more authoritative and reached further into popular culture. In this century of modernization and cultural change, scientists developed scholarly journals, professional associations, and university departments, elevating science to an unprecedented level of cultural power and prestige. As a result, other respected forms of knowledge, including theology in particular, were challenged and displaced. Nineteenth-century biologists, geologists, and physicists, for instance, produced new facts about the world that did not always comport with traditional Christian wisdom or doctrine. Scientific pronouncements on the earth's age and evolution contradicted older religious ways of thinking. New ideas in physics forced people to exchange an older, providential god who miraculously intervened in the natural world for a new god with little room to act in a universe of ironclad laws of cause and effect.[4] It was for this reason that the nineteenth-century Biblical scholar David Strauss, observing the matter with relative composure, quipped that deterministic natural laws had created an unprecedented "housing problem" for God.[5] In the modern world, God no longer had anywhere to live.

At the root of these specific difficulties, however, something deeper was in play, an alteration in background assumptions and worldview. Though specific Biblical stories and doctrines were challenged by new ideas, the deeper problem was the emergence of a new scientific world-view that glossed the universe as a closed system of facts governed by unchanging laws. According to this way of thinking, producing knowl-edge involved empirically studying nature's facts and using them to un-derstand better the laws that structured all aspects of the universe. The result was that talking about God, angels, or other invisible things sud-denly seemed hopelessly unempirical and thus unproductive of real knowledge. Historians examining this era have argued that the resulting "lust for empirical proof" eroded religious belief and "increasingly gave industrial man a worldview in which intangible reality had no place."[6] The great German sociologist Max Weber, who himself collected facts and discovered exact laws of human behavior, summarized the situa-tion, not without regret, by saying that the effort to master and control all things through scientific rationality meant the obliteration of the "mysterious incalculable forces" believed in by earlier generations. The modern world, he said famously, had become "disenchanted."[7]

But in the shadows of this outwardly secularized world of natural facts lurked elusive forces, energies, and other realities that remained stubbornly incalculable or defied simple explanation. Some of these realities were brought to light by Albert Einstein, whose theories of Special Relativity (1905) and then General Relativity (1915) seemed to demonstrate that nature behaved in unexpected and even confounding ways. His theories, for example, showed that clocks ticked more slowly the faster they traveled; that events that were simultaneous to one ob-server were not simultaneous to others; that gravity caused time to slow down; that space could be bent and distorted by large objects; and that energy and mass, which most people thought of as different entities, were actually interchangeable.

Then, in the 1920s, when quantum mechanical laws governing the behavior of elementary particles were discovered, nature came into focus as even more complex and difficult to fathom. The first baffling thing about quantum mechanics was that it could not (and cannot still) be combined or reconciled with Einstein's General Relativity. This immediately presented a difficult problem for those who believed that the universe was determined by one set of facts and laws. Relativity correctly described the behavior of large things in the cosmos, and quantum mechanics correctly described the behavior of small things in the subatomic world, but the two sets of laws did not fit together. How could the natural world be governed by two incompatible sets of laws and mathematical equations? Were there two (or more) separate worlds or layers within nature, worlds with different characteristics and rules? Moreover, if this were true, if there were separate layers or realms within nature, might there be other kinds of openings and layers—including, some audacious seekers wondered, a layer of supernatural things?

Quantum mechanical laws posed other puzzles and problems for the deterministic universe posited by earlier scientists, revealing a natural world with elusive and mysterious elements that were difficult to entirely map out, calculate, and master. The German physicist Max Planck was the first to notice that Newtonian physics could not explain certain phenomena, such as the odd behavior of light, which sometimes appeared to be a continuous electromagnetic wave and at other times seemed to be comprised of discontinuous energy packets. Planck, Albert Einstein, Niels Bohr, and others gradually demonstrated that light and indeed all other subatomic objects had both wave and particle characteristics. (Einstein was awarded a Nobel Prize in 1921 for discovering that light waves delivered their energy in particle-like packets.) In certain experiments elementary particles behaved like spread-out waves; in others they banged around like energetic marbles. Their appearance depended on how scientists observed them. A confounding puzzle emerged: Why would the smallest building blocks of nature appear different depending on how scientists looked at them? Max Born, who won a Nobel Prize in 1954, arrived at the startling formulation that elementary particles were merely "tendencies to exist," he said, that became (what we call) particles when we added the element of "looking" at them. Was physical reality somehow constituted or at least influenced by our observation of it? Today a number of physicists and even more mystics and spiritual seekers insist that consciousness somehow shapes physical reality.

(Convinced that nature operated according to more deterministic laws, Einstein could not embrace the accepted view that human consciousness somehow affected the nature of physical reality. "Do you really think the moon isn't there," he once quipped, irritated, "if you aren't looking at it?"[8] Of course the moon behaves in expected ways, but Einstein was wrong about super-small quantum things: They actually do exist in a fuzzy, indeterminate reality. Moreover, Einstein refused to accept an additional phenomenon described by quantum mechanical laws, the entanglement of particles separated across vast distances, such that what happens to one instantaneously affects the other. He derided this concept as "spooky action at a distance"—but this "spooky" phenomenon has now been experimentally verified many times over.)

One way of summing up the situation is by saying that physics has recently returned to the modern world-picture some of those "mysterious incalculable forces" that Max Weber thought had been banished forever. Though physicists generally eschew philosophical speculation, a number of prominent early quantum physicists, as well as mystically minded scientists beginning in the freewheeling 1960s, indulged speculative instincts and linked ideas in physics to philosophical issues such as free will, the mind/body problem, the mystery of consciousness, and the possibility that our world is an "open world" that incorporates a divine consciousness or transcendent dimension. Some of the boldest speculations have come from a post-1960s cabal of "hippie physicists" writing about human psychic powers, the wave/particle duality of matter, and eastern mysticism. (Ridiculed as bad science by many scientists, their increasingly popular metaphysical speculations might more profitably be understood as part of a changing western worldview, reminding us of Alfred North Whitehead's astute observation that inherited ideas, including religious ones, are modified and reimagined in every age as a result of new scientific advances.)[9] One of this group's best-known publications was Fritjof Capra's *The Tao of Physics: An Exploration of the Parallels between Modern Physics and Eastern Mysticism* (1975), which pursued in detail the physics-mysticism parallels initially identified by quantum physicists such as Bohr and Heisenberg.

The book has inspired numerous publications with similar aims and has been published in more than forty-three editions and twenty-three languages.[10]

In general, it is hard not to notice that apparently secular scientific discourses have become sources for new enchanted worldviews of uncanny invisible forces, and transcendent cosmic layers and spaces. It is this surprising development that forms the backdrop for this book.

∽∿∿∿∾

In the course of moving from the more closed, deterministic world of nineteenth-century science to this more open-world physics of uncanny wonders and hidden realities, there was one scientific notion above all that disillusioned skeptics, spiritual scientists, and religious seekers used to help them recover an imaginative sense for the supernatural—namely, the idea that the universe has higher dimensions. The notion that our universe has hidden locations, dimensions, or spaces is one that has fascinated Europeans and Americans, spiritual and secular, from the nineteenth century to today.[11]

In retelling the remarkable history of this concept, there is no better place to begin than with two British thinkers, Edwin A. Abbott and C. Howard Hinton, whose higher-dimensional thought experiments and imaginative stories have been borrowed and repurposed again and again. Abbott, who I examine in Chapter 1, published in 1884 a novel about higher dimensions that eventually would go through over twenty editions, be translated into twenty-three languages, and inspire at least six book-length spinoffs and three films, including a full-length 2007 animated film with voices by Martin Sheen and Kristen Bell.[12] *Flatland* is set in a two-dimensional universe where flat characters slide around in their 2D world unaware of the existence of a higher third dimension. At the novel's climactic moment, the main character, an unnamed flat Square, encounters a three-dimensional Sphere who suddenly inserts himself into the Square's world, insisting that there is another dimension, an "up" that the Square cannot perceive or even imagine. The Square finds this notion unbelievable until the Sphere, determined to win the argument, pulls the Square out of his flat world and up into three-dimensional space. It is there that the Square discovers something astonishing:

Flatland actually was part of a much greater, higher-dimensional world.

In *Flatland* Abbott borrowed mathematical ideas about higher dimensions in order to make higher realms seem more reasonable, to argue against older, religious ways of thinking about these higher realms, and to suggest that there might be a more credible, authoritative way of talking about the supernatural. Abbott's way of developing a more scientific supernatural would be borrowed by later thinkers struggling to imagine how there could be a higher, spiritual realm above our familiar world, thinkers that include the Christian writers C. S. Lewis and Madeleine L'Engle, the American evangelical megachurch pastor Rob Bell, and many others.[13]

Many readers were content to embrace Abbott's essential message, which was that human beings, like flatlanders, might live entirely ignorant of a higher-dimensional reality above them; but others wished to go beyond merely entertaining this stimulating conjecture, developing ambitious proposals to imagine and even see into higher-dimensional worlds. Abbott's contemporary, for instance, an Oxford-educated mathematician and social reformer named C. Howard Hinton, developed a system of visualizing higher dimensions that his mathematical colleagues found difficult to fathom, that detractors linked to hallucination and mental illness, and that religious believers used to develop mystical powers of vision and insight. He disseminated his ideas in a series of books and articles, including several articles in popular periodicals such as *Harper's Magazine,* attempting to show audiences that higher dimensions existed and that there were specific ways to train the self to "see" into them. Hinton's work was particularly effective in spreading higher-dimensional ideas to religious believers, artists, writers, and even mathematicians and scientists who felt that scientific materialism had imprisoned them in ironclad spaces bereft of human feeling, imaginative freedom, or spiritual transcendence. Hinton's controversial life and his arguments with other mathematicians are examined in Chapter 2, and the widespread impact of his ideas on conceptions of spirituality, social reform, race, and gender are surveyed in Chapter 3.

Though Hinton's meditations and imaginative exercises sometimes elicited denunciations from mathematicians who claimed he misused mathematical concepts, and though his work also provoked caveats and warnings from concerned physicians and other observers, his system also stimulated revelatory visions in people who believed that older, religious methods for finding God needed to be replaced in what was obviously a new era of scientific discovery and perceptive vision.[14] Several modern artists in particular took this view. Chapters 4 and 5 examine several of them, beginning with the American artist, architect, and spiritual seeker Claude Bragdon, who after Hinton's 1907 death became the preeminent public philosopher of higher dimensions. (Sometimes these thinkers are also called "hyperspace philosophers.")

Designing buildings in New York with mathematically balanced proportions borrowed from musical scales and other natural patterns; creating art and music festivals in parks such as New York City's Central Park with higher-dimensional lanterns and decorations; installing higher-dimensional designs in churches and theaters; and deploying a type of fourth-dimensional architectural ornamentation that he believed would counteract the ugliness and noise of the modern city, Bragdon tried to find ways of making the universe's underlying structures and higher spiritual spaces visible in geometric artwork and architectural design. He wanted to remind people that reality contained a higher world of perfect symmetry, unity, and composure.

Bragdon was not the only artist to use higher-dimensional motifs to attempt to probe the deeper, supernatural elements of reality. In the early twentieth century, many modern artists believed that poets and artists, not prophets and priests, saw into the deepest, spiritual dimensions of reality. Max Weber, Wassily Kandinsky, Francis Picabia, Juan Gris, Kazimir Malevich, and Salvador Dalí attempted to depict reality's more fundamental, spiritual elements by borrowing new ideas about geometry, space, and higher dimensions. The Russian-American painter Max Weber in particular, who is profiled in Chapter 5, used ideas from geometry and higher-dimensional theory in order to understand better the basic spiritual elements of reality and how these elements might structure new ways of seeing the traditional Judaism of his childhood, making it more scientific, modern, and (thus) believable. Like others in this book, Weber borrowed ideas from mathematics and science in order to develop a more authoritative way of talking about and representing spiritual realities.

When Hinton and others had momentary glimpses of higher-dimensional realities, they perceived that at higher levels all things, even all time frames, were united in a single, massive reality. This insight had various consequences in popular culture, examined in different parts of this book, including the idea, deployed by thinkers such as W. E. B. Du Bois, that a higher-dimensional perspective made possible new ways to imagine race and the social order.

But if everything was indeed contained within a single reality block at higher levels, what did this mean for our conceptions of time? Were "the past" and "the future" simply part of one unified and unchanging reality? Chapter 6 takes up this question by examining unusual wartime experiences of soldiers who had altered experiences of time and unusual dreams that seemed to predict the future. This chapter focuses in particular on the higher-dimensional time theories of the British aeronautical engineer John W. Dunne, whose widely read *An Experiment with Time* (1927) used Hinton's hyperspace theories and Einstein's ideas about relative time frames to explain his predictive dreams and nightmares. Arguing that consciousness contained multiple time "observers" that perceived things from different time dimensions, Dunne believed that everyone had a dreaming self that could rise up, like Abbott's Square protagonist, into a higher-dimensional space where it might view reality as a whole. Certain that predictive dreams were common, Dunne encouraged readers to keep their own bedside journals. Dunne's views and his journaling practices inspired many who were seeking ways of transcending the terrors of life during the First and Second World Wars, including H. G. Wells, the British broadcaster and novelist J. B. Priestley, and Christian writers such as J. R. R. Tolkien and C. S. Lewis.

The transcendent dreaming of Dunne, the visionary art and architecture of Weber and Bragdon, and the imaginative meditations of a host of higher-dimensional mystics and reformers can all be seen as ways of displacing traditional religion, which seemed dogmatic, unscientific, institutional, and impersonal, and substituting instead alternative modes of metaphysical speculation and spiritual imagining. This same substitution of imaginative and spiritual for dogmatic and religious continues in Chapters 7 and 8, which examine science-fiction and fantasy writers who used mathematical and scientific ideas to help themselves and others visualize, imagine, or believe in a level or dimension beyond the range of the senses. Here again those who lost or doubted childhood faiths would reimagine supernatural things by appropriating from scientific discourses discussing higher dimensions. Many well-known writers did this, including J. R. R. Tolkien, C. S. Lewis, and Madeleine L'Engle.

One of the best-known spiritual writers in the last fifty years, Madeleine L'Engle, has a particularly important story that is examined in Chapter 8. L'Engle used her fantastic fiction as the setting in which new scientific concepts could be combined with older Biblical tropes in more credible narratives that she thought were inspired and revelatory. Her new narratives drew on recent discoveries in physics and mathematics, and, as in her iconic *Wrinkle in Time* (1962), she used ideas such as Hinton's tesseract (a four-dimensional cube) to open imaginative doorways into other times, spaces, and dimensions. For L'Engle, however, making the supernatural and transcendent believable again also meant rewriting Biblical narratives and myths devised by male Christians such as C. S. Lewis, stories that had not granted girls and women a full humanity or a share in divinity. In L'Engle's work, then, tesseracts and other otherworldly openings did not just help readers imagine new spaces that liberated souls from our mechanized and secular world; they also opened up ways of thinking about the social order and laid out new possibilities for women and girls, who in L'Engle's hands became angels, heroes, and prophetic figures central to modern sacred narratives and other ways of thinking about ultimate things.

Today we live in a time of proliferating scientific theories of alternate worlds, parallel realities, and multiverses, not to mention the virtually unlimited science fiction and fantasy otherworlds imagined in ongoing entertainment franchises such as *Star Trek, Star Wars,* or *Harry Potter,* to name just a few. How is one to describe these recent developments and sum up a book on the imaginative and spiritual power of higher-dimensional ideas? In Chapter 9 and in the Conclusion I foreground recent fictional and nonfictional, scientific and spiritual, borrowings from the higher-dimensional tradition that began with Abbott, Hinton, and Bragdon. I examine spiritualists who saw spirits through TV static, spirit channelers who conducted technological séances, and Pentecostal televangelists who used electronic media as openings to other dimensions.

I investigate how sci-fi writers, scientists, mathematicians, and artists, attempting to expand the modern metaphysical imagination, have borrowed from and repurposed Abbott's classic novella *Flatland*. It turns out that physicists have used this story to introduce the public to higher-dimensional ideas in string theory, brane theory, and multiverse theory; that religious scientists and "spiritual but not religious" writers have borrowed it when trying to conceptualize what might lie beyond this world; and that many people who have studied or experienced near-death experiences have used it when talking about the altered geometry of a heavenly afterlife. Abbott's imaginative ideas, as well as Hinton's, have rippled through literature and television, fiction and nonfiction, reshaping how we see and depict the imagined worlds we live in.

This book assembles an unusual cast of characters—visionary mathematicians, mystical physicists, spirit channelers, fantasy writers, television producers, hippie scientists, New Age prophets, social reformers, indefatigable parapsychologists, and utopian artists. It brings them together in order to get at something elusive but important—how Americans and Europeans in the last 150 years, people with widely diverging temperaments and interests, with secular and spiritual commitments, with elite and popular sensibilities, strategically borrowed mathematical and scientific concepts to recover hope in a supernatural beyond.

Part of the reason I have gathered together this diverse group is to make a larger point that scientific and religious ideas always come braided together and that they influence and shape each other to a degree that has gone unnoticed for several reasons, including the fact that until recently cultural elites and other commentators have held simplistic, reified views about science and religion and have often understood them as implacable enemies. For many years, for example, those examining these subjects have focused on how doubt led to religious decline and secularization: Christians discovered critical perspectives and came to believe in, and practice, their religion with less and less fervor. But while certain forms of decline and negation did take place, there were other, equally important moments of reconstruction and affirmation. For even though some found they could not salvage doctrines and practices from their childhood religions, many others did not entirely abandon religious perspectives or ways of seeing the world. There certainly was, as I have said, a decline in traditional religion; but we might also say that the "religious" element in culture was refigured and changed, relocated in other activities, made more individual and private, shorn of institutional ties, and made more dependent on dual sources of authority in the self and a reconceived supernatural—in short, made into something many people now call *the spiritual*.[15]

How individuals did this, how they improvised new ways of talking about spirit and the supernatural, how they stitched together, using both secular and religious ideas, the spiritual worlds that many modern people now inhabit, is this book's focus. It is a process marked by rhythms of decline and revival, despair and hope, existential crisis and recovery. It involves painful and difficult change. The anthropologist Franz Boas once captured well the laborious, even traumatic, nature of this process while talking about cultural change in a different context—"It would seem that mythological worlds have been built up only to be shattered again, and that new worlds were built from the fragments."[16] The problem, however, is that when scholars talk about spiritual seekers such as those examined here—sometimes using the word "bricoleur" (tinkerers or handymen) for these figures—they tend to celebrate their expansive creativity, their unfettered freedom, their mix-and-match eclecticism. But there is an unseen, tragic dimension to their lives. Before they could develop new views, before they could build up new convictions or piece together a new sacred cosmos, their world had to become incoherent and full of gaps—"shattered," as Boaz astutely observed, into fragments. People who lived through these types of situations and had the courage to face them were not usually freewheeling iconoclasts who joyfully mixed and matched traditions; they were figures who struggled to prevent their lives from collapsing and falling apart.

And thus we return to the life and many tribulations of Edwin A. Abbott, who, before creating his other-dimensional landscapes in his classic *Flatland*, studied science and the humanities as a student at Cambridge University until one day when, to his surprise and terror, he felt the last inner supports of his faith wobble and crash to the ground.

1

Edwin Abbott's Otherworldly Visions

The problem, in short, was miracles. Like others coming of age during the middle of the nineteenth century, Edwin Abbott came to suspect that the Bible's miracle stories, long regarded as indisputable evidence of the truth and superiority of Christianity, might be myths of uncertain religious value and historical accuracy. There were different reasons miracle stories were called into question, but the most important was that they seemed to contradict a scientific idea that was just then gaining wide acceptance. The idea that emerged in this period, one articulated forcefully in such works as Charles Lyell's *Principles of Geology* (1830–1833) and William Whewell's *Astronomy and General Physics Considered with Reference to Natural Theology* (1833), was that there was one set of natural laws that governed everything that happened in the universe, at all times, past and present. Whewell called this "uniformitarianism," and this concept anchored a new nineteenth-century worldview. When this uniformitarianism was applied to religion, as it was, for example, by nineteenth-century Biblical scholars, it reinforced the idea that events in Biblical times, including Jesus's earthly life and ministry, must have unfolded according to the orderly laws of nature.

Like others, Abbott saw that holding this view and pressing it to its logical conclusion meant also calling into question several deeply held convictions. If Jesus's life proceeded merely according to nature's unchanging laws; if his extraordinary wisdom and healing power were somehow the result of universal natural forces operating everywhere in uniform ways; if even the most remarkable events of his life, including his Resurrection, long considered the decisive proof of the transcendent power of his religion, could now be understood merely as natural, psychological, or social facts—if these new interpretations were possible, and if Christianity was a natural rather than a supernatural phenomenon, what was the status of Christian doctrines and truth claims? Was it possible to talk any longer about Christianity as divine, supernatural, or extraordinary in any way?

The ability to ignore these unsettling questions was made difficult by a new group of Bible scholars who treated the sacred text not with warm sympathy but with a cool, analytical skepticism. Edwin Abbott encountered these scholars and their work while at Cambridge and was disturbed by the questions they raised. But the biggest jolt came three years after taking his degree, in 1864, when he read the German Biblical critic David Strauss's explosive *Life of Jesus* (1835), a book that caused Christians in Europe in America to be paralyzed, one commentator noted, "with terror."[1] The reasons were plain enough—Strauss's book scrutinized the New Testament's miraculous narratives and concluded that they were inconsistent and unreliable as history, contrary to the laws of science, and fabricated by a prescientific people out of their own expectations and superstitious imaginings. The book "made me miserable," Abbott told a friend, forcing him to "think little of my judgment" and question truths previously considered unassailable. At his lowest point he wondered if he could sustain basic religious beliefs. (His predicament was made more difficult by the fact that just months prior to reading Strauss he was ordained an Anglican priest.) He decided to try to ignore his most destructive thoughts, to "suspend" them, he said, and merely go through the motions of prayer and worship, acts of willpower and grit that not all of his clerical colleagues were able to muster.[2]

Gradually the environment of skepticism in nineteenth-century England became pervasive. The biologist then promoting Darwin's new theory of evolution, Thomas Henry Huxley, found it necessary to create a word that described the state of not knowing if God existed, "agnosticism," in 1869. Prominent Christians, such as the Cambridge philosopher Henry Sidgwick, whose work Abbott knew well, and the chaplain Stopford Brooke, abandoned their churches because they could no longer profess inherited creeds or believe in prescientific teachings. Even Abbott's close friend from Cambridge, John Seeley, published in 1866 a book analyzing Jesus as a Jewish reformer and moral teacher rather than a miracle worker, a book that raised such frightening religious doubts that the Seventh Earl of Shaftsbury, putting a fine point on popular reaction to the text, called "the most pestilential book ever vomited out of the jaws of hell."[3] These were signs of the times: Many wondered if one had to believe every word of the Bible in order to be Christian. Did one have to believe for instance that Lot's wife had been turned into a pillar of salt or that a fish swallowed Jonah—when these tales obviously contradicted reason and science?

In time Abbott was able to recover from these doubts and help others reimagine the Christian tradition in new ways that comported with modern conceptions of science and nature. He did this in many publications throughout his life. He wrote popular books that argued that some Biblical miracles conveyed deep spiritual lessons and might actually be "natural and credible" when understood using newer scientific principles. He wrote columns and tracts in which he promoted a rational Christianity positioned in-between unbelieving agnostics on the one hand and superstitious Roman Catholics on the other. He fashioned several book-length fictional narratives about reasonable figures who lived during the time of Christ's apostles. He wrote accessible theological works "to the very large number of the young who, year by year, are rejecting Christianity because they say they find themselves unable to believe in it," offering them a Christianity of "love, trust and awe" that did not require belief in "anything that is unnatural or incredible."[4] And between the 1870s and his death in 1926, he published a set of remarkably detailed and learned volumes of Biblical scholarship that carefully examined the gospel narratives in particular, volumes that he believed would be his lasting contribution to posterity.

Though Abbott was an astute observer of people and events, on this matter, on the matter of his legacy, he erred to a remarkable degree, for his many erudite volumes of theology and Biblical criticism, so urgently researched and carefully written, were within a generation almost entirely cast aside.

Instead, a most unexpected thing happened—a small work of fiction he published in 1884 became not merely his best-known book (by a wide margin) but also his most successful intervention in the ongoing struggle to develop a believable, modern form of faith. Since its original publication in 1884, *Flatland* has become a classic text, read by science fiction fans, mathematics students, and spiritual seekers. It has gone through numerous editions, been translated into twenty-three different languages, and inspired sequels, spinoffs, and films.[5] Written by a theologian and incorporating both mathematical and science-fictional elements, *Flatland* has sometimes puzzled commentators, but a close reading of the novel reveals it to be an ingenious way to speak in scientific ways to key philosophical and religious concerns. Here as elsewhere Abbott tries to show that apparently miraculous events could have reasonable and scientifically plausible explanations. In particular, *Flatland* uses mathematical and geometrical ideas to suggest that there were reasonable ways of both imagining the existence of supernatural entities and explaining how these entities might appear in our lower plane of existence.

The *Flatland* Narrative

Flatland is written in the voice of an unnamed narrator, a square-shaped Flatlander who experienced remarkable dreams and visions and decided to write about them. "I call our world Flatland, not because we call it so," the Square began, "but to make its nature clearer to you, my happy readers, who are privileged to live in Space." The Square described Flatland as a two-dimensional world, much like a world that might exist on "a vast sheet of paper." Various Flatlanders—lines, triangles, squares, pentagons, hexagons, and other figures—slid freely about on this surface world, though, of course, they did not rise above or go below their world. (In fact they had no knowledge of that third dimension, which is *up above* or *down below* their surface world.) In Flatland, one's status and class corresponded to one's number of edges: Soldiers and lower-class citizens were isosceles triangles, middle-class Flatlanders were equilateral triangles, professionals were squares and pentagons, and aristocrats had six sides or more. Members of the highest, priestly class had so many sides that they were almost perfectly circular. Individuals with irregular shapes or angles were assumed also to have inner irregularities, and offspring born defective in this way were destroyed. Women were the only creatures with no edges or angles: They were, in other words, one-dimensional lines.

Flatland was, in part, a parody of rigid British norms and social conventions. In the story Abbott made it clear for example that Victorian England, like his fictional flat society, was foolishly conventional, rigidly hierarchical, and, not least, misogynist. (Near the end of the story a higher-dimensional being with advanced knowledge and wisdom told the Square that he and others like him thought more highly of "your despised Straight Lines than of your belauded [priestly] Circles."[6]) Neither Flatlanders nor the English could think of much beyond their inherited traditions, ingrained prejudices, and daily preoccupations. Both societies were filled with people who could believe in nothing beyond what they saw or touched; they were empiricists destitute of real vision and insight. And, as our square hero would unfortunately discover, these types of myopic societies were not kind to reformers claiming knowledge from a source beyond the ken of social convention or the testimony of the senses.

Notwithstanding the many inducements to conform and stay in place, the Square found himself the recipient of visions and dreams that were revelatory and subversive. In one of them he dreamed of an odd world that was not two-dimensional like Flatland, with length and width, but one-dimensional—a "Lineland." All beings were either line segments or dots arranged in a single-file, lined-up world. In this dream, the Square called out to these line beings, saying that he was from a space above theirs that was two-dimensional. He had length, which they certainly understood, and width, which they unfortunately did not. He reasoned with them, but nothing penetrated their stubborn arrogance and dogmatism. They were certain that nothing existed outside of Lineland.

The next day brought a surprising reversal. If in his dream the night before the Square visited lower-dimensional Linelanders, in a new day-time vision he encountered a higher-dimensional being from a larger world. The evening had begun in the usual way, with the Square giving his hexagonal grandson lessons in geometry. The Square told him that a line three units long could be represented as 3^1, and that if one stretched this line three units in another direction one would have a square that could be represented by 3^2. This raised a question for the young Hexagon: What did 3^3 look like? Nothing at all, the Square assured him, "for Geometry has only Two Dimensions." But the grandson persisted. A point moving three units in one direction formed a one-dimensional line represented by 3^1. That line moving three units perpendicular to itself formed a two-dimensional square represented by 3^2. That square moving three units in a new direction perpendicular to the other two directions "must make a Something else (but I don't see what) of three inches every way—and this must be represented by 3^3." Was there a *Something else* that existed but could not be seen? At this point the Square upbraided the boy in a way that made it clear that such unconventional questions were intolerable in a conventional society. "If you would talk less nonsense, you would remember more sense," he said. Irritated, he turned to his wife. "The boy is a fool."[7]

At this moment, however, a voice announced that the boy was not a fool and that, contrary to what the Square was saying, "3^3 has an obvious Geometrical meaning." The voice came from a strange object that appeared suddenly in the center of a room in the Square's home. The Square initially thought it was a circular priest. He quickly realized, however, that this priest was able to do unusual things—he could shrink, expand, and perform miraculous feats such as seeing into closed rooms and cabinets. The Square began to wonder—Was this a hallucination, a nightmare, a sign of insanity? Was the intruding visitor a magician or a God?

The Sphere responded that he was merely a being with an additional dimension. He said that in addition to the two directions or dimensions of Flatland, forward/back and left/right, there was another dimension, an *up above and down below* the plane of Flatland that the Square could not perceive. The Sphere lived in that larger three-dimensional space and was himself three-dimensional. Flummoxed, the Square responded as Linelanders had: Such things had to be impossible.

The Sphere, however, did not give up. He reached toward the Square, pulled him out of the surface of his two-dimensional world, and cast him into three-dimensional space. Floating suddenly in this

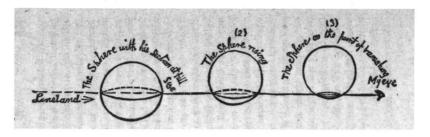

Figure 1.1   The Sphere descends into the plane of Flatland. The Square's eye (at right) sees an expanding cross-section of the Sphere as he enters this flat world. From Edwin A. Abbott, *Flatland.*

larger reality, the astonished Square looked down and saw all of Flatland below. Where, exactly, was he? Had he been thrust suddenly into a state of "madness" or the abyss of "Hell"? The Sphere calmly insisted that the Square was experiencing neither. "It is Knowledge; it is Three Dimensions: open your eye once again and try to look steadily." The Square looked and beheld something that went far beyond his familiar "poor and shadowy" world: He saw Flatland, but now he saw into all parts of it at once—all parts of the town and its residences, into all the closed-up parts of his home, into the rooms where his children lay asleep. He could see the precise angles and lengths composing all things. "All this I could now *see,* not merely infer," he said, amazed. He had been initiated into higher "mysteries."[8]

It was a transforming revelation. As a result, the Square became a Flatland seer and prophet—and, eventually, in the way of so many seers and prophets, an outlaw and outcast. In the initial stages of his ministry, however, he was buoyed by an otherworldly optimism. Certain that his "Gospel of Three Dimensions" would be simple for others to grasp, the Square began by telling others that imagining higher realities was as easy as thinking about mathematical analogies. If one could understand one-dimensional lines and two-dimensional squares surely one could imagine the existence of something with an additional dimension. The Square first targeted his precocious grandson, who already had pondered the existence of higher dimensions. He rehearsed with him how one might first stretch a point into a line, and a line into a square. Then came the difficult part: What about stretching every point in that flat square in a direction perpendicular to the other two directions, in an "up" direction to create a "sort of extra Square in Three Dimensions" or what the Sphere had earlier told the Square was a "*Something-which-you-do-not-as-yet-know-a-name-for-but-which-we-call-a-Cube*"? The Square's grandson momentarily considered this possibility. But very quickly he decided not to think about these notions in detail. It was not just that they were difficult to imagine; they also had been outlawed by priestly Circles and other authorities. Even discussing them was illegal.

It was not a good omen that the Square could not convince even a curious and open-minded child to consider such matters. How would he show people that there was something higher? Turning to other strategies, he attempted to compose a treatise on reality entitled "Through Flatland to Thoughtland" in which he carefully avoided illegal talk of higher *physical* dimensions by discussing higher realities as merely thoughts in a higher thoughtland. But while writing this treatise he could not figure out exactly what to say. (Alas, who would be foolish enough to write a book about something as esoteric as higher dimensions—let alone expect people to buy and read such a book?) He tried to remember what the Sphere had showed him, and he tentatively mentioned these things to others; but the topic was abstruse and forbidden and as a result friends started to avoid him. Increasingly agitated, the Square started to let slip expressions such as "the all-seeing land" in conversations even with circular priests, and at one fateful meeting of the "Local Speculative Society" he was provoked into giving an entire account of his journey into higher space, including his conversations with the Sphere. At first, he assumed the persona of a storyteller "describing the imaginary experiences of a fictitious person"; but carried away by an intemperate enthusiasm, he concluded his account by exhorting everyone to believe in the third dimension! His colleagues were stunned. He was arrested on the spot.

In *Flatland*'s final scene it became clear that things would not turn out well for the Square. Enduring sadness, self-doubt, and even concern about his mental soundness, the Square sat alone for seven years in prison. He was bereft of followers or disciples. All he could do was write down his incredible story, hoping he had not endured his unusual trials and tribulations in vain. He clung to hopes, he said, that his memoirs "may find their way to the minds of humanity in Some Di-

mension, and may stir up a race of rebels who shall refuse to be confined to limited Dimensionality." The Square spoke directly to his readers:
Were there rebels or visionaries out there who would refuse to be limited by conventional views and perspectives?[9]

If this was the Square's most urgent question, his final and most
pressing concern, it was Edwin Abbott's as well. Like the Square, Abbott
was frustrated with inherited pieties and traditions, curious about ways
of transcending empirical knowledge derived from the senses, and preoccupied with the revelatory possibilities of true spiritual visions and
dreams. (Among friends, Abbott was willing to admit that he shared
the Square's preoccupations, signing a copy of *Flatland* to his best friend,
for instance, "from the Square." Moreover, as one of Abbott's biographers has written, even the names of the two are similar: Edwin Abbott
Abbott, after all, is Edwin A^2—"A Squared.")[10] Like the Square, Abbott
was interested in how invisible, supernatural realities could appear in
visions that might be understood in terms of the math and geometry of
higher dimensions. In Abbott's real-life version of the Square's treatise
"Through Flatland to Thoughtland," for example, entitled *Through Nature to Christ* (1877), Abbott examined a variety of visionary experiences,
dedicating the book to departed souls who came back to comfort the
living, ghosts who, "next to Christ, have had the most power to help the
living by destroying death and by making things invisible real." Abbott
had no doubt about the reality of these hauntings and near-death
forms of touch and contact.[11]

His understanding of these matters, however, like the Square's, was
unorthodox. In a section of *Through Nature to Christ* that he excised (and
later self-published), for example, Abbott put side by side the inspired
utterances of Biblical prophets with newer revelations from radical poets
and prophets such as William Blake and George Fox.[12] Abbott would
spend a good deal of his life attempting to understand better how to see
and imagine higher, spiritual realities and develop ways of separating
true ecstatic visions from false ones.

The overall point of *Flatland* was that there might be dimensions, spaces, and realities beyond experience. The lesson was not that
Linelanders, who scoffed at the idea of things with both length and
width, were particularly obtuse, or that Flatlanders, who outlawed discussion of three-dimensional geometries, were particularly misguided—but

rather that there might be an "up above" or "down below" direction to our human world that, while uncomfortable to ponder and difficult to perceive, could nevertheless be real. The problem was that all creatures, as Abbott said once, including human beings, were "slaves of our senses, attaching too much importance to 'the things that do appear,' too little to unseen things."[13] Abbott worried about a general failure of the imagination that was exacerbated by living in a scientific time in which only empirical facts would be known or believed in. His genius was to attempt to use secular tools, dimensional notions in math and geometry, to pose the possibility that there might be invisible things existing just slightly beyond the reach of the senses. *Flatland,* he said once later in life, was intended to "lead us to vaster views of possible circumstances and existences."[14]

Other Higher-Dimensional Narratives

Abbott's *Flatland* was by far the most widely read fictional narrative about higher dimensions but it was not the first time someone used mathematical ideas about higher dimensions to direct attention beyond our familiar three-dimensional world. Beginning late in the eighteenth century, mathematicians and philosophers, including Immanuel Kant, had wondered about the nature of space and the possibility that it had unseen dimensions or layers. ("If it is possible that there could be regions with other dimensions," Kant said early in his career, "it is very likely that God has somewhere brought them into being."[15]) A number of mathematicians, including the great German mathematicians Carl Friedrich Gauss and Bernhard Riemann, of whom more will be said later, developed *n*-dimensional geometries, and Abbott, who was conversant with developments in math and science, probably knew their work well. But it was two prominent German thinkers with interests in mathematics, space, and visual perception, Hermann von Helmholtz and Gustav Fechner, whose imaginative thought experiments influenced Abbott the most. Fechner in particular worked out in detail what two-dimensional spaces might look like, how they might be structured, and even how beings living in those worlds might think or act.

Fechner was a "man of two minds," the American philosopher and psychologist William James once said, a divided soul who both pioneered the scientific study of psychology and wrote mystical essays about the spiritual lives of plants, the heavenly afterlife of the human soul, and the varied activities of angels living in invisible, higher-dimensional spaces. He started out at medical school at Leipzig, where he "came to see the world as a set of mechanical workings," confidently professed atheism, and became interested in physiology, perception, and vision in particular. Medical school gave Fechner both a lifelong interest in physiology as well as an abiding skepticism about the ambitious claims, and patently ridiculous treatment regimens, of medical science.[16] (Near the end of his medical education, he wrote, for example, a satirical piece entitled "Proof That the Moon Is Made of Iodide," which lampooned doctors for treating almost everything with iodide salts.) But Fechner's ongoing interest in mysticism and German Romantic philosophers meant that he refused to see nature as a "soulless mechanism." German Romantics believed that nature was the expression or emanation of a divine principle, and they insisted that understanding it properly involved not just the empirical study of the scientist but the vision and intuition of an artist. He completed a habilitation thesis on German Romantic views on nature in 1823, but soon found that, as important as these humanistic pursuits were, they did not bring him the sense of certainty he desired.

At this point, in the middle of the 1820s, Fechner turned back to scientific studies to find, he said, a "more exact path" to "clear, certain and productive findings," initiating a period of assiduous work in physics and physiology in which he not only translated the works of great French scientists into German but also conducted his own experiments. He continued to be interested in vision and he experimented on the subjective experience of seeing, which involved studying his own reactions to various kinds of optical illusions and flashes of light. Initiated around 1835, these experiments led to the onset of a number of medical and psychological symptoms. Fechner experienced an inability to concentrate, depression, loss of appetite, fatigue, visual disturbances, eye pain, and partial blindness. Even dim light hurt his eyes. "He was constantly experimenting on himself for subjective optical effects, even glancing at the sun, working with sudden lights, and straining his eyes to observe the electromagnetic scale, and this gradually led to his later calamity," an American graduate student, G. Stanley Hall, remembered. (Hall later became the founder and first president of the American Psychological Association.)

Fechner had worked on philosophical and experimental issues until it hurt—quite literally. Undoubtedly his optical symptoms made his psychological ones worse and vice versa. In any case, long-standing eye pain set in, forcing him to give up reading and sit for long periods in a darkened room. He made his way through the streets of Leipzig, Hall recalled, "almost like a blind man." In 1838 he stepped down from his physics professorship at the University of Leipzig. He remained for long periods in his darkened room, communicating with his family through an opening in the door. When he went outside, he insisted on wearing metal cups over his eyes.[17]

Then, in 1843, Fechner had a mystical experience that healed him of his physical ailments and helped him reconcile his scientific and metaphysical interests. After three years of hardly being able to see, he suddenly opened his eyes and saw things he had never seen before. During a walk one spring morning his diseased eyes somehow saw the world in a beautiful, vibrant clarity, shimmering with light and vitality. He saw a pulsing consciousness in everything around him, noting that even plants were "glowing." Fechner began to see that there was an overall consciousness to the earth, and that our individual minds were merely waves on the surface of that larger consciousness. To Fechner this event was miraculous and life changing. Before it he had lived in the shadows; now he saw that everything was full of light.

From this time forward he developed a worldview using metaphors of dark and light, calling his new metaphysics of hope and immortality "the day view" (*Tagesansicht*) and the dreary materialism of positivist scientists "the night view" (*Nachtansicht*). Fechner's "day view" held that everything was alive with consciousness and that human beings were analogous to sense organs—we all were the individual sense organs of the earth, so that we added to the life of the greater consciousness as we lived and perceived the world. "When one of us dies," William James wrote, summarizing Fechner's arguments, "it is as if an eye of the world were closed."[18]

There were nested realms of consciousness, and as one rose through them they became more and more inclusive. Fechner believed that our cumulative perceptions live on after death, as we live on as part of the greater absolute consciousness.

When one believed that we were connected to a higher consciousness in this way, Fechner argued, one saw connections between material and spiritual, higher and lower, by reasoning with analogies, something that characterized Fechner's later metaphysical writings. This most likely was another way that Fechner influenced later narratives of shadow worlds and higher dimensions, including Abbott's *Flatland*.

Even before his mystical experience of illumination, Fechner appears to have nourished a mysticism of shadow and light. Beginning in the 1820s he wrote pseudonymously (as "Dr. Mises") about shadow worlds, angels living near the sun, and the possibility of higher dimensions. He wrote three pieces in particular that may have influenced Abbott, "The Comparative Anatomy of Angels" (1825), "The Shadow Is Alive" (1846), and "Space Has Four Dimensions" (1846). The first is interesting because in it Fechner reasons by analogy from our imperfect human forms to higher forms that might exist in the universe, forms of being without human "irregularities, elevations and depressions." Borrowing from ancients such as Plato and Xenophanes, Fechner supposed that the highest forms must be perfectly symmetrical spheres. These highest forms, which he called "angels," were spheres of light. Though Fechner adopted a playful voice in this piece, we know from other writings that he believed earnestly many of these ideas. In "The Shadow Is Alive" on the other hand, Fechner speculated about the difference between higher and lower forms of life, discussing the existence of two-dimensional shadows that might possess their own kind of life. Perhaps shadows saw themselves as the essence of selfhood, while we lumbered about in dull three-dimensional bodies. Were shadows dependent upon us or were we dependent on them? Were their speculations about other worlds ridiculous or were ours? Did they have greater freedom or did we? Were they epiphenomenal or were we?

In the third and final piece, "Space Has Four Dimensions," Fechner asked readers to imagine the existence of a two-dimensional being living on the paper surface of a camera obscura. This being might use its own scientific instruments or philosophical categories to search for some higher reality, just as our scientists and philosophers did, but in the end its study of the cosmos, its view of all things, "cannot be lifted above the plane." We were in the same position: We were three-dimensional creatures, and we saw three-dimensionally, but there was no reason to suppose that nature had not created dimensions higher than our own. The change from one to two or from two to three was no different from the change from three to four or four to five. Is it more likely that nature stopped making new dimensions or that our limitations prevent us from seeing beyond our familiar three? Fechner also discussed raising a two-dimensional flat being into a third dimension and the ways that this might change that being's ability to see and perceive things.[19]

There are several ways in which Abbott, who was fluent in German, borrowed from Fechner. First, Abbott's higher creature from the third dimension resembled Fechner's highest beings, his "angels": All of them were spheres. Second, Fechner and Abbott both reasoned with analogies from lower forms of life to higher ones, developing ways of stretching the imagination in order to envision things above our three-dimensional reality. Third, there are surprising similarities between Fechner's flat world (with its sentient beings) in "Space Has Four Dimensions" and Abbott's classic text. Fechner's flat creatures, like Abbott's Flatlanders, wondered about the nature and meaning of their flat world, even pondering the existence of dimensions that went beyond their own. Fourth and finally, both Abbott and Fechner lampooned unimaginative and conventional thinkers in similar ways. In "Space Has Four Dimensions," for example, Fechner identified two types of people who would never understand his innovative ideas and narratives—"those who only believe what they see and those who only see what they believe. I put the natural scientists who base everything on their senses in the first category," he complained, "and philosophers in the second." Abbott would have embraced this formulation.[20]

There was one other scientist who influenced Abbott in crucial ways—the great nineteenth-century German scientist Hermann von Helmholtz. Helmholtz was the only other figure who wrote about beings who lived in other dimensions, and though his discussions of these matters were less detailed than Fechner's they reached wider audiences. In a lecture given in 1870 and reprinted in different forms thereafter,

Helmholtz said that through his work on optical phenomena, including visual distortions and illusions, he had come to question the transcendental quality of ideas about space. Perhaps we believed space was three-dimensional because we had learned this to be the case through our (limited) senses—not, as Kant had argued, because of some *a priori* in the human mind. Were there other dimensions beyond the ken of our powers of perception? To help his readers consider this possibility Helmholtz spoke of "reasoning beings" who lived on two-dimensional surfaces. He argued that beings living on the two-dimensional surface of a sphere would arrive at different geometrical (actually, planimetrical) ideas from beings who lived on the surface of an infinite plane.[21] The former would develop axioms appropriate to their non-Euclidean surface, while the latter would develop geometrical axioms that were more similar to ours. Another race of beings living on the surface of a pseudo-sphere would develop wholly different geometrical axioms. Helmholtz was arguing that our ideas of space were not metaphysically given but created through experience: We had learned to perceive three dimensions because we lived (apparently) in three-dimensional space.

Was it possible, however, that we actually lived in a more dimensionally complex world and that our normal forms of three-dimensional seeing merely scanned the surface of reality? Was it possible, in other words, that the types of seeing we normally performed were distortions, illusions, or perceptual mistakes—and that there was another higher form of seeing into reality? If future higher-dimensional thinkers pondered this question, and they did with enthusiasm, perhaps none explored its many elements and angles, its mathematical and metaphysical implications, as searchingly as Edwin Abbott and his fictional alter ego, the Square.

Illusions

Flatland itself was preoccupied with issues of seeing, but so were several other books Abbott wrote around the same time. Taking up these questions in both *The Kernel and the Husk* (1886) and *The Spirit on the Waters* (1897), Abbott wrote that just as new physiological studies showed that human vision was flawed, so also had theologians discovered that Christian beliefs had been mixed up with mistakes and illusions. "Do you suppose, when you see anything, that you see that which the thing *is?*" Abbott asked, introducing his readers to scientific questions about the accuracy of vision. There were two reasons that our vision came mixed with illusions—first, that the categories we assigned to things we saw were based on our limited experiences, and, second, that our visual apparatus itself provided incomplete and sometimes distorted information. On the first matter, the characteristics we assigned to different things were merely categories we used based on our limited experiences and perspectives. We assigned colors to things, for example, but those colors represented not some absolute quality in objects but rather our imperfect attempts to characterize them. Was it conceivable that someone with finer sensibilities, someone or something with a greater understanding of color or shape, might produce a different picture of reality? "We do not see things as Superior Beings see them," Abbott wrote. One sees something for example as "yellowish-green" but a superior intelligence might wonder "which of the one hundred and fifty shades of yellowish-green" it was. "You might as well tell me," Abbott continued, "when I shew you a sheep, 'This is a *being,*' as tell me simply this is 'yellowish-green.'" Our categories and language shape quite dramatically how we "see" things.[22]

Then there were problems with the eye and brain, which, it turned out, were beset by many kinds of flaws and infirmities. Abbott pointed out that what were called "illusions of sense" were common and universal, and he offered several examples. When your hand was pricked by two compass points that were close together, we felt it as one sensation. When you crossed your middle finger over your index finger and held a marble between them, the marble felt like two marbles. (Both of these examples were commonly cited illustrations of sensory illusions in contemporary texts.) But visual illusions were particularly prevalent, Abbott argued. Because of light refraction we seldom see things where they actually are. In misty weather and underwater, objects appear in one location but actually reside in another. Also, because it takes time for light to travel, what we see in the heavens is not how things really are. In general, there were so many problems with seeing that, as Abbott wrote in another book, "sight itself is an illusion."[23]

It was no coincidence that Abbott linked scientific ideas about vision with theological notions of miracles and spiritual truth. Discourses about the eye and vision were important in the dimensional writings of Helmholtz and Fechner, of course; but the connection between the eye and religion was most powerfully articulated in a text that virtually every British and American child living in the nineteenth century was required to study, William Paley's *Natural Theology* (1802). In this book Paley examined nature's providential design, and though he surveyed a range of animal and human anatomical features in order to show God's astonishing handiwork, one of his first (and certainly best-known) examples was the human eye, an organ of consummate design and unmatched mechanical perfection. Such an organ could never have come about by chance.

Abbott read Paley carefully but he also studied the most famous response to it: Charles Darwin's *Origin of Species* (1859). Darwin also knew Paley's work well, and though for a time he agreed with Paley's arguments, in his *Origin* he developed a different way of explaining nature's design. In one section of the *Origin* he mentioned Paley by name and, in a subsequent passage that exemplified his approach, he discussed the human eye's design.

Darwin's tone in this passage was understated but his arguments, when pondered carefully, were destructive of inherited views. He said that the eye had been developed and improved through natural selection over millions of years, insisting that while it was a remarkable organ *it was by no means perfect*. Natural selection undoubtedly made things better over time but it did not "produce absolute perfection." It produced merely a relative perfection. "Natural selection tends only to make each organic being as perfect as, or slightly more perfect than the other inhabitants of the same country with which it comes into competition," Darwin argued.[24] So the eye was relatively good, refined over many millennia, but not perfect. Summarizing recent physiological studies, including those of Helmholtz,[25] Darwin pointed to the eye's many ways of producing errors, illusions, and mistakes. Darwin knew that this was a crucial issue: He knew that it was conventional to see the eye as unassailable evidence of the Creator, and he also understood that his views about the eye would be a barrier to the acceptance of his theory. Pious readers of Darwin's text could point out that even if God had not created the eye per se, he had devised a perfect framework of natural laws that in time shaped everything for the good. Many argued this, even if it was not faithful to Darwin's theory in every respect. It was apparent to those who read Darwin's text carefully, however, and indeed it was apparent to Darwin himself, that if God could be removed one step from nature he might be removed yet another—and another. In time, Darwin wondered if God was necessary at all.[26]

Darwin and Helmholtz were the most widely read scientists in England during Abbott's lifetime and though Abbott did not usually cite sources, he clearly borrowed from both. In his discussion on vision and illusion, Abbott followed Helmholtz's ideas in his *Popular Scientific Lectures* (1883), particularly the chapter on "The Recent Progress of the Theory of Vision." Abbott appears to have borrowed from Helmholtz much of what he had to say about vision, including examples related to illusions of refraction, the different ways that erroneous inferences produced illusions, and even specific examples of illusions such as the marble between the finger and the problem of perceiving different color shades, including shades of "yellowish-green." (Abbott appears to have taken this verbatim from Helmholtz.) Abbott also discussed the problem of a color-blind observer attempting to distinguish the red and green of train signals, another example contained in Helmholtz's *Scientific Lectures* and in his work on color-blindness.[27]

Abbott used all of this to argue that if the science of vision proved material knowledge was beset by difficulties, so spiritual knowledge and tradition were characterized by mistakes and exaggerations. Illusions permeated the book of nature and the book of revelation, and in both realms advancing toward greater truth meant understanding and overcoming them. This brought Abbott back to miracles, which he understood as illusions that mature Christians might now understand in their proper context. Children developed by gradually learning that they had made erroneous assumptions and inferences and then by improving their abilities to see the world correctly. It was a process of overcoming illusions. The same thing was happening in the history of the Church. The Word of God contained a permanent "kernel" of truth but this kernel was obscured by the transient "husk" of historic doctrines and interpretations. (Abbott drew this directly from Strauss's *Life of Jesus,* where the Biblical scholar spoke of the "husk" of Christian stories and distinguished them from the more important, spiritual kernel of truth they contained.) There were many illusions in the history of the

Church—the doctrine of Christ's divinity, the common interpretation of Christ's ministry as miraculous, the belief in his physical Resurrection, historical notions about his second coming, and so on.[28] "The history of Christianity," Abbott wrote, had been "the history of profound religious truth, contained in, and preserved by, illusions; an ascent of worship through illusion to the truth."[29] Astronomers and psychologists, Newton and Darwin—all showed Christians how to see through older illusions to the eternal truths behind them.

Inner Eyes and Spiritual Visions

In some ways all of Abbott's talk about illusory doctrines and Church teachings, about the distortions of Christian history or the myopia of Christian theologians, or even about sciences of vision and visual illusion were merely prologue to something else he wanted to argue, which was that people could sometimes actually see supernatural things. They could have real visions of angels and spirits. Abbott believed that the ghosts of departed souls in particular appeared regularly to people living in our earthly world. He thought carefully about how to understand this kind of visionary experience and other forms of spiritual seeing.

Flatland itself moved from a consideration of vision and sight to spiritual seeing and mystical insight. In sections on eyes and vision early in the narrative, *Flatland* discussed how individuals in this two-dimensional world saw and recognized each other. Though they were two-dimensional, Flatlanders approaching one another saw only one-dimensional lines. A circle, a hexagon, a square—all appeared simply as lines as individuals encountered each other in this flat world. Of course this made recognizing others somewhat difficult. Flatlanders distinguished one another by voice and sometimes by feeling the angles on approaching strangers, though the upper classes relied solely on "Sight Recognition." (Vision was considered the preferred and most reliable sense.) Recognizing someone else's shape by sight was possible because Flatland, like nineteenth-century London, was shrouded in gray fog, a fog that made it possible "to infer with great exactness the configuration of the object observed." As Flatlanders approached objects, they could see their sides shading off into the fog and infer their angles and overall shape. (See

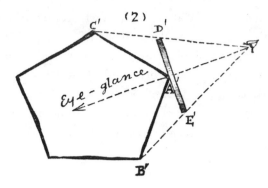

Figure 1.2   Abbott incorporated several drawings showing how a Flatlander's eye (upper right) perceived oncoming shapes. Here the eye sees a pentagonal physician approaching and, because of subtle shading caused by ambient fog, is able to perceive the oncoming physician's angles and therefore his class. From Edwin A. Abbott, *Flatland*.

Figure 1.2.) If a figure approached and presented its side rather than its angle, it was not improper to ask this oncoming figure to rotate.[30]

At the climactic moment when the Square encountered the Sphere, however, the story's discussion of sight moved in a new direction. At this point, the narrative pivoted from focusing on eyesight and vision to ways of cultivating the ability to see reality in its wider, spiritual context.

When discussing higher dimensions, for example, the Sphere noted that he came from a "direction in which you cannot look" because the Square's eye was on his side, on his perimeter. In order to see into a higher dimension the Square needed an eye "not on your Perimeter, but on your side, that is, on what you would probably call your inside; but we in Spaceland should call it your side." The Square needed an inner eye, so to speak. When the Sphere pulled the Square out of Flatland, the Square spoke of the experience as seeing more completely and perfectly. "I looked, and behold, a new world!" He looked down on Flatland and for the first time saw it as it truly was. "All this I could now *see*, not merely infer." Then, in a final dialogue with the Sphere, the Square made it clear that the ability to see in higher ways existed in everyone. "Just as there was close at hand, and touching my frame, the land of Three Dimensions, though I, blind senseless wretch, had no power to touch it, no eye in my interior to discern it, so of a surety there is a

Fourth Dimension, which my Lord perceives with the inner eye of thought." Yes, the Sphere admitted to the Square, he had heard reports of an even higher, fourth dimension. But the existence of it was contested, he said, and perhaps visions of such things came merely "from the brain" or from a person's "perturbed angularity."[31] The Sphere himself was not certain. Were such visions evidence of higher forms of seeing? Were they truly ways of perceiving something beyond the senses?

Abbott discussed these questions in *Flatland* but he pursued them in more detail in other writings. Explaining his beliefs in his *Apologia*, for instance, he insisted that there was a form of spiritual seeing that was indubitable, that there were "certain 'words,' thoughts, and (so to speak) invisible visions, spiritual visions, that 'will never pass away'"— and furthermore, he wrote, it was on this assumption that *all of his work was based*. Abbott believed that spiritual visions were not limited to Biblical prophets or Jesus's apostles but that God revealed himself to individuals "from the first dawn of human consciousness up to the present day," a view that he said was suggested to him by reading Darwin's *Origin*.[32] He was fascinated by visions of recently departed spirits and had no doubt that such visions were common. He had friends, for example, who in dreams and waking visions were visited by dead friends and relatives. (One of them, a skeptical physician, saw his mother shortly after her death. "I was as much awake as you are now," he had told Abbott. "And I saw her as clearly as I see you. But of course I knew it was a mere optical delusion.")[33]

But were such visions merely *optical delusions*? Abbott did not think so. He dedicated *Through Nature to Christ*, to the "blessed dead," who, he said, "next to Christ, have had the most power to help the living by destroying death and by making things invisible real." Abbott believed that the dead could reach out and touch people in visions or in other experiences, and he even pointed to Tennyson's trance in his famous poem *In Memoriam* as an example. Here the Poet Laureate, while reading old letters from a departed friend, was "touched" until "all at once it seem'd at last // His living soul was flashed on mine." If mere mortals could inspire these kinds of fleeting visions, Christ could create even more dramatic "flashings," his powerful personality producing visions in believers, Abbott argued, "in forms indistinguishable from those of physical vision."[34] These were not, as the skeptical physician had said, "mere optical delusions." Abbott averred that these visions sustained "the sense of the presence of an invisible world acting upon the visible, and of possibilities of things in heaven and things on earth more than are dreamt of in our philosophy." Be alert for things not dreamt "of in our philosophy"—this was Hamlet's instruction to the rationalist Horatio, who had just seen the ghost of Hamlet's slain father. Abbott quoted from the same dialogue in the epigraph on *Flatland's* cover.[35] Unexpected supernatural things, including ghostly visions, happened. In *Flatland*, confounding visions of other worlds were crucial to the narrative—the Square had dreams and visions of a higher-dimensional world, a one-dimensional Lineland and a zero-dimensional universe called Pointland.

It may not seem unusual for a clergyman to call attention to the possibility of perceiving invisible worlds or spirits, but in fact Abbott's writings on the subject were radical in many respects. To his editor at Macmillan, Abbott worried that his chapter on unusual "visions and voices" in his forthcoming *Through Nature to Christ* would get him blacklisted as a preacher and fired from his job as headmaster of the City of London School. He ended up omitting this chapter and Macmillan, apparently, was pleased.[36] The heterodox nature of this chapter is best indicated by the fact that it treats more or less equally Biblical visions and revelations, the inspirations of Romantic poets such as William Blake, and the ecstatic rantings of radicals such as George Fox. (In fact, Abbott wrote elsewhere that "many of the visions in the Bible are inferior to that of George Fox.")[37] Abbott took the visions of Fox and Blake seriously at a time when Christian contemporaries were writing that both figures were unhinged madmen. Abbott argued that God inspired visions in seers throughout history, especially at times of desperation, decline, or crisis. He developed an impressive roster of authentic seers that included Ezekiel, Isaiah, Jesus, Dante, John Milton, Fox, William Wordsworth, George Whitefield, and Blake. (We might add to this list the Square.)

Of course, true visions always came mixed with other elements, including human wishes, imaginings, and idiosyncrasies, and these "illusions" and distortions needed to be understood. One needed to evaluate the circumstances and effects of spiritual visions carefully. Were visions caused by intemperance, sin, or rage—or were they preceded by sober reflection and piety? Did they result in new light on philosophical problems? The true seer, Abbott believed, had a passivity and openness about him, which he called, modifying a phrase from Helmholtz, an "unconscious receptiveness." Real spiritual visions came in moments of "patient and quiet waiting," when the senses and consciousness were quieted, as they were for George Fox.[38] Finally, true visions often discomfited or disturbed people, forcing them to think and act in new ways.

Abbott's preoccupation with spiritual seeing was also on display in his many works of Biblical criticism. In several books he examined visionary experiences in the Bible and how Biblical authors understood these experiences. Abbott developed sophisticated analyses of Greek words such as *Horao* (ὁράω) and discussed the appearance of these words in the Gospel of John in particular. *Horao* (ὁράω) was used in the sacred text mostly to refer to seeing spiritual objects or entities such as God, miracles, or the resurrected Christ. Abbott noted that in the Gospel of John, which used this word nineteen times, the author used this term to distinguish between a pagan notion of physically seeing a fleshly god and a spiritual form of seeing experienced by the apostles. The seeing of *Horao* was powerful and vivid but was not a physical kind of seeing—it was an insight, a recognition, and a "participation in" the object seen. It was not a fleshly form of seeing. There was no fleshly seeing of God.[39]

Understanding what the Bible meant by spiritual seeing was a key step in separating the church's illusions from Christianity's essential truths, and it was especially important in reimagining two crucial Christian teachings—the Incarnation and the Resurrection, that is, how God descended into our world and how he eventually rose up and out of it. These, we might say, were the two key miracles of Christianity, and if in an age of science miracles were hard to believe, it was logical that these teachings also would be called into question. *Flatland* dealt with precisely these issues, if in a veiled way: It was a story about a higher being who first descended into a lower world and then rose up above and out of it.

On the Resurrection in particular, a controversial subject in the nineteenth century, Abbott argued that the earliest gospel, Mark, had no resurrection narrative and that other early accounts of this event, such as St. Paul's, used words that indicated the event's spiritual rather than material reality. (St. Paul, Abbott wrote, used the word the synoptic writers used for angelic visions to talk of what he saw.)[40] It was a visionary experience given "only to the eye enlightened by spirit," not to modes of fleshly seeing, even if some later thinkers exaggerated about the event by talking about it as a physical thing. Christ's resurrected body was not a tangible body. These events were not miraculous but they were supernatural, which meant that while they did not contradict natural law they were "above" it. Contemporary believers held tightly to an older view of Christ's bodily Resurrection, Abbott wrote, because they had not yet grasped the fact that some gospel traditions were clouded by errors and illusions. Eyewitnesses mythologized and exaggerated. They sometimes used ambiguous words to describe their encounters with the risen Jesus—*meeting, seeing,* and *touching.* And there were ambiguities concerning what evangelists meant by "body" and "spiritual body" as well. But perhaps the most important reason believers clung to the older view was a "fleshly unwillingness to believe in the reality of anything that cannot be seen and touched by the flesh." This fleshly unwillingness may have had roots in antiquity but it was thriving as never before in modernity, with agnostics such as the mathematician William Clifford insisting that it was "wrong, always, everywhere, and for anyone, to believe anything on insufficient evidence." Abbott's position was that when disciples saw, heard, "met" or touched the risen Jesus they did so with spiritual senses. It was the same way with figures in the Hebrew Bible. Isaiah's lips were not actually "touched" by a live coal from the fire on the altar, nor was Exodus's burning bush actually on fire. These were spiritual, not material, realities.[41]

Abbott saw a regrettable lack of imagination in those who did not believe in things that could not be seen or touched. He thought the remedy for this was to "liberate" one's thinking from material views and "take a more ample view of the Universe." But how could modern people get this more ample view? How might they learn to see or imagine something *beyond* the senses—especially at a time when agnostic scientists and other critics insisted that miracles and other supernatural phenomena could neither be seen nor believed? While this was a great intellectual and theological problem, it was also a personal problem for Abbott, and not merely because as a young man this empirical world-view threatened to take away his comforting faith in an unseen world. It was personal because as an Anglican priest, teacher, headmaster, and, by all accounts, devoted friend, Abbott was confronted with other people's real-life problems—with students who said they wanted to believe but could not, with clerical colleagues who had had to abandon the ministry, with despairing friends facing sickness and death.

Abbott himself spoke of these burdens and dilemmas. Sometime in the early 1880s, for example, as Abbott wrote *Flatland,* a dying clergyman who was struggling to hold on to his faith sought Abbott's help. Diagnosed with a fatal disease, with weeks to live, this anxious man had lost his sense for the reality of another world at precisely the moment when he needed it most. He had fallen into the darkest of places, into "that abyss of agnosticism," he said. "It would comfort my short remainder of life," he wrote Abbott, "if you would come and look me dying in the face and say, 'This theology and Christology of mine is not merely literary: I feel with joy of heart that God is not unknown to man: try even now to feel with me.' "[42] Abbott arranged a meeting. The challenge of that moment should not be underestimated: How, in an age of empiricism, does one explain to a dying friend that God or a spirit world might be known or believed in? How might one respond to this man's request to see or feel such a reality?

Abbott was remarkable because he retained a vital belief in that unseen spiritual world and because he argued that certain scientific discourses, when properly understood, pointed to the existence of this world. He did this by redefining miracles as supernatural events that were above the laws of nature in some way while not in conflict with them. In his theological writings and in *Flatland,* he made these realms above nature seem credible by talking about them in mathematical ways as higher spatial dimensions. It was not that Abbott thought spirits existed in a higher, fourth dimension, though other Christians would make such arguments, as we will see. It was more that the overall aim of the *Flatland* narrative was to expand the imagination, to show that extra-empirical realms might exist. "I hope," Abbott once commented about *Flatland,* that it "may prove suggestive . . . to those Spacelanders of moderate and modest minds who—speaking of that which is of the highest importance but *lies beyond experience*—decline to say on the one hand that 'This can never be,' and on the other hand, 'It must needs be precisely thus, and we know all about it.'" Elsewhere he arrived at a similar formulation, saying that he hoped to help others "conceive that there may be a Thoughtland, as much more real than Factland as the land of three dimensions seems to us more real than the land of two."[43] To suggest the existence of something higher, to merely help others conceive of it—these might seem modest aims, but in an era defined by empirical science, perhaps showing that a higher realm was scientifically plausible was enough to console dying clergymen and others who suddenly were unable to see life's meaning or death's inevitable approach with the eyes of faith.

2

The Man Who Saw the Fourth Dimension

Though religious doubts and feelings of uncertainty were common in nineteenth-century Europe and America, only occasionally did they produce the kind of despair and paralysis described by the British mathematician Charles Howard Hinton, who at one point found himself unable to say or do anything at all. At the Rugby School and then at Oxford for bachelor's and master's degrees, Hinton wrote letters home about his deteriorating condition. The first indication that something was wrong was contained in a note to his father in 1870, where he admitted that religious doubts were preventing him from proceeding with confirmation in the Church of England. But this was only a beginning, for Hinton's skepticism was running in deeper channels. When he left Oxford in 1877 and began teaching at a private secondary school he started to feel not just that everything he knew about philosophy and religion had to be discarded but that our basic perceptions of the world were illusory. Could we ever say that we knew anything with certainty? Could we believe what we saw or touched? Did our eyes tell us anything true about objects? These kinds of doubts were not merely philosophical; they were personally distressing in a way that obliterated Hinton's basic sense of security and competency in the world. He experienced a sickening vertigo as the ground tilted beneath his feet. When he looked to friends for cues on how to act or speak truly, he could not right himself. Speech became difficult. "For to a mind that enquires into what it really does know," he explained later, matter-of-factly, "it is hardly possible to enunciate complete sentences." "I was reduced," he wrote once of this time in his life, "to the last condition of mental despair."[1]

Hinton's despair was deeper and more damaging than Edwin Abbott's and in the end his effort to overcome it was more innovative and radical. Unlike Abbott, who was content to cobble together older Christian notions with newer mathematical ones, Hinton set out to develop a wholly new spiritual philosophy and a new ethics. He anchored these new ideas in a complex set of visualization exercises that (he believed) gave people unusual powers of imagination and insight, exercises that Hinton's mathematical colleagues found both difficult to master and hard to believe but that many others embraced as a pathway to mystical forms of knowledge, spiritual powers, or profound feelings of peace and composure. Hinton disseminated these exercises and his higher-dimensional ideas in a series of books and articles, including several articles in popular periodicals such as *Harper's Magazine*, attempting to show that there were spatial dimensions beyond our familiar three-dimensional world and that the human self could be trained to "see" into them. His ideas had an astonishing reach into popular culture. They were studied by modern artists, Modernist writers, mystical mathematicians, and even maverick political revolutionaries who rejected traditional religions as antiquated or superstitious but who also yearned, in some cases quite desperately, to recover an imaginative sense for the unseen and transcendent.

Seeing Higher-Dimensional Cubes

C. Howard Hinton was a student and then a teacher of mathematics, and when he fell into his paralyzing depression, he naturally turned to mathematical ideas to find something certain he could believe in. In fact, turning to mathematics to find metaphysical certainty was not an unusual strategy in nineteenth-century Europe, where, especially in England, mathematics and theology had long been seen as complementary ways of discovering ultimate truths.[2] Hinton wrote his father that while older sources of certainty were collapsing, mathematics offered ways of accurately glimpsing the outer forms of the natural world and even its deeper spiritual truths. Geometry in particular was an "exercise in direct perception," he wrote, a way of seeing into the heart of reality and beyond it to the realm of ideal or ultimate truths.[3] Geometry's ideal forms and unchanging truths were undistorted by individual wishes, biases, and perspectives. Was it here that Hinton might find a certain foundation for reasons for acting, speaking, and, eventually, believing? He sensed that if he could learn how to see things as they actually were—that is, not as they appeared to a single observer but as they might appear from all perspectives at once—he might be able to recover a sense that he was seeing the world truly.

If these initially seemed like modest aims, they eventually led to an ambitious system designed to do nothing less than entirely rework our ways of thinking about and perceiving the world. Believing that the properties of geometric objects and their arrangement in space was something that could be known with certainty, Hinton constructed a set of wooden cubes that he organized and then memorized in different configurations. At first, the set of cubes he used was 36 by 36—it was a flat arrangement of 1,296 one-inch cubes, which itself was no small accomplishment. He gave each of the cubes a unique two-word Latin name, and started memorizing as many different arrangements of the cubes as he could. (This kind of memorization amounts to an astonishing feat—but, as one biographer notes, his father was known for a remarkable memory and Hinton also had a system for reducing the total number of facts to be memorized.)[4] Later Hinton developed and recommended a smaller set of cubes that was three by three by three, twenty-seven cubes in all that were arranged in a larger Rubik's cube, though with this simplified system he assigned unique names to all sides, edges, and points of each of the twenty-seven cubes—still a formidable set of things to remember. He arranged his set of cubes in one configuration, memorized the entire thing, and then rotated the cube set and memorized it again. He gradually developed an ability to see all of the different elements and features of the cube set at once—to, in his words, have a "direct feeling of what the block is."[5]

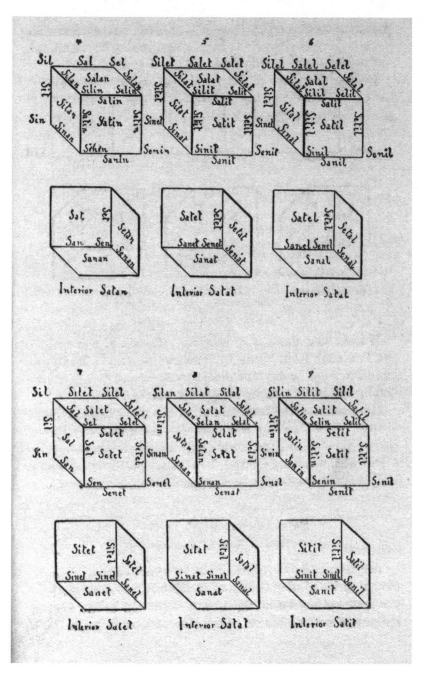

Figure 2.1 Hinton named all parts of the cubes in his system. Each face, edge, and point of each cube in the twenty-seven-cube system was given a unique name. From C. Howard Hinton, *The Fourth Dimension* (London: George Allen and Co., 1912; orig. 1904), 265.

Arranging and memorizing his cube sets had the desired effect: Hinton began to feel that he could know at least some things with certainty. Perhaps there was a stable set of realities in the world and a reliable way to approach them. "It is not a high form of knowledge," Hinton admitted once about his cube memorizations, but it was "a bit of knowledge with as little ignorance in it as we can have," and "just as it is permitted a worm or reptile to live and breathe, so on this rudimentary form of knowledge we may be able to demonstrate the functions of the mind."[6] It was not a "high form" of knowledge, but it was *certain* knowledge, and it gave Hinton something possessed by even the lowliest creatures—the ability to be at home in the world again, to live and breathe.[7] He worked outward from this small circle of certainties, beginning with his cubes and moving from there to other things in nature or his surroundings. "As the mass of known cubes became larger in number," he wrote, "a group of them would fairly well represent a wall, a door, a house, a simple natural object such as a stone or a fruit."[8] Could he now organize the flux of daily events, his work schedule, family responsibilities, and interpersonal relationships into a grid of things that, while they remained impenetrable at some ultimate level, could be anticipated, ordered, and controlled? Could he now name and manipulate more easily the inner stuff of the self, his emotions and dispositions, arriving at a more orderly geometry of human nature and human relations?

These were exciting possibilities and Hinton eagerly pursued them, but it happened that there was another form of knowledge to be found in these imaginative exercises. When Hinton discovered this new and unexpected form of knowledge, he saw that everything that he had previously learned was by contrast trivial and insignificant.

This was so because as he memorized his cube configurations he gradually developed an ability to see something invisible, a *fourth*-dimensional cube, something he dubbed a "tesseract," which is a higher-dimensional object that has since found its way into an astonishing range of twentieth-century sci-fi novels, superhero films, and comic books, not to mention modern mystical literatures. (A tesseract or hypercube is a geometric object created by stretching a three-dimensional cube into an additional fourth direction that is perpendicular to the other three directions, a direction that we cannot perceive. Geometers today use computerized images of rotating hypercubes to try to see what these objects might look like.)[9] As he learned to see this fourth-dimensional hypercube, Hinton came to believe that there was a mystical significance to seeing four-dimensional objects. When we learn to do this, he lectured once, we wake up "an intuition of [a] higher world," an inner sense that there was a higher, more real, more dimensionally complex world above our own.[10] Our three-dimensional world was only a flat shadow or projection of that higher, fourth-dimensional world. Glimpses of this higher existence put the material world into a new perspective, and, as he confided to a friend, he began to doubt if the materialist worldview was an accurate representation of the universe.[11] Though Hinton, like other intellectuals, was sometimes wary of the imagination and the ways it contaminated observation and abetted credulity, the imagination also helped him see something new, and this intrigued him. Did his imaginative exercises offer a new possibility, a method for being both reasonable and scientific, and imaginative and spiritual, at the same time?[12]

He had come a long way—from being confounded by the most trivial facts of everyday living to seeing somehow into the most abstruse matters of ultimate reality. In 1880, while in his fifth year of teaching at the Cheltenham Ladies College, Hinton married Mary Ellen Boole, the daughter of the self-taught progressive mathematician Mary Everest Boole, an event that, with the publication of his first published article on the "fourth dimension" signaled the end of his earlier crisis. Then in 1881 he became Science Master at the well-regarded Uppingham School, where Edwin Abbott's best friend, Howard Candler, was Mathematics Master. Hinton was beginning to write articles and books about seeing the fourth dimension and was now quite certain, as he wrote early in the 1880s, that no one "who spent a few years in becoming familiar with the facts of space, not by means of symbolism or reasoning but by pure observation, could doubt that there are really four dimensions."[13] He offered this kind of "pure observation" to his pupils,[14] tutored students privately, and thought about the best ways to present to the public this astonishing new method of perceiving transcendent objects. For the first time in his life, he experienced self-confidence and professional success.

Complications

But there were some matters, some facts about romantic relationships in particular, that Hinton, for all of his success in this period, had not quite worked out. On the issues of love and sex for example, he wrestled with a confusing inheritance of ideas from his father, James Hinton, a skilled ear surgeon, author of books on moral and social issues, and agitator for liberal causes. Like other reformers in his era, James Hinton insisted that marriage was oppressive and unjust to women. Why should women who want to devote themselves to art, literature, or science have to give up these pursuits and live a two-dimensional existence as wife and mother in a monogamous marriage? James Hinton believed that the constraints of monogamous marriage also caused unnatural and excessive desires in men and women, leading to infidelity and prostitution. Victorian codes about sexuality and modesty only "foster & intensify the desires that they seek to repress," one of Hinton's colleagues insisted.[15] To James Hinton, the solution was that men might take additional "spiritual wives" and that people ought to practice generally freer sexual relationships.

If James Hinton called for remarkable new freedoms, however, he also required his followers to take on certain novel moral constraints. He advocated freer sexual relations to be sure, but this teaching was contextualized in language about service, altruism, and self-abnegation, principles that he identified with the best teachings of Christianity and the true state of nature. Victorian restraints hatched by the orthodox were prudish and unnatural, he complained; the alternative was a less inhibited, more natural way of thinking about the body and sex. So he advocated freer sexual relations, female nudity, and "serving" others sexually. He regarded himself as a kind of prophet to modern women, joking once to his wife, in a phrase put to service by detractors in the 1880s, "Christ was the savior to men, and I am the savior to women, and I don't envy him one bit!"

He almost certainly had sexual relations with women outside of his marriage, and his wife was probably aware of it. A formula that James Hinton liked to quote was "truth is truth to Nature; goodness is the goodness of Nature"—but he appears to have underestimated how difficult it was to derive ethical guidelines from a reimagined Christianity and the study of nature's principles. As his friend, the writer and social reformer Havelock Ellis, wrote, "The principle was so large, and the moral field so unfamiliar, that he himself seems often to have been bewildered and confused over its meaning." Ellis, an early convert to James Hinton's brilliant ways of harmonizing science and religion and a passionate exponent of his ideas on sexuality and ethics, was in the end confused too. As we watched James Hinton, he wrote, we were sometimes "conscious of [seeing] a prophet who is caught up from the earth in a whirlwind he cannot control, and borne away in a chariot we cannot follow." Practicing a higher altruism by having additional spiritual and sexual partners; wholly reimagining Christian ideas about sin, selfishness, and what was considered "natural" and moral—these were radical new directions, and James Hinton and his followers, as they experimented with new ideas, did indeed find themselves caught up in a disorienting whirlwind.[16]

James's son, C. Howard Hinton, was also caught up in this tempest of change and experimentation. Though he married Mary Boole in 1880, by 1882 at the latest he was in a romantic relationship with a second woman named Maud Florence. Before his father James's death in 1875, Howard had pressed him about the ethics of extramarital relationships. James announced enigmatically that sometimes the remedy to such problems was worse than the disease itself.[17] This was hardly clear advice. Given his father's principles, and given the fact that Howard embraced these principles in general if not in all of their specifics, it is possible that Howard started his extramarital relationship as a way of forging ahead with James Hinton's new ethical program. Howard was casting off unnatural and prudish Victorian constraints and seeking a higher, more natural way of acting.

Though this experiment in "serving" more than one woman, if that is what it was, may have worked for a while, there surely were strains in negotiating Florence's loneliness, domestic arrangements with Boole, and the demands of the young children he and Boole were beginning to raise. How would he manage these competing claims on his time and affection? Could he "cast out" his selfishness so completely that everyone around him could be satisfied, and all tensions either reconciled or contained? This might be a good time to recall that it was relatively easy for Hinton to use his "mass of known cubes" to make sense of "a wall, a door, a house, a simple natural object such as a stone or a fruit"—it had been easy to understand and arrange these inanimate things. But human facts were more difficult to sort out, and, again, his father's contradictory inheritance was not helping. By 1882 or 1883, Howard, like other reformers charting new paths, was improvising.

Then came unexpected complications. Sometime in late 1882 Florence announced she was pregnant—with twins, it turned out. Apparently she was not as sure as he was that "spiritual" wives and legal ones had equal privileges. She proposed that they marry. For Hinton this was a difficult moment: He was confronted with consequences of his radicalism that were quite unexpected, and he did not have a clear map to follow. He did what he felt was best, and he agreed to marry her in January 1883, though this decision also had unfortunate consequences. He may have married Florence because he loved her, or because he wished to appease her, or because he wanted to give legitimacy to the children. In any case, he was now raising two sets of children, managing two different residences, loving two wives, living two lives. It is not clear if his first wife knew of his relationship with Florence, but she certainly did not know that Howard and Florence were *married*—at least for a while. Oddly, some among Howard's immediate family and friends do seem to have known about it, a few of them from the beginning, including an aunt who, a friend recalled, "says she doesn't quite take Howard's view, & feels, too, the difficulties for the children."[18] The issue of the children looms large. Whose children was she worried about: Boole's or Florence's?

Alone most of the time, Florence appears gradually to have grown resentful, emotionally disturbed, and, after everything unraveled, justifiably vindictive. The relationship deteriorated. She and Hinton may also have argued over how properly to support and care for the infant twins.[19] In any case, by 1885, Howard approached the physician and social reformer Havelock Ellis, who was his friend as well as his father's. Ellis, however, had tired of the drama. Feeling entirely lost and unsure about where to begin, Howard initially told Ellis about his many experiments in seeing tesseracts, but Ellis knew something more puzzling was coming. Howard "came to see me yesterday," Ellis wrote in a letter, and "plunged at once into a favorite question of his—'Space-relations'— walking eagerly up and down. But I knew he had something more definite than that to talk about/& by & bye he plunged into it with a good deal of confusion & hesitation."[20] The juxtapositions in this breathless encounter are fascinating—the relations of geometrical space and the confounding realities of love and marriage. In this case, apparently, the one could not solve the other.

Then, in the summer of 1886, things deteriorated when Boole became pregnant with their fourth child and someone told her about Hinton's other marriage. Boole, who is upset but not irate in the sources, insisted Hinton go to the police to confess the crime of bigamy. Together they first went to Howard's supervisor, the headmaster at the Uppingham School, Edward Thring. "What a piteous and strange thing," Thring confided to his diary the same day. "Hinton came in with his wife and his sister (I understand) to say he had committed bigamy and that they had persuaded him to give himself up to justice." The next day he and Boole went to the police station, he confessed, and, according to the *Times*, Boole "said she did not wish to prosecute," explaining that the "prisoner had only given himself up as a matter of conscience as they did not wish to have a secret in the house." Howard was jailed briefly. Maud Florence, who had disguised her identity by taking the pseudonym Maud Wheldon, was located and deposed. A trial date was set for October 15, 1886, and the whole affair was covered by all three major London papers and papers as far afield as Birmingham. When Florence was deposed, she was asked if she thought what she did was wrong. She said no; she loved C. Howard Hinton. But when the deposition was over she was full of despair and confusion. When the moment came to sign the papers she had to turn and ask, "What is my name?"[21]

Howard had ruined several lives, including, for the moment at least, his own. He was convicted of bigamy and fired from Uppingham. Maud Florence's passionate love for him had turned into the coldest hate, and reports from mutual friends on Florence's condition pointed to alarming levels of despair and despondency. She told one friend she was going mad. She told another she wanted revenge. Another thought she might kill herself.[22] Howard tried unsuccessfully to find work lecturing on fourth-dimensional space—about which, one friend said, no doubt accurately, that "he was becoming an obsessional." He tried to get students for private mathematics tutoring. None of it was enough to support Boole and their children. Elisabeth Cobb, a friend who appears to have wanted the best for both of them, stated the situation plainly. "All the family . . . have to join together to support this man & wife & all the children, in their utter material ruin."[23] A campaign against James Hinton's visionary ideas was already under way by the 1880s and his son's troubles were used to great effect by those who hated James for espousing irresponsible teachings on free love, female nakedness, and "serving" young women in sexual relations. As Howard's broken life plainly demonstrated, such behaviors "served" no one especially well.

A "New Era" of Thought

After searching unsuccessfully for work and enduring ignominious rumors and innuendos, Hinton did what disgraced reformers and prophets have done for centuries: He left town. He packed up Mary and their four boys and left for a new job as headmaster of the Victoria Public School in Yokohama, Japan.[24] Nine days after the birth of his fourth son and just before leaving for Japan, he wrote a frank letter to his editor, who had by this time published one of his books on higher-dimensional seeing, and in the letter he insisted that a more complete knowledge of higher dimensions would help him navigate this difficult time. "What I have come to see is that in the mere facts of the material world there is an evident and clear proof of a higher existence than that which we are conscious of in our ordinary bodily life," he said. Knowing the higher existence was accomplished not via some "historical 'revelation'" but from a "purely scientific" process, Hinton wrote, a process that led to psychological comfort and ethical direction. "However much or little these [ideas] may seem in the reflections of others, they have been of vital importance to me—and the effect has been thus far simply ruinous—for I found myself in a false position—and the first & absolute condition of any true life as I understand it now lies in absolute openness."

The meaning of this despairing confession is not immediately clear, but what Hinton seemed to be saying was that his higher-space knowledge had brought into focus the immorality, the lies and illusions, that characterized his double life. Now that he knew this, he would rebuild his life on surer foundations. "I have had to give up everything and go through disgrace such as rarely falls to anyone's lot—and have to put up with misconception on every side. But still although I have lost all outward things I have got on the right basis of life." He had been lost, but now armed with his metaphysical system he was on track. Casting out one's selfish perspective, learning to see things from all sides at once, put the end to his experiment in bigamy. "Knowing yourself as 4-dimensional," Hinton once wrote in an unpublished set of notes, "makes you know the world differently."[25]

In Japan, and then as a mathematics instructor at Princeton and an assistant professor at the University of Minnesota, Hinton developed his thinking and pedagogy of higher dimensions. Because he believed that our normal perceptions were merely the result of learning to experience life in three dimensions, he devised ways of familiarizing children and young people with a wider range of experience. "The first step in the cultivation of the imagination is to give a child 27 cubes, and make him name each of them according to its place, as he puts them up." Hinton also devised games with the cubes. For instance, he had a cube set represent a house, with certain cube locations symbolizing chairs, beds, clothes, and even people. He asked students to do these visualization exercises daily so they could imagine themselves inside this gridded three-dimensional landscape. Sometimes he would ask them to walk imaginary routes up and down, back and forth, through the block of cubes. Sometimes he asked students to build a multistory building in their heads with cubes or he would have them play chess blindfolded, which required knowing the positions of all chess pieces at each moment. When a child succeeded in memorizing a set of cubes, his imagination, his "power of inward drawing or modeling," Hinton wrote, summarizing his own experience, was greatly increased and a "type of absolute knowledge" took shape, a knowledge "to which he will strive to make all his other knowledge conform." Each cube, or each position in space, Hinton exclaimed, "is a type of what a piece of knowledge ought to be, simple, definite, and limited in itself, yet capable of being brought into relation with every other piece of knowledge."[26]

There were still other ways to teach children to visualize moving in space. Hinton's son Theodore remembered that during their years in Japan his father constructed a three-dimensional climbing frame out of bamboo. Most people moved in only two dimensions, left/right and forward/back, but Hinton's climbing structure allowed children to move up/down as well. "He believed that if people could become comfortable in a real three-dimensional space," Theodore remembered, "the intellectual step to the fourth would be easier." One of Hinton's boys went on to develop and sell these climbing structures, the first ever "jungle gyms."[27]

Hinton also published articles and books on his higher-dimensional discoveries. (When people have rapturous experiences along the lines of Hinton's mystical revelations, they generally do not keep such things to themselves, and Hinton was no exception.) He published several articles on the fourth dimension, epistemology, and the imagination, including one in *Harper's* in 1904, and a number of books, including *Scientific Romances* (1884), *A New Era of Thought* (1888), and *The Fourth Dimension* (1904).

Responses to Hinton's publications varied. The harshest criticism came in an unsigned review of *The Fourth Dimension* in *Nature,* a review that criticized Hinton for mixing legitimate mathematics with illegitimate speculations about metaphysical problems and the human soul.[28] Other reviews, however, were more sympathetic. When the British philosopher and logician Bertrand Russell reviewed *The Fourth Dimension* he wrote that while he was not (yet) persuaded about the existence of higher dimensions, speculations about higher dimensions nevertheless seemed useful in certain ways. Such speculations "stimulate the imagination, and free the intellect from the shackles of the actual. A complete intellectual liberty would only be attained by a mind that could think as easily of the nonexistent as of the existent. Toward this unattainable goal, non-Euclidean geometry carries us a stage; and some degree of emancipation from the real world is likely to be secured by the readers to whom this book is addressed." (He also said that Hinton's cubes, "as ingenious as they are," required "as much thought for their use as would suffice for the understanding of the fourth dimension without their aid." In his diary he dubbed Hinton the "conscientious bigamist.")[29]

Earlier mathematicians such as James Clerk Maxwell, an evangelical, and William K. Clifford, an outspoken agnostic, also believed that the idea of higher dimensions was liberating in certain ways. (The philosopher George Santayana by contrast thought thinking about unobservable things such as higher dimensions was useless. Imagined facts, he said once, in a statement that directly contradicted Hinton's cherished beliefs, can never "become parts or extensions of the experience they are thought to explain.")[30] Others debated whether it was possible for human beings to visualize a higher dimension, how to achieve such an accomplishment, and whether the effort to do so was worthwhile at all. Some were enthusiastic about Hinton's ideas. In the journal *Science,* one physicist discussing Hinton's work argued that developing our abilities to see fourth-dimensional spaces might help biologists better understand nature, physicists better understand natural forces, and theologians understand better new religious truths. Letters to the editor in subsequent issues took issue with some of these claims.[31] Reviewers writing for the *New York Times* and other periodicals were sometimes puzzled by Hinton's cube exercises but they generally praised his imaginative thinking.[32]

Hinton was working with the same concepts that Abbott engaged in *Flatland,* concepts related to geometry, mathematics, and spatial dimensions, though he understood better than Abbott the mathematics of higher dimensions as that field developed. The beginnings of the field can be traced to 1854, when a young German mathematician, Bernhard Riemann, who was a student of the great German mathematician Carl Friedrich Gauss, gave a lecture suggesting that our three-dimensional space was warped or bent in higher dimensions. Riemann's work generated widespread academic discussion in Europe and America. A number of people interpreted and popularized Riemann's ideas in subsequent decades, including the British mathematicians W. K. Clifford and J. J. Sylvester. Clifford translated Riemann's paper and published it in *Nature* in 1873; he also gave a popular digest of Riemann's work in public lectures at the Royal Institution in 1874. The most important person interpreting Riemann, however, was Hermann von Helmholtz, whom we already discussed, an expert on issues related to perception and space and the person who contextualized discussions about spatial dimensions in broader conversations about how we sense the world around us. Helmholtz argued that we were able to sense three dimensions not because of innate categories of thought (as Kant had said) but because we had learned to experience three and only three dimensions.[33]

This meant that it was possible to learn to imagine a fourth dimension if we could develop ways of seeing and touching it, an idea that directly influenced Hinton. Historians have documented how Helmholtz and other academics were preoccupied with the idea of higher dimensions between 1870 and 1920.[34] Though Helmholtz did not necessarily believe in the existence of actual higher dimensions, his popular lectures on the subject made such speculations seem appealing and respectable. Many people started to think about, and some tried to imagine, a separate, invisible fourth-dimensional space.

Merely Modern Superstition

It is an understatement to say that not everyone was pleased with this development. Professor Helmholtz "tickles the popular consciousness" with tales of flat worlds and intelligent two-dimensional beings, one scientific colleague groused. The regrettable result was a compromising of the objectivity of science and a trickling down of imaginative errors in which less intelligent people, indulging their mythopoetic instincts, now talked about higher-dimensional realities and a fourth-dimensional "spirit world."[35] This was a gross misunderstanding of scientific concepts. Insisting that an accurate view of the world meant expunging imaginative inclinations, fanciful over-beliefs, and wild speculations about unseen realms, this same scientist objected to the increasingly bold, and inanely conceived, popular appropriations of reasonable mathematical ideas. The overheated imagination and human mythopoetic instincts led people to see things, including ghosts, that simply did not exist, and it was these instincts that drove fourth-dimensional enthusiasts like Hinton.[36] In the face of such stubborn superstitions, intellectuals were forced to stand up and police the line between flights of imaginative fancy and sober, scientific knowledge. They were not afraid to humiliate anyone who crossed it.

It was the prevailing (though by no means universal) view among professional scientists that imaginative fantasies and beliefs were the preoccupations of mystics, oddballs, clerics, and people who read too much fiction. Given this, it is not surprising that some mathematicians objected when their geometrical concepts were used to buttress mystical beliefs. Arthur Crathorne, a professor of mathematics at the University of Illinois, for example, complained in 1910 that mathematical ideas relating to the fourth dimension had been

> immediately seized by the romance writers, the prestidigitators, and a certain class of spiritualists. To the first it gave a new method for the disappearance and reappearance of the hero or the villain. As a rule, he returns as a reflection of his former self, having become turned over in the fourth dimension. To the second class it gave a new set of catchwords and phrases for use in sleight-of-hand performances. To the third class, led by Professor Zollner of Leipsic, the fourth dimension became the abode of the spirit world. For them it solved a great problem, and many are their arguments to prove their contentions. The Bible is brought in to testify, and an extra dimension is read into the meaning of such verses as, "May be able to comprehend with all saints, what is the breadth and length and depth and height." (Ephesians iii, 18)[37]

Crathorne was right: Writers, magicians, entertainers, spiritualists, and religious believers of different inclinations had appropriated the fourth dimension for different purposes. The problem that Crathorne identified was that while the fourth dimension was certainly useful in the context of mathematical calculations, there was no reason therefore to believe in or try to imagine an actual fourth spatial dimension.[38] There was a difference between the conceptual spaces of mathematics and the empirical spaces of real life.

When he edited essays submitted for *Scientific American's* 1909 contest for the best explanations of the fourth dimension, the Brown University geometer Henry Manning made similar points. He reminded readers that geometries were mathematical systems that did not necessarily comport with reality. "Geometry does not deal with material things like a string or sheet of paper, but with abstract lines and surfaces. Nor does geometry deal with actual facts. It only shows what would be true if certain other things are true. We apply some statement of geometry to a string or to a sheet of paper whenever the conditions of the statement seem to be fulfilled, and the correctness of the result depends upon whether the conditions are fulfilled." People who understood this had no difficulty understanding how mathematicians could develop higher-dimensional geometries—and they had no difficulty understanding that just because these geometries could be developed it did not mean that they pointed to real, higher-dimensional spaces, to say nothing of ghosts or other such entities.[39] (The *Scientific American* contest elicited 245 essays from the United States and "almost every civilized country.")

Both Manning and Crathorne seemed absolutely certain on these matters, though in actuality the problem was complex, as we will see, for not everyone understood in the same way the relationship between the imaginal worlds of mathematical variables and the material realm of real things in the physical world. In any case, when true believers such as the British journalist and spiritualist W. T. Stead exclaimed that "we are on the eve of the fourth dimension," an era in which "the limitations of time and space furl up and disappear," sober mathematicians were forced to clarify what they meant by the fourth dimension. We have been talking about linear algebraic equations, the British mathematician E. H. Neville grumbled, not about "a new heaven and a new earth."[40]

On the other hand, some intellectuals felt torn between pleasing mostly skeptical scientific colleagues and following their own furtive, spiritual curiosities. One of these intellectuals was the Canadian-American astronomer Simon Newcomb, who knew Hinton's work well, almost assuredly knew Hinton personally, and probably even helped get him a job at the National Bureau of Standards in Washington after he left the University of Minnesota. Newcomb expressed interest in new higher-dimensional concepts in an article in *Harpers Magazine,* noting how strange it was that in his time "the most rigorous mathematical methods correspond to the most mystical ideas of the Swedenborgian and other forms of religion."[41] In this article and in articles written for scientists, such as an 1898 piece in *Science* and his 1897 presidential speech to the American Mathematical Society, he argued that imagining higher dimensions was a useful exercise. In these pieces he raised the possibility that there might be actual higher dimensions, other spaces or universes, all around us. But physical evidence of these other worlds had not yet materialized. In other writings Newcomb struck about the same posture—he admitted that different perspectives were possible but maintained the scientific position that affirming the existence of these other spaces required empirical proof. Newcomb became well known for his interest in higher dimensions and was even mentioned as an authority on the subject by the Time Traveler in H. G. Wells's *The Time Machine* (1895).

In other contexts, however, and especially in private, Newcomb was less inhibited. A student of Newcomb's at Johns Hopkins University recalled that Newcomb admitted in private that a spirit world might be explained by the fourth dimension. "To admit this conception of a fourth dimension," this student recalled, "would give a sort of reality to an invisible world of spirits all about us and would help to explain not a few of the old mystical ideas of the human race." Newcomb carefully broached this issue with others, including academic colleagues, though encounters with hardheaded scientists sometimes yielded predictably disappointing results, as they had for Hinton. At one point, Newcomb announced a lecture on campus on the fourth dimension and was keen to get his colleague in physics, Henry Rowland, to attend. Like Newcomb, Rowland was a distinguished scientist. He had been the first president of the American Physical Society, and, according to Rowland's own testimony, he was the "ablest physicist in America." (When subjected to questioning on this matter, Rowland raised the issue while in the presence of Thomas Edison and the great mathematician Sir William Thompson. Evidently both luminaries agreed.)[42]

When Rowland heard about Newcomb's upcoming lecture on the fourth dimension, he promptly scheduled another activity. Before beginning the lecture, Newcomb dispatched colleagues to locate the absent Rowland, who (it turned out) was horseback riding. Though the assembled audience included some traveling from long distances, Newcomb insisted on postponing for a week. A week later, everything went as planned, with Rowland in attendance, and at the end Newcomb turned for his colleague's opinion. "Rowland looked as though awakened from a deep study," a student recalled, and "then in a jerky manner, he answered, 'I'm a practical man. I don't know anything about a fourth dimension.'" He then rose and walked out. Newcomb was "a bit embarrassed," observers noted, perhaps even hurt. It was an idiosyncratic moment in the history of science and the fourth dimension, but it pointed to something larger: Those who, like Newcomb, were personally interested in higher dimensions had to face the fact that respectable scientists, insisting that science was concerned only with empirical realities, might respond with irritation and avoidance.[43]

The Fourth Dimension as Hallucination

But reactions to fourth-dimensional speculation went beyond disdain, wariness, and avoidance to encompass genuine fear that these ways of "reeducating" the senses could imperil human health and sanity. Such fanciful speculations and imaginative exercises, some observers worried, might lead to perceptual mistakes, hallucinations, and even permanent mental instability. Edwin Slosson, an American chemist and popular science writer, argued that efforts to imagine a higher dimension strained "the imagination to the breaking point," while others cited documented cases where the effort to imagine higher dimensions led to insanity or suicide.[44] In fact it is not difficult to find notices in British and American periodicals discussing the problem of the fourth dimension and mental illness. Contemporary fiction also dealt at length with the idea that the fourth dimension could be an unhealthy obsession, though the topic was sometimes dealt with humorously. (One notice in *Life Magazine* from 1912, for example, warned readers about professors who taught esoteric higher-dimensional notions that entangled one's mental faculties.) Though Howard Hinton denied that developing fourth-dimensional vision caused mental problems, he often encountered these criticisms. It did not help that there were widely publicized cases linking fourth-dimensional enthusiasms and mental illness, including one notice, picked up by a number of British newspapers, that an Oxford undergraduate and son of a local priest committed suicide after studying the fourth dimension. Newspapers reported his brother saying that the evening before the suicide the troubled undergraduate "wished to discuss the 'fourth dimension,' [and] higher mathematics. He was very excited. The next morning, he was very white, and his eyes were staring. He said he had been out of his mind, but was then sane, and that he knew it at that time, but might forget it. . . . He also said, afterwards, 'I'm going mad.' "[45] Did transcending normal perceptual abilities make one unfit for regular, three-dimensional living?

When doctors and psychiatrists heard about fourth-dimensional visions they worried that such experiences were a dangerous type of hallucination. Beginning in the late 1880s, scientists deployed debunking categories such as hallucination for religious experiences of all kinds, using the term to talk about people who had heavenly visions or saw spirits and ghosts. (The 1880s and 1890s was an era of great popular interest in ghosts and ghost seeing. In fact, when Hinton published his 1884 pamphlet "The Fourth Dimension," his publisher appended the subtitle "Ghosts Explained.") Skeptics insisted that ghost seeing was a kind of hallucination, by which they meant a form of perception that seemed real but actually existed only in the brain and mind. Scientists generally were not surprised to find people dreaming about, hoping for, or imagining things that were not real. Their studies showed that hallucinations and perceptual mistakes were quite common. The British Society for Psychical Research, for example, carried out a "Census of Hallucinations" from 1889 to 1892 that showed that one in ten people had a vivid hallucination at some point in their lives. William James, in his key 1890 psychology textbook and in the *Varieties of Religious Experience* (1902), confirmed that a range of healthy people experienced visions or heard voices. And Francis Galton, in his studies of mental imagery, found that people were generally susceptible to many different types of hallucinations, including oscillating color patterns, number forms, synesthesia, involuntary waking visions, and even seeing ghosts. (Galton himself confessed to a remarkable visionary experience, which was undeniably Hintonian, though he did not mention Hinton by name. "An eminent mineralogist assures me that he is able to imagine simultaneously all sides of a crystal with which he is familiar," Galton wrote. "I may be allowed to quote a curious faculty of my own in respect to this. It is exercised only occasionally and in dreams, or rather in nightmares, but under those circumstances I am perfectly conscious of embracing an entire sphere in a single perception. It appears to lie within my mental eyeball, and to be viewed centripetally.")[46] Galton could see all sides of a sphere at once.

The category of hallucination was often applied to fourth-dimensional visions in the same way that it was used to understand ghost sightings or phantasmagoria—that is, as a way to disabuse and debunk. It was used to reveal visionary experiences as symptomatic of an unsound mind. All kinds of pathological conditions were said to cause hallucinations—hypochondria, hysteria, insanity, obsessive thoughts, intoxication, anxiety, wishful thinking, excessive credulity, and excessive emotionalism.

There were some, however, who, while recognizing the power of scientific studies of hallucination, nevertheless refused always to interpret hallucination as a wholly false form of seeing. Their thinking brought into focus a set of mediations between scientific categories and religious notions that generated new ways of thinking about visionary experiences and how to understand them. For instance, William James and others associated with the Society for Psychical Research used categories such as hallucination but they remained agnostic about the truthfulness of hallucinations and often found ways of marking these experiences as worthwhile and useful. James did this most famously in the *Varieties,* a book with an astonishing reach in popular and intellectual circles in Europe and America. James's narratives of visions, revelations, and intuitions introduced a huge audience to different types of experiences and ways of understanding them. When, for instance, he spoke of the hallucination of a friend who sensed a presence around him and then felt himself physically grasped, James discussed this hallucination as a phenomenon that pointed to hidden capacities in the self. This example suggested "the existence in our mental machinery of a sense of present reality more diffused and general than that which our special senses yield." Like Edmund Gurney, another investigator of psychical phenomena, he wondered if there was another, little understood mental faculty that could sense things beyond the normal range of perceptions. James and others associated this realm of the self with the "subconscious," arguing that this faculty might be able to perceive things above the senses—spiritual realities and truths. If there was such a subconscious realm, hallucinations could therefore be both "inside the head" and also true.

William James and C. Howard Hinton carried on a remarkable correspondence about these and other matters for about a decade around the turn of the century, both equally interested in the possibility of a higher sensibility somewhere in the self. James liked Hinton's ideas, taught them to his students at Harvard, invited Hinton to lecture at Harvard, and even supported him with a loan.[47] Hinton argued that the best way to activate this higher sensibility in the self was by putting it in contact with higher objects, which could be done by constructing and rotating his cube sets. "Our limitation must be one of consciousness—the totality of sense organs working under this condition—of perceiving in 3 space," he wrote James. "And the only way in which the higher space existence can be seen is in the change of our existing objects."[48] If one studied, sensed, and experienced the cube sets, one could develop crucial inner sensibilities. Perhaps, Hinton said, refining these inner sensibilities would lead to other discoveries such as "the existence of personality outside the individual man; the object, and possible unity, of mankind as a whole; the connection between ethical conceptions and individual existence—i.e. the notion that in a sense of right there is a reference to a deeper being than is exhausted by the description of the vicissitudes of life as we actually know it."[49] Hinton, James, Frederic Myers, the English mystical poet and philosopher Edward Carpenter (who was influenced by James Hinton), and many others linked the mysterious realms of consciousness to the fourth dimension and spoke of fourth-dimensional "hallucination" as a projection of real truths from deep inside the self. Like other religious virtuosi, these thinkers believed that the outer world was an empty show, a shadowy illusion, insisting that the real world was the inner world of ideals or *spirit*. This was how they domesticated the hallucination critique, insisting that once people experienced the fourth dimension they would see how pallid three-dimensional realities were. They would see, as the Russian esoteric philosopher Pieter Ouspensky put it, that the three-dimensional world "was the creation of our own fantasy, a phantom host, an optical illusion, a delusion—anything one pleases excepting only reality."[50] Real fourth-dimensional imagination turned the material world into its own kind of fantasy and phantom.

Could Higher Spaces Be Imagined?

These kinds of epistemological questions were important not just for psychologists and philosophers but also for mathematicians, physicists, and other scientists. They too wanted to know if people came to know the real and true via the senses or if other capacities played a part. Could one carefully use the imagination, or train the self to appreciate beauty, or develop certain intuitions or feelings—were these also ways of probing truth? These questions were fiercely debated by intellectuals and other commentators, including scientists such as T. H. Huxley and John Tyndall, beginning in the 1840s. Though he admitted that science sometimes incorporated a form of disciplined imagination (especially during hypothesis construction), Huxley generally believed that imagination, speculation, and faith were destructive of clear thinking. True knowledge was arrived at by one method only—experimental verification of empirical facts. For these reasons, Huxley had little interest in mathematics, which he believed was purely deductive and thus unproductive of new knowledge. Mathematics neither advanced our knowledge of verifiable facts nor usefully expanded our range of thinking.

Mathematicians, of course, disagreed. The president of the Mathematical and Physical Section of the British Association for the Advancement of Science, J. J. Sylvester, responded to Huxley in an address to that body in 1869, claiming that mathematics incorporated both empirical observations and "the exercise of the highest efforts of imagination and invention."[51] It was both empirical and imaginative. As an example of how these practices were harmonized, Sylvester pointed to non-Euclidean geometry. Different geometrical systems could be developed, but in order to understand the geometry of the phenomenal world we had to compare these geometric systems with empirical facts. Thus the details of our three-dimensional geometry were not merely mental constructs derived from deductive reasoning. They also were tested by empirical observation.[52]

On the other hand, Sylvester also believed that mathematics had an imaginative power that went beyond empirical facts. That mathematicians could imagine alternate geometries, he argued in the same speech, pointed to a kind of creative power that mathematicians used to uncover unseen elements of the universe that might someday be verified empirically. Mathematics pointed in new directions, probing deeper, more fundamental realities that were beyond experience. Sylvester even quoted the great mathematician Carl Friedrich Gauss, who had quipped that though for a time he had worked on non-Euclidean geometries, he eventually put them aside until after death when his "conceptions of space should have become amplified and extended."[53] Sylvester had made his point: Mathematical reasoning pointed us in transcendent directions. It was a supremely important discipline, he concluded, because of the "world of ideas which [it] discloses or illuminates, the contemplation of divine beauty and order which it induces, the harmonious connexion of its parts," and "the infinite hierarchy and absolute evidence of the truths with which it is concerned."[54] In contemporary debates between empiricists and idealists, debates that animated academic and popular discussions, mathematicians often argued that mathematics uncovered logical, ideal truths. Sylvester made similar kinds of arguments.[55]

Sylvester expanded on these points in an edited version of this address subsequently published in *Nature* in 1870, pointing out in a lengthy footnote that there was something appealing about speculations on the fourth dimension. "Dr. Salmon, in his extensions of Chasles' theory of characteristics to surfaces, Mr. Clifford, in a question of probability . . . and myself in my theory of partitions, . . . have all felt and given evidence of the practical utility of handling space of four dimensions, as if it were conceivable space."[56] Such a thing could be conceived and used in equations, but what was the relationship between conceiving of a thing in mathematics and asserting its truth in reality? Was the fourth dimension merely a mathematical variable or did it force us to make new metaphysical claims?[57]

Sylvester did not answer directly, but he clearly believed that the conceptions of the greatest mathematical minds probed ideal spaces that others could not see. "If an Aristotle, or Descartes, or Kant assures me that he recognizes God in the conscience I accuse my own blindness if I fail to see him. If Gauss, Cayley, Riemann, Schalfli, Salmon, Clifford, Kronecker, have an inner assurance of the reality of transcendental space, I strive to bring my faculties of mental vision into accordance with theirs."[58] Sylvester was not the only British mathematician using theological language to describe the relationship between geometry and absolute truth. In his 1883 presidential speech to the British Association for the Advancement of Science, to cite just one example, Arthur Cayley developed the point by saying that "the truths of geometry are truths precisely because they relate to and express the properties of what Mill calls 'purely imaginary objects': . . . I would myself say that the purely imaginary objects are the only realities . . . in regard to which the corresponding physical objects are as the shadows in the cave."[59] In

England, mathematical truths, like religious truths, had long been considered ways of seeing beyond the shadowy phenomenal world to the highest realities beyond them.

Thus, while many mathematicians and scientists did not embrace the fourth dimension as a pathway to ecstatic religious visions the concept nevertheless did important imaginative work for them. Some, including the mathematical physicists James Clerk Maxwell and Peter Tait and the Canadian-American mathematician and astronomer Simon Newcomb, seemed to think that the fourth-dimension concept made the existence of heaven or a spirit world more plausible.[60] In *The Unseen Universe,* for example, Tait and his coauthor speculated that the soul was like a knotted vortex ring that came from an invisible dimension.[61] Others thought that our ability to conceive of higher dimensions was itself evidence for a transcendent dimension to reality, a formulation structurally similar to older ontological arguments for the existence of God.[62] Still others who remained agnostic about the existence of real higher-dimensional spaces nevertheless insisted that the effort to imagine such spaces was itself emotionally or intellectually liberating. Professed agnostics such as Bertrand Russell and William Clifford embraced the fourth dimension as a way to emancipate the self from the imaginative limits imposed by scientific positivism. Clifford, who, like Hinton, experienced a despairing crisis of faith, admitted in 1873 that higher-dimensional geometries made "the whole of geometry . . . far more complete and interesting. . . . In fact, I do not mind confessing that I personally have often found relief from the dreary infinities of homoloidal space in the consoling hope that, after all, this other [geometry] may be the true state of things."[63] As late as 1940, writing in their bestselling *Mathematics and the Imagination,* the mathematicians Edward Kasner and James R. Newman pointed to the importance of reflections on higher dimensions. "No concept that has come out of our heads or pens marked a greater forward step in our thinking, no idea of religion, philosophy or science broke more sharply with tradition and commonly accepted knowledge, than the idea of a fourth dimension."[64]

What was the nature of the relief and liberation experienced when mathematicians and scientists pondered the fourth dimension? Part of it was simply that these new ideas led to a deeper understanding of space and an expanding sense of its possibilities. But for some it involved something more, a sense of wonder and awe at the mysterious depth of the universe. This extra sense of mystery and wonder is hard to identify in mathematical papers published in professional publications, but it comes into focus when examining the lives of more philosophically oriented mathematicians, such as Cassius J. Keyser, Adrain Professor of Mathematics at Columbia University between 1904 and 1927. Keyser insisted that geometers delighted in a kind of spiritual practice when they imagined these new higher-dimensional structures and pondered how they expanded the mind. "He beholds them with the eye of the understanding and delights in the presence of their supersensuous beauty. It is by creation of hyperspaces that the rational spirit secures release from limitation. In them it lives ever joyously, sustained by an unfailing sense of infinite freedom." He linked this sense of freedom with human progress and argued that hyperspace was the amplest "freedom ever won by the human spirit." Human progress meant being released from life's limitations and changes, from the world of the senses, from the contingent and mortal. Higher-space ideas liberated us because they made accessible a stable world of pure thought free of temporal and spatial limitations. As a way of breaking free of the limitations of our senses, mathematics was similar to theology; both were "sciences of idealization" that helped us conceptualize transcendent things.[65]

Keyser, for one, was sure that the tragic move of modern culture toward agnosticism could be reversed by deploying the ideal realities discovered by mathematics. Keyser's point was not so radical, for many would have agreed that mathematics accessed ideal truths beyond the ken of empirical science. The fourth dimension was another ideal truth that mathematicians probed in order to understand better the world and its parts. Though at least one of Keyser's colleagues at Columbia was astounded that "several distinguished geometers" were insisting they could actually intuit or visualize a fourth spatial dimension, Keyser and others did not equivocate. He wanted to restore an imaginative, even spiritual, element to western culture and thus mitigate the "tragedy" of our modern loss of imaginative vision.[66] Keyser believed that more mathematicians and scientists needed to write about the deeper, philosophical, and religious implications of the scientific worldview, offering scientific concepts and ideas as new ways to inculcate enchantment, awe, and wonder.

⌒⌒⌒

Hinton too was beset by worries about agnosticism and sometimes spoke of his cube system as a way of overcoming the limits agnostics placed upon knowledge. Sometime between 1902 and his death in 1907, he complained to James that "the whole idea of explaining us as digestive process or physical bodily affections is utterly absurd." "I am a higher being," he insisted, adding that his consciousness "is not limited in the same way my sense perceptions are."[67] In an unpublished, fictionalized account of his life, Hinton spoke to similar issues in a dialogue with a Mr. Thicket, a hard-hearted agnostic with "a dogged and resolute countenance." There had been a lot of "destructive materialism through which the old ideals disappear," he told Thicket. But there were constructive possibilities too, "through which new [ideals] rise up, or the old ones reappear under a different form." Thicket, who was more interested in the destruction of the old than the creation of something new, asked if he had read the great agnostic Robert Ingersoll. "You couldn't bring a boy up on Ingersoll," Hinton told the thickheaded Thicket, responding in a way that reminds us that it was Hinton's need to have a *philosophy to live with* that started him on his path in the first place. But he had another reason for wanting a philosophy to live with, for he and Mary Boole now had five sons—the fate of his children with Maud Florence is unknown—and like others of his era, he wondered how to raise them during a time when everyone was casting off the old. Mr. Thicket, he said, speaking now to a sympathetic friend, had "sterling qualities but has parted company with nearly all those ideas in connection with which those qualities originated. I wonder what the effect will be on the coming generation?"[68] What would be the sources of the coming ethical and spiritual worldview?

This was the crucial dilemma of Hinton's age, which Matthew Arnold characterized, writing slightly earlier, as "Wandering between two worlds, one dead / The other powerless to be born."[69] But understanding better the lives of both Abbott and Hinton and their considerable legacies helps us see that many people overcame doubt and despair and forged ahead with constructive projects of their own imagining. In

Hinton's case, the ideas he developed and promoted helped him and others find a sense of certainty about what could be known, a set of moral guidelines to shape what should be done, and a sensibility of higher realities that satisfied spiritual longings for something beyond. His ideas were embraced by many.[70] To be sure, writers, artists, social reformers, mystics, and intellectuals all embraced Hinton's ideas not merely because they suggested the existence of a space that somehow existed outside of the ironclad laws of nature; they embraced his ideas also because they represented an underlying order that might anchor them in a twentieth-century world that, as we will see, would be marked by confusing prophesies of religious change, social reform, and cultural revolution.

3

New Heaven, New Earth

It was an enchanting vision—somewhere above the suffering and pain of everyday life existed a higher realm, a space above the linear timeline propelling us from birth to death, a realm that we might access in meditative practices and even return to at death. This Hintonian vision appealed to many who sought new ways of thinking about transcendence, new methods of cultivating spiritual practices, and new traditions that might replace older religious ones that now seemed unpalatable. The twentieth century was obviously a new age, and higher-dimensional ideas were embraced as the way forward by many—by rural preachers, urbane liberals, spirit channelers, itinerant lecturers, inspired visionaries, and even Ivy League academics. Some were liberal Christians who reimagined the Resurrection and Christ's miracles in fourth-dimensional terms, as Abbott and his admirers did. Others were mystics and radicals who studied mathematical essays by C. Howard Hinton or Hermann von Helmholtz and saw in them the seeds of a new metaphysical worldview or social order. And there were still others who treated Hinton's cubes as objects of spiritual power, as tools that bestowed visionary capacities when used in private meditations, public meetings, or séances. It was quite understandable then that sober mathematicians observing the situation would grouse that "a certain mythical concept, described as '*the* Fourth Dimension'" had become irresistible to gullible people, complaining furthermore that these people linked this new concept to mystical entities such as electricity, energy, the inner stuff of matter, human thought, or an eternal spirit.[1] These were clearly unintelligent things to be doing. In any case, such complaints did not prevent true believers from insisting that the math of higher dimensions, far from being merely an intellectual exercise, was actually a pathway leading a new chosen people to the Promised Land.

Like the Israelites of old, however, they would get there without their Moses. On April 30, 1907, C. Howard Hinton and his wife Mary attended the annual dinner of the Society of Philanthropic Inquiry in Washington, D.C. Hinton did not know it, but it would be not just his last time socializing with friends but also his final exit from three-dimensional existence. The evening began auspiciously, with printed programs that featured Hinton's talk at the end of the night. When his turn came, Hinton stood up and gave what his wife remembered, writing in a sad letter to William James, as a "wonderful speech." By the end of it, however, something was wrong. Hinton finished his remarks, walked out of the banquet, and fell to the ground dead. Hinton generally promised a lot, but that evening's remarks were particularly ambitious—a brief talk, the program announced, on "Psychic Entrance into Life in the Fourth Dimension or Heaven or any Other Place." On this occasion at least, Hinton succeeded in ways no one could have imagined.[2]

Religious Uses of Abbott and Hinton

It is worth beginning this chapter on fourth-dimensional mystics and visionaries by pointing out that their lives took place during a time of widespread spiritual and social experimentation. In the decades before the Great War, many searched for new ways both to conceive of heaven and to organize matters on earth. The iconoclastic progressive philosopher and activist Edward Carpenter located the beginnings of the modern revolt against Victorian culture slightly earlier, in the 1880s, using an apt metaphor for this period's elusive boundaries. "The Socialist and

Anarchist propaganda, the Feminist and Suffragist upheaval, the huge Trade-union growth, the Theosophic movement, the new currents in the Theatrical, Musical and Artistic worlds, the torrent even of change in the Religious world—all constituted so many streams and headwaters converging, as it were, to a great river."[3] Artists, writers, philosophers, and politicians penned manifestos and experimented with different ways of thinking and acting. The art critic Holbrook Jackson, writing in his classic 1913 assessment, recalled a period of intense cultural change, a moment when a new age was born. Older aristocracies and monarchies were attacked by Young Turk democrats, political revolutionaries, and firebrand socialists who saw the turn of the century as the time to act. Older regimes, such as those held together by the Russian Czar and the Ottoman Sultan, were swept away, while other governments were dramatically reformed. Though scholars of religion working (like other scholars) within their specialties have sometimes ignored these widespread social changes, they have not overlooked the period's tectonic religious rumblings. The American religious liberal Octavius Frothingham may have said it best—"Ours is an age of restatements and reconstructions, of conversions and 'new departments' in many directions. There is an uneasy feeling in regard to the foundation of belief. The old foundations have been sorely shaken."[4]

Edwin Abbott was not the only Christian who felt the foundations shake and rumble. Nor was he the only one to attempt hastily to reinforce them. There were many in fact who appropriated the fourth dimension to argue that science proved that our world was merely a part of a greater heavenly world, or that unseen things were not necessarily unimaginable, or that apparently miraculous events, such as Marian apparitions, healing miracles, and Jesus's Resurrection, could be accounted for by understanding them as higher-dimensional phenomena. This was not, however, merely a way of finding modern ways of supporting older doctrines; it was a way of changing fundamentally the tradition, a way of using new, scientific ideas to reform and purify it, and most liberal thinkers who engaged in this kind of thinking spoke openly about this. They were part of a burgeoning group of liberal or "Modernist" Christians who tried to make Christian traditions more believable in the modern world, and their formulations would become dominant by the early twentieth century.

Those borrowing dimensional ideas, such as the Anglican priest Arthur Willink, believed that using these notions would help modern people limn a middle path between an arid agnosticism on the one hand and credulous over-beliefs on the other. Willink argued that Christ was a higher space being; that spirits lived in the fourth dimension; that higher dimensions strongly suggested the existence of heaven and immortality; that the idea of dimensions made Christian doctrines such as the Incarnation seem more reasonable; and that apostolic visions of the resurrected Christ really amounted to what we could call higher-dimensional vision. (If in Willink's expository prose these ideas were presented as arguments, in the fiction of the day they animated everyday conversations about transcendent things. A vicar visited by an angel in H. G. Wells's *The Wonderful Visit* [1895], for example, remarked casually that angels came from the fourth dimension.[5]) Another Anglican, whose works were widely reviewed, Alfred Schofield, made arguments that were similar to Willink's, insisting that dimensional analogies and related ideas "serve to show that the scriptural way of entering the Kingdom of God is the only way possible." If these new ideas "assist to rouse enthusiasm in believers, to convert unbelievers, and to silence materialists," Schofield concluded, his aim would be achieved.[6]

But if some were sure that dimensional ideas proved the superiority of Christian ways of thinking about salvation and the supernatural, others correctly pointed out that there was nothing specifically Christian about higher-dimensional notions. In fact, most people who used higher dimensions did so not to buttress Christian doctrines but to argue for more general spiritual notions such as the existence of a spirit world, life after death, or transcendent intuitions and visions. Certain that modern people needed religious ideas even if they could not accept them on dogmatic authority, W. F. Tyler argued in a thoughtful book on *The Dimensional Idea as an Aid to Religion* (1907) that the dimensional idea might "be grafted on to any existing religion," lifting all religious believers out of the "quagmire" of superstition and irrationality. Establishing religions on this principle also could lead to important ethical outcomes, the cessation of Christian sectarianism, and a "liberality of feeling" toward people with different beliefs.[7] That higher-dimensional ideas might lead to a new religious universalism and help people overcome narrowness, bigotry, nationalism, or sectarianism—these were common ideas in the religious literatures of higher dimensions. The Great War, which produced shockwaves of exhaustion and disillusionment, provided a context in which such universalist ideas found favor.[8]

Then there was a set of more restless reformers, teachers, and prophets who believed that Christianity was incompatible with modernity and who developed alternative metaphysical systems. They produced an astonishing number of groups that went by different names—mystical, occult, spiritualistic, theosophical—but in reality they were part of a single cresting wave of religious creativity. Europeans and Americans were discussing spirit mediums, visionary experiences, séance sittings, and hitherto unknown psychic powers that everyone (apparently) had had all along. Participants in this new age of spiritual discernment often commented on the charged atmosphere of change and expectation. The psychologist Carl Jung, for example, who would become one of the twentieth century's most influential religious innovators, participated in séances during this period and wrote his doctoral dissertation on the "unbelievable rise" of spirituality "in every form in all cultured parts of the western world since the late nineteenth century," observing that people flocked to these "modern gnostic systems" because they "meet the need for expressing and formulating wordless occurrences going on within ourselves better than any of the existing forms of Christianity." (During one of Jung's séances his cousin fell into a trance; produced remarkable, prophetic statements later confirmed true; created mysterious rapping sounds; and even channeled Carl's grandfather, the reverend Samuel Preiswerk, who chided Carl from the grave for reading too much Nietzsche.[9] Not everyone on earth or in heaven was happy about the spiritual revolutions afoot.)

Having jettisoned the certainties of traditional religion, the mystics and psychics that Jung discussed found spiritual assurance elsewhere, often using new scientific notions and technologies. Microscopes, telescopes, and other inventions enabled people to see into the invisible. Wireless telegraphy made a type of disembodied communication possible across great distances. Could these technologies and others like them probe into unseen realms, allowing us to see spirits and communicate with those living in hidden, heavenly landscapes? Could the electrical/spiritual energies around a séance table be so strong as to send sparks and vibrations across the great divide between earth and heaven? Could new visual technologies such as cameras take photographs of emotions, spiritual vibrations, or ghosts? Could these new technologies expand our senses so that mind reading, clairvoyance, or other remarkable powers were possible? These were all questions that spiritual seekers and iconoclasts asked.

British and American Spiritualists, for example, embraced fourth-dimensional notions as a sign that new sciences might one day probe into supersensible realms. It was not uncommon in Spiritualist periodicals, for example, to find announcements that C. Howard Hinton had proven the existence of a spirit world. As we have seen, mathematicians and other intellectuals sometimes called Spiritualist higher-dimensional "visions of a happy otherworld" "silly and sad" but such critics had a persistent problem: Prominent scientists, including leading lights such as the British chemist and physicist Sir William Crookes and the German astrophysicist Johann Karl Friedrich Zollner, believed both in spirits and in our ability to communicate with them in their happy otherworlds.[10]

Zollner's activities were greeted with the greatest outcry, for this Leipzig professor did not restrict himself to measured statements about the possibility of higher spaces, which would have been enough to elicit irritation; rather he asserted definitively that higher dimensions existed, conducted séance sittings with an American medium named Henry Slade, whom many thought an opportunistic fraud, and published a book affirming that higher dimensions were accessed by psychics. The title of his book on these matters announced a new kind of science—a *Transcendental Physics* (1880) that studied forces and energies that operated in spaces above our familiar three. As might be expected, this book set off an explosion in Europe, generating a controversy that lasted a decade. A few of Zollner's longtime friends accused the great scientist of being senile or insane. An official panel of experts that was convened to investigate the matter thought Zollner was engaged in wishful thinking and was "of unsound mind." The same commission cast doubt on the testimony of other scientists at these sittings, complaining that one was "advanced in age" and another "was afflicted with defective vision." Academics, editors, and reporters attacked Zollner for lending his considerable authority, and the prestige of science, to the Spiritualists. Scientists could be stupid privately, one editor vented, but to support séances publicly and thereby lead the masses toward superstition was something that ought to be prevented by the state.[11]

British and American Spiritualist publications followed the Zollner affair closely—with one periodical calling Zollner's book "one of the most valuable works in the whole range of spiritual literature." Reviews and columns were dedicated to the works of Hinton and Abbott. Like others living at the time, Spiritualists embraced contemporary discourses of empiricism and called for proof of spiritual things; and they were inspired by new energetic technologies such as the wireless telegraph, which showed the very real possibilities of communication across distances, even into the beyond. "I know that one might almost call it an exact science but for the difficulty of defining what constitutes that fourth dimension," one American Spiritualist wrote, adding that the science of a higher dimension, once understood, would be one that allowed people to communicate with spirits in the "Beyond." The study of modern physics, of wireless telegraphy and radio, of X-rays and other invisible, psychic, or spiritual forces—all were constituent parts of new sciences that revealed hitherto invisible things. This person had had his own psychic experiences, had heard voices of departed souls (including his mother's), and knew enough to know that in the spirit world there were no jealous guardians of orthodoxy, intolerant prigs or frowning clergymen. These new spiritualist revelations showed just how wrongheaded modern Christianity was.[12]

Higher-Dimensional Visions

Then there were religious mystics and prophets who read Abbott and Hinton or worked with Hinton's cubes and had remarkable visions of rotating geometric shapes, guardian angels, departed loved ones, or ghosts from fourth-dimensional heavenly landscapes of varied description. Johan Van Manen, for example, a Dutch Theosophist living in and traveling around northern England, journeyed through the countryside lecturing on the fourth dimension, Hinton's works in hand. After meditating one night on the fourth-dimensional problem and trying to visualize fourth-dimensional objects, Van Manen saw the luminous heavens open before him, with mystic threads of light shimmering in

Figure 3.1   Van Manen's sketch of a fourth-dimensional globe. From Johan Van Manen, *Some Occult Experiences* (Madras: Theosophical Publishing House, 1913), 59.

his previously dark room. He then beheld several fourth-dimensional shapes. "To my great astonishment I saw plainly before me first a four-dimensional globe and afterwards a four-dimensional cube." He sketched the globe in his journal. (See Figure 3.1.) "I saw the forms as before me in the air (though the room was dark), and behind the forms I saw clearly a rift in the curtains through which a glimmer of light filtered into the room." He described the four-dimensional globe he saw as an ordinary globe "out of which on each side, beginning at its vertical circumference, bent tapering horns proceeded, which, with a circular bend, united their points above the globe from which they started." It was a three-dimensional globe that was wrapped around itself in a fourth dimension, a mysterious, ineffable object recognizable only to others with astral sight. (Visionary experiences seem to have accompanied Van Manen wherever he went. At his lectures people reported seeing luminous halos around him or ghosts on the stage. Once an audience member recalled that next to Van Manen appeared "a stately Hindu wearing a turban." Van Manen himself could not explain the appearance of the turbaned Hindu.)[13]

Others had visions of fourth-dimensional objects or luminescent geometrical shapes. The German religious liberal and founder of Anthroposophy, Rudolf Steiner, toured Europe in 1905 and 1906 lecturing on Hinton and higher dimensions. Steiner used fourth-dimensional analogies, thought experiments, and cubes of various colors to help people "at least gain some idea of the so-called astral realm and still higher forms of existence." He had almost as much enthusiasm as Hinton, offering complex methods of visualizing fourth-dimensional objects such as hypercubes. Others participating in what scholars have described as a European revival of mysticism and the occult, especially among educated, upper-class liberal Christians, pursued methods of seeing higher or heavenly objects. The Irish poet and playwright W. B. Yeats had visions of geometric shapes and saw them as emblems of deeper truths of the universe. Yeats and his wife, George, developed an esoteric religious system and wrote about it in *A Vision: An Explanation of Life,* an enigmatic book in which Yeats explained the sources of artistic creativity, the journey of the soul, the passage of time, and many other matters. Much of the book was channeled by George Yeats, while other sections came in dreams or remarkable visions. The ideas in *A Vision* are symbolized with a diagram of two cones overlapping one another so that the open end of one cone touches the tip of the other, and vice versa—in some ways quite like Van Manen's four-dimensional sphere. Yeats believed that these interlocking cones represented the cyclical nature of time, patterns of growth and decay, the interlocking dimensions of the self, the eternal oscillation between subjective and objective— everything, really, in one image. One of the revelations that inspired the book showed that there were other dimensions beyond the familiar three. "When I saw this," Yeats wrote, "I tried to understand a little of modern research into this matter but found that I lacked the necessary training." Had he wrestled with Hinton's books and cubes? Though he could not master this esoteric discipline, he knew it held a clue to the mysterious ways his cones rotated and to the enigmas of cyclical time, historical cycles, and the "eternal return" spoken of by eastern religious teachers.[14]

No one, however, could equal Charles Leadbeater's imaginative feats of fourth-dimensional sight. Leadbeater was a charismatic lecturer and writer in the Theosophical Society at the turn of the century, a man who, a recent biographer insisted, was in many ways the most influential mystical leader of the twentieth century. He either fashioned or popularized many of the key ideas still used in New Age circles today, ideas such as the astral plane, the Akashic Records, the Occult Hierarchy, the Masters, Atlantis, Lemuria, and so on. Leadbeater grew up in England as the son of a railroad clerk who died in 1862. He was then brought up by his mother, took a series of jobs, and was ordained an Anglican priest in 1872. Like others during this period he was curious about new mystical and religious groups and was introduced to the Theosophical Society by the author Alfred Percy Sinnett, one of the first Theosophists and a friend of Helena Blavatsky. He was officially inducted into Theosophy during a ceremony in 1883 at Sinnett's London home, the same ceremony in fact where William Crookes, a professor and fellow of the Royal Society, also was initiated.[15] From there, the Masters (via Helena Blavatsky) instructed Leadbeater to travel to India, where he achieved a certain status as the first Christian minister to become a Buddhist.

Like other early Theosophists, Leadbeater was keenly interested in communicating with the Masters—and, as it turned out, he was particularly good at it. The Masters visited him regularly, blessed him with many psychic powers, and transmitted their words to him, which he communicated in lectures and in a remarkable series of books read by Theosophists and many others around the world. Leadbeater had phenomenal energy: His prolific books rewrote the geological and cultural history of the world, chronicled the lost histories of the continents of Atlantis and Lemuria, and reexamined the history of Christianity, the nature of the atom, and the methods of cultivating psychic powers. He made missionary trips to America, Europe, and Asia.

Leadbeater used Hinton's ideas and techniques with extraordinary results. He confirmed that fourth-dimensional objects actually existed because he saw them on the heavenly, or astral, plane. "I can . . . bear witness that the tesseract or fourth-dimensional cube which [Hinton] describes is a reality, for it is quite a familiar figure upon the astral plane," Leadbeater wrote once. In *The Astral Plane* (1894), Leadbeater described seeing various inhabitants of higher realms, including angels, departed spirits, and menacing demons, and he coached his readers on how to acquire the ability to see these things. Leadbeater could magnify atoms to see them up close, view other people's desires and feelings, and even see objects that were far away. (Not everything he saw with fourth-dimensional vision turned out to be correct, of course. He said for instance that there were humanlike creatures on Mars—not an uncommon belief at the time, but also an incorrect one.)

Higher-dimensional vision also meant you could do what Hinton did—namely, see all sides of a thing at once, so that "every particle in the interior of a solid body is as fully and clearly visible as those on the outside."[16] All sides of a cube, for instance, would appear equal, as they actually are, rather than distorted by our limited powers of perception. This kind of "sight in the fourth dimension" also included the ability to see through things (clairvoyance) and perceive etheric vibrations and energies, luminous mists around us (or "auras"), and ghosts or other spectral presences around séance tables. Though not everyone was gifted with this kind of insight, it was not uncommon for religious liberals to talk about cultivating spiritual visions of "auras," energies, chakra fields, departed spirits, or other intangible things like feelings and attitudes. In an era of science, these visions were ways of empirically verifying hitherto invisible realities.[17]

Hinton's published meditations and his cubes elicited revelatory visions in much broader liberal circles—in London and New York, among Christian Science practitioners, New Thought lecturers, and spiritual wanderers moving among different groups. Mabel Shine, a religious seeker who read avidly in New Thought spirituality and the latest "mental science magazines," focused on the "power of concentration for developing the higher faculties" as the antidote to her persistent unhappiness. Perhaps New Thought literature primed her to see thoughts actually becoming real things, for, as the saying went, all "thoughts are things." And so one night her thoughts became things, and she saw them take on objective shape before her eyes. She described these detailed visions in her book *Little Journeys into the Invisible: A Woman's Actual Experiences in the Fourth Dimension* (1911). Her meditative procedure began by sitting in a chair and reading the Bible for a few minutes; she then described how she would "lean my head back and fix my gaze on a flower in the border of the wall paper," quieting her thoughts until her mind became empty. She got proficient at this and was able to meditate in this way for three hours a day, finding those three hours "short and most delightful."[18] Sometimes she would focus on one thought or affirmation, or send healing thoughts to sick friends or humanity in general.

One night a strange feeling caused her to open her eyes and see a wall of remarkable lights. Looking for the source of the lights, she turned to the fireplace, which was dark, and then the window, which was an inky blackness. The moving golden lights, "with bright particles shining out," formed into flowerlike images, human faces, and geometric shapes. She sensed a presence in the shapes and knew that these shapes were portals to higher dimensions. The geometric forms communicated something to the effect that all was well, that all things "are one," and that physical matter, vibrating energy, and human beings are all shadows of a higher fourth-dimensional world. "I had raised my consciousness to a higher plane of vibration," she wrote, "which means a higher plane of realization; the figures and flowers are the first things one sees on the threshold of that plane. All thoughts are in form; the geometrical figures were the orderly reasoning or putting together of different forms of truth." Mabel Shine had an angelic visitor in these visions too, a male spirit who took her across rivers and into cities, where she saw poor people in tenements. The things she saw all came to pass later in real life, and the angelic visitor turned out to be a New Thought healer she was soon to meet, court, and marry. Had she created a reality by wishing and thinking it with a fourth-dimensional consciousness? From my experiences, she said, "may be learned what and where is the Fourth Dimension. It is the dimension of the thought world, which is the creator of the physical world. It is the world which this physical world objectifies or pictures forth. . . . All is born first in the 4D and then descends into the physical to grow. Souls are created in the soul plane, then to 4D world, then to earth."[19]

There was no shortage of self-help books and manuals describing how to develop fourth-dimensional consciousness. Like Mabel Shine, Charles Brodie Patterson was interested in mental science and he wrote in detail about how to discipline the mind in order to leave behind the body and enter the fourth dimension. It was through states of "mental abstraction" achieved in meditation, Patterson wrote, that people were able to see fourth-dimensional planes, images, and departed spirits. There were different steps in the process—controlling emotions and thoughts, practicing breath control, and meditating. Mastering these practices enabled people to "liberate the mind and soul from the physical organism" and, if they were very skilled, enter into the fourth dimension. Patterson himself had seen things in that dimension—beautiful colors, symphonic sounds, and a variety of developed (and undeveloped) souls. This was not wishful thinking but actual experience. ("In writing as I have done I have not recorded my belief, but what I know, and before one can speak knowingly he must have had experience. This is a leaf out of my personal experience.")[20]

There is no doubt that these efforts to see the invisible were related to contemporary preoccupations with visual perception and its limits. Historians have long associated modernity with ocularcentrism,[21] but in the nineteenth century this preoccupation deepened as new medical and psychological studies drew attention to the human eye's power, inner workings, and limitations. Did the eye see accurately or was it routinely fooled by perceptual mistakes, wishful thinking, mental illness, or optical illusions? In an important book on nineteenth-century visual culture, Jonathan Crary showed that nineteenth-century physiological investigations exposed the eye's susceptibility to mistakes and illusions of various kinds. The result was a decisive break with older ways of thinking about vision, a moment when attitudes toward seeing were destabilized and new questions emerged about how to discipline the self in order to see truly. As a number of scholars have shown, understanding the eye's abilities and limitations was interesting not only for scientists in this period but also for anyone who enjoyed optical parlor games, kaleidoscopes, magic lantern shows, phantasmagorias, or scientific and magical performances. As Iwan Morus has argued, this new visual culture made people aware of their perceptual limits and the possibilities of illusion, deception, and other forms of false seeing. Scientific lecturers in particular warned about religious credulity, showing that supposedly supernatural phenomena were illusions or deceptions that could be explained using naturalistic terms.[22]

But there was a doubleness to this culture of visual play and performance, for while lecturers sometimes debunked religious visions they also could open up astonishing new vistas on mysterious, invisible realities. Scientific lecturers put projecting microscopes and powerful telescopes on display and produced explosive chemical reactions or crackling electrical jolts. All of these spectacles called forth awe and wonder at the mysterious and hidden natural phenomena that scientists were discovering. What must it have been like to look through a microscope and see for the first time the physical features of a flea or the astonishing aquatic environment of an amoeba? What was it like to experience the unexpected shifts in scale involved in going from the microcosmic to the macrocosmic, from seeing the tiniest unseen creatures through a microscope to viewing distant planets through a telescope? The microscope in particular was a source of virtually endless comment in the popular press on how the invisible had now been brought into view. Other new visual technologies included the stereoscope, the zoescope, photography, chronophotography (later, cinema), and x-ray photography, which brought previously invisible facts to light in striking ways. In the 1890s people collected x-ray photographs (often of their hands) and pasted them into family albums, astonished that a new kind of "ray" could pierce their outer bodies and see unseen dimensions of the self. It was not uncommon to speak of x-rays as miracles, which one of Hinton's friends defined simply as "a manifestation of power new to experience, and counter to the current thought of the time," a technology that put pressure on us to think and perceive in new ways.[23] He was not alone in believing that x-rays suggested that an expansion of the senses was possible and that clairvoyance and other mystical ways of seeing were within reach. Hinton agreed that scientific wonders such as the telescope, microscope, and x-ray photography proved that science provided new ways of seeing the invisible. Science was ushering in a new, spiritual dispensation of seeing beyond conventional realities into the heart of all things and beyond.[24]

Evolving a Higher Consciousness

It was not uncommon for dimensional philosophers and visionaries to talk about the immanent approach of a new age of spiritual evolution.

Darwin's recently articulated theory of evolution, and the widespread use of evolution as a trope and master narrative, led to a battery of evolutionary social and spiritual theories. Races evolved, societies evolved, even human consciousness evolved. Two crucial figures who discussed the evolution of a new spiritual consciousness were the Canadian psychiatrist Richard Maurice Bucke and the British liberal reformer and writer Edward Carpenter. Bucke was interested in mysticism and consciousness, and he did more than anyone to popularize the notion of a cosmic consciousness. In his best-known book, *Cosmic Consciousness* (1901), which he managed to complete the year before his death, he summarized his own mystical experience and the dramatic experiences of others, including Walt Whitman, Emmanuel Swedenborg, St. Paul, the Buddha, and Sri Ramakrishna. From this data he developed a theory of evolutionary consciousness that included three grades of awareness—the simple consciousness of animals, the self-consciousness of human beings, and a final state of awareness of the total life of the universe that he called cosmic consciousness. A number of attitudes and feelings accompanied cosmic consciousness, including a "feeling of elevation, elation, and joyousness," a "quickening of the moral sense," and an immediate and present sense of immortality. Bucke promoted the optimistic notion that races were gradually evolving greater mental powers and that the next stage of development would bring to all races a wider range of perceptive abilities, including especially the "Cosmic Sense." He saw glimmers of this psychic achievement among the most advanced human beings, who, it turned out, were usually middle-aged men "of good intellect, of high moral qualities, of superior physique." They could be men of different races, it seems, but they were indeed usually men. Bucke's notions of cosmic consciousness informed a generation of intellectuals and artists, including the American psychologist William James, who wrote about Bucke in his *Varieties of Religious Experience* (1902).[25]

Then there was Edward Carpenter, who began his career as an assistant to the great British theologian F. D. Maurice, but who swapped interests in the Anglican ministry for preoccupations with Indian religion, psychical research, Walt Whitman, and mysticism.[26] (Carpenter was a contemporary of James Hinton and the two had mutual friends such as Edith Ellis and Olive Schreiner.) He discussed evolving consciousness in his *From Adam's Peak to Elephanta* (1892), a narrative of travels in India and Sri Lanka, where he observed local customs and spoke to gurus about their mystical powers. He left convinced that it was possible to cultivate an advanced form of consciousness, a "supramundane" mind that allowed some to perform remarkable feats. Indian adepts had demonstrated that they could see events at a distance, pass objects through walls, and levitate; these and similar behaviors reported sometimes in the West could be explained by new studies on the fourth dimension. The fourth-dimension idea made it "conceivable that apparently separate objects, i.e., distinct people, really are physically united; that things apparently sundered by enormous distances of space are really quite close together," or that solid objects might be moved through other objects. Carpenter also thought that the fourth dimension suggested that behind the world of appearances there was a realm of ideality and ultimate unity, a unity that Carpenter called the "great Self." He drew this idea directly from Hinton, who, we might recall, believed that in higher dimensions all people, and all things, became one. Carpenter supported new psychical research and nursed a millennial hope that humans were developing psychical powers that would also lead to new ways of knowing ultimate truth and organizing society. Alongside these hopes and convictions, Carpenter also developed socialist political views.[27]

A third thinker, the Russian mystic and fourth-dimensional philosopher Pieter D. Ouspensky, borrowed from Bucke and Carpenter, translated Carpenter's mystical works (as well as Hinton's) into Russian, and spread these ideas to Russian avant-garde philosophers and artists. In many ways, Ouspensky was Hinton's European successor. Born and raised in Moscow, Ouspensky worked in the editorial office of the Moscow daily *The Morning* in his twenties, during the years around the turn of the twentieth century. For over a decade he searched for religious truth at home and abroad, traveling to Egypt, Turkey, India, and Sri Lanka and encountering along the way a number of gurus and teachers, including, back in Moscow in 1915, the influential esoteric teacher George Ivanovich Gurdjieff. In 1909 he moved to St. Petersburg, where he held court at a bar called the Stray Dog, a seedy, foul-smelling, and badly lit bar where metaphysical seekers talked all night long. The Stray Dog crowd called him "Ouspensky Fourth Dimension" and dancers, poets, painters, musicians, and radicals came to smoke, drink, and listen, day and night, as Ouspensky expounded with authority on the Tarot, yoga, "reality," time, consciousness, God, and higher dimensions. Even Leo Tolstoy listened patiently over lunch one day as Ouspensky drew multidimensional diagrams on the tablecloth. This metaphysical bar chatter was collected in Ouspensky's *The Fourth Dimension* (1909) and *Tertium Organum* (1911).

As one who had experienced altered states of consciousness that were both frightening and revelatory, Ouspensky spoke with some authority. He studied James's *Varieties of Religious Experience* and other books on consciousness, and he experimented with nitrous oxide and hashish. His experiences varied. In one he realized that the outer world of material objects was unreal, witnessing his inner world of thoughts enlarge to become an overwhelming presence. He saw a gigantic lotus blossom before him, from which streamed intense emotions, new forms of knowledge, light, movement, color, and a sense of unceasing growth. He was approaching the absolute, and he felt its danger expanding in front of him. A presence in the vision warned him not to proceed, and he turned away. But he continued to pursue altered states of consciousness. At another time, high on nitrous oxide, he was filled with onrushing sensations and profound thoughts, which he hurried to write down. In the morning he searched for and eventually located the scribbled note, which said simply, "Think in other categories." He could not recall what he had meant.[28]

Ouspensky argued that the way to think of the fourth dimension was neither as a mathematical space nor as a realm of spirits but as a dimension of our consciousness. Ouspensky thought other approaches were limited. The mathematical approach did not lead to real perceptions or intuitions of the fourth dimension. Hinton's cube system expanded the imagination but probably worked only for those with a similar kind of mind. And arguing about dimensions from analogies— as in Abbott's *Flatland*—was indirect and ultimately inconclusive. To Ouspensky, the key was consciousness. "We shall find the conditions of the three-dimensionality of the world in our psyche, in our receptive apparatus—*and shall find exactly there the conditions of the possibility of the higher dimensional world.*" With this, Ouspensky turned his attention to sensation, perception, and other mental faculties, developing an interesting, speculative argument that all beings perceived higher spaces as time. Snails, for instance, moving through life in a one-dimensional line, experienced two- or three-dimensional objects only because those objects moved through their perceptual field. They experienced those objects as motion through time. Similarly, an animal unable to see three dimensions would perceive a sphere as a flat circle that rotated as it moved around it. Again, it saw a higher dimension as motion through time. It seemed reasonable that as this animal saw the immobile curves of a three-dimensional object as time, so human beings saw the immobile angles and curves of higher-dimensional things as temporal phenomena. Perhaps, Ouspensky speculated, all of our sensations of changing things—sounds, lights, moving objects—are the immobile sides and angles of things we know nothing about, things that merely appear to us as motion. Perhaps our consciousness, "not being able to embrace these things *with the aid of the organs of sense, and to represent them to itself in their entirety, just as they are,* and grasping only the separate moments of its contact with them, is constructing the illusion of motion." The world, Ouspensky thought, was "immobile and constant," something that moved and changed only because "we are looking at it through the narrow slit of our sensuous receptivity." Ouspensky's views here were indebted to Hinton's in obvious ways: Both spoke of how consciousness divided reality, which was ultimately one thing, into parts.[29]

These views were often articulated together with enthusiastic prophesies of a coming social(ist) society. In a manifesto about the fourth dimension indebted to Hinton, Abbott, and the mystical writings of Madame Blavatsky, the American Claude Bragdon insisted that human consciousness was changing and that social forms also would soon transform. He spoke of human beings as two-dimensional squares who lived, like Abbott's fictional Square, mostly unaware of the higher dimensions around them. Bragdon began an essay on "Man, the Square," by quoting both Helena Blavatsky and the Book of Revelation. Man, Blavatsky wrote, "is the mystic square," and he "becomes the cube on the creative plane."[30] Human beings were squares within a higher reality—an idea that Bragdon also rendered in an illustration of a bisected cube. (See Figure 3.2.)

There was both an "archetypal world" of higher realities and a "phenomenal world" of human beings in the material world. Bragdon

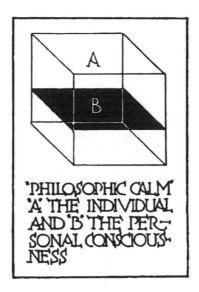

'PHILOSOPHIC CALM'
'A' THE INDIVIDUAL
AND 'B' THE PER-
SONAL CONSCIOUS-
NESS

Figure 3.2   Our "personal consciousness" was merely a cross-section of a larger reality. From Claude Bragdon, *A Primer of Higher Space (The Fourth Dimension)* (Rochester, N.Y.: Manas Press, 1913), 68.

thought it possible for human squares to stretch themselves higher, imagining a more complete world of things where everything was connected. He borrowed the Book of Revelation as he discussed what that higher reality was—"And the city [the New Jerusalem] lieth four square, and the length is as large as the breadth. The length and the breadth and the height of it are equal." That made things very clear: Somehow, the New Jerusalem was a cube in which all of our small lives were layered together.

Individual human beings existed not as flat squares but as higher cubes, and these individual cubes gathered together in a higher realm into an enormous single entity—it was, in short, Hinton's composite cube, spinning in some bigger space. Though individuals appeared separate in this world, we were "under the illusion that each person is unique and singular, that some are better and some worse." But these differences did not exist in the higher, heavenly world. Realizing this, and living a life of high moral purpose, led to geometric and spiritual alignments in which "you will make vertical and parallel the axes of your higher, or cube bodies; and as the sides of your square bodies cleave

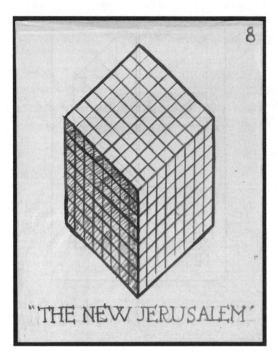

Figure 3.3   All individuals merge into one: Bragdon's cubic vision of the New Jerusalem. From a lecture drawing, ca. 1912. Courtesy Special Collections, Rare Books and Preservation, University of Rochester Libraries.

together, so will the faces of your cube bodies coalesce." When we con-join in these ways, and practice love to one another, Bragdon exclaimed, "individuality is transcended" and everyone merges.[31] (See Figure 3.3.)

Many thought that new spiritual methods for spiritual seeing and higher-dimensional thought might hasten the coming of a long-promised utopia. C. B. Patterson, in his *New Heaven and New Earth*, saw signs of the new age in the psychic and spiritual powers demonstrated in séances, and he said that gradually everyone would evolve until these powers were common. "As men rise from dimension to dimension their powers are changed and increased in many ways," another spiritually minded author wrote.[32] Still others argued that a new spiritual or higher-dimensional sensibility would awaken first in a vanguard of committed visionaries. Leadbeater, who believed that all human ac-tivities were somehow part of a higher whole, insisted that studying Hinton's books and cubes would help rid us of selfishness and individualism and help us develop toward a higher social organization. Lead-beater developed remarkably detailed schemes of evolution and development in which human beings gradually reached the level of the ascended spiritual Masters, who might then mentor aspiring souls, progressing through further "initiations" and stages.[33] When Leadbeater talked about social unity he sometimes borrowed Hinton's way of talking about this. It was like a series of threads passing through a plane world, he said. These threads appeared only as moving points to flatlanders. But a being in a higher dimension knew that these threads were fingers of one hand. Though Leadbeater's colleague in the Theosophical Society, Annie Besant, argued that humans were not quite ready for socialism, others formed intentional communities to put these notions into practice.[34]

Patriarchal Spaces and New Possibilities

Though they spoke a great deal about universal brotherhood and uto-pian communal spaces, white Protestant and post-Protestant men like Hinton and Leadbeater found it difficult not to privilege white men in the futures they imagined. Leadbeater affirmed that people evolved from lower, primitive races into beings that looked suspiciously like British gentlemen. And as Gauri Viswanathan points out, the medium-istic channeling of Oriental mahatmas, a kind of racial ventriloquism that people like Blavatsky and Leadbeater practiced, could be seen merely as one way for white, British colonizers to control "eastern" philosophical and religious messages.[35]

But if some reformers like Leadbeater produced predictions that were patriarchal and racist, others imagined fourth-dimensional uto-pias that inverted the logic of western ethnocentrism and empire. H. G. Wells's *The Time Machine* (1895), M. P. Shiel's *The Purple Cloud* (1901), Richard Jefferies's *After London* (1885), Grant Alien's *British Barbarians* (1895), and Ford Madox Ford and Joseph Conrad's *The Inheritors* (1901), among other works of fiction, used dimensional ideas to play out anxieties about imperial power and western progress. Deploying the fourth dimension to allow characters to accomplish miraculous feats or travel across vast spaces or times, H. G. Wells transported readers into the future via the fourth dimension in *The Time Machine*. In this novel, the England of the future was not the apogee of progress but a frightening dystopia in which the British race, made weak by years of reliance on technology, devolved into a weak, enslaved people. This was quite a reversal, for in this vision of the future, it was the intellectual and industrial superiority of the British that destroyed them. Of course, visions such as Wells's may have been produced less by dissatisfaction with western society than by fears of a kind of future reverse colonialization. That same fear animated alien invasion narratives, including Wells's *War of the Worlds,* in which interplanetary invaders (hailing, in some narratives, from "other dimensions") came to destroy human civilization and colonize earth. Anxieties about the wisdom of British imperialism surface in other ways in *The Inheritors* by Ford and Conrad, a book that begins with a dialogue between a writer named Granger and a female visitor from the Fourth Dimension. The visitor offers Granger a vision of "something beyond, something vaster—vaster than cathedrals, vaster than the conception of the gods to whom cathedrals were raised." She convinces Granger that he should "consider [himself] as relatively a Choctaw," for just as colonizing Europeans obliterated Native Americans, so too would the denizens of the Fourth Dimension "come in swarms" and "devour like locusts."[36]

It is not an insignificant detail that this fourth-dimensional visitor was a woman. A number of hyperspace writers and thinkers linked women to higher-dimensional ways of thinking and acting or used dimensional ideas to rethink gender. This tendency began with Abbott and Hinton, who certainly believed in the transformative possibilities of seeing the social order from a higher vantage point and who also were dissatisfied with conventional ways of thinking about sex and gender. Abbott, who detested the prejudiced and one-dimensional way his contemporaries viewed women, parodied rigid gender binaries in *Flatland,* demonstrating that it was dehumanizing and destructive to assign rigid characteristics such as rationality to men and emotion to women. In the hierarchical and misogynist *Flatland* social order, women were one-dimensional lines, with no brains and little sense. There was therefore no need to educate them. (A *New York Times* reviewer critical of *Flatland* nevertheless appreciated its clever assault on British morays and its implicit "appeal for the education of women."[37]) Abbott hoped to change how the British thought about gender, believing that the binary way of thinking about men and women was harmful to both sexes. He worked alongside female leaders in the Women's Education Movement and in organizations such as the Headmaster's Conference and the Teachers' Training Society to buttress women's secondary education and prepare them for entrance into Oxford and Cambridge.[38] By the end of *Flatland,* the Square realized that seeing the world properly involved combining male qualities with female ones. In fact, in one dialogue between the Sphere and the Square the Sphere disclosed the remarkable fact that he and other denizens of the higher realm thought more highly of "your despised Straight Lines than of your belauded [priestly] Circles."[39]

In Hinton's case, as we might recall, he and his father experimented with new ideas concerning gender and marriage, with limited traction or success. Hinton believed that enantiomorphs (mirror images) in natural phenomena—mirror-image isomers (stereoisomers), opposite electrical charges, the mirror symmetry of the human body and male and female sexes—suggested the existence of a higher dimension. In a *Flatland*-like narrative called "A Plane World," Hinton created a female character who was rotated through a third dimension, inverting herself into a man. Hinton did not consider the subversive or emancipatory possibilities of this higher-dimensional transformation, but a few other thinkers would.

Female writers, activists, and spiritual seekers saw women as more evolved and sometimes spoke of themselves as penetrating into higher modes of four-dimensional consciousness. Like contemporary Christian women who argued that their sex was "naturally" more ethical and religious, these women argued that their status as more dimensionally evolved meant they could claim authority over their children, their husbands, and even their religious communities. A number of scholars have emphasized the links between new spiritual movements, including Spiritualism and Theosophy, and a powerful feminist activism in the late nineteenth century.

Different impulses fed this movement, including changing notions of gender and domesticity, evolutionary social theories emerging in the wake of Darwin's *Origin of Species,* and burgeoning interest in the evolution of consciousness.[40] Many believed, as the southern author Mary Johnston did, that women who had evolved higher-dimensional capacities would lead the way toward social redemption. Her title character in the novel *Hagar*, a gentile Southern advocate of progressive socialism and women's suffrage, became a leader of others because she had learned about the fourth dimension, had developed her fourth-dimensional consciousness, and thus knew that God's immanent spirit was shaping all things toward the progressive evolution of the race. Johnston thought women, naturally nurturing and constructive, would lead the way in the new century. In her diary she rejoiced that women would lead the race into the future with a "new conception of space and time. New consciousness." Her fourth-dimensional consciousness liberated her—it was "inner freedom, ability to work, personal independence, courage and sense of humour and a sanguine mind, breadth and height of vision, tenderness and hope." (In *Hagar*, however, Johnston contrasts the heroine's liberating higher-dimensional vision with the atavistic and superstitious sensibilities of black characters, who, in her rendering, did not have access to the highest levels of spiritual or social reality.)[41]

Still other women used higher dimensions to develop new self-created spaces where gender might be reimagined. Grace Thompson Seton's travel narrative *A Woman Tenderfoot in Egypt* (1923), for example, lays out an alternative geography in which Seton, who said she wrote the book to understand better the "complex picture of womanhood in Egypt," examined her own complex understanding of gender roles, eastern mysticism, and visionary experience. A leading American activist for women's causes, Seton described in this book not merely her journeys to the pyramids, the Sphinx, and the Nile, but also several visionary, higher-dimensional experiences that transported her into alternative times and spaces. After joining a caravan of (male) Bedouins and attending a feast in the desert, she was propositioned by one of them but somehow hypnotized him merely by staring into his eyes. He wondered if she was a goddess. Later she had visionary experiences "excursioning into the fourth dimension" in which she was transported to the "Fire Chamber of the Great Pyramid" where she performed the postures of some "strange rite of worship" while "repeating strange words"—all before witnessing a special ritual for King Sethron from "the XIII Dynasty." She had another vision on a Nile steamer in which she saw a priest in the Temple of Edfu selecting a young woman to sacrifice for the god—another odd vision sent from some mythical past. The next day she actually traveled to the Temple of Edfu and saw the rooms and spaces laid out just as they had been in her vision. Had she become initiated into old, Egyptian mysteries, acquiring the higher-dimensional powers of a goddess? She called her book about Egypt and its many dimensions not a guide book but a "kaleidoscope"—a dynamic vision of things that combined Egypt's alternate landscape with reflective mirror images of her own deeply felt desire to escape the flat western social geography and its limiting possibilities.[42]

A Black Fourth Dimension

The existence of a fourth-dimensional space made possible other unexpected ways of viewing social conventions, unchallenged assumptions, and ubiquitous prejudices. A student at Harvard when Hinton and Abbott developed their ideas, W. E. B. Du Bois was introduced to these ideas by William James in his Philosophy 4 course (1888–1889) on "recent contributions to theistic ethics," a course that ranged from ethics to philosophy and the academic study of religion. We know that at the time James was corresponding with Hinton. We also know from Du Bois's Philosophy 4 notebook that James held in-class discussions on Hinton, including his *Scientific Romances* (1886), a collection of essays that included explanations of the math of higher dimensions and a fictional piece imagining a Flatland-like world. "That there is a fourth dimension in life every sensible man must say," Du Bois jotted in his notebook. "We have a 4th moral dimension separating us from animals. Thus we are cut off certainly from the whole universe only part of which we see." Du Bois here captures James's enthusiasm for a higher space that might constitute a separate, transcendent department of the world or self. How might this new conception change how people understood ethics, ontology, or theology? By altering one's view of space in these ways, Du Bois noted, God "becomes non-human"—by which he probably meant nonanthropomorphic. Here was "the dif. between the speculative and common sense gods." These new higher-dimensional notions put pressure on us to exchange a personal God for an impersonal transcendent space or higher modes of consciousness.[43]

Du Bois took these ideas in novel directions. Sometime in 1889 he produced an incomplete fictional narrative that used dimensional ideas to critique racial attitudes in the United States. The title of the work,

"A Vacation Unique," suggests a narrative that takes place outside of everyday life, in a location that might provide a new perspective on reality. (James believed in the importance of occasionally taking a "moral holiday," a break from conventional ethics that allowed one to develop a new perspective.) In this fragmentary piece, a black Harvard undergraduate convinces a white classmate to undergo a "painless operation" that would turn him into a "Negro." Then the two of them would entertain audiences around the country, making money to offset college expenses. This idea might not have been appealing; the black protagonist was forced to enumerate the useful aspects of such a transformation. "By becoming a Nigger you step into a new and, to most people, entirely unknown region of the universe," he insisted. It was a chance to "break the bounds of humanity and become a—er—colored man." And this was not all. "Again you will not only be a Negro but a Negro in an un-thought of an astoundingly incongruous role"—he would be both races and neither, visible and invisible, rising above everything to a position in which he might even "solve in a measure the problems of Introspec-tion and [the] Fourth Dimension." He would see things others could not see. "Have you heard of the Fourth Dimension, Fool?" the black student probed. "Spend summer in that portion of space, viewing [the] world's intestines from [a] new point of view." His view of things would "have a striking resemblance to the view which Mr. Field [?] of Flatland had . . . of Lineland intestines." Seeing things from a higher dimension offered a kind of clarity: Hinton said he could see metaphysical rela-tions and human facts from a high vantage point, and Du Bois bor-rowed this idea to argue that there was a kind of clarity provided by the outside vantage point of blackness.[44]

Once transformed from white conventionality to black four-dimensionality, even a Caucasian Harvard undergraduate could see how everything had been laid out in America, with its carefully gridded hierarchies of decorum and privilege, with its invisible class and color lines. The traveling pair toured the United States and many formerly invisible features came into focus—they were eyed suspiciously, asked for character references, denied lodging, assaulted with stories about "how much I did for your People," and subjected to "gaping" looks from American men, women, and even ministers of the Church, some of whom muttered incredulously about "Niggers in *Harvard!*" Du Bois's exploratory piece is interesting for a number of reasons, including the fact that Du Bois deployed the metaphysical fourth dimension in order to locate another geography, an "impossible geography" above inflexible American hierarchies, in which white people might see their privilege and black people might find freedom. Shamoon Zamir analyzed the extensive links between this work and the social and racial hierarchies in Abbott's *Flatland,* concluding not just that Du Bois borrowed Abbott's ways of using a higher geographic space to relativize lower social spaces—to get a critical view on society "from nowhere"—but also that Du Bois's formulations in this fragmentary story influenced the first chapter of *The Souls of Black Folk.* "So when Du Bois in *The Souls of Black Folk,*" Zamir writes, "asserts his right to cross the color line and 'sit with Shakespeare,' he isn't disproving his blackness, he instead is disproving the validity of limits on the mind and the imagination."[45] Du Bois also used higher-dimensional language at other times in the twentieth century to imagine utopian social spaces beyond the color line and racial inequality.[46]

If Du Bois was borrowing from Hinton and Abbott, other African Americans turned to more esoteric notions about our spiritual evolution to reconceptualize the history of race and their place in it. Many who used these concepts were influenced by Theosophical notions of "root races" and their evolution. In *The Secret Doctrine,* for instance, Blavatsky said that the stages of our rise from material to heavenly races would culminate in a twenty-eighth-century race of advanced beings, the Sixth Root Race. This race would have the advanced physical and spiritual powers that fourth-dimensional mystics were beginning to master. Leadbeater and other Theosophical thinkers developed other schemes of racial evolution, and while they tended to associate the most advanced races with whiteness, as we have seen, their evolutionary perspectives would be appropriated in unexpected ways. The Harlem Renaissance poet and novelist Jean Toomer, for example, identified himself as one of the new supermen of the Sixth Race and introduced esoteric evolutionary theories to other important writers and artists in Harlem in the 1920s. Like others interested in the coming higher-dimensional consciousness, Toomer read carefully Ouspensky's *Tertium*

Organum, a book that Bragdon called the "long sought New Testament of the Sixth Race which will justify the meekness of the saint, the vision of the mystic, and create a new heaven and a new earth."[47]

If we were to take Blavatsky's chronology seriously, Toomer and other supermen had arrived a tad early; but neither Blavatsky nor other Theosophists nor the spirit Masters they channeled were beholden to limited human constructs such as timelines. (After all, as the Bible says of such things, "the wind bloweth where it listeth.") In 1926 Toomer had a religious experience that convinced him that he had mystical abilities like those characterizing advanced races in esoteric timelines. He stood on an elevated train platform in New York City and was seized by a Power. He then entered a mystical state of "higher consciousness" in which he experienced the world as a place of joy, harmony, and brotherhood. This state of mind lasted two weeks. In his long poem "The Blue Meridian" (1936), Toomer rendered this experience in verse, suggesting the possibility of a new consciousness that transcended barriers. The poem borrowed its title from the "Meridian of Races" in Blavatsky's *Secret Doctrine* and her description of "azure seats" as special dwelling places, now empty, for representatives of a future race. "Who of the brown, who of the red, or yet among the black (races), can sit in the seats of the blessed, the seats of knowledge and mercy!" Blavatsky wrote. As Stephen Finley argued in his important examination of esotericism in African American experience, Toomer "interpreted this passage to apply to himself—so that he saw himself as a member of the blue race endowed with a fourth-dimensional consciousness." The concluding stanza of Toomer's poem announced an unexpected future in which the white world was turned upside down: "Above you will arch a strange universe, / Below you will spread a strange earth, / Beside you will stand a strange man." Toomer represented only one way in which esoteric notions of higher dimensions and future races influenced Harlem Renaissance figures.[48]

The African American intellectual Robert T. Browne, who wrote a book on conceptions of space and dimensionality in 1922, represented a different strategy—higher dimensions not as a way to critique American racism but as a refuge from it. Browne's life reminds us that the categories we use to understand other people's deepest commitments are often transgressed in real life, for Browne maintained commitments to

Methodism, Marcus Garvey, Theosophy, and, later in life, a wholly new esoteric spiritual fellowship. He was born in Texas but by his thirties was living in Harlem, where he became friends with the Harlem Renaissance intellectual and Freemason Arthur A. Schomburg. Attracted by Theosophy's rhetoric of brotherhood and ecumenism, Brown embraced Theosophy in 1915 and began his study of esoteric philosophy. In 1919 he published *The Mystery of Space*, concealing his race from the publisher, fearing that editors and critics would not take an African American philosopher seriously. Writing to a colleague, Schomburg said that "Browne doesn't want to be advertised, not even his publisher knows his identity." Browne captured in the book the esoteric language of the evolution of human consciousness toward higher racial conceptions without being overly specific or explicitly polemical. "The evolution of consciousness," Browne said, from simplicity to complexity, "is first made by the most advanced of the race and that only in a dim, vague way." This advance is registered at first in a small number of advanced individuals and only gradually was becoming "the normal faculty of the entire human family cropping out in each individual." Browne speculated that in this advanced, modern era the evolution of these faculties would be swift, especially because so many were cultivating new psychic and "intuitional" powers. These capacities will "make for union, for the brotherhood of man" and through them "man will come gradually into the consciousness that fundamentally, in his inner nature, in every respect of vital concern, he is at-one with his fellowmen." The human race was "nearing the time when it shall actually be able to function consciously in some higher sphere."[49]

Browne's learning, charisma, and proficiency at meditative and visualization techniques made him a hero to thousands of fellow prisoners in a Japanese POW camp in the Philippines in the early 1940s. Teaching visualization techniques, this mystical philosopher helped many overcome anxiety, despair, and the health and morale problems that came with starvation. (During this time he himself went from 212 to 120 pounds.) The historian Christopher Paul Moore has brought to light Browne's remarkable story—

Of all the courses and lectures taught by the teachers among the internees, none seems to have had more impact on the camp's population than Browne's mind-power techniques. . . . Browne's philosophy spread throughout the camp and may have actually helped defer or at least delay some of the intense psychological pain associated with malnutrition and starvation. The visualization technique became a camp phenomenon.[50]

After the war, Browne founded his own esoteric religious society, the Hermetic Society for World Service, which still exists today.

∞∞∞∞

The mood among spiritually minded reformers in this age of transition could be optimistic in the extreme, and this attitude was by no means confined to Theosophists who saw a new age of spiritual evolution on the horizon. Liberal Protestants in Europe and America spoke with excitement about a coming "religion of the future"; millenarian prophets in America waited for the imminent return of Jesus; Spiritualists thought new technologies would bring an age of technological contact with the dead; and artists such as Wassily Kandinsky issued self-confident proclamations that art would bring a new era. As we have seen, certainties about the fourth dimension and a coming dimensional consciousness fueled these speculations.

Yet at the same time there were complaints that the ubiquitous cant of spiritual evolution was a misreading of contemporary events. Modern society needed not a spiritual evolution but a material revolution. Progress depended not on renewing spirituality but on overcoming its harmful illusions.

For those holding such convictions, the idea of the fourth dimension came freighted with possibilities that seemed sinister and atavistic. In Russia, for example, where the sense of social and political experimentation was acute, arguments broke out about the precise nature of the coming changes. The 1905 revolution had eased censorship restrictions and Russians quickly discovered Theosophy, Steiner's Anthroposophy, and other mystical teachings. Poets, writers, and the artistic avant-garde, many of whom were ready to replace the Church with something else, discussed new ideas in cafés and at lectures on mysticism and the fourth dimension. Perhaps the best-known Russian influenced by these ideas was the abstract painter Kazimir Malevich, who experimented with different geometric forms and incorporated squares and cubes into his designs, hoping his work would usher in a spiritual revolution. Malevich believed that his famous painting of a single *Black Square* (1915) represented the Absolute more perfectly than earlier religious icons and images. He also saw that meditating on it brought a type of "cosmic" or higher-dimensional consciousness. "I see in it what people at one time used to see before the face of God."[51]

Meanwhile, the Bolshevik reformer and future communist leader Vladimir Lenin, who sensed (correctly) that mystical ideas were spreading among the European masses, warned in *Materialism and Empiro-Criticism* (1908) that questioning mathematical and scientific certainties such as three-dimensional space would lead to disorder and confusion. Mathematicians might explore new dimensional ideas, he complained, but "the Tsar can be overthrown only in the third dimension!" In the same book Lenin responded to a group of younger Bolsheviks within revolutionary Russia who wanted to increase the emotional power of Marxism by importing "religious" sensibilities and emotions. Lenin saw as counterproductive any form of faith, religious emotion, or philosophical idealism. He argued that those entertaining the reality of a separate world independent of our senses, thinkers as diverse as the philosopher Henri Poincaré and the physicist and philosopher Ernst Mach, were led directly to religious faith or philosophical idealism. Those speculating about higher dimensions were part of the problem. "If Mach is entitled to seek atoms of electricity, or atoms in general, *outside* three-dimensional space, why should the majority of mankind not be entitled to seek the atoms, or the foundations of morals, *outside* three-dimensional space?" Lenin grumbled.[52]

Of course, revolutionaries, seers, and prophets used the fourth dimension in precisely this way—as an opening to something outside of three-dimensional space, as a portal to other ways of thinking about the social order, race, or inherited morality. In short order Lenin achieved power and Malevich achieved fame, and when Lenin died in 1924 Malevich, then director of the government-sponsored Petrograd State Institute of Artistic Culture, proposed that Lenin's body be placed in a cubical mausoleum. Malevich had since become famous for painting squares that, according to him, had mystical significance. "The cube is no longer a geometric body. It is a new object with which we try to portray

Figure 3.4 Malevich lies on his deathbed beneath his famous *Black Square* (1915)—a square opening to the afterlife.

eternity, to create a new set of circumstances to maintain Lenin's eternal life, defeating death," he wrote. Lenin's cubical mausoleum would be a symbol of the eternal fourth dimension. Moreover, Malevich wrote, "every working Leninist should have a cube at home, as a reminder of the eternal, constant lesson of Leninism, which will establish a symbolic, material basis for a cult." When Malevich died of cancer in 1935 his disciples created a similar higher-dimensional exit point for him. On his deathbed he was arranged with the *Black Square* above him; mourners at his funeral waved a banner with a black square; and his ashes were buried in a grave marked with a black square.[53]

Malevich was not unlike earlier visionaries who meditated on Abbott's sentient square beings or Hinton's rotating cubes, people who wanted not just to transcend earthly life but transform it as well. In Malevich's case, as in others, the idea of higher dimensions both transported people to new heavenly realms and helped them reimagine social circumstances on our lower-dimensional, earthly plane.

4

Cathedrals without Walls

If revolutionaries in Europe used dimensional notions to shift the philosophical and political landscape, reformers in America used similar ideas to catalyze a series of their own unsettling tremors and disturbances. In both places individuals groped toward new, modern ways of being religious or spiritual and all of them borrowed the authoritative categories provided by science. But there were unmistakable differences between Americans and Europeans. Unlike Europe at the end of the nineteenth century, America at the time was concluding an era of astonishing transformation from rural to urban, a transformation marked by considerable cultural strain. Exacerbating the sense of strain and upheaval was a robust public discourse that emphasized freedom from authority, individual liberty, and rule by the people. Moreover, though commentators have sometimes overemphasized the transformational power of the western frontier, there is no question that westward-traveling American pioneers were developing new ways of living and thinking—and East Coast customs and creeds, not to mention the clergymen superintending them, struggled to keep pace.

In short, if Europeans experimented with new social and ideological formations, Americans considered themselves a nation of social and ideological experimenters. Though many Americans celebrated this fact, there were some who saw it as an ominous sign. Jacksonian democrats could enthusiastically pursue new enterprises with an unrestrained, entrepreneurial spirit, but there was mounting evidence (for those willing to see it) that democratic license was giving way to dangerous licentiousness. For those so worried, the vexatious problems of American individualism were plain to see. In his 1914 diagnosis of modern *Drift and Mastery*, for instance, a book Theodore Roosevelt encouraged every American to read, the New York journalist Walter Lippmann complained that waves of iconoclastic prophets, rebellious artists, Protestant sectarians, and individualistic democrats roaming the new country had fostered a distressing level of confusion. "What nonsense it is, then, to talk of liberty as if it were a happy-go-lucky breaking of chains," Lippmann wrote. "It is with emancipation that real tasks begin, and liberty is a searching challenge, for it takes away the guardianship of the master and the comfort of the priest." To Lippmann the result was a loss of authority, an unmoored drifting. "The iconoclasts didn't free us," he complained. "They threw us into the water, and now we have to swim."[1]

This chapter begins in the anarchic spiritual imagination of Americans living on the western frontier, where the American successor to C. Howard Hinton, Claude Bragdon, grew up learning what it meant to feel psychologically adrift. There were two religious strategies for developing a sense of mastery on the frontier—religious liberalism and Christian orthodoxy—and Bragdon, whose parents disagreed on such matters, found himself somewhere in-between the available options. He was raised in an area of upstate New York with a reputation for religious agitation, a region on the edge of what was known as "the Burned-Over District" because the fires of revivalism had burned intensely there earlier in the nineteenth century. The Burned-Over District was a wild western frontier of end-time prophets, overzealous converts, antisocial radicals, comeouter sectarians, disillusioned freethinkers, and spirit mediums who talked to the dead. It was in this region, for instance, that Joseph Smith created his new religion, Mormonism; that the end-time preacher William Miller waited on high places for Christ's Second Coming; that the Fox sisters began the American version of the Spiritualist movement; and that John Humphrey Noyes, whose divine revelations outlined new ways of organizing society, founded a socialist utopia.

Bragdon had his own notions of utopia and his own plans for reform. He would revive America's spiritual imagination by creating an art and architecture of higher dimensions.

Religious Restlessness

Bragdon was descended from generations of religious strivers. On his mother's side was a set of orthodox Christian warriors, including Bragdon's maternal grandfather, a Congregationalist minister named Fayette Shipherd, who spent his time battling the disorderly and doctrinally lax. In prayer Shipherd had had the unusual experience of hearing clearly God's voice, which had informed him that his purpose in life was to seek dispirited Christians, broken-down parishes, and other difficult situations, fix them, and move to the next town. This evidently was precisely how he lived his life.[2] Something of Shipherd's intense personal style can be gleaned from an address he gave to officially welcome a new ministerial colleague to (he said) a lifetime of "exhausting study and unwearied toil, with *persecution* in its varied forms." And these were not the only inducements to a ministerial career. There was also, he continued, the *esprit de corps* made possible by likeminded ministers arrayed in battle against sectarians, drunkards, infidels, and slave owners. Shipherd concluded with this rousing encouragement—"But my brother, if at any time you betray the confidence we repose in you—if you corrupt the 'faith once delivered to the Saints,'" we will "cut the cord which links you to the brotherhood and send you forth to wander vagabond, like Cain, the hapless victim of merited disgrace, until, like Peter, your bitter tears and sound conversion, give lucid proof that you are penitent."[3]

Obviously, he had a certain intensity about him: He was "single eyed," as he would have put it. He wrote a spiritual autobiography that chronicled his efforts to imitate Christ and communicate directly with God, efforts that (it should be said) not every minister of the gospel pursues with equal determination.

Though we know less about her, Shipherd's wife was every bit as single-eyed. Catherine Schermerhorn described herself as a "she-preacher" and was an outspoken advocate for women's rights, two facts that place her within the ambit of Burned-Over District evangelical reform culture. We know that she traveled through upstate New York, insisting that good Christians abstain from alcohol. For these reasons she was not a beloved figure, irritating Christians who abhorred female preachers and terrifying bartenders who saw she was bad for business. Owners of local "grog-shops," her grandson Claude remembered, sometimes "threatened physical violence." But Schermerhorn persisted.[4]

If Bragdon's mother's family carefully patrolled the borders of orthodoxy, his father's family tilted toward unconventional, even liberal ideas. His father's parents, George L. and Eliza Salisbury Bragdon, were abolitionists whose farm was the last stop on the Underground Railroad. They fed and housed runaways, gave them clothes and Bibles, and took them in the middle of the night to Henderson Harbor where they boarded schooners for Canada. George and Eliza had ecumenical sympathies and founded with a few others a nonsectarian church, the Bethel Church, in Selkirk, New York, which explicitly barred membership to "proselytes for party or sect."[5] (The great revivalist Charles G. Finney experienced his conversion in this area in 1821, conducted revivals here, and was the first to call western and central New York the "burnt district.") Bragdon's father, George, went to Union College, read Enlightenment philosophers, attended lyceum lectures, and became a writer and newspaper editor with anticlerical views and doubts about Christianity. He became a disciple of Emerson and was attracted to liberal theological works such as *Ecce Homo*, written by Edwin Abbott's close friend John R. Seeley. His son Claude called him "restless," perhaps because he moved from one newspaper to the next, from one town to another, or from one religious persuasion to another. Eventually George and his family settled in Rochester, where burned-out evangelicalism had (in time) abetted unconventional forms of spirituality, including Spiritualist and Theosophical societies sprouting there like weeds. The Theosophical Society's first American branch was founded here in 1882. In Hydesville, New York, about twenty miles southeast of Rochester, the Fox sisters claimed to communicate with the dead, launching the American version of Spiritualism. (In 1906 nearby Rochester became home to the world's largest Spiritualist church.) At some point, George joined the Theosophical Society and developed an extensive library of books by Theosophists and other religious liberals— Blavatsky, Mabel Collins, Annie Besant, Emerson, and many others.[6]

This diverse frontier of fire-and-brimstone revivalists, new prophets, and intolerant sectarians made finding one's way, especially as a young person, somewhat difficult. This was certainly the case for the area's most controversial prophet, Mormonism's Joseph Smith, who was confounded by the many contending sects. To make matters worse, he was caught in the middle of his mother's Presbyterianism and his father's Unitarianism. When God and Jesus appeared to him one day in the woods, he did not waste time. Which of the many competing sects were true? he asked. (God responded that they were all mistaken and that Joseph would need to restore the one true religion.)

Claude also had to find his way amid the contradictory claims of contending sects, and, as with Joseph Smith, his parents' differences were not helping. What are we to make of the fact, for instance, that his father, George, critiqued churchgoers as "quite religious one day in each seven" while his mother required attendance at services every Sunday and Wednesday?[7] Claude's father venerated Emerson's writings and installed a life-sized portrait of the great seer on the stair landing, and it was just a matter of time before Claude appropriated Emerson's legendary antinomianism. One morning he picked up Emerson's *Conduct of Life* and lost track of time while others prepared for church. When his mother called out he answered with remarkable boldness—"I don't think I'll go to church this morning, Mother." His mother's response is not recorded, but the episode was shocking enough that Claude remembered and wrote about it over sixty years later. The exclusivity and sectarianism of the churches bothered him; the sermons and singing bored him; and the weekly witnessing seemed formulaic.[8] At some point he told the local minister not just that he wanted to disaffiliate but also that he wished to announce this intention publicly as well as all of his reasons for it. The harder he tried to be a real Christian, he told his minister, the less he felt he could be a regular churchgoer. (The minister politely declined Bragdon's offer to complain about the church in public.)

Mathematical Mystic

This put Bragdon in a particularly modern predicament: He had the sensibilities of a believer but no longer accepted the religion of his childhood. His way of solving this dilemma followed the pattern we have seen in this book—that is, he developed a more universal spiritual perspective anchored in mathematical and scientific notions. Like many Americans embracing liberal religious views, Bragdon was disillusioned by Christianity's unseemly sectarianism, and he used the universals of nature and science to locate truths that transcended parties and factions. Modern science, technology, and commerce were making wider bonds of unity and friendship possible in the modern era, Bragdon wrote, while religious hatred retarded these processes. "Every spiritually enlightened person, belonging to any religion or to none, knows that all worship is of the same divine through different rituals and symbols," he once wrote. ("The spiritually enlightened are not numerous enough, however," he added, apparently without irony, "to impose this realization upon those religious sectarians, bigots, formalists and fanatics of whom there are still so many.") "The very thing which might and should be the most powerful of all unifying forces—the recognition of a universal and ubiquitous spiritual life—has come to operate, by reason of certain forms of priestcraft and churchianity, as a separative force."[9] In the modern age, the new religious spirit would be transmitted using a new vocabulary. Modern people had turned decisively to new truths in science and mathematics and it was here that a new language for meaning and metaphysics might be forged.

In Bragdon's life, and in the lives of so many other Americans journeying toward a liberal universalism, the American Transcendentalist Ralph Waldo Emerson was crucial. Emerson introduced Americans to other religions and located the deepest spiritual truths in nature's patterns, rhythms, and laws. When Bragdon began his career as a draftsman, architect, and architectural theorist, Emerson's influence was central. The impact of Emerson's *Conduct of Life*, which Bragdon studied as his mother brooded in church, was particularly important. In this book Emerson spoke of Nature as the perfect reflection of the divine, as "philosophy and theology embodied," and thus as the most important source of moral, aesthetic, and metaphysical truth.[10] Emerson wrote about Nature's ultimate structure as a "Beautiful Necessity," insisting that nature incorporated an indwelling harmony, a design that was perfect and divine, and one that, when understood, bestowed rapture, joy, peace, and awe.

In his earliest publications, Bragdon developed these concepts and made them central to his thinking. He wrote that all things had an underlying order, a set of laws that could be reduced to basic laws in mathematics and geometry. "Number is the *within* of all things,—the 'first form of the Brahman.' It is the measure of time and space; it lurks in the heart beat and is blazoned upon the starry canopy of night." All things—space, music, color, the body—were physical manifestations of an underlying language of God, the language of mathematics. In passages reminiscent of Hinton's work, Bragdon insisted that even human emotions and wishes were an unfolding of numerical ratios and patterns. ("Everything is some number made manifest," for "all thoughts, all emotions, all passions have their numerical coefficients.")[11] In his architectural work, Bragdon made architectural ornamentation that incorporated these patterns and thus made the divine visible again, making esoteric spiritual truths public. He was responding to the encouragements of Emerson and Whitman, who called for American seers and prophets to rise up and forge a spirituality for modern democracy.

In these ways, with these intellectual and philosophical moves, Bragdon replaced his feelings of being spiritually adrift with a sense of mastery. But there was an additional step that Bragdon had to make, a still deeper probing into the invisible beyond. Emerson knew nature's laws and numbers were suspended in some greater whole, in some kind of divinity or "Over-soul," that at an ultimate level collected all things into Oneness. What was the nature of this Over-soul and how could it be approached in a way that was more certain and reasonable than the dogmatic assertions of self-assured frontier preachers and prophets?

In the late 1890s Bragdon found his answer: The exact nature of the elusive Emersonian Over-soul had something to do with the mathematics and geometry of higher, invisible dimensions. The "Higher Space Theory" that Bragdon was then reading about represented a "new way of looking at the world," a way of comprehending "regions where the senses fail us, and the mind alone can lead." Quoting Emerson's dictum that "Nature Geometrizes"—the saying was originally Plato's—Bragdon argued that there was no reason that nature would stop at three dimensions: The patterns went higher and higher.

In 1907, Bragdon heard about these matters directly from Howard Hinton, who, as we have seen, had organized his life around them. They met at the New York apartment of their mutual friend, the writer and humorist Gelett Burgess. It was just two months before Hinton's death. To his mother Bragdon reported that Burgess introduced him to "Hinton the 4 dimension man," who enthusiastically "demonstrated the 4th dimension with different colored cubes of his own invention."[12] Like others, Bragdon could not quite grasp the details of Hinton's cube system, but he appreciated the main point, which Hinton still conveyed with the passion of a convert: that learning to think about or visualize nature's higher geometries made possible a new sense of mastery amid modernity's anxieties. The new mathematics of higher dimensions, Bragdon once proclaimed, using a phrase that captured both the personal and the social possibilities of this system, brought into focus "new vistas of progress, new possibilities of power."[13]

Higher-Dimensional Art and Design

Whatever it is that allows one to sketch effortlessly an object's likeness, whatever capacity in the brain or hands that makes this possible, Claude Bragdon had it. By all accounts (including his own) he was a gifted graphic artist, draftsman, and architect. As a young man he spent spare time drawing from anatomy books, studying the principles underlying the organization of nature and human nature, a passion abetted by his reading of Emerson and other Transcendentalists. By the 1890s he was a draftsman in local architectural firms and was winning drawing prizes. His skills impressed supervisors and coworkers, some of whom said Bragdon was the most talented draftsman they had ever seen. A young colleague in Rochester, Myron Bement Smith, who went on to become an expert in Islamic art and architecture, remembered that Bragdon was "fully as great an architect as Frank Lloyd Wright but he lacked Wright's talent for ballyhoo and self-promotion. Indeed, in my mind, Bragdon was the greater man." Another colleague recalled that Bragdon would sit down, "tear off a sketch, view it with apparent admiration, and then say, 'I think that is about perfect.'"[14]

Many marveled at Bragdon's ability, but a few also were irked by what they saw as his arrogance. Bragdon's close friend, Fritz Trautman, once attempted to set the record straight by pointing out that Bragdon was guided not by self-confidence or arrogance but by a kind of unconventional spiritual faith. He "was possessed of a boyish enthusiasm and a sense of wonder that he never outgrew," Trautman wrote once to Bragdon's younger son, Chandler. "He felt that he was the agent of some ineffable but perfect intelligence which at propitious moments guided his hand. The results . . . often delighted and surprised him, not at all as if they were his own work but the work of his jinnee [genie]. This of course was the exact opposite of self-conceit. But few of his associates understood his spiritual side."[15]

Had they taken the time to read his publications, they would have understood. For decades after Hinton's death, Bragdon wrote books and articles about the fourth dimension, becoming the most important popularizer of a new mysticism of mathematics and dimensions. It is likely that his books were read and used by many artists and writers, including Francis Picabia, Marcel Duchamp, Max Weber, Gelette Burgess, Kasimir Malevich, Salvador Dalí, Emil Bisttram, and Buckminster Fuller.[16] Bragdon's writings are notable in their use of illustrations to convey ideas about the basic patterns in nature, how dimensions shape our space, and how we might imagine invisible, higher spaces. During business hours, Bragdon worked as an architect; at night he wrote books such as *The Beautiful Necessity* (1910), *Man the Square* (1912), *A Primer of Higher Space* (1913), *Projective Ornament* (1915), *Four-Dimensional Vistas* (1916), and *Architecture and Democracy* (1918). In these books and many articles, Bragdon introduced his readers to the fourth dimension with drawings and essays about perception and perspective. Borrowing from Bergson, Hinton, and Abbott, he developed, for instance, drawings in which cubes represented the higher self (or soul) and two-dimensional squares represented the human self (or "personality") on earth. We came into this world when our higher-dimensional selves descended into this flat world. As we did so our cross-sections grew larger, changed, grew smaller, and finally disappeared. The perimeter of the cross-sections changed as our bodies grew, aged, and then disappeared at death, but the higher self remained. This was Bragdon's way of imagining the spiritual self in a material world. (See Figure 4.1.) The same point was made in another drawing that examined how higher-dimensional objects cast shadows onto lower worlds. Were we merely flat shadows of a higher-dimensional world that was more rich and complex?

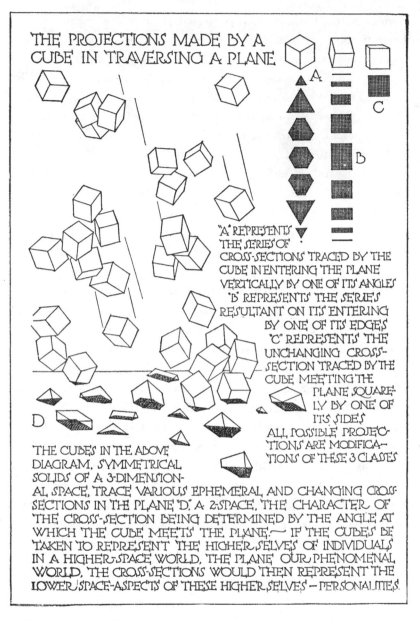

The diagram contains the following text:

THE PROJECTIONS MADE BY A CUBE IN TRAVERSING A PLANE

A

B

C

D

"A" REPRESENTS THE SERIES OF CROSS-SECTIONS TRACED BY THE CUBE IN ENTERING THE PLANE VERTICALLY BY ONE OF ITS ANGLES "B" REPRESENTS THE SERIES RESULTANT ON ITS ENTERING BY ONE OF ITS EDGES "C" REPRESENTS THE UNCHANGING CROSS-SECTION TRACED BY THE CUBE MEETING THE PLANE SQUARELY BY ONE OF ITS SIDES ALL POSSIBLE PROJECTIONS ARE MODIFICATIONS OF THESE 3 CLASSES

THE CUBES IN THE ABOVE DIAGRAM, SYMMETRICAL SOLIDS OF A 3-DIMENSIONAL SPACE, TRACE VARIOUS EPHEMERAL AND CHANGING CROSS-SECTIONS IN THE PLANE "D" A 2-SPACE, THE CHARACTER OF THE CROSS-SECTION BEING DETERMINED BY THE ANGLE AT WHICH THE CUBE MEETS THE PLANE. — IF THE CUBES BE TAKEN TO REPRESENT THE HIGHER SELVES OF INDIVIDUALS IN A HIGHER-SPACE WORLD, THE PLANE OUR PHENOMENAL WORLD, THE CROSS-SECTIONS WOULD THEN REPRESENT THE LOWER SPACE-ASPECTS OF THESE HIGHER SELVES — PERSONALITIES.

Figure 4.1 Higher-dimensional objects appear as lower-dimensional cross sections when they intersect with a simpler world. From Claude Bragdon, *A Primer of Higher Space (The Fourth Dimension)* (Rochester, N.Y.: Manas Press, 1913).

Like other religious people in this new era of knowledge and technology, Bragdon was interested in psychic phenomena, altered states of consciousness, spirit channeling, and other spiritual occurrences. His interest in these subjects was abetted by Theosophy, a religion that he followed, with more or less enthusiasm, beginning in his twenties. He had an unshakable belief in spiritual intuitions and visionary experiences throughout his life, and the notion of higher dimensions helped him account for these experiences. He illustrates, for instance, how clairvoyant vision might be possible in one drawing in *A Primer of Higher Space* (1913). (See Figure 4.2.)

In the illustration he explains how a higher, three-dimensional being can see "into" all sides—and into *the insides*—of a being in a lower, two-dimensional world. In a flat-plane world, as he says here, a two-dimensional shape living on that flat surface can only see the lines that outline the borders of those flat beings. In other words, when one flat square sidles up to another in this world, all they see of each other are lines. (He got this idea from Fechner, Hinton, and Abbott.) But if one of these squares could, like the Square in *Flatland*, rise into a third dimension "above" this flat, two-dimensional world, he would see not just the boundaries of his fellow creatures but also their insides. In the same way, while in our three-dimensional lives we see only the boundaries of our bodies, if we were to rise up somehow into a fourth dimension, we would see all sides of the human form at once, including, somehow, the body's insides. Our three-dimensional bodies "would in turn appear transparent and be perceived to be but boundaries or cross sections of 4-dimensional solids." Spiritual seers with "x-ray vision" into impossible regions or far distances, or people who could perceive auras or emotions, had developed some kind of four-dimensional ability. In another drawing in the same book, Bragdon illustrated how higher-dimensional seeing might account for all types of remarkable forms of perception. "Possession, obsession, automatic writing and allied phenomena are susceptible of explanation by means of the higher-space hypothesis. It is only necessary to realize that from the higher region of space the interior of a solid is as exposed as the inside of a plane figure is exposed from the region of the third dimension."[17]

Bragdon believed that specific types of art and design could help people develop this kind of higher-dimensional sight. His pen and ink

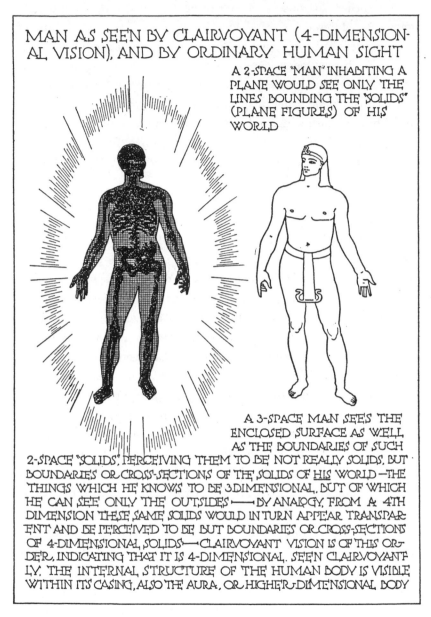

MAN AS SEEN BY CLAIRVOYANT (4-DIMENSIONAL VISION), AND BY ORDINARY HUMAN SIGHT

A 2-SPACE "MAN" INHABITING A PLANE WOULD SEE ONLY THE LINES BOUNDING THE "SOLIDS" (PLANE FIGURES) OF HIS WORLD

A 3-SPACE MAN SEES THE ENCLOSED SURFACE AS WELL AS THE BOUNDARIES OF SUCH 2-SPACE "SOLIDS", PERCEIVING THEM TO BE NOT REALLY SOLIDS, BUT BOUNDARIES OR CROSS-SECTIONS OF THE SOLIDS OF HIS WORLD —THE THINGS WHICH HE KNOWS TO BE 3-DIMENSIONAL, BUT OF WHICH HE CAN SEE ONLY THE OUTSIDES —— BY ANALOGY, FROM A 4TH DIMENSION THESE SAME SOLIDS WOULD IN TURN APPEAR TRANSPARENT AND BE PERCEIVED TO BE BUT BOUNDARIES OR CROSS-SECTIONS OF 4-DIMENSIONAL SOLIDS—CLAIRVOYANT VISION IS OF THIS ORDER, INDICATING THAT IT IS 4-DIMENSIONAL. SEEN CLAIRVOYANTLY, THE INTERNAL STRUCTURE OF THE HUMAN BODY IS VISIBLE WITHIN ITS CASING, ALSO THE AURA, OR HIGHER-DIMENSIONAL BODY

Figure 4.2 Someone with fourth-dimensional vision could look "down" on our three-dimensional world and view all parts of three-dimensional things at once. From Claude Bragdon, *A Primer of Higher Space (The Fourth Dimension)* (Rochester, N.Y.: Manas Press, 1913).

renderings, for instance, instead of using vanishing-point perspective, were isometric, employing a kind of perspective in which objects that are drawn seem to oscillate between different views. Isometric drawings oscillate in this way because parallel lines are drawn parallel on the page instead of receding in a triangle toward a vanishing point. There are a number of famous examples of isometric depth ambiguity, such as Escher's drawings, which have unstable corners and thus cause the eye to move between different views. Bragdon used the technique because it put the viewer in simultaneous multiple positions vis-à-vis the drawing, forcing a kind of higher vision upon the viewer: The viewer saw different sides of a thing at once. Bragdon insisted that isometric perspective was a "projection of the mental image" that rises above "earth-bound perspective" because "isometric perspective shows things as they are *known in the mind*: parallel lines are really parallel; there is no far and no near." As Paul Emmons has written, Bragdon's way of talking about isometric perspective was similar to Theosophical ways of discussing astral vision. "Isometrical perspective is therefore more intellectual, more *archetypal*, it more truly renders *the mental image*—the thing seen by the mind's eye."[18]

Probing higher and deeper, seeing the *mental image* in the outer reality—these were unusual preoccupations, perhaps, for an architect who spent his time designing homes, buildings, and bridges. But work did not take up all of his time or exhaust his prodigious energies. A young assistant in Bragdon's Rochester office recalled that he was a great talker who liked to speculate about the inner meaning of apparently mundane things. He "found time almost daily to come to my table and talk to me for an hour or more while I folded my hands and listened." "The topics ranged from abstract aesthetics to theories of the fourth dimension. All that was being done at the office was explained carefully, but most of the talk ran to philosophy and metaphysics. To all this flood of pearls I registered dumb amazement. One day when my expression must have been particularly blank, he told me, confidentially, that he knew well enough that I didn't understand then what he was telling me but he was assured that it was making a subconscious impression which would eventually emerge as conscious realization."[19]

Bragdon shared the deeper truths of architecture at the office, in lectures, and in writing, speaking of how beautiful art and architecture copied the Beautiful Necessity, those deep natural structures, patterns, and numbers discussed by Emerson. He thought architects should divide space with numerical ratios and basic geometric shapes in mind, as all great architecture had done in the past. Divided-up portions of space should be metered out by using "significant, quantitatively small and properly contrasted" numbers, and they should obey some clear numerical progression. By designing buildings that displayed these patterns Bragdon made the divine visible for everyone using these spaces. "In every excellent work of architecture, there dwells an esoteric and universal beauty, following as it does, the archetypal pattern laid down by the Great Architect."[20] The patterns Bragdon saw in nature included harmoniously balanced oppositions (yin/yang, male/female, light/dark, freedom/fate), the deployment and combination of basic geometrical elements (the circle and square), and the unfolding of correspondences between large and small. Aspects of nature have corresponding structures, from the smallest leaf to the largest tree, and architectural ornamentation can have that same kind of overall unity, though built at different scales. The human body, of course, represented this same kind of overall unity, a unity made up of scaled repetitions, harmoniously reconciled oppositions (left/right), and mathematical relations between different parts (e.g., the length of the hand is the same as the length of the face; the distance between outstretched hands equals our height, and so on). "The human body," Bragdon insisted, "is beautifully geometrical, being founded on the square, the circle and the equilateral triangle," all entities that, like major chords in music, had a special appeal to our senses.[21]

Seeing Spirit in the City

In the first decades of the twentieth century, Bragdon developed a reputation among progressives as a talented architect and critic. He represented progressive architects in upstate New York, was well known nationally as an architectural theorist, and was in touch with the era's most prominent architects, such as Irving Pond, Emil Lorch, and Louis Sullivan. Bragdon was a close correspondent with Sullivan and later his most visible interpreter, becoming, according to the architectural historian Jonathan Massey, the "single figure most closely associated with Sullivan in the architectural press." In the years after Sullivan's death in 1924, Bragdon published excerpts from his correspondence with Sullivan, compiled Sullivan's correspondence for publication in *Architecture* magazine, wrote the foreword to Sullivan's *Autobiography of an Idea,* and edited, introduced, and republished Sullivan's *Kindergarten Chats.*[22] The *New Yorker* writer and architectural critic Lewis Mumford, who admired Bragdon's aesthetic and democratic principles and found his public festivals remarkable, said Bragdon's theories had as great an influence on culture as the work of the American architect Irving Pond.[23]

Bragdon began with smaller, private commissions but as his reputation grew he took on larger projects such as Rochester's First Universalist Church, its Chamber of Commerce Building, and the New York Central Railroad Station. The train station is an early example of how he tried to create structures that made visible nature's "Beautiful Necessity." When he began work on the train station in 1909, he thought about how to make those invisible patterns and harmonies visible. Borrowing inspiration from the five driving wheels on locomotives, he designed the four-story building with five aligned, tangential circles. He designed the circles and the spaces inside the building using musical ratios—the ratios of length, width, and height, for example, were built on musical intervals such as octaves, major fifths, and diminished sevenths. Those with eyes to see and ears to hear could perceive the harmonies. Before the building opened, Bragdon took a friend with him to tour the building, a Theosophist and former opera singer named Marie Russak, who, like many Theosophists, had ways of perceiving deeper truths. "As we were standing in the gallery overlooking the waiting-room, she ran up the notes of the diatonic scale in her full, powerful voice. At the utterance of a certain note the entire room seemed to become a resonance chamber, reinforcing the tone with a volume of sound so great as to be almost overpowering." Everything vibrated. "There!" she said, as the sound faded. "Now your railway station has found its keynote—now it is alive."[24] Overwhelmingly satisfied with the building, Rochester officials asked Bragdon if they could reward him in some way. He "requested that he be allowed to attach small boxes, holding theosophical literature, to the inner walls of the station." Bragdon had to replenish these pamphlets constantly and was astonished that they were so popular—until he discovered that they were simply being discarded by a rival religious group.[25]

Figure 4.3   A postcard of the New York Central Railway Station, which opened in 1913 and was demolished between 1965 and 1973. A new Rochester transit station is being designed using aspects of the original design. Courtesy Special Collections, Rare Books and Preservation, University of Rochester Libraries.

There is perhaps no better symbol of industrial modernity than the railroad, which inaugurated an era of disorienting speed, dissonant noises, and artificially built environments that were out of touch with nature's underlying beauty. City dwellers had lost their "intimate communion with [nature's] visible forms," Bragdon complained.[26] "The railroad, the factory, and the mine are the sources of the strength of the modern world," he wrote, "and it should be our task to convert this strength from ugliness and injury to beauty and beneficence."[27] When he designed the New York Central station (in Rochester) he took up the task with enthusiasm, developing ways to transform ugly icons of industrial modernity into things that were simple and beautiful. His station design was grand, symmetrical, and formal like other railroad stations during the period, incorporating contemporary ways of dividing space from the water table and base levels to the attic. In its decoration, however, Bragdon's design was novel. He used large, open arches, geometric decoration, and simple natural colors to create a sense of aspiration, harmony, and repose. In the central waiting room, for instance, with its sixty-foot Guastavino tile vault ceiling, Bragdon used autumnal colors reminiscent of the woods behind his home. Primarily browns and yellows, the waiting room had darker colors near the floor and lighter yellows for the ceiling. The entablature and strips of decorative tiles below and above the wainscoting incorporated bright yellow, green, and blue.[28] Bragdon spoke of cultivating a sense of repose in this room to counteract the station's buzzing intensity, drawing on the ideas of his friend Irving Pond, a Modernist architect who spoke at length about using nature's forms to induce a sense of rest. Bragdon's interior color scheme, harmonic proportions, and simple geometric decoration were ways of deploying nature's forms to counteract the worrisome psychological and social effects of the unnatural industrial landscape.

The problems that confronted Bragdon on the railroad project became lifelong preoccupations. In journals and magazines he discussed how new design principles might remedy modern industrial nervousness, reduce social fragmentation, and create responsible citizens. In letters and in more personal settings, Bragdon gave voice to even stronger complaints, arguing that the root of the problem was a pervasive materialism that did not just drain the cityscape of beauty but also caused an inner, spiritual destruction. To other architects he spoke about the dangers of American materialism, of the ugliness of advertising, of the spiritual aridity of modern industrial society. In dour moods, his warnings became urgent. "The insane speed of our industrial production destroys human values," while the "insane speed of our automobiles will continue to destroy human lives," and the towering skyscrapers of the city stole everyone's air and light, manifestations of the ruthless "will-to-power of a man or a group of men." Higher-dimensional spiritualities sometimes led to talk about "brotherhood" or socialism; in Bragdon's case, these views led to a critique of American capitalism, which he associated with selfishness and greed.[29]

What was the solution? Bragdon hoped architects might develop, following Emerson and Whitman, a uniquely American form of public spirituality. "We people of America, obsessed by materialism, forgetful of the past, heedless of the to-morrow, if we would not perish unhonored on the rubbish-heap of our civilization, must needs produce men—seers, philosophers, poets, artists,—who shall reaffirm in no uncertain terms, the sovereignty of the spirit, for it is the spiritual element in nations, as in individuals, which makes for greatness, for immortality."

These new designers and artists needed to create a new set of outer symbols for a new spiritual life stirring within. Though older scholarly narratives about Modernist architecture have characterized it as rationalist and pragmatic, Bragdon was not the only Modernist who saw architecture as a site of possible spiritual insight or comfort. Bragdon and Sullivan were both deeply influenced by Transcendentalism, while many others, such as those in the circle of Hendrik Petrus Berlage, for instance, were influenced by mystical movements, including Theosophy. "The times are critical," Bragdon cried, even if they did not appear so to the "skeptically minded, who, since they never look for portents never perceive them."[30]

Bragdon thought that a new system of decorative ornamentation might help him draw attention to natural and spiritual beauty, solving some of these problems, and when he designed the railroad station he experimented with ornamental designs. The problem he faced was that the mood of modern architects went exactly the other way: The contemporary strategy was to keep ornamentation to a minimum. Other architects considered ornamentation wasteful, degenerate, and immoral. "The evolution of culture marches with the elimination of ornament from useful objects," the influential Austrian architect Adolf Loos wrote.[31] It was a "strip-tease stage of architectural development," Bragdon said later, recalling Modernist preferences for purely functional structures that left behind styles based on limited nationalistic sentiments and cultural ideals. But Bragdon never completely assimilated this naked functionalism, dubious that it could ever satisfy the human soul. He experimented with eclectic, improvised ornamental details in the railway station and used them sparingly. He decided to combine "some of the canonical ornamental motifs with a free hand, much as a jazz-band leader might syncopate, swing, or otherwise distort" older motifs. He used triumphal arches reminiscent of great entryways of Roman cities. He incorporated stylized pattern work in his capitals and entablature.[32]

But these compromises also did not entirely satisfy him. He began to wonder if it would be possible to develop a wholly new system of ornamentation based on geometric patterns, mathematical ratios, and nature's deep, universal structures. These elements might bring repose to a world of clattering trains, humming engines, and bustling factories. Bragdon also wondered if it was possible to take an additional step—to create a type of architecture that brought into public view the hidden, higher-dimensional realities visualized by geometers, avant-garde artists, and visionaries like Hinton. If this could be done, Americans stuck within an ugly industrial cityscape might be able to see once again the outer forms, and perhaps even the inner spirit, of something higher.

Architectural Esperanto

The result of this kind of thinking was a 1915 manifesto entitled *Projective Ornament*. In this book and in several related articles Bragdon attempted to show that a new kind of architectural ornamentation could be created out of representations of higher-dimensional objects such as Hinton's tesseract. To begin, he discussed how ordinary three-dimensional figures appeared when they were rendered on a two-dimensional, flat surface. A three-dimensional pyramid, for example, can look like several different objects when projected onto a two-dimensional screen, just as a three-dimensional cube can take on different shapes when projected onto a two-dimensional surface. Representing a four-dimensional object on a two-dimensional surface was a bit more difficult, but because the basic properties of four-dimensional objects (also called "polyhedroids" or "4-polytopes") were clear—we know, for instance, exactly how many edges, faces, and cells make up a four-dimensional cube—it was possible to represent these objects in drawings. Bragdon explained this in detail and included illustrations, such as the illustrations of the tesseract in Figure 4.4.

Here Bragdon showed two ways that a four-dimensional cube could be represented in a lower space. It could be either projected or "folded down." The representations he drew at the bottom of the page were different plane projections of a tesseract. The ornamental patterns he developed in these ways, though, went beyond tesseracts to include other higher-dimensional objects. In another illustration Bragdon showed how he proceeded from three-dimensional solids (on the left) to representations of four-dimensional objects (in the middle), to stylized ornamental designs (on the far right). (See Figure 4.5.) At the bottom of the figure Bragdon represented another higher-dimensional object, a six-hundred

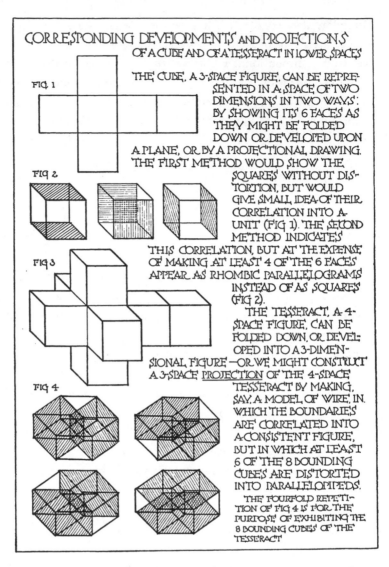

The figure contains the following text:

CORRESPONDING DEVELOPMENTS AND PROJECTIONS
OF A CUBE AND OF A TESSERACT IN LOWER SPACES

FIG 1

THE CUBE, A 3-SPACE FIGURE, CAN BE REPRESENTED IN A SPACE OF TWO DIMENSIONS IN TWO WAYS: BY SHOWING ITS 6 FACES AS THEY MIGHT BE FOLDED DOWN OR DEVELOPED UPON A PLANE, OR BY A PROJECTIONAL DRAWING. THE FIRST METHOD WOULD SHOW THE

FIG 2

SQUARES WITHOUT DISTORTION, BUT WOULD GIVE SMALL IDEA OF THEIR CORRELATION INTO A UNIT (FIG 1). THE SECOND METHOD INDICATES

FIG 3

THIS CORRELATION, BUT AT THE EXPENSE OF MAKING AT LEAST 4 OF THE 6 FACES APPEAR AS RHOMBIC PARALLELOGRAMS INSTEAD OF AS SQUARES (FIG 2).

THE TESSERACT, A 4-SPACE FIGURE, CAN BE FOLDED DOWN, OR DEVELOPED INTO A 3-DIMENSIONAL FIGURE —OR WE MIGHT CONSTRUCT A 3-SPACE PROJECTION OF THE 4-SPACE

FIG 4

TESSERACT BY MAKING, SAY, A MODEL OF WIRE, IN WHICH THE BOUNDARIES ARE CORRELATED INTO A CONSISTENT FIGURE, BUT IN WHICH AT LEAST 6 OF THE 8 BOUNDING CUBES ARE DISTORTED INTO PARALLELOPIPEDS.

THE FOURFOLD REPETITION OF FIG 4 IS FOR THE PURPOSE OF EXHIBITING THE 8 BOUNDING CUBES OF THE TESSERACT

Figure 4.4   Representing four-dimensional cubes (tesseracts) in two dimensions. From Claude Bragdon, *A Primer of Higher Space*.

hedroid, which is a shape containing six hundred equal, regular tetrahedrons. Bragdon pointed out that these representations of polyhedroids, like two-dimensional drawings of three-dimensional objects such as cubes, rendered them as if they were transparent. The result was that when people viewed these representations they saw through their

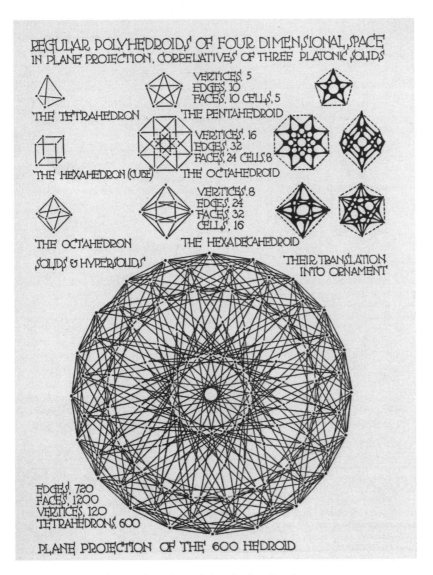

Figure 4.5   Claude Bragdon, the architect Irving Pond once wrote, was a "reincarnated Brahmin" with uncanny abilities as a draftsman. "I never could have the patience to produce his brilliant and syntilating [*sic*] projective ornament, cold as ice in its cut diamond clarity, which I have seen him make with such technical perfection and such seeming ease." From Irving Pond, *The Autobiography of Irving K. Pond: The Sons of Mary and Elihu* (Oak Park, Ill.: Hyoogen Press, 2009), 301.

outer surfaces with a kind of "x-ray" or higher-dimensional vision. Those who viewed these shapes thus acquired a new kind of sight.[33]

It does not do Bragdon any injustice to call his hopes for these ornamental designs utopian. He believed that this new ornamentation could change human beings in several ways. He believed that projective geometric ornament was not just a beautiful "rhythmic subdivision of space" but that it also trained attention on nature's deep geometry and the transcendental reality beyond nature. Like others during this period, he embraced evolutionary social and psychological theories and argued that projective ornament would help retrain the senses and consciousness so that people might perceive something higher, something *more.* "It is possible that by dwelling on elementary higher space concepts, by an intention of consciousness upon the fourth dimension we may push back the psycho-physical boundary and capture for sense the now transcendental fourth dimension."[34] In other words, these designs might reshape the architecture of the brain. Bragdon thought his designs also suggested ways that all material things were projections of higher realities. "These figures illustrate anew the idea, old as philosophy itself, that all forms are projections on the lighted screen of a material universe of archetypal ideas: that all of animate creation is one vast moving picture of the play of the Cosmic Mind." Finally, Bragdon insisted that ornamentation based on nature's universal mathematical and geometric principles might be a way to overcome differences of class, culture, nationality, and religion. America wrestled with strikes and labor unrest, with an increasingly diverse society of immigrants, with urban poverty and slums. Knowing that architects in the past had used ornamentation to demarcate rank or display status, Bragdon forged a new ornamentation that was simple and natural, one that drew attention away from rank, class, culture, or nationality. His universalism would be an antidote to international disorder, excessive nationalism, and race prejudice, all of which nourished the conditions for the Great War that was just then beginning. His ornamentation was a universal "form-language," an architectural Esperanto, which might counteract these dangerous trends.[35]

By the end of 1915, the year that Bragdon published his *Projective Ornament,* he had completed the New York Central Railroad Station; had won other commissions, including the new Rochester Chamber of

Commerce Building; and had designed many other buildings and homes. But at about this time everything changed. In *Projective Ornament* and in other writings he articulated a desire to help reform American culture—to be one of those American "seers" called for by Emerson and Whitman—and increasingly his life in Rochester felt stifling and conventional. He confided to a friend that in Rochester "I have never been able to do my best work: no one is willing to let me be radical enough."[36] Designing commercial buildings, private homes, and small renovations—was this the best use of his ideals and energy? This question became more urgent as America's social problems mounted. There were labor strikes and violence in the streets; there were emphatic editorials calling on capitalists to temper their greed and accommodate the working classes; there were fears that alternative social and political systems, especially communism, might supplant democracy; and there were the ubiquitous problems of the city—overcrowding, poverty, unsanitary conditions. The world was balanced between old and new, between an older culture, now irreparably damaged, and a new world order struggling to be born. The visionary, idealistic side of Bragdon yearned to be involved. Did he want to be a servant of the soaring American capitalist enterprise, with its ugly buildings, ubiquitous advertisements, and detestable, driving profit motive, or would he become a master of his own life and an architect of reforms that might save America from its alarming drift?[37]

"I long for real architecture," he confided to his wife. "Something big."[38]

"Cathedrals without Walls"

These expansive aspirations led him to Progressive-era reform efforts and more public design projects that involved bringing his four-dimensional ornamentation to civic pageants, public festivals, church services, and Broadway theater sets. He also spoke widely about his ideas for architectural renewal at conferences, churches, lecture halls, retreat centers, salons, libraries, New York clubhouses, and civic associations. In 1914 he proposed that the Rochester Chamber of Commerce build a civic theater where citizens could stage pageants to "unite the arts of poetry, the drama, music and the dance in one synthesis of beauty" that might portray "the drama of democracy finding itself."[39] Democracy, he said, found its spiritual foundation and purpose in a crowd consciousness that developed when people came together to pursue common interests. This kind of crowd consciousness could mitigate the divisive effects of differences of class and race. Bragdon's plan for a civic theater fell apart, but the idea of creating spaces where Americans could come together stayed with him. With his wife, Eugenie, and their friend Harry Barnhart, a Rochester native and the founder of the community singing movement, Bragdon staged in his backyard an ambitious party that would incorporate choral singing and multicolored lamps suspended in midair. The illuminated lamps were covered with "glass-covered circular screens" that were "made to look so like rose-windows as to suggest a cathedral without walls." They were decorated with his projective ornament patterns.[40] After this event, Rochester officials asked Barnhart and Bragdon to organize a civic festival with community singing and ornamental lanterns, which was staged in Rochester's Highland Park in September of 1915.

At the time, Progressive reformers, liberal Protestant activists, and local politicians were preoccupied with developing a spiritual element in American democracy as a way of counteracting social fragmentation. Bragdon's civic festivals were his way of advancing this effort by bringing his previously private higher-dimensional convictions to larger, public audiences.

The "Song and Light" movement that Bragdon created built in particular on the community singing movement, a nationwide initiative fashioned by settlement-house reformers, musical organizations, and local governments. The originator of the movement, Harry Barnhart, who started on the streets of New York City with a broken-down car and portable organ, established community choruses in Rochester, New York City, Buffalo, Syracuse, and several suburban New Jersey towns. Above all he sought enthusiastic participation, coaching crowds to sing in order to generate feelings of community and lift "people out of their own self-consciousness."[41] Evidently he was quite charismatic. "Never mind what they say about your voice at home!" he told audiences in places such as Madison Square Garden and Central Park. Called the "Billy Sunday of Music," Barnhart exchanged the classical repertoire for popular standards, national anthems, and religious songs. Always in the background was Europe—aristocratic, antidemocratic, fragmented, degenerate. Community singing would buttress democratic feelings, neighborliness, and universal participation and would shape a new spiritual sensibility of self-expression, freedom, and love of God and others.[42]

By designing these public festivals, Bragdon, Barnhart, and Arthur Farwell, another leader of the movement, hoped to give voice to a deeper, spiritual element of American democracy. Farwell, a composer, settlement-house administrator, and music educator, wrote articles about the community music movement and democracy in widely available periodicals such as the *Atlantic Monthly*, the *North American Review*, and the *Review of Reviews*. Like many reformers, Farwell drew on Bergson's idea of a life force (*élan vital*) that moved civilization forward; inspired great scientific, social, and technological changes; and would usher in a new era of universal, spiritual brotherhood. The particular form of spirituality that would help us evolve was a mixture of mysticism, scientific insight, and democratic thought. Farwell quoted Christian mystics, New Thought writers, Whitman, Emerson, and William James. Farwell also believed that the arts would play a key role in this evolution, arguing that music in particular was "a spiritually centripetal force, drawing men together into a single emotion or idea." Combining insights from Whitman, New Thought, and social psychologists, Farwell argued that when large groups of Americans gathered, a kind of spiritual electricity developed that eroded individuality and difference. "It is no longer the separate minds which listen, it is the over-soul of the mass, and . . . in its capacity to assimilate the most real essence of all that vibrates upon it, no limits can be ascribed."[43] Gathering and singing in large groups momentarily dampened the intellect and opened powers of emotion and fellow-feeling. Bragdon knew a lot about the choral organizing in New York and was friends with both Barnhart and Farwell. As far back as 1913 he was talking to Barnhart and Farwell about the unifying and spiritualizing effects of large-scale community events.

Though largely forgotten today, Song and Light festivals were remarkable spectacles witnessed by many with awe and astonishment. In the Song and Light festival in New York's Central Park in 1916, for instance—the first of three annual Song and Light events there—a crowd of sixty thousand onlookers sang popular standards, the national anthem, and religious songs in a setting decorated with lighted lanterns and panels that incorporated Bragdon's projective ornament designs. On a temporary stage erected across the lake from the Bethesda terrace and fountain in Central Park, Barnhart coordinated a sixty-five-piece orchestra and a professional chorus of eight hundred. Audience members gathered around the stage and the lake. At dusk the musicians struck the first note of "America" and light fixtures and panels were suddenly illuminated, projecting Bragdon's higher space patterns in different colors throughout the park. After "America," the chorus sang pieces by Wagner, Offenbach, and Strauss before Barnhart moved to the climax of the event, the communal singing. As Barnhart turned to face the massive audience, people slowly joined until thousands of voices created a remarkable wall of sound. When Barnhart silenced the professional chorus, the audience carried the tune. At that instant

> a great voice, the voice of the people, rose out of the darkness and rolled out across the water, to be finally taken up, echoed and reinforced, by the waiting chorus and orchestra. This was done again and again, with ever-increasing success, in subsequent numbers, and when "Nearer My God to Thee" was rendered in this fashion, deep calling to deep, the light to the darkness, the crowd was wrought up to such a pitch of emotional excitement that many an eye was dimmed by involuntary tears, and many a heart was invaded by a new, great, and impersonal love for all the others, brought suddenly inexplicably near, become suddenly inexplicably dear.[44]

These were Bragdon's words, but the next day, the *New York Times* focused on the same moment. "As the song rolled across the water from the absolutely invisible thousands, it had a strangely stirring effect, something that could not be duplicated in a thousand years of concert halls and opera houses. . . . It seemed as if all the 60,000 were trying their best."[45] The art critic and writer Lewis Mumford, who was twenty years old when he attended this event, recalled that "in this communal drama Bragdon's faery geometry counted for as much as the choral music floating over the water. The enchantment of that scene has never quite faded from my mind." The whole spectacle gave Mumford the sense, he said, that "we were on the verge of translation into a new

Figure 4.6 The Song and Light stage, Central Park, 1916. Courtesy Special Collections, Rare Books and Preservation, University of Rochester Libraries.

world, a quite magical translation, in which the best hopes of the American Revolution, the French Revolution, and the Industrial Revolution would all be simultaneously fulfilled."[46]

The lanterns and screens that Bragdon created for these festivals were ways of pointing to deeper correspondences undergirding all things. Bragdon made them by layering colored tissue paper over black construction paper with stenciled cutouts of projective ornament designs. The designs were then set into wire or wood frames (Figure 4.7). He used bright colors such as orange, green, yellow, and pink, combining these colors in ways that corresponded to the music. (He used an ophthalmic scale that linked colors and musical tones.)[47] Bragdon hung these colored screens from cables that stretched across the proscenium, where the panels, when illuminated, lit up the stage and chorus. Bragdon also placed circular screens and lanterns around the conductor's platform and in different locations in Central Park. The idea was to project calming color and sound vibrations that integrated audience members into a single, harmoniously acting (and singing) group. He sought an

Figure 4.7 One of Bragdon's projective ornament panels used in Central Park, 1916. Courtesy Special Collections, Rare Books and Preservation, University of Rochester Libraries.

effect here not unlike the effect created in a cathedral. Song and Light, he said once, created a "cathedral without walls"—it reproduced the light and shadow of a Gothic cathedral, with its "vast shadowy interior lit by marvelously traceried and jeweled windows, which hold the eyes in a hypnotic thrall." Farwell also noted that Bragdon's "new art of design in colored light . . . turned the entire landscape into a veritable 'temple built without hands.'" After all, Falwell wrote, the true church was not an institution or form; it was a living community of faith. Like cathedrals of old, these modern spaces shaped a new spiritual subjectivity. "By dint of continued gazing . . . and by trying to recognize all its intricate inter-relations," Bragdon explained, viewers "may come finally to the feeling that it is not merely a figure on a plane, but that it represents a hypersolid of hyperspace."[48]

Seeing through Bragdon's illuminated panels to a higher, fourth dimension was a spiritual act with social implications. Because it was based in universal patterns, and because these patterns drew observers up into higher levels of seeing, Bragdon's projective ornament would lift people above social, racial, and national distinctions. "All elements of city life were represented" in Central Park's 1916 Song and Light, Bragdon wrote, "Italians, French, Russians, Germans, forgot their racial antagonisms for the time being under the spell of the music in which their voices joined." At first the universalist aspirations of festival organizers distinguished this American effort from Old World antagonisms in Europe, prejudices that had produced full-scale war. But when America entered the First World War in 1917, Bragdon, Barnhart, and Farwell staged Song and Light festivals in different locations that were more nationalistic. Their festivals in 1917 incorporated military bands and processions, the American national anthem, and the anthems of other Allied powers. Some of these events celebrated or bade farewell to soldiers ready for deployment.

The meaning of these more militarized festivals is interesting to ponder. Had Bragdon and others been co-opted by the U.S. government for its own purposes? Had the ultimate aim of social solidarity been sacrificed for something more expedient—namely wartime mobilization and military morale? Like other Progressives, Bragdon saw the war as a moment not to give up on his goals but to realize them. He glossed conscription, army camp life, and even combat as propelling Americans into a new type of existence, with new, higher democratic ideals, more integration across class and race, and deeper convictions about community. Bragdon did not see his festivals as corrupted; he saw the war as a chance to forge ahead with a more robust democracy. "In our army camps social life is truly democratic," he wrote, justifying his war work. "Not alone have the conditions of conscription conspired to make it so, but there is a manifest will-to-democracy—the growing of a new flower of the spirit, sown in a community of sacrifice, to reach its maturity, perhaps, only in a community of suffering."[49] Bragdon's way of talking about the war as a purifying contest was similar to how reformers, Protestant ministers, and social scientists spoke of the war, at least in the beginning: It was a refining fire and an agent of social evolution.

Nevertheless, it is hard to deny that by deploying higher dimensions in mobilization efforts, Bragdon engaged in a kind of nationalist myth making he had earlier regarded as distasteful, jingoistic, and narrow. The best that could be said about Bragdon is that he failed to resist a temptation most other religiously minded Americans, including the vast majority of American clerics, also failed to resist—he conflated God's will with America's political and military objectives.

At the beginning of the Depression, in 1931, Barnhart and Bragdon collaborated again to create Song and Light events at Madison Square Garden that were incredible spectacles, combining elements of the circus, community singing, Bragdon's fourth-dimensional lanterns, a one-thousand-person African American chorus, and bikes and motorbikes racing around the Garden's track. Admission was inexpensive (a mere $1.50) because the Garden's president wanted to sell tickets. Illuminated by powerful yellow spotlights and decorated with sunflowers, the center of the arena, where Barnhart coordinated the action, was encircled by the band (wearing black and white) and the massive chorus (in red gowns). "Clad all in white, like an angel of the Lord," Barnhart held forth with charisma. His amplified voice boomed "like a message from Jehovah" through the arena, one reporter remembered, as he called out directions to the choir, barked encouragement to the audience, and, near the conclusion, called for the bicycles and motorcycles to begin racing on the outer track. The electrical lights above and around the arena projected Bragdon's ornamental, consciousness-raising designs in every direction.

Reviewers offered different opinions on the event, calling it "exciting," "stimulating," "weird," "insane," and "beautiful." Born of financial necessity, designed by a higher-dimensional proselytizer, and hosted by a man who believed that such spectacles brought into existence a spiritual principle animating democracy, the event captured in one evening the incongruous impulses and aspirations that defined early twentieth-century American culture. "If ever the vulgarity, the rush and hurry, the new and incredible artistic standards, and yet, too, the underlying spiritual beauty of which humanity is capable, the restless, changing Twentieth Century, was typified," one observer insisted, "it happened in Madison Square Garden last Friday night."[50]

Higher Dimensions in the Pulpit, on the Stage

If Bragdon created new outdoor sacred spaces, he also brought higher-dimensional designs to many other settings. His ideas on light, color, and spirituality altered how a number of churches designed their worship practices. Religious notices in the *New York Times* and correspondence to and from Bragdon indicate that his books were read by a variety of religious Americans, studied in church-sponsored study groups, and discussed in sermons given especially by liberal Christian pastors.

Bragdon's designs were dramatically incorporated, for example, in the church of his friend William Norman Guthrie, a tall, garrulous Episcopal priest at St. Mark's Church in the Bouwerie, a downtown Manhattan church attempting to bolster sagging membership by attracting artists and intellectuals. The grandson of the Scottish-born abolitionist, feminist, and freethinker Fanny Wright, Guthrie inherited some of his grandmother's spirit of radicalism. He was well known for a social gospel ministry that included feeding the city's poor and even housing them in the rectory, acts that caused reporters to dub the church "St. Marx." He also was known for opening his pulpit to Native Americans, Hindus, members of the Baha'i Faith, and others. In 1922 he allowed a Parsee priest to set up an altar where he said prayers. A 1931 *New Yorker* profile of Guthrie found it necessary to say that "this was the first time such a thing had been done in the history of the Episcopal Church," noting further that the act "caused appreciable numbers of wealthy Episcopalians to look on Guthrie as the Wild Man of Borneo."[51] Guthrie also was interested in the arts and invited artists and dancers, including Martha Graham, to speak or perform. (He also invited the dancer Isadora Duncan, who detested churches, to come and speak of dance as a spiritual practice; but the presiding Episcopal bishop, wary of Guthrie, canceled the event.) Guthrie was known to participate in ritual dances conducted by others during services, acts that on balance increased church attendance, even if "a few of the old ladies dropped out."[52] No matter—a stuffy, wealthy church for the elderly was not what he was after.

Bragdon knew Guthrie because they had been involved in reform activities on behalf of the poor and unemployed during the years after the First World War; both had also been involved in community singing events by and for the unemployed masses. Bragdon spoke at Guthrie's church several times about the fourth dimension and ways of accelerating the evolution of human consciousness. In 1921 Guthrie asked Bragdon if he would use his expertise in sound, light, and design to enhance the emotional power of the service at St. Mark's and create an atmosphere of beauty and mystery. Bragdon constructed projective ornament lanterns and screens similar to the ones he used at outdoor festivals. He hung them from the ceiling so that they projected light downward, leaving the vault of the church dark. He also manipulated lights during Guthrie's sermons. When Guthrie told tales of sin, crime, or murder, the spotlights turned from blue to red. When Guthrie spoke of love and virtue, the lights were dimmed and accompanied by transient flashes of bright purple, red, pink, and yellow. Bragdon used spotlighting to highlight the choir or the pulpit, to focus attention, or to create moods of surprise, awe, or wonder.

The reforms at Guthrie's church were part of a wider impulse to renew church architecture, design, and liturgy in the early decades of the century.[53] The American pageantry movement, which presented pageants and plays as ways of educating citizens about American democracy, inspired liturgical innovation in the Protestant churches, and many pastors and religious educators incorporated dramatic arts into religious events. Christian writers such as Martha Candler embraced Bragdon's ideas and called on Christians to incorporate them, believing that his ways of using color and sound made services more powerful and appealing.[54]

Bragdon was happy to see his art and design used in any context, including churches, but he had little hope that the church would be in the vanguard of the coming new spiritual age. Though he was polite when sitting in the pews or speaking from pulpits, his intuitions told him that older religious forms were breaking apart and new ones would take shape in their place. "That the church has more or less ceased to function, especially with our young people," Bragdon wrote in a typical passage, "is not open to question. It is a self-evident fact."[55] Modernity had brought a new world, and modern believers had to invent new forms, including, as we have seen, new public forms of transcendent art and design.

One new, public form of transcendent art was the theater, and after 1919, when his friend Walter Hampden asked for his help, Bragdon turned to the theater as a way to develop spiritual spaces and narratives. A Broadway actor, manager, and (later) film actor, Hampden asked Bragdon to be the artistic director of his production of *Hamlet*. This involved designing everything—all the costumes, sets, stage elements, and lighting. The close friendship between the two turned into a successful collaboration, and by 1923 Bragdon had closed his architectural practice in Rochester and moved to New York City, where he became a full-time stage designer. He moved into the Shelton Hotel, sharing the building and often his breakfast table with Alfred Stieglitz, Georgia O'Keeffe, and other likeminded artists, writers, and spiritual seekers. For the remainder of his life he sustained himself financially by designing Broadway sets, publishing books, creating book jackets for Alfred Knopf, and giving lectures. (Some of Bragdon's books that he had previously published via his own Manas Press in Rochester sold well enough that Knopf took them over and kept them in print.)

At the time of their collaboration, Hampden was on a remarkable trajectory from Broadway actor and manager of the Colonial Theater (subsequently renamed Hampden's Theater) to acting in silent and sound films. During the post–First World War period, he and Maurice Evans were the only actors to play Hamlet three times on Broadway. Bragdon and Hampden shared interests in Theosophy and eastern religions and had similar ideas about the theater as a religious vocation. (Hampden had resigned from Theosophy in 1915, though was still interested in eastern religions.) "My art to me is a religion," Hampden explained once to a reporter. "It is something sacred, and I feel that while I am engaged in the presentation of a play, especially a tragedy, that it is more or less of a sacred function and that I am enacting the part of a priest. I am interpreting the essence of Beauty to the audience." The first play they did together, a production of *Hamlet* in 1919, was to Bragdon a wonderful example of a spirituality of what he called "exquisite acquiescence." (The spirituality of "acquiescence" in the play had to do with Hamlet's sacrificial submission to a fate that was predestined and communicated to him in a ghostly visitation.[56]) Bragdon aped the style and approach of what was called the "new stagecraft," preferring abstract and symbolic rather than realistic sets, and he also found ways to incorporate his higher-dimensional ornamental motifs. He felt his projective ornament patterns reinforced the spiritual message of the play, because an important aspect of projective ornament designs was that they harmonized individual freedom, represented in arabesque curves, with the iron boundaries of fate, symbolized by the regular, crystalline shapes. The mysterious relationship between fate and freedom was another cosmic truth that Bragdon made visible in these geometric designs.

Their productions of Shakespeare continued to be successful and lucrative, but both Hampden and Bragdon wanted to stage something more closely aligned with their religious interests. In 1918 Hampden had been involved in a Theosophical production of Edwin Arnold's classic story of the Buddha, *The Light of Asia* (1879), at the Krotona Institute of Theosophy, a one-thousand-acre property in the Hollywood hills of Southern California. Part of the motivation for the play came directly from Madame Blavatsky, who before her death asked Theosophists to gather on her death's anniversary to read *The Light of Asia* and the *Gita*. Theosophists were staging dramatic renditions of the Buddha's life at Krotona and at many other society meetings, including at meetings in India and in Ojai, California, where Krishnamurti lived. The version at Krotona had a large cast with Hampden playing the Buddha. The dancing was choreographed by the modern dance pioneer Ruth St. Denis, herself a religious seeker and an admirer of Bragdon's writings. (St. Denis read and studied the works of both Bragdon and Ouspensky and used their ideas for inspiration as she pursued hidden realities through dance. She would reiterate Bragdon's view that "form determined by the evolution of changing nonmaterial nature corresponds to psychic forces"—that, in other words, dance and other art captured or harmonized with spiritual forces or energies. She also recommended Bragdon's books to her student Martha Graham.)[57] The production of *The Light of Asia* did well in California. The *Los Angeles Times* praised the outdoor amphitheater setting, the dancing, and the costumes and said Hampden's acting captured the "essence of the spirit of the Buddha." Referring to the annual Passion Play in Bavaria, which for centuries had dramatized the life and suffering of Jesus, the newspaper called Krotona's "Life of the Buddha" the new "Oberammergau of the West."[58]

Hampden was determined to stage a similar play in New York and by 1928 he had developed a script and wished to move forward. It looked like it would be a terrific production—Hampden was famous as an actor and director, Bragdon was known for his set designs, and Ruth St. Denis would choreograph. Unfortunately, reviewers detested it. Though some praised Bragdon's sets or St. Denis's efforts, most thought the production was shallow, predictable, amateurish, and preachy. "Most sumptuously uninspired," wrote one of them. "Is it to be treated as a dramatic entertainment or a piece of religious propaganda?"[59] In California, they had worked with true believers; in New York, they had to face cagey skeptics. Nevertheless Bragdon continued to work in the theater and was certain that drama (and early television) were media that might be used to discipline the senses in ways that led beyond them.

Bragdon's ideas informed still other performances, spectacles, and spaces. In 1921 Bragdon met a young Broadway set designer, Norman Bel Geddes, after one of Hampden's performances. Bel Geddes was a set designer and director for plays in Los Angeles but later opened an industrial design studio that became widely known for designing commercial products and futuristic automobiles, houses, and airplanes. By the 1930s he was a prominent designer and a leading thinker on social and technological trends. Bel Geddes borrowed Bragdon's higher-dimensional ideas, embracing his notion, which was ultimately traceable to Hinton, that human consciousness was evolving capacities to perceive higher dimensions. Bel Geddes popularized these ideas in articles and built them into design projects, including his designs for the 1939 New York World's Fair. At the fair Bel Geddes created the

Futurama exhibit for General Motors, a futuristic model of America in the 1960s, complete with highways, glass skyscrapers, cities, suburbs, and aerodynamic automobiles.

But Bel Geddes also created another exhibit at the fair, the Crystal Palace, an eight-sided building made to resemble a tesseract. He positioned this building at the center of a large reflecting pool, so that the reflected image of the elevated prism in the water would be its mirror image (rotated in a fourth dimension). Visitors paid fifteen cents, entered the polygonal structure, and chose one of three levels from which to gaze into a polygonally shaped room with white, female dancers, bare-chested, dancing and spinning around in light fabric skirts. Just as the structure itself was reflected in a pool below, the dancers inside were spotlit and reflected in mirrors that covered the platforms below and the walls and ceilings. The ubiquitous mirrors meant that each dancer was "reflected to infinity in all directions." Bel Geddes called this show a "polyscopic prismatic show" but it was really a sophisticated peep show. This was "seeing all sides of a thing" in a way that even Hinton couldn't have imagined.

The exhibit demonstrates how Bel Geddes and other men of the time conflated sexual and spiritual longing. Bel Geddes talked about this exhibit as both a way of training the senses to see higher things and as a "very high-class Peep Show" that could be "as naughty as you might at any time decide" but one that was not in essence vulgar but artistic.[60] Bel Geddes and others believed women passively embodied the fourth dimension (and, more generally, the spiritual), and thought that female spirituality was enlivened by interaction with the more active male force. The active male and spiritual female forces were combined in the Crystal Gazing Palace, in which women produced fragmented four-dimensional mirror images that only men could "put together" visually. Women fluttered by one-way mirrors that made the audience invisible, breaking themselves into moving parts. They could not see the whole as the audience might have seen it (had they looked for it). Scientific men who were privy to the esoteric logic of fourth-dimensional vision may have been looking for a spiritualized, higher whole in the moving, fragmented parts—but commentators were sure most men were content with glimpses of "polyscopic" flashes of a female breast or inner thigh. (After viewing the exhibit one alarmed offi-

cial exclaimed, "For God's sake get some underwear on these girls!"[61])
The male gaze filled up this exhibit's empty spaces, bringing four-
dimensional imagination into life.[62] Bragdon probably was too reserved
and Victorian to have gone along with Bel Geddes's polyscopic nudity,
but he too conceived of the feminine as somehow essentially spiritual
and higher dimensional.

◠◡◠◡◠

Because so many Americans today pursue their religious lives outside of
churches and other religious institutions, it is easy to overlook the fact
that Bragdon's way of relocating religiousness was unconventional and
disturbing during his time. To him the spiritual was located in nature
and in its deepest structures, as Emerson had insisted, rather than in
churches or other traditional religious institutions. Several earlier
fourth-dimensional philosophers believed this as well, but Bragdon did
more than anyone to make these private and sometimes esoteric notions public, to create new ways to educate the higher senses through
art, architecture, theater, and public festivals. So, while many higher-
dimensional thinkers used scientific ideas about higher dimensions in
order to develop *new ways of thinking* about the supernatural, Bragdon
took up the difficult task of developing a lived, material culture. "Spiritual verities can never be matters of tradition," an Indian missionary
to America, Swami Vivekananda, once said. "We can never believe in
things until we become acquainted with them through our own direct
perception."[63] Bragdon found ways to provide direct perception of these
spiritual verities for the public, helping others see, touch, and live in a
world of higher sensations.

He did this in different ways. His architectural ornamentation
helped Americans see in new ways the layers and dimensions of the
built environment. In Song and Light he fashioned new public spaces
that conveyed a sense of awe and wonder at something beyond. In theatrical spaces he used geometric designs and colors to add depth and
beauty to older myths and stories. Through midcentury and beyond,
Bragdon influenced many people—writers such as Charles Tart who
were interested in expanded consciousness; designers such as R. Buckminster Fuller who wanted to develop higher-dimensional built environments; sci-fi authors such as Robert Heinlein who created dimensional

otherworlds; sculptors such as Peter Forakis who wished to explore natural laws and geometry; and artists such as Marcel Duchamp who strove to understand and even depict the deepest parts of reality.[64] Some of their stories and the stories of other artists and writers attempting to think about or visualize higher dimensions occupy us in the chapters that follow.

5

Max Weber and the
Art of an Invisible Geometry

I f Edwin Abbott believed that we were higher-dimensional beings living
in a world of flattened-out squares, if C. Howard Hinton resolved his
existential dilemmas by imagining them as aspects of a massive cube
structure, and if Claude Bragdon developed hypercubes and other
higher-dimensional objects into an otherworldly ornamentation, none
of these thinkers exhausted the meaning of cubes and hypercubes in
European and American cultures. In fact, by the first decade of the
twentieth century, Europeans and Americans saw cubes and other elementary geometric shapes everywhere—or so it seemed. Nowhere was
this more the case than in the art world, where modern artists com-
peted with one another to discover ways of breaking down reality's
outer forms by reducing them to their basic, and often geometrical,
parts. As artists looked for new ways to represent reality, some of them
turned to math and geometry, including new geometries of higher-
dimensional space.

The beginnings of this impulse were initiated by the French Post-
Impressionist painter Paul Cézanne, who was interested in perception,
optical phenomena, and geometry. In 1904 Cézanne wrote to a friend
that "everything in nature is formed upon the sphere, the cone and the

cylinder," a formulation that, according to the art historian and journalist Alfred Werner, gave "the growing generation of painters . . . a means by which they might render the apparent 'chaos' of nature into patterns that made sense, aesthetically speaking."[1] Cézanne's work inspired a number of different styles, including the first abstract form of modern art, Cubism, developed in Paris beginning in 1907 by Pablo Picasso and Georges Braque. Picasso, Braque, and other Cubists broke down, analyzed, and reassembled objects as abstract entities fashioned out of cylinders, triangles, circles, or cubes. Many Cubists working in this manner also studied the ideas of Hinton, Bragdon, and other hyperspace philosophers, using these ideas to attempt to represent in different ways things beyond our everyday, three-dimensional world.

Though many Cubists read and discussed new works in mathematics and geometry, including hyperspace geometries, they were not the only artists to do so. As Linda Henderson has shown, higher-dimensional ideas were deployed by Cubists, Futurists, Suprematists, American Modernists, Dadaists, Surrealists, and others.[2] Henderson has argued in particular that while Einstein's notions of space were dominant by the 1920s, Hinton's were more important in the period before then, especially in art and culture. "In the first two decades of the twentieth century," she has written, "the idea promulgated by Hinton and many others that space might possess a higher, unseen fourth dimension was the dominant intellectual influence."[3] Of course not all artists used these ideas in order to probe into what they called the spiritual, the infinite, or "the Absolute." But those who did believed that higher-dimensional art helped them both see how nature was structured and capture once again, as great artists always had, that elusive spiritual element in reality that made art enduring.

One artist who embraced higher-dimensional ideas for these reasons was the Russian-American Cubist painter Max Weber. Raised in an observant Jewish home in rural Russia until immigrating at age ten to Brooklyn, Weber found himself in between a traditional Judaism attuned more to the lifeways of the Russian shtetl and an avant-garde sensibility that characterized artistic and literary New York. When as a youth he discovered a talent for drawing he gravitated toward the New York art scene, which was wholly unfamiliar and certainly unappealing to his orthodox Jewish parents. The feelings of disapproval and revulsion were mutual: Modernist artists, of course, were not known for their fondness for tradition. There was for instance the Russian painter and theorist Wassily Kandinsky, who announced to those who had not yet perceived such things that Catholicism, Protestantism, and Judaism, rotten with unbelief, were tottering and crashing to the ground. These religious traditions would be replaced by artist-seers who, like prophets of old, would usher in an era of divine wisdom and perceptive vision.[4] Weber embraced this new iconoclasm, at least initially, but found that pursuing it led him unexpectedly back to traditional Judaism. He would come to see that fundamental geometries and higher-dimensional objects structured Jewish life, and he would use these insights to reimagine Judaism in art that made this ancient tradition seem vital and believable once again.

An Old and New Me

Before giving birth to this new synthesis, however, Weber had to labor through considerable strains and tensions. His *Cubist Poems* (1914) are filled with disruptive feelings of loss, what he called an expanding "time space between the old me and the new me," a sensation of tearing away.[5] The first difficulty he encountered came from embracing art as a profession. Some Jews, including Weber's parents, considered the mere act of producing art an unacceptable form of idolatry. Weber's reflections on Judaism and art show how concerned he was about this matter. In traditional Russian Jewish communities, where many believed the Second Commandment ruled out making images of any kind, iconoclasm had a strong hold. Weber's upbringing in Bialystok, Russia, was probably similar to the childhood of the painter Maurice Stern in Latvia, where "religious Jews took very seriously the injunction against 'graven' images," Stern remembered, "and I was punished badly one day by the rabbi of the school for drawing his picture on the ground with a stick."[6] (One wonders exactly what the image looked like.) As a young man, Weber hid his artwork from his parents. A friend and fellow Russian Jewish émigré to America, the Modernist painter Abraham Walkowitz, offered Weber a refuge. "His father and mother were very religious. And he couldn't even open a drawing there. So I said, 'Max, you come to my studio.' I had a studio on 23rd Street, right near the

Parke-Bernet at that time. So he came the following day, and I had a cot, and by pulling out the cot this way, we slept in one cot. Almost three months he was with me."

Later, after Weber had become famous, he was asked how his parents felt about him becoming an artist. He said that as a young man he attempted to convince them that *teaching art* was not only a lucrative profession but also one that allowed him to avoid working on the Sabbath.[7] When Walkowitz's hospitality waned, Weber, with no money and little to eat, turned to Alfred Stieglitz, who had a small gallery called 291. Stieglitz was not interested in Weber's art but he pitied him and allowed him to live temporarily in a friend's apartment next to 291.[8]

Many in Weber's situation outgrew their revolutionary impulses or encountered doubt, but Weber always remained certain of his talent and his place in history, even when neither were apparent to anyone else. He studied art at the Pratt Institute in Brooklyn and began teaching art at different locations in the United States, borrowing inspiration and ideas not just from his art teachers but also from a set of familiar crusaders against buttoned-up Victorian culture, including, of course, Emerson and Whitman. (Weber supplemented this with readings from Young Turk artist-revolutionaries such as Kandinsky.) Over time it became clear that moving to the center of the avant-garde art world meant going to the source in Paris, and, having saved enough money, Weber departed in 1905. He traveled and studied art in France, Spain, and Italy, spending most of his time in Paris, where he frequented the salon of Gertrude and Leo Stein, took classes at Henri Matisse's private "Academie," and became acquainted with Guillaume Apollinaire, Henri Rousseau, Picasso, and others. Though Cubism had not yet developed, Paris's artists had begun their revolt against the naturalism taught in art academies, turning gradually to an abstract style that attempted to capture not outer, natural forms but inner emotions, deep design principles, or spiritual impulses that animated all things. At the Steins' salon, Weber studied paintings by Cézanne and took part in arguments about abstract art and cultural renewal, while Leo Stein presided over these gatherings "as moderator and pontiff." There was an atmosphere of expectation and change. It was a setting in which "one felt free to throw artistic atom bombs," Weber remembered, adding, "many cerebral explosions did take place."[9]

In Paris, Weber experienced his own cerebral explosions. For him, the works of Matisse, Cézanne, and other modern artists were liberating. They showed the way toward a style that no longer imitated nature but used form and color to reveal deeper emotions, natural laws, or geometric fundamentals. The results were sometimes dramatic, with distorted perspectives and intense colors. In 1906 Weber saw Cézanne's works exhibited at a large retrospective at the Salon d'Automne, an exhibit that greatly influenced the direction of the Paris avant-garde. "As soon as I saw them," Weber remembered, "they gripped me at once and forever." Weber later recalled that Cézanne inaugurated a new age, the end of the dry, imitative tradition taught in art academies. When I saw Cézanne's work, Weber once said, "I said to myself 'this is the way to paint. This is art and nature reconstructed by what I should call today an engineer of the geometry of aesthetics.'" Cézanne was rediscovering the essential structures and emotional intensity of great art, things that had been lost in art academies where young people learned merely to imitate nature. This new art, Weber wrote, "goes to the birth-giving source for its idea. It is a rejuvenation and a cleansing after a period of academies whose ideals are no more than the acquisition of technical skill which is mere penmanship."[10]

Weber's paintings during this period (1906–1912) incorporated these principles. He began to take liberties with natural forms, though his work was still closer to Post-Impressionism than Modernism. By 1909, when he returned to Brooklyn, he was developing a kind of abstract art virtually unknown, and certainly unappreciated, in America. Though later seen as a gifted painter and one of the first American modern artists, in 1909 he was an outcast. Those few reviewers who saw his work called it "ugly," "brutal," and "vulgar." His paintings, one confounded critic wrote, "served as an object lesson of the ends to which a painter will go to assert his freedom from the trammels of tradition, whether these be sane, reasonable, sound and constructive ones or not."[11] His religious and political opinions, when he shared them, also elicited outcries of complaint and recrimination. By the time of his 1909 return from Europe he was, as he put it, a Bolshevik "communist." When he visited the Pratt Institute, his alma mater, to see if they might exhibit his new work, the president swiftly declined. From a friend,

Weber heard that the president was referring to him as "the disgrace of Pratt Institute."[12]

Though Weber would soon become known as America's first Cubist painter, when returning to New York in 1909 he had neither developed his abstract Cubist style nor incorporated into his thinking higher-dimensional notions. But this would soon change. By the second half of 1910, he set out in a new direction, borrowing elements from the early Cubism of Picasso and Braque. The seeds of this change may have been planted during conversations in Paris, but some historians and critics, including Percy North and John Lane, have pointed to the key role of the publication in America of Gelett Burgess's influential article "The Wild Men of Paris" in a leading periodical, the *Architectural Record,* in May 1910. In this article, Burgess reproduced for the first time the works of Picasso, Braque, and others and discussed their surprising new styles. There is no evidence that Burgess and Weber met in Paris, but such a meeting would have been possible, for they had mutual friends and shared interests in modern art, geometry, and the fourth dimension. They also both were certain not just that inherited traditions had to be abandoned but that new artistic methods might be developed to renew culture and revive a spiritual sensibility that had been lost in modernity.

Gelett Burgess's Dimensional Spirituality

It turns out that the writer of the influential "Wild Men" article, Gelett Burgess, was an unconventional spiritual seeker, an enthusiast for higher dimensions, and a close friend of C. Howard Hinton. An avant-garde writer, art critic, and cartoonist, Burgess was best known for both humorous poems and aphorisms and also books about oval-headed, rubber-limbed cartoon characters he called "Goops." Though born in Boston and educated at MIT, Burgess left behind the buttoned-up East Coast in 1887 to be a land survey draftsman for the Southern Pacific Railroad in San Francisco, where he sought a less conventional lifestyle. He felt the weight of eight generations of Puritan ancestors and wished to leave all of them behind. "I have to laugh when I hear anyone boast of having Mayflower ancestors," he wrote in an unpublished manuscript. "Why one should be particularly proud of being distantly related to that hard, dry, cheerless bunch of religious mechanics and tradesmen

I don't know. By all accounts they were pretty disagreeable and more afraid of a good time than they were of the devil himself." In California he found what he was looking for, exchanging his ancestors' "sabbatarianism, chastity, temperance, rigid truthfulness and . . . habit of churchgoing," with activities such as drinking, flirting, writing, and hatching practical jokes.[13]

Dismantling his Puritan heritage was a task that he pursued with genuine enthusiasm. For instance, on New Year's Eve in 1894, Burgess concluded an evening of celebration by destroying a statue of a wealthy temperance crusader, Henry Cogswell, in San Francisco's Embarcadero district. Cogswell believed that if people had access to clean water at public drinking fountains they would drink less alcohol, and he made it his life's mission to design and build elaborate public fountains in cities across America, including the one Burgess ransacked in 1894. (Grandiose Cogswell fountains and statues erected in other cities were not always well received. A Cogswell statue in Connecticut was thrown into a nearby lake; another in Dubuque, Iowa, was knocked down and buried.) Evidently Burgess thought the Embarcadero statue of Cogswell, with Cogswell's "whiskers flung to the rippling breezes," was aesthetically and morally reprehensible, and he and several colleagues, working late at night, removed it. The next day, the *San Francisco Call* surveyed the destruction.

> Some iconoclastic spirits, probably made bold by too freely indulging in the convivialities of New Year's day, found vent for their destructive proclivities in the small hours of the morning yesterday. With the greatest deliberation, apparently, a rope was coiled around the mock presentment of Dr. Cogswell and with a strong pull, and all together, he was toppled from his fountain pedestal at the Junction of California and Market streets.[14]

A mechanical drawing instructor at the University of California, Berkeley, Burgess was soon implicated in the crime and fired. Though suddenly without an income, Burgess discovered an upside to unemployment: He was now free to escalate his war on Victorian prudes and ignorant philistines.

He edited a literary magazine (*The Wave*) and founded and edited a humor magazine called *The Lark*, which developed a significant following, produced a spinoff magazine, and made it possible for him to collect and republish his essays in a few books. He made enough money to pay his rent. In 1897 Burgess moved to New York and continued to write for magazines such as the *Century* and *Collier's*. By this time he was becoming well known for his humorous poems—including, most famously, "The Purple Cow"—and his oval-headed, goopy cartoon characters who, by being ill-mannered and uncouth, demonstrated how not to live one's life.

> The Goops, they lick their fingers,
> and the Goops, they lick their knives;
> They spill their broth on the tablecloth,
> Oh, they lead disgusting lives!

(Of course, Burgess conveyed Goop misdeeds with conspiratorial delight.) As we have seen, Burgess himself was not above devising his own mischievous conspiracies, and San Franciscans were sometimes amused to find Burgess's peculiar Goops painted on city buildings, with unsettling captions such as "SOMETHING TERRIBLE IS GOING TO HAPPEN."[15] Juxtaposing his goofy Goops and pessimistic warnings made for a humorous effect, but those who knew Burgess understood that dire predictions were not merely a comedic strategy; they reflected a deep melancholy that characterized Burgess's inner life. Reporters who sought him out were often disappointed during interviews. "Isn't life awful?" Burgess said once to a reporter. "Awful funny?" was the tentative reply. "No," Burgess said, "just plain awful, so awful that if we had no escape from reality we'd curl up and die." Claude Bragdon, who knew Burgess well, remembered that in private the humorist was usually sad and saturnine. He called him a clown with a broken heart.[16]

Things changed for Burgess, however, when he met a quirky philosopher with a suitcase of colored cubes, a man named C. Howard Hinton. Higher-dimensional notions appealed to Burgess for the same reasons that they appealed to Hinton: They were a rational way of finding a wider, spiritual context for life. (It was refreshing, Hinton wrote Burgess, referring to his MIT pedigree, that someone with a mathematical background "doesn't dismiss the whole thing with benevolent contempt.") The extant correspondence between Hinton and Burgess (from 1903 to 1907) contains some of Hinton's most detailed spiritual speculations.

Figure 5.1 Burgess had the idea that his humorous "nonsense" verses, here taught to students by a round-headed Goop, suggested not just life's absurdities but also gaps, mysteries, and disjunctures that existed outside the range of familiar, sensible discourses—in a "fourth dimension." From Gelett Burgess, *The Burgess Nonsense Book: Being a Complete Collection of the Humorous Masterpieces of Gelett Burgess* (New York: Frederick A. Stokes Co., 1901), frontispiece

There was a whole "world which stretches away from the 3 dimensional limitations," Hinton assured Burgess, a universe we could perceive if we trained our senses and intuitions in certain ways. The process involved rigorous steps—logical reasoning, the training of the senses to imagine geometric objects and their cross-sections, and learning how to put together higher wholes in the mind. Hinton was getting good at it, he said, and he told Burgess that he now had the feeling "sometimes of being on the edge" of something great, a feeling that scientific materialism was merely a partial representation of reality. Hinton argued that his methods led to stretching the mind to find the "unitary conception" that was behind reality.[17] Many mathematicians and intellectuals approached the issue from the wrong direction, that is, by trying to break down complex things into simpler elements. Hinton told Burgess he wanted to see the whole thing, the essence and foundation that harmonized and kept reality together.

Burgess thought Hinton was a "genius," saying once in a lecture that Hinton was simply "the greatest man I ever met."[18] Like Hinton, Burgess embraced higher-dimensional notions as a way to feel a sense of wonder, hope, and astonishment at the universe. He believed higher-dimensional notions suggested both the existence of God and a kind of personal immortality. These rational theories provided spiritual comfort without having to rely on outmoded forms of doctrinaire belief. In different unpublished writings Burgess developed the view that there might be a creator God existing on a different dimensional plane. He also embraced Hinton's idea that we were three-dimensional cross-sections of some larger reality. This formulation, he said, was "the only consolation I have in this puzzle of identity. There must be in this continuance of constant change," he continued, "a unifying and unchanging reality." All past experiences, he said, were "different aspects of an unchanging and absolute I." The self existed as one timeless thing if we could see it from a higher-dimensional perspective. As for Hinton, for Burgess the higher space hypothesis was a way of tentatively holding spiritual beliefs while setting oneself apart from irrational and credulous religious believers.[19] These notions might not be appealing to simple-minded religious believers, but, unfortunately, Hinton complained to Burgess, they were also being resisted by mathematicians and scientists. Perhaps, he told Burgess, it was something "which only poets can see through."[20] Burgess agreed—it would be literary people, poets, and artists who could see into the deeper, fourth-dimensional properties of things.

This conviction inspired Burgess as he set off for Paris to understand better what modern abstract painters were doing. The article that he produced, "The Wild Men of Paris," which drew from interviews with Picasso, Braque, Matisse, and others and reproduced for the first time Picasso's *Les Demoiselles d'Avignon,* profiled artists who seemed so strange that Burgess's editor initially dismissed the article as a practical joke.[21] When the essay finally appeared it included wisecracking commentary on these wild artists and astonishment at the art they were producing. The colors in these paintings were atrocious! The landscapes were indecipherable! The nudes inhumanly distorted! Why paint housecats composed of cylinders and human figures out of triangles? "There was," Burgess wrote, "no limits to the audacity and the ugliness of the canvasses."

> Still-life sketches of round, round apples and yellow, yellow oranges, on square, square tables, seen in impossible perspective; landscapes of squirming trees, with blobs of virgin color gone wrong, fierce greens and coruscating yellows, violent purples, sickening reds and shuddering blues. But the nudes! They looked like flayed Martians, like pathological charts—hideous old women, patched with gruesome hues, lopsided, with arms like the arms of a Swastika, sprawling on vivid backgrounds, or frozen stiffly upright, glaring through misshapen eyes, with noses or fingers missing. They defied anatomy, physiology, almost geometry itself.

But as the article proceeded, the significance of this new art came into focus. These artists were not attempting to capture or imitate reality, something artists had done for millennia. They were revealing hidden aspects to reality that no one had seen before—subjective experiences, deeper essences, principles of natural wholeness and harmony. Braque told Burgess he was trying to paint the emotional experience of seeing a woman rather than the woman herself. "Nature is a mere pretext for decorative composition, plus sentiment," Braque said. "It suggests emotion, and I translate that emotion into art. I want to expose the Absolute, and not merely the factitious woman." Picasso too, with his "monstrous, monolithic women, creatures like Alaskan totem poles, hacked out of solid, brutal colors," spoke of trying to render the subjective experience of seeing, of depicting emotion, instinct, volume, and other unseen aspects of reality. A cylindrical cat or a triangular nude was a way of probing beyond surface appearances to the underlying structures of things. "I don't distort Nature," Auguste Herbin responded to Burgess's questions. "I sacrifice it to a higher form of beauty and decorative unity."[22] These artists located a higher beauty that existed beyond the senses, searching for underlying mathematical and spatial dimensions. "To portray every physical aspect of an object," Braque said, obviously influenced by mathematical and higher-dimensional discourses then circulating, "required three figures, much as the representation of a house requires a plan, elevation, and a section."[23] These artists were experimenting with seeing all sides of something at once. Some of them had begun reading Hinton's works, though Hinton, who died the year before Burgess's article appeared, never knew how important his work would become.

Perhaps wild artists and other outcasts could see into the deepest and most vital aspects of reality. Was it this notion that prompted Burgess to conclude that, as odd as these artists were, they were capturing something "virile," "ecstatic," and energetic? Their art "was the product of an overplus of life and energy," he said; it was "alive and kicking, not a dead thing, frozen into a convention." Perhaps they were "ahead of the rest, blazing out the way of progress for the race."[24] If there was anything Burgess could appreciate, it was blazing a way out of convention. He was similar in many ways to the modern artists he interviewed, people who had rejected tradition and turned to new forms of literary and artistic expression, trying to get beneath the chaotic, tragic surface of life to find something deeper, simpler, and vital. Both Burgess's humorous "nonsense" verses and modern art were ways of ridiculing, problematizing, and, sometimes, escaping reality.

Art as "Spiritual Expression"

After returning to Brooklyn from Europe in 1909, Weber also attempted to sketch and paint the deep essences and realities undergirding all things. He began a decade of artistic experimentation that would make him America's greatest Cubist painter. As John R. Lane and Percy North have argued, beginning at this time Weber adapted techniques seen first in Burgess's reproductions of Braque, Picasso, and Jean Metzinger, even borrowing ideas and phrases from Burgess's article.[25] In several of Weber's 1910 compositions, for instance, Weber used for the first time geometric faceting; dramatic angles in faces, heads, and shoulders; Braque's square feet; and three-figure sketches that depicted one model from three different angles. Braque had told Burgess that to show every aspect of something one had to use three figures, and in 1910 Weber composed a number of crowded three-figure studies that used this technique.[26] In a series of drawings between 1910 and 1912 that Weber called "crystal figures," for instance, we can see Weber's developing interest in geometry, blocky forms, and an art that probed the elementary architecture of forms. Alfred Stieglitz, who exhibited Weber's crystal figures and other paintings at 291 in 1911—a show panned by puzzled critics—said that Weber was not trying to reproduce nature but study it. "It is analyzed into its constituent parts, its bulk is emphasized, the relationship of lines and masses is explained," he wrote. Weber's works, Stieglitz continued, challenge the mind rather than please the senses.[27] These works by Weber were among the earliest Cubist art forms produced in America.

It would become common for modern artists to turn reality into crystalline forms, which many Modernists saw as openings into underlying, eternal forms and nature's ultimate geometry. This was particularly the case for Modernists with mystical interests who studied crystal balls or globes (smooth or faceted) for signs, portents, predictions, or other occult messages. (Weber's friend Alvin Coburn, a photographer who produced portraits with multiple exposures, much like Cubist portraiture, also kept a crystal amulet, photographed transparent crystals, and wrote about how staring at photographed crystals led to "an intensified search for things of the spirit." Weber painted Coburn's portrait in 1911 and dedicated his book *Cubist Poems* to Coburn and his mother.[28]) Weber also believed in the occult power of reality's basic geometry. In an unpublished reflection in which he borrowed from Plato and Emerson, Weber insisted that geometry was God's architecture and he averred that in skilled hands geometric elements "become the vehicle or means for spiritual expression in the purest language of placid plastic beauty of the highest conceivable form." These geometric elements, he continued, "may be charged so as to emerge or reappear as informing spirits—voices from the inherent." This formulation was obviously indebted to Plato's notion that "nature geometrizes" and Emerson's re-purposing of those ideas as he wrote about nature's "Beautiful Necessity." Weber also seemed to believe that the mysteries of human emotion and personality could be rendered in points, lines, and various shapes—a symphonic geometry of the human condition in plastic form.[29]

In Weber's paintings in the 1910s he experimented with ways of organizing landscapes, cityscapes, and the human form into geometric elements. In *Woman and Tents* (1913), a painting that appears to depict several women in tents, Weber actually renders one woman from different vantage points. (Later *Woman and Tents* was exhibited as *Women and Tents*, a change that obscured Weber's original intentions.) Like French Cubists he broke surfaces into facets, but his geometric designs were less angular and more graceful. The result was a combination of Cubist faceting and the curvilinear lines of aboriginal sculpture. Elements of the woman's face and body are intermixed gracefully with the curved lines of the tent in a way that simulates the effects of a kaleidoscope mirror. The fragmentation of the subject here is reminiscent of other Cubist work, including Picasso's much later *Portrait of Dora Maar* (1937), which shows the subject's face from different angles. This was a way of capturing all aspects of someone in a single, synoptic view. It was, to use Hinton's higher-dimensional lexicon, seeing all sides of a thing at once. (See Figure 5.2.)

Though higher-dimensional notions influenced many Cubists in the 1910s and 1920s, Weber was the first to publish an essay about higher dimensions and art, entitled "The Fourth Dimension from a Plastic Point of View," which appeared in 1910 in Stieglitz's *Camera Work*. Weber linked the fourth dimension to "consciousness of a great and overwhelming sense of space-magnitude in all directions at one time," insisting that the concept was not merely a mathematical variable but that it was real and could be "perceived and felt." "It exists outside and in the presence of objects, and is the space that envelops a tree, a tower, a mountain, or any solid. . . . It is the immensity of all things."[30] This characteristic immensity in all things stretched from its outer form toward an infinite energy Weber wanted to capture in art. He studied

Figure 5.2   Max Weber, *Woman and Tents* (1913). Courtesy of William Marklyn.

edges, gaps, and in-between spaces to see if he could find the elusive qualities of extension toward infinity. He studied elementary geometric forms not because they captured the essence of things but because they taught him how forms stretched outward into something higher. This way of moving from elementary to complex forms, from lower to higher, is depicted in the first poem of his *Cubist Poems*, a poem called "The Eye Moment." The poem begins with a Bragdonian image of cubes tumbling outward to infinity. "Cubes, cubes, cubes, cubes//high, low and high, and higher, higher//far, far out, out, out, far,//Planes, planes, planes,//Colors, lights, signs, whistles, bells, signals, colours,//Planes, planes, planes,//eyes, eyes, window eyes, eyes, eyes . . . Millions of things upon things,//Billions of things upon things."[31]

It is easy to see how Weber moves from elementary cubes to infinite dimensions in paintings composed in the 1910s. In *Interior of the Fourth Dimension* (1913), for example, Weber examined New York City at night, an abstract view across the harbor with a sailboat in the foreground.

Figure 5.3 Max Weber, *Interior of the Fourth Dimension* (1913). Courtesy of the Estate of Max Weber.

Tall buildings surround the harbor and take on more complexity as they rise and fragment into smaller geometrical shapes. Finally they dissolve into a negative space that surrounds the painting on all sides. Because the light fades as you move from center to periphery, Weber creates a cinematic effect: "The negative space that frames the central overlapping shapes and the flickering light simulate the sensation of watching cinema."[32] The effect makes the center of the city alive with light and color while drawing attention to its smallness within the context of an infinite cosmic expanse. This painting suggests the immensity of a multidimensional world by showing that as you move from the illuminated center of civilization to the dark cosmos, you proceed through layers—a human world of curved lines and warmer colors to a shrouded realm of geometrical scaffolding and finally to an undifferentiated immensity. Great art, Weber thought, conveyed that feeling of reaching toward a dimensionally complex world.

For Weber and other young artists, the fourth dimension, like other scientific notions and technologies, was helping modern people see into hitherto invisible realms. It was a "wonderful age" of discovery and creative liberty, Weber wrote, one in which human beings were finally penetrating the infinite.[33] "There are dimensions in space and matter not yet known," he told the art collector Mabel Dodge Luhan. "There are colors, odors, sounds, motions, weights, not yet known and they may have been always. Our sense may not yet be what they might yet be. Then, new thoughts, ideas, new objects will arise, measures will change; differences, nuances will be other than what they are now. There will be other numbers or units."[34] If this sense of millennial enthusiasm marked fin de siècle reformers it also characterized the proclamations of visionary artists. All of them were inspired by scientific discoveries that opened up astonishing new vistas into impossibly small worlds and immeasurably far-off spaces. People who looked through telescopes or peered into microscopes saw for the first time previously hidden worlds. And there were other new technologies that saw into the invisible, including for example x-ray photography.[35] Because scientists opened up new revelatory vistas every day, when people heard about a fourth dimension it was only natural that they embraced this concept as another hidden reality that would soon be revealed. "Looking back upon it now," Mabel Dodge Luhan wrote in her memoir, "it seems as though everywhere, in that year of 1913, barriers went down and people reached each other who had never been in touch before. . . . Men began to talk and write about the fourth dimension, interchangeability of the senses, telepathy, and many other occult phenomena without their former scoffing bashfulness, only they did it with what they were pleased to call a scientific spirit."[36]

Weber believed that creating visionary art was above all an inner discipline. He may have been drawing on hyperspace philosophers who located higher-dimensional capacities in deep states of consciousness. "We with our senses are the master works of God—governed by intellect and possessed of a spirituality limitless, of infinite power and quality," and we thus were able to animate material objects when we rendered them using plastic arts, pushing them higher into the mystical fourth dimension. Real seeing, he wrote, was not "a lens process" but a kind of "mind sight." This process took place best "under a dome of silence," during a stillness that "ferments [sic] a mood of peace, of contemplation," Weber insisted.[37] "Communicate with God and the great masters, and do your practical work in the practical world for practical purposes," Weber wrote to a friend. "And then lock yourself up in your silent chamber of Art, and pour out your woes and pangs and sound them with beautiful melodies, harmonies and variations masterly, pure and ideal—such as God enabled you to do. . . . Silence and solitude are great factors in the lives of creators." (Like other artist-visionaries, Weber did not suffer from personal doubts and insecurities. He also told this friend, speaking now of his own work, "I paint so that my future with God's help is assured, for I see in my work some of the highest qualities, and I compare it justly with masters' work and works of high standing."[38])

Weber argued that during contemplation we accessed memories that somehow linked us to spirit. Our memories of a symphonic performance, for example, "binds scene with scene, act with act," filling the gaps and spaces. In our memories of visual objects, on the other hand, we fill empty spaces and rearrange and reorganize visual objects. Weber tended to write aphoristically, imitating Emerson's style, and in Weber's case his meaning was not always clear. "With memory of sight I lift and transport whole spheres. Then I live and possess all that my eyes ever beheld, and my imagination projects that memory into still more infinite spheres." "Memory of sight," Weber wrote, "is the great spiritual vision windowed into the infinite. . . . To see, to remember, is to prepare as for prayer."[39] Weber believed that in memory and in consciousness there were spiritual truths that could be used to reimagine material things.

Weber's way of talking about memory and contemplation relied on a set of Neoplatonic ideas widespread among artists in this period. Mark Cheetham makes the point that this Neoplatonism was not derived from a philosophical tradition in Europe but from a popular pattern of thinking fed by Romantic writers, idealist poets such as Goethe, religious mystics, and Theosophists such as Charles Leadbeater and Annie Besant who were popular among artists. Paul Gauguin, Piet Mondrian, and Kandinsky wanted to get beyond the superficialities of nature to an abstract art that began from the inner self. Earlier artists, Gauguin complained, "heed only the eye and neglect the mysterious centers of thought." Borrowing an image from Plato's cave analogy, Gauguin proclaimed that "painting is now freed of its chains." Weber used these ideas as well as Neoplatonic glosses on art found in the works of other artists. Kandinsky, who believed that artists were modernity's prophets and seers, announced that real artists worked in silent (Platonic) contemplation, for the artist must "immerse himself in his own soul" in order to arrive at a pure, abstract vision.[40] It was possible in contemplation to come to recollect the ultimate laws of nature and the supernatural. "These laws are known to us unconsciously when we come close to nature, not in an external way, but inwardly," Kandinsky said. "It is necessary not just to see nature, but to experience it."[41]

Weber worked from within this tradition in obvious ways. Both he and Kandinsky borrowed the platonic theory of anamnesis, which held that knowledge of eternal realities was something we already possessed and simply needed to remember. In platonic philosophy, we retrieved knowledge of eternal things, including transcendental Ideas the soul knew in a previous existence, through recollecting things we forgot when we were incarnated in a body. (Following this logic, bodily or sensate knowledge is a source of error while true knowledge comes from either reason or this type of mystical recollection.) This, Weber said, was the purpose of art: To find by combining inner recollection and outer form an expression of the "spirit that emanates only from the spiritual and mystical realms, from the nether and the astral."[42]

Weber's use of the term "astral" for a heavenly dimension reminds us how central Theosophical categories were for artists attempting to see and represent the invisible. Theosophical notions moved into art circles via routes of exchange and conversation that have been expertly scouted by Tom Gibbons, Sixten Ringbom, and Linda Henderson. In particular, Theosophists gave modern artists a vocabulary for what it might mean to probe beyond traditional three-dimensional perspectives. Hinton wanted to overcome three-dimensional perspectives for his own existential purposes, as we have seen, but in the hands of slightly later, more mystical interpreters, including Bragdon and Leadbeater, dispatching three-dimensional perspectives was something you did for spiritual purposes, to see beyond the epiphenomenal world of "maya," or illusion, and discover the invisible beyond. Hinton's ideas were extensively summarized by Leadbeater in particular, who recommended Hinton's thought experiments and books as ways of preparing the self for visionary experiences. Leadbeater influenced Mondrian, Kandinsky,

František Kupka, Kazimir Malevich, and others. "The knowledge of the Theosophists, culled from books and temples and audacious dreaming," the art historian Roger Lipsey has written, "was powerful enough to point artists toward a new inwardness and the possibility of translating that inwardness into visible form."[43] French painters at the time were also reading Leadbeater, whose *Astral Plane* was translated and published in Paris in 1899. Other Leadbeater works were translated and published in 1910–1912, and still other Theosophical publications brought ideas related to astral vision and dimensionality to Paris beginning in 1911. In any case, there is an unmistakable affinity between Friedrich Zollner's "cubical vision," Hinton's fourth dimension, Leadbeater's notion of clairvoyant vision, and certain techniques used by Cubist painters. The Cubist habit of combining several views of an object on a single canvas is indebted to Leadbeater's notion that astral sight involved seeing all sides of an object at once, an idea, of course, derived from Hinton's cube exercises. Also, the overlapping geometric planes of Cubist art, such as those in Weber's *Woman and Tents* can be related to the higher-dimensional notion that higher forms of seeing enable you to see through walls, as the Sphere did in *Flatland* and as Leadbeater and other visionaries claimed to be able to do while having inspired visions. "It is difficult to resist the conclusion," Tom Gibbons has argued, "that the new pictorial language of the Cubist painters constitutes a deliberate attempt to represent, point for point, the detailed phenomena of this transcendental mode of perception."[44]

Not every Cubist was interested in mystical visions or the Absolute— some thought of our many-dimensional world in merely naturalistic terms—but Weber, both early and late in his career, took the position that visionary, religious art was the only true and lasting form of art. If modern art was to be worth anything, it had to be like great art of the past—that is, it had to be religious in some way. Weber appears never to have doubted that he could produce this kind of great art, but at different times he wondered exactly how to do it. What outer forms most powerfully represented inner spirit? In his Cubist decade, from 1910 to 1920, he experimented with mystical visions in a style limned by Kandinsky and other abstract painters. But he came to believe that modern abstract painters were missing something. Those who were secular, such as Picasso, he said, attempted to produce "a transcendental art without transcendental ideas."[45] Picasso had new artistic methods and he produced interesting representations of nature, but he did not perceive those most important elements that lay beyond nature. Other artists attempting to uncover Absolute truth produced schools that were as contentious as religious sects. "We have had whole ship-loads of Italian, French, Spanish and English flavors of art, hastily manufactured. But who can manufacture or ship real inspiration?" In our haste to jettison the old we created new directions and styles, but just as one is hastily constructed another supersedes it.

Perhaps the effort to throw out the old and create something new was itself ill conceived. Perhaps true art, "if art it is," Weber wrote, "has its own reward in living through whole ages of darkness."[46] And with this, Weber began to think in a new way about tradition and its ways of memorializing and transmitting spirit.

Jewish Geometries and Infinities

Though I see continuity in Weber's oeuvre, many critics have divided his career into a Modernist period before 1918 and a return to figurative art and Jewish subjects after 1918. There is something to be said for this perspective, for Weber himself acknowledged changes in his work that came near the end of the First World War. In fact many artists experienced a "crisis of style" during this period, when the war's astonishing destruction dimmed enthusiasm for modernity and forced people to reconsider the wisdom of casting aside traditions that had long anchored western civilization. Other life changes at this time undoubtedly made Weber think carefully about deep questions and his relationship to Judaism. He married in 1916, his father died in 1917, and his mother died in 1918. In other words, his connection to tradition was vanishing just when he needed it the most. These factors likely played a part in his renewed interest in Jewish subjects after 1918. Also, though scholars have complained that we know little about Weber's reasons for turning more to Jewish subjects, in interviews and letters he did offer hints about why he became restless with abstract art and interested in art that eclectically borrowed old and new.

In a letter to Henry Hurwitz in 1935, he revealed some of the reasons he turned to more figurative art and Jewish subjects during the first war. He had been confronted with images of "archaic" Jews in New York and at the cinema. "The spirit that moved me to write the poems 'Jerusalem' and 'Melodic Rage Hebraic' in 1914 after seeing several reels of 'Scenes in the Holy Land' in a little cinema theatre in a remote corner of the East Side is the very same spirit that prompted me to paint 'Talmudists' last winter (1934) after a pilgrimage to one of the oldest synagogues of the East Side," he wrote.[47] His letter points to the power of that most modern art form, the cinema, as a technology that represented images of the old and archaic. In that small cinema on the East Side, the ancient Judaism of Weber's imagination flickered to life.

But if the cinema brought those "archaic" traditions to life again, Weber's friends and mentors already had shown him that the old and primitive had a raw power and spirit pulsing though it. European artists in the first decade of the twentieth century, such as Gauguin, Matisse, and Picasso, believed that while western, civilized societies had in some cases experienced decadence and decline, other so-called primitive societies retained a raw, pure, undisciplined spiritual power. These artists turned to African sculpture in particular to discover the deepest, most powerful artistic elements and forms. In his proto-Cubist period (1906–1909), Picasso, for example, incorporated the contoured, masklike facial features of African sculpture into his paintings. Maurice Raynal, a French art critic and proponent of Cubism, noted the extent to which Cubists believed that both native art forms and the fourth dimension led them to the universe's basic design elements.

> The Primitives . . . obeyed a very exalted need, that of the mysticism which illuminated their thinking. . . . Instead of painting the objects as they saw them, they painted them as they thought them, and it is precisely this law that the cubists have readopted, amplified and codified under the name of "The Fourth Dimension." The cubists, not having the mysticism of the Primitives as a motive for painting, took from their own age a kind of mysticism of logic, of science and reason, and this they have obeyed like the restless spirits and seekers after truth that they are.[48]

Modern artists took something essential from the primitives in order to create a modern mysticism that was both enchanted and scientific at the same time. For artists who worried that modern civilization was decadent, materialistic, and spiritually enervating, the primitive represented something original, vital, natural, and spiritual.

Weber operated with a similar set of assumptions. "A Peruvian, Mexican or Congo savage," Weber pointed out in an unpublished manuscript, "in making a pot or shaping and moulding the handle of a tool" perfectly embodies his desires, putting them into his work. His artistic creations grew organically. "It is to me similar to the fruits and flowers or other plant life," he reasoned, which exist in incipient form in nature and grow naturally.[49] Primitive art brought deep, spiritual design elements to the surface. In Paris, Weber studied African art in museums and upon his return to New York he studied Mexican and Peruvian art at the Museum of Natural History, where he also sat and composed many of his "Cubist poems." "It was grand, refreshing and reassuring to see the great Mexican Primitives at the [American] Museum of Natural History," he wrote in a remarkable letter to the American sculptor Louise Nevelson. "I wish I too could be a primitive. But the primitives, *having been*—we can't be primitive! . . . It is indeed compensation enough to be privileged to understand their art—the ecstasy, exaltation, austerity they embodied in their sculpture. . . . It would be wonderful if we could recapture or discover their virginal spiritual conception and a key to their plastic values and processes."[50] Modern people feeling this primitive nostalgia could study primitive art and feel its powerful, mystical vibrations.

Of course, it was not only modern artists who objectified other races and peoples as simple, childlike, pure, or powerful. Social scientists studying aboriginal peoples found something enlivening in them, a power undimmed by the enervating effects of modern culture. The American psychologist of religion William James, for example, knew he could not *be* primitive but studied what he saw as the most primitive religious experiences because he hoped to experience something himself—a frisson of vicarious excitement, a shudder of religious emotion or primitive awe.[51]

When Weber painted more figurative Jewish-themed works after 1918, he was still trying to find the raw power and spirit of ancient and primitive art, only this time he turned his attention to a different "primitive" tradition, the traditional Judaism of his childhood. In comments about different paintings, Weber clearly equated Jewish tradition

Figure 5.4 Max Weber, *Invocation* (1919). Courtesy of the Estate of Max Weber.

with the primitive or archaic. Of his *Invocation* (1919), a painting of rabbis studying, praying, and gesticulating, he said, for instance, that his "chief aim was to express a deep religious archaic spirit in fitting attitudes and gestures." Moreover, in this and in other pieces, Weber incorporated characteristics of African masks and sculpture. Rabbis and Jewish mystics are rendered with powerful, angular heads and exaggerated, expressive features that radiate power and simplicity. Weber sets these Jewish figures not in urban Europe or America but in older, European settings—in a Yeshiva (*The Talmudists*), around a study table (*Invocation*), in an ecstatic religious dance (*Hasidic Dance*), or alone in nature (*The Worshipper*). Weber's Jewish-themed works focus not on modern Jews but on Jews who prayed and studied in traditional contexts. As Matthew Baigell has argued, Weber's Jewish subjects appear "on the edge of religious ecstasy and call to mind the many Hasidic legends and stories with which Weber might have been familiar."[52] The Judaism of Weber's art was the Judaism of a mythical European shtetl from the past.

Judaism, the primitive, geometry, and infinity—these characteristic preoccupations animate Weber's work, early and late. The subject matter of *Woman and Tents,* for example, a work usually regarded as one of Weber's important Cubist paintings, incorporates Biblical elements that Weber understood as "primitive." Where other than "Holy Land" pilgrimage narratives or the Hebrew Bible would Weber have read about the "tent life" of women and men? Different people in the Hebrew Bible lived in tents, as did the Hebrew patriarchs and the Israelites during their forty years in the wilderness. To be sure, *Woman and Tents* is layered with familiar primitivist motifs. The faceted angles of the woman's face, for example, frame the same bold and exaggerated lips, nose, and eyes that characterize Weber's rabbis. Moreover, the intersecting pale-green planes of the tent's folds are not harshly angled as they might have been in works by other Cubists such as Picasso. Instead they are gracefully layered, reminiscent of the lush jungle foliage foregrounded in Rousseau's tropical landscapes. That Weber homologized these green tent folds and leafy jungle foliage is suggested also by the fern fronds and leaflike patterns he incorporated into the tent's surface. He was probing what he called the "inherent"—that is, the deep geometrical patterns that undergirded nature, human life, and even spiritual realities. Thus Weber weaves together nature's deep structures, the primitive, and Jewish elements in a painting that is neither traditionally Jewish nor wholly Cubist but a new hybrid form.

If *Woman and Tents* is an earlier work that incorporated religious motifs, many of Weber's later "religious" works employed Cubist elements. In *The Worshipper* (1918), for example, Weber foregrounds a long-haired, white-robed believer oriented vertically like a totem pole. With his hands folded across his chest and eyes glancing upward, he studies an open circle in the heavens. In the background a darkened silhouette doubles as a tree and the figure's shadow. It was another way of pointing to the "inherent" patterns that linked all life, and another example of how Weber linked the traditionally Jewish with the most vital, primitive, and natural.

These same preoccupations are clear in *The Talmudists* (1934), another later work that gives a religious moment great power and solidity by structuring it with geometric elements. Here rabbis gather to study and debate scripture. "Pictorially, plastically, 'Talmudists' was approached and solved in the very same manner as an abstract problem in painting," Weber wrote. "The group of figures around the table was spacially [sic] encased in and interlaced, as it were, with the arches of an ecclesiastical interior. The lesser pictorial accessories—chairs, benches, books and even the skullcaps—are incidental geometric elements made to function simultaneously with other integral parts and elements of the picture in the construction of a pyramidic architectural rhythm and equilibrium." There also appears the same kind of upward extension toward infinity in which forms become simpler and more geometric as they move toward the topmost levels of the canvas, as was the case in *Interior of the Fourth Dimension*. Weber captures the felt presence of the Absolute here by showing how it moves simultaneously in two different directions: It comes up from the text and down from a brightly illuminated, geometrical infinite. "I find a living spiritual beauty emanates from, and hovers over and about, a group of Jewish patriarchal types when they congregate in search of wisdom in the teaching of the great Talmudists of the past."[53] Weber was doing here what he described in lectures on art—the artist, Weber said, "should seem to angle the light and to impregnate the three dimensions with a spiritual fourth dimension."[54] (See Figure 5.5.)

Instead of understanding Weber as someone who moved from abstract art to figurative and Jewish subjects, it may be more accurate to see a single, consistent purpose behind his different styles: He wished to develop a geometric and higher-dimensional art that could reinvigorate traditional images and sources of truth. Tradition and innovation were always important to him. In his early Cubist period he maintained a respect for tradition and a consistent desire to engage it. Drawing and

Figure 5.5   Max Weber, *The Talmudists* (1934). Courtesy of the Estate of Max Weber.

painting became a new kind of ritual prayer, even during this earlier, rebellious period. "You must live in seclusion, in hopefulness, and in consciousness of a beyond: that is prayer,—and it is art also," he wrote.[55] Though in this earlier period he sometimes spoke like other artist revolutionaries, he still was a practicing Jew who observed holy days, kept kosher, painted Biblical scenes, and believed that great art had to be religious. Like other modern artists, he studied and used different sources of tradition or "the archaic," especially the art and statuary of African and Native American people. Later, he turned to Jewish subjects as another way of understanding the deepest, essential elements of reality. In all periods of his life, he identified these deep essentials not just with traditional societies but also with basic geometric forms, and throughout his life he conflated the higher dimensional, the "infinite," and God. In 1915, amid the confusing efflorescence of art schools and avant-garde ideologies, he was asked what he *was*. Was he a Futurist? Was he doing Futurist work? "I am not!" he insisted. "What, then, a cubist?" "Certainly not! I am Max Weber," he responded. He had no single style but he did articulate one overall aim—to use art to try to "know the infinite."[56] Critics who have not understood this fact have not perceived the underlying purpose of both his Cubist abstractions and his later "religious" art.

Weber helps us understand better how Modernists used dimensional notions not just to replace tradition but to reinvigorate it. We witnessed this pattern with Abbott and Christian interpreters of the fourth dimension who spoke of higher dimensions in order to offer modern proof for theological doctrines and heavenly otherworlds. Modern Jews also produced their own new spiritualities by deploying tradition in new ways—by refiguring Jewish practice, as was done in Europe and America in many different ways; by redescribing revelation in modern terms such as altered consciousness, archetypal memory, or "aura" (as in Walter Benjamin); or by re-presenting the original purity of the "archaic" Biblical world.[57] Known for his eclecticism and for holding together contrasting impulses, moving back and forth between old and new, Max Weber shows us that a complete break with tradition was never desirable. Instead the strategy was, as he himself said, to shape in "modern hands" the "raw power of tradition." What was the location, the nature, the structure, and the geometry of the Biblical sacred? How might one render the auratic presence of the spirit that animated Hasidic dances? What exactly *was* the elemental force that drove the rabbis to study the text and imagine the holy? What was it like to see the thunder and lightning on Sinai? In the end, Weber used dimensional ideas in order to answer these questions, rework traditional religious notions, and render these traditional notions in ways that seemed more real and believable.

6

The Spacetime of Dreams

One does not need to experience situations of extreme danger to have altered experiences of space or time, but for whatever reason it does seem to help. In combat experiences during the First World War, for example, soldiers sometimes slipped out of the flow of regular time or saw reality from an altered vantage point. The unusual wartime experiences of John G. Bennett, for example, who fought not just in the muddy trenches of France and Belgium, which was traumatic enough, but in dark caves underneath them, changed forever his thinking about life, death, and time. In an underground network of chalk caverns that stretched for miles, from British-held areas in northern France to German-held Belgium, Bennett joined thousands of British, Canadian, and German soldiers stalking each other in a dark and terrifying underworld. Bennett was stationed in a cave filled with buzzing radio equipment, where he sat, day and night, intercepting fragmentary German messages and occasional SOS signals from doomed ships in the North Atlantic. As he sat there, sometimes for days without sleep, his sense of place and time became confused. He mistook stalagmites and shadows for approaching German soldiers. He thought falling water droplets were German pickaxes coming for him.[1] The anxiety of the moment was heightened by a growing sense of anticipation, for like everyone else Bennett knew the enemy was preparing a final offensive. He listened to his radio hiss and crackle, and he waited.

On March 21, 1918, the offensive came. Before sunrise on a morning shrouded in fog, the German Spring Offensive (*Kaiserschlacht*) began with an astonishing artillery bombardment that was the largest of the entire war. It thundered across 150 square miles, with over a million shells fired in the first five hours. During the attack's first twenty-four hours, the Germans killed 20,000 British soldiers and wounded another 35,000. Very quickly there was chaos behind British lines, with both communication networks and infrastructure destroyed, and by the end of the day the British were conducting a fighting retreat. Bennett's response to the chaos of the German artillery and advance was a renewed feeling of temporal and spatial disorientation. Exhausted by weeks of intelligence work, Bennett felt psychologically removed from the noise and activity. "The physical sensation is of a kind of disembodiment. There is a headache that is painful and even frightening," he remembered, "but with it a sense of being set free from the limitations of ordinary existence."[2] In the middle of this experience, he gathered his equipment and retreated, escaping danger for the moment. But three days later, as the German offensive continued, he rode his motorcycle through a recently demolished Monchy-le-Preux and came under fire. He was injured in the head and thrown to the ground. He woke up in a hospital.

The next thing he remembered was seeing his dead body in an army cot. While doctors rushed around his body he hovered above it, watching.

> I gradually became aware that there were other men present, and somehow I was seeing what they saw and even feeling what they felt. I am quite sure that my eyes did not open and that I had no sensation of my own body. Yet I was aware that stretcher after stretcher was being carried in and that there was no place for them all. . . . I knew there were wounded and dying men, but I heard no sound. I knew that we were being bombarded—not because I could hear the shells—but because I could feel the shock with which the people present reacted to them.

One very clear memory is of a man in a nearby bed. I knew he was an army padre and I knew that he was afraid of dying. I knew that in some way he was stuck to his body and I was not stuck. Some thought passed through me like: "How strange—he doesn't know that it will not hurt him if his body is destroyed!"[3]

After six days in a coma Bennett recuperated for several months in military hospitals, gradually recovering from shrapnel wounds and a brain injury that immobilized part of his right side.

It is not an exaggeration to say that Bennett spent the rest of his life trying to understand his extraordinary combat experiences. How had he slipped out of our everyday reality both during combat and during his near-death experience? When Arthur Shipley, Vice Chancellor of the University of Cambridge, made arrangements for Bennett and other wounded officers to retrieve university books and meet faculty, Bennett spoke with mathematicians such as Joseph Larmor and Ernest William Hobson as well as the physicist J. J. Thompson, discussing Relativity, the experience of time, and the geometry of higher dimensions. (Bennett had been offered a mathematics scholarship to Oxford before the war and considered himself an amateur mathematician.) But Bennett found no one who could answer his questions. His grasp on his extraordinary experiences faded. "I often tried later to recapture the certainty that made me say: 'If my body is destroyed, what does it matter?' but there was no bridge by which I could pass from this world to that."[4] He yearned with nostalgia for those moments of extreme experience when he was removed temporarily from what he called later, writing in his first book, "the bitter taste of life in time."[5] This became the crucial question for Bennett—was there a way to transcend the terrors of time?

For Bennett and many others the war made time itself seem mysterious, irresistible, and frightening. This was so not just because the arc of time in these years propelled so many soldiers unexpectedly to their destruction, but also because time now seemed behind a world-historical process that led to civilizational decline and moral dissolution. The war showed that dreams of social progress, ubiquitous before the war, were illusory, and that in fact everything marched forward into decay and oblivion. Looking back at the "time-haunted" writers and artists of the period after the war, the critic George Kernodle attempted to summarize the era's ethos. "Time has ceased to be a mere setting for human history; it is an active force, a force of evil. It seems to be going faster and faster, always bearing man nearer to some frightful finish." One soldier whose disorienting combat experiences gave him a fragmented sense of time, a man who later became one of the best-known time-haunted playwrights, J. B. Priestley, knew that above all "modern man is haunted by the idea of inexorable passing time." The "problem of Time was the particular riddle that the Sphinx has set for this age of ours," Priestley insisted in a different context. "It was like a great barrier across our way and we were all squabbling and shouting and moaning in its shadow." If this barrier could be crossed and this problem solved, he continued, "there might follow a wonderful release and expansion of the human spirit."[6]

But what would it mean to solve the problem of time? What if it could be shown that time was not uniform but layered in many levels and dimensions, and that human beings, rather than being trapped in an irresistible trajectory toward death, could in certain situations move freely through these cosmic times and spaces? Was it possible that in altered forms of consciousness or perhaps in dreams we could achieve this kind of transcendence?

Dreams of the Future

The person who offered answers to these questions was a most unlikely candidate to resolve his era's urgent philosophical or spiritual concerns. A quiet, conventional member of the Anglo-Irish aristocracy, John W. Dunne initially followed his father into the military and fought for the British in the South African (Second Boer) War from 1899 to 1902. After contracting typhoid he was sent back to England, where, after recovering, he pursued interests in engineering and science and worked for the British War Office on the development of gliders and airplanes. By 1904 he had invented a tailless aerofoil and he soon developed other, similar airplane designs. He designed and built one of the first British military airplanes, which was tested covertly in 1907, and his airplane designs were later used by other nations. Slight in build and taciturn in his personal style, Dunne presented himself as a rationalist and a scientist. One person who met him, someone who, like everyone else, knew of

MR. J. W. DUNNE.

Figure 6.1 A depiction of Dunne that illustrated how the public saw him—a prodigious intellect. Friends reported that he actually was a bit lopsided. "He was a slightish man with a good big head," Priestley once recalled. From J. B. Priestley, *Man and Time* (London: Aldus, 1964), 244.

Dunne's book on precognitive dreams, was surprised not to find more of a visionary. "He looked and behaved like the old regular-officer type crossed with a mathematician and engineer." He was, this same writer continued, "as far removed from any suggestion of the seer, the sage, the crank and crackpot as it is possible to imagine." Certainly during the first half of his life, Dunne cultivated the persona of a scientist—insisting for example in the very first sentence of his dream book, and at more or less regular intervals thereafter, that it was "not a book about 'occultism.'" He was not, he said again and again, developing a new form of mysticism. There are reasons, however, to suspect spiritual motivations behind his work.[7]

Like others, Dunne was disoriented by traumatic combat experiences. While fighting in the Second Boer War, he started having remarkable dream experiences and writing them down. At the end of 1900 he got typhoid fever and was sent to a hospital in Italy to recuperate. There his dreams began to disturb him. In one he found himself in the Sudan in North Africa, where he encountered exhausted comrades with whom he had fought in South Africa. Dressed in the usual ragged khakis, these soldiers had faces that were so weathered and sunburned that they were almost black. Dunne could not believe what they told him—that they had just walked the length of Africa, from South Africa to the Sudan. No one had done it before. They assured him that this was precisely what they had done. One said he had nearly died from yellow fever along the way. When Dunne woke up and opened the newspaper at breakfast, he saw a headline about a "Cape to Cairo" expedition of Boer War soldiers. Not all of the details in his dream were correct, but enough of them were that it shocked him.[8]

This was only the beginning of Dunne's unusual dreams. In 1902, when fighting against Boer guerrillas near the destroyed town of Lindley, South Africa, Dunne slept fitfully and had vivid, frightening dreams. In one of them he stood on the upper slopes of a hill. The ground had white formations with fissures that released jets of vapor and gas. He recognized the place as one he had visited before in dreams, an island, and he perceived that it was in imminent danger from a volcano. "Forthwith I was seized with a frantic desire to save the four thousand (I knew the number) unsuspecting inhabitants. Obviously there was only one way of doing this, and that was to take them off in ships. There followed a most distressing nightmare, in which I was at a neighbouring island, trying to get the incredulous *French* authorities to despatch vessels of every and any description to remove the inhabitants of the threatened island." He was sent from one official to another, his anger rising, until finally he found himself begging one "Monsier le Maire" for his horse-drawn carriage. Dunne woke up pleading with Monsieur le Maire—"Listen! Four thousand people will be killed unless...."[9]

The next newspaper he read ran this headline—

Volcano Disaster in Martinique
Town Swept Away an Avalanche of Flame Probable Loss of over 40,000 Lives

The French-speaking island was devastated by what would be the twentieth century's most destructive volcanic eruption. The town of Saint-Pierre and surrounding areas were entirely destroyed. The total number of fatalities was different in real life, as were other aspects of the disaster. But some parts of his dream did seem to predict the future.[10] Was it possible that dreams could probe the future?

Dunne pondered this question, but his dreams subsided for a few years and his curiosity subsided with them. Then the Great War came, an event that brought on disturbing dreams and experiences all over Europe. Typhoid had weakened Dunne's heart, so instead of reporting for combat he found himself in a London hospital in 1917 for a heart procedure. In this hospital his odd experiences resumed. He dreamed one night of an explosion. The next day (January 19, 1917) the great Silvertown munitions factory exploded nearby, shattering the hospital's windows and shaking its foundations. Fearing German Zeppelin bombers overhead, the nurses quickly extinguished the lights.[11] In the middle of it all Dunne lay in bed wondering about time. Was it possible that traumatic or violent events somehow fragmented time itself? Was it possible that these events stimulated some type of inner capacity to perceive time differently? Or, more frightening still, was it possible that these events had disturbed his sanity?

He began diligently recording and studying his dreams, and he came to believe that predictive dream experiences were not unusual or abnormal. He developed these thoughts in his 1927 book *An Experiment with Time,* which became well known. In the early chapters of the book Dunne recounted dream experiences and discussed ways that they drew from events that happened in the future. He theorized that everyone's dreams were "composed of *images of past experience and images of future experience blended together in approximately equal proportions.*"[12] Anyone could discover this by following the procedures that Dunne had followed—that is, by keeping a journal at one's bedside and writing dreams down immediately upon waking. In the later chapters of *An Experiment with Time* and in *The Serial Universe* (1934), Dunne developed a theory of time to explain the dreaming self's temporal freedom. It was a theory that posited the existence of multiple conscious observers within the self. Dunne spoke of Observer 1 as our waking consciousness. Observer 2 was our sleeping consciousness, a consciousness that existed in a higher dimension that could move freely across past and future events. Upon waking, Observer 1 could sometimes recall the perceptions of the dreaming Observer 2. Dunne focused his analysis on just these two observers, but he also argued that the nested, inner observers continued to an "observer at infinity" who represented the immortal aspect of each person. Thus, there was always a higher-dimensional, observing part of the self that witnessed the self watching other things.

This infinite regress was unpalatable to some reviewers, but as two historians of interwar British culture have pointed out, this aspect of Dunne's theory also was "more comforting than any conceivable form of traditional life-after-death. Whatever happened, one was always *somewhere,* looking attentively at oneself."[13] This kind of reasoning nicely accounted for dissociative experiences and near-death experiences of soldiers like Bennett as well: In dissociative states, dreams, and apparently even in death, you were always *somewhere,* floating freely across time, observing yourself.[14]

As he developed these ideas, Dunne drew on new scientific notions about space and time, particularly the theories of the German-born physicist Albert Einstein and popular overviews of Einstein's theories by the Cambridge University astrophysicist Arthur Eddington. Though Einstein developed and published his ideas early in the century, they remained unknown to the public until scientists confirmed General Relativity's conception of gravity by observing a solar eclipse in 1919. At this point, Einstein became a celebrity, and his ideas about time, space, light, and gravity were covered extensively in newspapers around the world. He advanced a number of astonishing claims—that our three dimensions of space and our one dimension of time were not independent but were rather united in a single four-dimensional fabric called spacetime; that energy and mass, which most thought of as different things, were interchangeable; that space and time were warped and altered by gravity; that gravity caused time specifically to slow down; and that events that were simultaneous to one observer were not simultaneous to others. There was no absolute frame of reference. Time, which most people had thought of as linear and absolute, was fragmented and variable, existing in different and relative frameworks. This last idea strongly influenced Dunne. "What is future to Jones may be present to Brown," Dunne wrote, drawing the inference that, in some sense at least, the "future" could already exist in someone else's present. Times were different for different observing selves.

How did the sleeping consciousness, that is, Observer 2, actually perceive images from future times, however? Answering this question involved using not just Einstein but C. Howard Hinton as well. Dunne argued that in higher-dimensional contexts everything existed at once—that all spaces and times, as Hinton had said, existed in this higher space as one massive entity. Dunne liked Hinton's notion that we experienced this stupendous time/space entity through a flickering consciousness that perceived only sequential time/space slices. Dunne argued further that the sleeping consciousness had a measure of freedom to move through the time/space whole. He argued for this kind of freedom by pointing to the work of Eddington, whose popular books on Einstein's theories argued that individuals were four-dimensional objects greatly extended in the time dimension. Dunne believed that the sleeping consciousness existed at a right angle to the self and observed it moving through time. (To Dunne, anything that perceived a three-dimensional whole in its entirety must exist in a higher spacetime, just as seeing completely a two-dimensional flat world required one to see it from a higher, three-dimensional level.)[15] So, at a higher level, time existed as one entity, even if our three-dimensional waking consciousness experienced it gradually, or serially.

"Personal Access" to Time Dimensions

Dunne's book sold briskly and was widely read and reviewed. His ideas became an important part of the interwar zeitgeist, and predictive dreams were spoken of colloquially as "Dunne Dreams." And while his writings received appreciative reviews even in science journals,[16] there were many skeptics. Some complained that his predictive dreams could be mere coincidences; they objected to how he stacked up observers in an infinitely regressive chain; they disagreed with how he reified categories such as "time"; they worried that his block universe actually took away human freedom; and they questioned why he needed so many complicated diagrams and ill-defined neologisms such as "Reagent."[17] The most deeply felt objections came from professional philosophers who felt (with some justification) that Dunne was borrowing their categories and developing philosophical arguments without consulting their more sophisticated work. The logical positivist philosopher of science Ernest Nagel, for instance, was not impressed by Dunne's uncritical attempt to shore up human freedom and divine ontology and was irritated that Dunne presumed to educate others about complex philosophical categories such as time, sensation, and attention.

But if Dunne was critiqued by some for being uninformed he was praised by others for developing novel arguments for human dignity and freedom. Another philosopher, the Oxford pragmatist F. C. S. Schiller, thought Dunne's was a welcome provocation, a book "well calculated to flutter the dovecotes, or rather rookeries, of the philosophers" because it used their categories in different ways and pursued them to different ends. Schiller and others thought his book opened up important new questions.[18]

Outside of university faculty clubs, Dunne's ideas had a greater appeal. An important literary critic and exponent of new ideas in the Modernist avant-garde, J. W. N. Sullivan, put Dunne's theories in context in a wide-ranging piece that asked apprehensively "What and Where Are We?" In 1937, few answered that question optimistically. Sullivan attempted to identify sources of disillusionment. An earlier generation of scientists unsettled dogmatic certainties about human purpose and God's providence, he claimed, while the war shattered the West's sense of progress and confidence. There was no abiding God in the universe, no hope for an upward march of civilization. But nested in new sciences were possibilities for hope and even new arguments for human meaning and transcendence. Relativity and quantum mechanics made human consciousness central to our understanding of time, space, and other aspects of the natural world. Sullivan thought that Dunne and others offering examples of precognition had given convincing evidence that we existed (most of the time) in one dimension of existence, one time, but that there were other temporal layers. On the basis of Dunne's work and the studies of the Duke parapsychologist J. B. Rhine, Sullivan claimed that "there is something in man which is independent of space and time," a discovery that he was sure had wide-ranging implications.

> If man's independence of space and time be a genuine discovery, then the question of a purpose in life, together with many other questions, acquires a profoundly different significance. Although subject to space and time, he is not wholly conditioned by them. Even if all of his activities and aims have reference to his spatial and temporal existence, these things are not exhaustive of the nature of man.[19]

If true, Dunne's new ideas made a new basic outlook possible: Human beings transcended space and time.

It is worth emphasizing that Dunne developed these ideas not because he wanted to buttress older religious claims or church doctrines. To be sure, in *Experiment with Time* and *The Serial Universe* he had nothing to say about traditional religion. What he wanted to do was develop a new way of talking about human freedom and immortality, two issues he worried about at least since his wartime experiences. As early as 1904, for example, in a letter Dunne wrote to his friend H. G. Wells, he alluded to the power of inner flashes of insight that were not quite "religious" but that defied "the authority of our little observing and calculating machines." There was something in us that sensed things beyond our technologies and our senses. Dunne perceived this power in himself and knew that others had also experienced uncanny dreams, psychic experiences, and near-death visions. For Dunne the testimony of experience was powerful, but it was supplemented by new developments in physics that pointed to a much larger universe of things that could never be seen or perceived by human beings. (In this period, both Einstein and Eddington, for example, insisted that at deeper levels the universe's temporal and spatial realities eluded us.)[20]

Dunne's system was appealing because it took esoteric scientific ideas and used them to speak to deep religious and philosophical issues. While Eddington spoke of hidden times and spaces and Einstein spoke of the world's many time frames, Dunne took people to these places in their dreams. In the words of one historian, he transformed esoteric, scientific notions about time and dimensionality and gave individuals "personal access" to these dimensions.[21]

For much of his life, Dunne disguised his metaphysical interests, but beginning in the late 1930s he made these interests public in two books about immortality. Then, in 1955, six years after his death, his wife edited and then published an additional manuscript in which Dunne spoke directly about God and a set of visionary experiences that he had had during his lifetime. In this book Dunne recalled how he struggled as a young man to believe in Christianity even though its miracles and stories didn't comport with reason. He discussed how by the end of the Boer War he was mentally exhausted by the question of religion. Around this time he repressed his doubts and officially became a Christian, an act that brought an unexpected but temporary sense of relief and spiritual certainty. His doubts reemerged quickly, however, and he became convinced that he lacked sufficient warrants for belief. Could he be a Christian without adequate evidence for the Christian story, with all of its supernatural miracles and wonders? Adding to his doubts was the fact that the Biblical world and worldview had faded into an inaccessible and prescientific past. It had lost the ability to inspire and stir him inwardly. "Jesus of Nazareth had died nearly two thousand years ago. He was not present in this lovely 'now,'" Dunne thought.[22]

But while Dunne felt an unsettled sense of religious absence he also experienced a compensating sense of presence during dreams and, sometimes, in waking moments of inspiration. He wrote about hearing voices from a transcendent source, a Universal Mind that filled all of the dimensions of space and time. The intruding voices he heard convinced him that a Universal Mind existed and that this Mind communicated with individual minds via what Dunne called "intrusions."

God did not contravene physical laws with preposterous miracles, but he did intrude himself into individual minds, and these intrusions were the way that the Universal Mind guided people at crucial life moments or at crucial times in history. These divine intrusions had guided Dunne throughout his life, and, though he had not mentioned them in his dream book, they had in fact guided him through his dreams and encouraged him to interpret them. Dunne said that these intrusions were common in world history, that they guided people out of spiritual malaise, and that they were crucial during this time of widespread doubt about traditional religion. It was easy to imagine, Dunne wrote in this last book, that "occasional intrusions might still be needed to save men from, e.g., a culminating fury of mutual destruction due, psychologically, to the gloomy teachings of ignorant materialism." In one vision discussed by his wife at the end of the book, Dunne encountered an angel in the midst of a frightening, black storm. "The question which had always worried him came out—'Christianity, is it true?'" The intruding angel replied: "God lets it be true for those who want it to be true."[23]

This was an angel for the modern world, to be sure. Though miraculous religious narratives were increasingly unbelievable, a thoroughgoing skepticism also was unappealing, for this kind of skepticism meant there was no way to transcend the confinements of material space and time. In fact, Dunne's intrusions made possible a new middle path toward spirituality for people who were both wary of superstition and credulity on the one hand and apprehensive about skeptical modernity on the other. In short, Dunne produced the kind of middle position we have seen many times before, finding a more natural type of supernatural that could be both reasonable and spiritual, both in nature and beyond it, at the same time.

Dunne's Dreams in Fiction

The sense of being shackled to time's destructive march through history was pervasive in the interwar period, and many writers, armed with Dunne's ideas, used fiction to perform their own Houdini-like escapes. Writers and playwrights experimented with nonlinear timelines, flashbacks, flash-forwards, time slips, and predictive dreams and many borrowed from Dunne's notions in particular. Dunne's *Experiment with Time* "was very widely and eagerly discussed" in the interwar period, a writer for the *New York Times* remembered, helping "to form something of the imaginative climate."[24] Dunne's ideas influenced a generation of British and American writers, including the poet T. S. Eliot, H. G. Wells, the novelist and screenwriter James Hilton, the journalist and playwright J. R. Priestley, and the fantasy writers C. S. Lewis, Charles Williams, E. R. Eddison, and J. R. R. Tolkien.

Sometimes authors used Dunne's time speculations to understand better the era's psychological traumas and plot ways of overcoming them. A Scottish writer named John Buchan, for example, did this in several novels, including *The Gap in the Curtain* (1932), in which a mathematics professor asked the narrator and others at a house party to participate in an experiment on the perception of time. Many of the characters had already commented on the unsettled quality of their age and articulated nostalgia for a more tranquil prewar England. But their encounter with Professor Moe signaled a turn toward a different kind of escape from time: movement into the future. Peace, happiness, success—they all depended not on a past that could be discovered but on a future that might be seen more clearly. After explaining time in a Dunnian mode, Professor Moe told them about the experiment: The men involved in the experiment were to try to catch a glimpse of an issue of *The Times* published one year in the future—an obvious recapitulation of Dunne's experiences. To prepare, Moe gave his subjects a training regimen in which they would read *The Times* and attempt to predict the style and content of the next day's issue. After this preparation, Moe gave them a drug that stimulated the part of the brain associated with time perception, and they saw fragments of the future. In the end, characters saw elements from the future, and while this remarkable feat provided comfort for some, it also raised difficult questions about how to interpret the future and how to understand human freedom in a predetermined world.[25]

Professor Moe was not the only fictional character to embrace Dunne's books as ways of understanding uncanny dreams of the future. In novels by Olaf Stapledon, James Hilton, H. G. Wells, C. S. Lewis, and others, characters read, studied, and recommended Dunne's books. In James Hilton's *Random Harvest* (1941), for instance, the main character,

Charles Rainier, experienced a traumatic war injury that led to memory loss and a disturbed perception of time. Over time he struggled to understand the Great War, his memories of it, and unusual flashes of "memory" that predicted the future. At one point another character interpreted Rainier's experiences of time as evidence of Dunne's theories. H. G. Wells, for his part, in 1933 crafted *The Shape of Things to Come* as an extended reflection on the precognitive dreams of a distinguished British diplomat named Dr. Philip Raven, a fictional character who had read Dunne's *Experiment* and believed that his own experiences were striking examples of "Dunne Dreams."

Characters in a number of C. S. Lewis novels turn to Dunne's theories as ways of reimagining time and making more plausible human superpowers, such as seeing into the future. In Lewis's unfinished time-travel manuscript *The Dark Tower,* three academics at Cambridge, MacPhee, Orfieu, and Ransom, discussed the possibility of traveling across time. One of them, Orfieu, talked about how memories, dreams, or altered states of consciousness enabled people to glimpse other times. This moved the topic of conversation, of course, to Dunne. Though many treated Dunne's dream experiences as mere hallucinations, Orfieu complained, there was no doubt that the mind had access to a broader range of times and experiences. "Of the innumerable things going through your mind at any moment, while some are mere imagination, some are real perceptions of the past and others real perceptions of the future." Orfieu's colleague MacPhee snorted in disbelief, but Orfieu continued. Orfieu insisted that if MacPhee had carried out Dunne's dream experiments himself and "got the same results that he got, and I got, and everyone got who took the trouble," MacPhee also would see that seeing the future was a scientific certainty.[26] (Had C. S. Lewis himself studied his dreams for evidence of precognition?) And in *That Hideous Strength,* Lewis used Dunne's ideas in a story about a Ph.D. student named Jane Studdock who wrote a thesis about John Donne—which is close, but not quite *John Dunne*—and tried to understand her uncanny dreams. Studdock's dreams and other mystical experiences enabled her and others to battle against scientific materialists who were leading society toward a dystopian future.[27]

Dunne's theories also influenced several of J. R. R. Tolkien's key works. Writing in the dirty mess-tents of the Great War, "in huts full of blasphemy and smut, or by candle light in bell-tents, even some down in dugouts under the shell fire," Tolkien initially conjured stories to distract himself from the monotony and terror of trench warfare. But while war was detestable, peacetime was not much better, for modern Europe to Tolkien had an industrial "rawness and ugliness" that he intensely disliked.[28] He would have escaped it if he could have done so—after reading F. M. Stenton's *Anglo-Saxon England,* for instance, he said to his son that "I'd give a bit for a time machine"—but bereft of such things he would journey into other times in his imagination. He carefully annotated his copy of *Experiment with Time* and used Dunne's ideas in many places in *Lord of the Rings.* For instance, he used both *before* and *after* when referring to the future, spoke of human lives as "an endless column moving forward" through a static time field, and developed characters who experienced déjà vu, odd flashbacks, or uncanny "memories" of future events.[29] Tolkien also experimented with characters who could see with the multiple perspectives of an "Observer 2," as Aragorn did when standing on the hill of Cerin Amroth in timeless Lorien.

In other books, including *The Lost Road* and *The Notion Club Papers,* Tolkien used dreams in order to question conventional distinctions between past, present, and future. In *The Notion Club Papers,* a fragmentary record of the meetings of a group of Oxford artists gathering in the future, the conversation often turned to dreams and what they meant. One of the members of the club, Michael George Ramer, experienced precognitive dreams and even saw the tsunami that sank Numenor, the large island in the Sundering Seas west of Middle-Earth described in the appendices to Tolkien's *Lord of the Rings.* Like Dunne, Ramer was recording and studying his dreams. "A pretty good case had been made out for the view that in dreams a mind can, and sometimes does, move in Time," Ramer said, attempting to persuade his colleagues. There were, he continued, "authenticated" modern accounts of the dreaming mind traveling into the future.[30] Tolkien himself was haunted by uncanny dreams he thought gave him access to inherited (racial) memories and events in the future. He drew some of these ideas from the Swiss psychotherapist Carl Jung.[31]

Finally, H. G. Wells, whose hyperspace ideas have been mentioned in earlier chapters, had a personal relationship with Dunne and used his ideas in fictional and real-life forms of spiritual escape. Wells had long sustained an interest in higher-dimensional ideas, using them in early novels and even arguing in a nonfiction work that such ideas could form the foundation of a credible faith in a higher-dimensional God.[32] When Dunne's dream book appeared in 1927 Wells gave it positive reviews in a couple of well-known publications, calling it "fantastically interesting" and confessing that it "stirred my imagination vividly." Most imaginative people, he said, "will be stirred by the queer things he has advanced in it. I do not think it has yet been given nearly enough attention."[33] Wells even let Dunne convince him to "keep a notebook at my bed-head and jot down my dreams fresh and hot." (I did this, Wells admitted, but "I do not remember making a note.") In fiction, Wells incorporated Dunne's ideas in many ways. Protagonists such as the narrator in Wells's *The Shape of Things to Come* (1933), claimed J. W. Dunne had accomplished "subtle thinking upon the relationship of time and space to consciousness" and documented "a series of very remarkable observations" to support his ideas.[34] In other books, such as *When the Sleeper Wakes* (1899), *The Dream* (1924), *The Autocracy of Mr. Parham* (1930), *What Dreams May Come* (1933) and *The Happy Turning* (1945), uncanny dreams structure the plot.

If Wells used dreams in fiction to drive narratives about fantastic escape or remarkable forms of temporal freedom he also studied his own dreams to uncover life's mysterious meaning and structure. "Wells was a dreamer," one of his many biographers has written, "but what is less clearly understood is how he used his dreams, fostered them, and created a world from those dreams in his novels."[35] Throughout his life Wells referred both to nighttime dreams and to a kind of waking dream during which he accessed his subconscious and brought its contents to the surface. When these ideas surfaced, he used them to understand the underlying pattern behind life's outward appearances. (Though he sometimes doubted the existence of God, Wells seems never to have questioned the idea that his life had an overall meaning and shape to it.)[36] Wells also turned to his dreams for consolation, writing that dreams compensated for life's disappointments and stimulated hope for a better future. He hoped for a future in which "one's best dreams could be recalled or re-dreamed as solace and for the alleviation of bad times." Finally, as biographers have noted, Wells used dreams to help him devise fictional storylines, characters, or sci-fi technologies.[37] Many of the things he dreamed about—air travel, "atomic bombs," wireless communication—have magically materialized into existence. We might say that Wells's "Dunne Dreams" have become everyone's future.

J. B. Priestley: "At Home" Again in the Universe

One person above all others carried forward Dunne's legacy, developed its evidentiary foundation, and used his ideas to buttress a metaphysics of extraordinary psychical and supernatural possibilities, a man who insisted that human beings were more free and transcendent than usually understood. After seeing the spectacle of the Great War up close, the British writer and journalist J. B. Priestley came to believe what so many others believed during this era—that time was an active force propelling us to destruction. "Above all," he said, "modern man is haunted by the idea of inexorable passing time."[38] The modern timeline had led to war, economic depression, and a sense of spiritual malaise. And now it ushered western civilization into another, greater war. But Priestley also sensed a way out of this destructive trajectory, and he spent a good portion of the second half of his life trying to imagine and write about it.

Born in Manningham, England, Priestley fought in the First World War until one day in 1916 when a German bomb buried him and the meal rations he was organizing. He was fortunate to have been in charge of the food: Survivors dug for the meal rations, he remembered, and also found him.[39] By the mid-1920s he was a well-known humor writer and critic. In 1929 he published the first of many best-selling books, *The Good Companion,* after which he became a national figure. Several additional popular novels came—twenty-six in all by the end of his life—and in the early 1930s he began writing plays as well. He was a regular broadcaster on the BBC during the Second World War. Priestley wanted to develop new forms of culture that would cross over from high literary culture to mass culture, hoping to replace the highbrow / lowbrow binary with (to use his word) "broadbrow."[40] Like others he was troubled by modern consumer culture, the soullessness of industrial production, the mechanization of culture, and above all the problem of time, believing that if someone "could find a key to fit this lock we might open a door into a new universe."[41]

He found that doorway in the scientific and speculative writings of Einstein, Hinton, P. D. Ouspensky, and Dunne. Priestley knew Hinton's works well and had spoken to Claude Bragdon about him. (Hinton "was obviously not only an original thinker of some power," Priestley said once, nicely summing up Hinton's personality, but also was "a delightful odd fish."[42]) It was, however, Dunne's work, less abstruse and mathematical than Hinton's, that convinced Priestley there were practical ways for individuals to overcome their fears of time and death. Dunne's *Experiment* book, Priestley insisted, was "easily the most fascinating and probably the most valuable book of our day."[43] Dunne showed that we were not "the slaves of chronological time" but "more elaborate, more powerful, perhaps nobler creatures than we have lately taken ourselves to be."[44] Priestley believed that recording one's dreams and using them to reimagine time would liberate people psychologically and allow them to see their lives as part of a larger and more meaningful whole that extended beyond this life. Borrowing from Carl Jung and the religion scholar Mircea Eliade, he understood the acquisition of a multiple time sense not as a futuristic innovation but as the recovery of a primordial, mythic sensibility. "Passing time, once almost meaningless, is now the inescapable beat, like that of the engine of some space ship, of the whole vast universe; we seem to be utterly at its mercy; while any idea, once so all-important, of the Great Time, the eternal dream time, the other time of gods and heroes of mythology, seems to have vanished."[45] From the depths of disenchanted modernity, with its relentlessly ticking clocks, Priestley would resurrect mythologies and dreams pointing to an eternal time.

Reading the more popular works of Einstein and Eddington made Priestley entirely comfortable talking about a universe that had not one but many time trajectories. He saw that we were "complicated creatures living in an extremely elaborate universe" and that our minds were only capable of grasping fragmentary images of it. "If this is a universe of many dimensions, as it now appears to be, I felt there is something in us that would come at last to explore and know them all. There was room for the grandest immortality, not an endless and senseless going on and on in one direction, but a complicated growth, forever adding new powers, new responsibilities, new chances of disaster or triumph." It may be, Priestley continued, that this life "is simply the creation of a fourth-dimensional body that, when it is completely discovered to us, will begin to move across a new field of Time, starting with the whole content of its first life as a dramatist might start with so many actors, costumes, scenes, and properties."[46] Dunne might have been right when insisting that we currently lived in a wider universe of Time, though "only shadows and whispers of their existence come to us because our attention is rightly fixed on this immediate time." Priestley argued that this kind of belief, far from being an opiate that deadened our senses, was a stimulant that augmented them, making our lives vigorous and joyful and sharpening our sense of brotherhood and community. "You have only to add a dimension—the fourth—to discover how our isolation vanishes, and what seemed a heap of branches, twigs, leaves, and fruit now appears as a growing tree." Here was indeed the key that unlocked the door to life's meaning and coherence. "If there is no invisible sphere, no great communion of mind, no shared adventures of the spirit, no reality unknown to outward sense, and all's plain sailing, why do we seem to move through a haunted world?"[47]

Wishing to bring these ideas to a wider public, Priestley wrote plays and novels examining time and the meaning of mortality and redemption. He did this most famously in his "Time Plays," which are still performed around the world and which experiment with different conceptions of time. In his first Time Play, *Time and the Conways,* Priestley introduced audiences to ways of sensing multiple time frames by beginning the play in the past in act I, moving to the future in act II, and ending back in the past in act III. The three-act play examined the life of a wealthy Yorkshire family over a period of nineteen years, from 1919 to 1937. In act I, which was set in the Conway house in 1919, the Conways celebrated Kay Conway's twenty-first birthday and looked forward to a postwar future of hope, prosperity, and progress. Act II, however, which took place in 1937, brought into focus a family devastated by career missteps, marital problems, death, and financial failure. In this act, Kay Conway, who was the central character in the play, vented to her brother Alan. "Remember what we once were and what we thought we'd be. And now this. And it's all we have, Alan, it's *us.* Every step we've taken—every tick of the clock—making everything worse. If this is all life is, what's the use? Better to die . . . before Time gets to work on you."

But Alan demurred, offering what amounted to Dunne's theory as metaphysical comfort. "There's a book I'll lend you—read it in the train. But the point is, now, at this moment, or any moment, we're only a cross-section of our real selves. What we *really* are is the whole stretch of ourselves, all our time, and when we come to the end of this life, all those selves, all our time, will be *us*—the real you, the real me. And then perhaps we'll find ourselves in another time, which is only another kind of dream."[48] In act III the play returns to 1919, where we now see elements of the future clearly adumbrated. At the end of the act, the Conway children gathered to hear Mrs. Conway foretell their future, and Kay, in a moment of déjà vu, briefly recalled episodes from the future already staged in act II. Kay turned to Alan and asked him, "Please tell me....I can't bear it...and there's something...something...you could tell me." Alan was not sure what to say; but he comforted her by saying that in the future he would know what to say and do. "There will be—something—I can tell you—one day. I'll try—I promise."[49]

In this play Priestley invited audience members to think about time in a new way—not as an ironclad linear process but as multiple frames of reference and activity, past, present, and future, that could be perceived in different ways. Kay saw future events dimly, and Alan knew enough of Dunne to know that time only appeared linear because of the limitations of human consciousness. The play encouraged the audience to "sharpen our vague sense of what is to come, and, in so doing, avert disaster and even realize a fuller form of life." A reviewer correctly noted that Priestley's aims were to "popularize" the kind of temporal experimentation written about by Dunne.[50] In fact, Priestley had Dunne work with the play's original cast. He wrote Bragdon to say that Dunne was delighted by the play and that Dunne had "insisted on giving all the members of the London company a signed copy of his book and a lecture on the nature of Time."[51] Not all members of the cast, however, seem to have understood Dunne's notions. "At his own suggestion, [Dunne] explained his ideas to the cast of my play *Time and the Conways*," Priestley wrote in his *Man and Time*, "a cast that always played well but never better than when they were pretending to understand what he was telling them."[52]

Priestley used this play to promote Dunne's alternative theory of time and human immortality. In the same week as its New York premiere

Figure 6.2 Priestley (left), the actress Jean Forbes-Robertson, and J. W. Dunne talk during Dunne's meeting with the London cast of *Time and the Conways* (1937). From the Personal Papers of J. B. Priestley, Special Collections, University of Bradford, Bradford, U.K.

in January 1938, *Time and the Conways* was performed for the American and Canadian radio audience of the music and variety show *The Royal Gelatin Hour*. The host of the show, the American singer and band leader Rudy Vallee, interviewed Priestley on the same episode. This was an exciting age of discovery, Priestley told Vallee, an age with new views of our destiny and cosmos. There was one new perspective, he continued, that time did not really destroy anything and that past, present, and future all remained in existence, even though we only perceived the present moment. Priestley saw evidence for this everywhere. Everyone knew people who saw glimpses into the future, who had intuitions and hunches. There was a kind of "freedom of movement" in the fourth dimension, he said, the same kind of freedom that Kay had sensed in his play. At this point, Rudy Vallee asked for clarification and Priestley mentioned the book of a "hardheaded" aeronautical engineer named Dunne, who brought an original mathematical mind to this important problem and proved the existence of immortality. "Now, that, Mr. Priestley does sound tremendously important," Vallee interrupted. Important and urgent for our times, Priestley confirmed, for the world was in a "very dangerous condition"—pessimistic, violent, nihilistic. "What we urgently need is a change of mind and heart."

> Men have got to feel at home in the universe again and I believe a great deal of the despair of our time is due to the fact that men have a false picture of the universe and of our destiny. Having lost religion and gained nothing in its place, too many people have come to believe that life doesn't amount to much. But actually as Kay and Alan say in my play, we are immortal beings engaged in a tremendous adventure. These new theories of time link up with some very old pieces of wisdom such as the kingdom of heaven is within us. If as I believe we live on after death as our fourth dimensional selves, then we ourselves establish the conditions and the quality of that future life. The heaven or hell waiting for us is of our own making. If time were really ticking our lives away, it might not matter how we live. But time is not ticking our lives away, and therefore it matters enormously and urgently how we live just because we are really outside of time and because we are immortal beings.[53]

Then the music began and Vallee sang about dreams and love in "Let's Make It a Lifetime." Priestley looked back on this night with astonishment. "What would Hinton have thought if he could have wandered into the large studio of the N.B.C. in Radio City and heard me, as one of the performers on the *Royal Gelatin Hour*, discussing the fourth dimension, for an audience of millions and millions, with a singer and danceband leader, Rudy Vallee?"[54] There is no doubt about it—Hinton would have been amazed.

Dunne and a New Spirituality of Dreams

Though Dunne spent much of his life hiding his spiritual interests and inclinations, glossing his dreams not as revelatory or mystical but as reasonable and mathematical; though he chose to speak about his new ideas at places such as (for instance) The Royal College of Science rather than the local Theosophical Society; and though he consistently projected the self-image of an unsentimental soldier and engineer in his public talks and private encounters—though these were the ways he usually proceeded, there did come a time when, suffering from illness and approaching death, he was candid about the spiritual things that had happened to him and why he was preoccupied with predictive dreams. In the final days of his life he rushed to finish a book that explained how he had been the subject of remarkable visions and dreams in which he had not just glimpsed the future but also received divine guidance and spoke to angels. He had seen things in dreams and daytime visions and had heard voices that instructed him to understand (and publicize) his precognitive dreams. He had seen scenes of bright illumination in which he, like Edwin Abbott or Gustav Fechner or others in this book, had sensed the divine around him. He had spoken with angelic beings who revealed that while Christianity itself was of dubious usefulness in the modern era, there was no doubt that a Universal Mind cared enough about human beings that it had inspired thoughts, dreams, visions, and higher-dimensional experiences of altered time and space in many people. These "intrusions," as Dunne called them, were not (unlike older miracles) against the laws of nature, but rather were events that operated in and through the inscrutable layers and compartments of human consciousness.[55] Dunne's intrusions made possible a new middle path toward spirituality for people who were both wary of superstition and credulity on the one hand and apprehensive about skeptical modernity on the other.

In short, Dunne produced the kind of middle position we have seen many times before. His work pointed the way to a more scientific type of supernatural that could be both reasonable and spiritual, both inside nature and beyond it, at the same time.

Dunne's views on dreams and time were part of a culture of scientific empiricism that dramatically influenced all aspects of life in the twentieth century, including, of course, religion and spirituality. When he advanced metaphysical truths anchored in the evidence of experience rather than the authority of tradition, he was not alone. Many religious thinkers, including twentieth-century Jews and Christians, embraced the idea that real religion could be probed, evaluated, and verified empirically. These thinkers developed arguments for God's existence and religion's usefulness by pointing to the universality of spiritual feelings, the naturalness of human belief in God, and the power of extraordinary experiences of sudden insight or illumination. All these things could be measured by experimental psychologists, analyzed by attentive clinicians, and even cultivated by the burgeoning ranks of pastoral psychologists.

Outside of churches and synagogues, in the many mystical fellowships and spiritual movements that flowered in modern Europe and America, an empirical orientation also was taken for granted. Intellectuals, cultural elites, and ordinary people attempted to (empirically) detect spirit manifestations in séance sittings; capture evidence of ghosts in spirit photography; transmit nonphysical energies from mind to mind in laboratory tests of extrasensory perception; document and study colorful, energetic auras; collect and share accounts of near-death experiences; and, of course, write down dreams that contained spiritual meaning, messages from the dead, or sights and sounds that somehow were conveyed from the future.

On this last matter, on dreams, a robust culture of dreams expanded far beyond Dunne. It drew from psychoanalysis, which was preoccupied with dreams and the unconscious; from a new literature on directed dreaming; from parapsychological researchers like Louisa and J. B. Rhine, who discovered ESP events in dreams and argued for a nonphysical dimension to the mind; in essays, art, and criticism by artists, including especially Surrealists who experimented with and recorded their accounts of dreams and hypnotic states of consciousness; and in literature that, as we have seen, deployed dreams and other forms of altered consciousness in order to transport characters into new times or bestow on them unexpected forms of knowledge.[56] In all of these ways and in others a pop-cultural network developed of people both seeking and finding empirical evidence for supernatural things.

Dunne contributed to this culture of empirical seeking but it was J. B. Priestley who advanced it far beyond anything even Dunne could have dreamed. Priestley made Dunne's redemptive theory of time available not just to millions of readers but to television audiences that watched adaptations of his time-haunted plays; and he promoted Dunne's theory on radio and in TV interviews as well as in nonfiction books such as *Man and Time* (1964). In 1963 he appeared on BBC television to discuss time theories and had the host Huw Wheldon ask viewers "to send me accounts of any experiences they had had that appeared to challenge the conventional and 'common-sense' idea of Time."[57] Notices about the interview and Priestley's research project subsequently were published in many periodicals. Priestley received over 1,500 letters in response, many of which still survive. The letters describe many kinds of experiences—unsettling presentiments of coming disaster; daytime visions of occurrences in the future; déjà vu dreams that foreshadowed unremarkable events such as reading a book or seeing a play. There were even dreams in which dreamers apparently slipped into someone else's point of view and odd, circular dreams in which the dreamer saw herself awake and remembered the dream she was just then having. Considering these experiences as a whole, Priestley insisted that they showed that human beings were not "the slaves of chronological time" but "more elaborate, more powerful, perhaps nobler creatures than we have lately taken ourselves to be."[58] As he told Rudy Vallee during the *Royal Gelatin Hour* radio broadcast, these experiences might help make unsettled and fearful modern people "feel at home in the world again."

Two final uncanny dreams take our analysis of dimensions and spirituality in new directions. In the first, Priestley, sleeping sometime in the 1920s, experienced a moment of sitting "in the front row of a balcony or gallery" in a theater with colossal proportions. On the stage in front of him was a scene that expanded the stage into impossible dimensions—a brilliantly colored canyon, apparently bottomless, stretched across his visual field. Later, in the 1930s, he visited Arizona and saw the real thing—the Grand Canyon. In the second dream, one of J. W. Dunne's correspondents dreamed parts of the 1932 novel *The Gap in the Curtain* before the book had been written. In the first example, Priestley dreamed a dramatic production that had not yet been staged in real life; in the second, Dunne's correspondent dreamed a fictional narrative that had not yet been written in real life.[59] Did these dreamtime ways of probing fiction and reality suggest that there was a single imaginative capacity behind both dreams and stories, a capacity that could see into other times and places or probe realities beyond ordinary spacetime? Could dreams, when studied in certain ways, and stories,

Figure 6.3 At his home in Stratford-on-Avon, Priestley sorts and examines the many letters he received about unusual time experiences. From J. B. Priestley, *Man and Time* (London: Aldus, 1964), 191.

when crafted in certain ways, peek into the real future, open doorways to higher levels of consciousness, or transport people somehow into reality's transcendent dimensions?

These ideas, which might strike reasonable people as farfetched, seemed preposterous indeed to another veteran of the First World War, a man who had come to believe, like the young Priestley, that time and fate and even God, if he existed, had conspired to send civilization crashing into oblivion. But then he picked up a book of fiction at a train station and, reading through it, glimpsed a light coming from it that illuminated his surroundings. The book was George MacDonald's fairy-tale *Phantastes*. "I saw the bright shadow coming out of the book into the real world and resting there, transforming all common things and yet itself unchanged." In that mystical moment, C. S. Lewis was confronted with the extraordinary possibility that certain kinds of made-up stories could connect human beings to real otherworlds and transcendent levels of reality—that the literary imagination, like the dreaming observer, when properly trained, could lead one into those higher worlds that illuminated everything from above. It was this idea that he used both to transform himself into a Christian and to create fantastic fictional work that would become some of the most influential spiritual literature of the twentieth century.

7

Mirrors, Doorways, and Otherworldly Openings

Efforts to shape a new popular culture of the supernatural went far beyond the mystical dreams and imaginative narratives of "time-haunted" writers such as John Dunne and J. B. Priestley, gathering momentum in the twentieth century and following a logic that was sometimes hard to predict. An important element of this new popular culture was imaginative fiction in which authors fashioned narratives that featured supernatural phenomena, gods, angels, spirits, and visionary prophets. For instance, beginning in the late nineteenth century, there were Modernist writers who sensed that Christian stories were inadequate and developed new mythological narratives (and mythopoetic verses) by borrowing and reworking ancient myths and cosmologies from the world's indigenous people. (Conveniently, Victorian anthropologists and scholars of comparative religion, such as James Frazer and F. Max Mueller, were at this time collecting and analyzing mythological stories from around the world and making them available in edited texts.) D. H. Lawrence, Ezra Pound, W. B. Yeats, and other Modernist mythmakers made sense of suffering, death, nature, time, modernity, and other concerns using these raw materials. In his imaginative novels and short stories, for instance, D. H. Lawrence, who saw himself as a "passionately religious man" and wrote his novels "from the depths of [his] religious experience," mined non-Christian traditions for insights into mystical experiences that predated the distortions of Christian history and dogmatism.[1] Essentially pagan in orientation, Lawrence and like-minded Modernists developed new supernatural narratives that could replace unbelievable or outmoded Christian notions and institutions.

But if efforts to shape a new popular culture of the supernatural had been restricted to these neo-pagan literary mythologies, they would have inspired far fewer people than they actually did. In fact, writers creating some of the era's most enduring fictional otherworlds and alternative universes built these worlds and related narratives not by using indigenous mythologies but by borrowing elements from what was to them the ultimate and highest myth, the Christian narrative. Several Christian writers of fairy tales and fantasy novels drew on Romantic ideas about the power of stories as ways of preparing the imagination for understanding and believing again in Christianity. If God was the supreme Creator, fiction writers were "subcreators" participating in a form of divine creativity—this was how J. R. R. Tolkien, for one, understood the imaginative power of his stories about fictional worlds such as Middle Earth. The creative writing of the fantasist, when crafted properly, was a redemptive act, because fairy tales and fantasy worlds prepared one to believe in the real, spiritual world.[2] It was fine that rebels, mystics, and pagans created imaginary places in fiction; but in order for these worlds to point effectively toward something real and true; in order for them to help human beings see something beyond their own faulty mythopoetic instincts and impulses; in order for them to truly satisfy the yearning for transcendence that originated in a single Source and animated every human heart, they needed to be crafted more deliberately with Christian elements and tropes. This was the ambitious goal of Christian fantasy and science fiction writers during this era.

This chapter examines how Christian writers such as George Mac-Donald, J. R. R. Tolkien, and especially C. S. Lewis developed otherworldly stories in order to help themselves and others imagine the possibility that there might be a real other world—a spiritual world in which Christian saints and martyrs somehow triumphed over evil, guardian angels helped and healed genuine believers, and a loving God welcomed souls in a heavenly afterlife. The books they wrote incorporated Christian tropes and narratives, as well as higher worlds, dimensional doorways, and other concepts borrowed from authoritative disciplines such as math and physics. The impact of this literature has been widespread. Over time, the fantasies of Tolkien and Lewis have become astonishingly popular, spawning sequels, spinoffs and films that have successfully re-presented the Christian story in a new mode that is neither theological nor liturgical, but literary and fantastic. In fact, in many ways, these new fictions have become the predominant way that the Christian narrative is introduced, discussed, understood, and imaginatively *lived in* today. Remarkably, a literary movement that began tentatively, in the midst of a culture wary of imagined narratives and fantasies, revived the Christian imagination in the disenchanted West and came to overshadow all other forms of Christian argument, apologetics, and self-formation.

George MacDonald, Lewis Carroll, and the Imagination

We have seen it again and again—before new myths can be fashioned older ones have to break down, become incoherent, or be destroyed. This process was at work in unexpected ways in the nineteenth century, a century that witnessed the unsettling of many religious narratives, including the rather dramatic unraveling, and in some settings the total obliteration, of Calvinist Protestant views in Europe and America.

The great Scottish writer of fairy tale and fantasy, George MacDonald, was caught in the middle of these changes. Born into a strict, Calvinist family, MacDonald, like many of his generation, became uncomfortable with Calvinist doctrines and sought alternatives. Known for his handsome appearance, his innovative Christian fantasy novels, and a Romantic mysticism that was unconventional for a Christian, MacDonald associated with the era's great poets and writers and became the kind of figure about whom people told stories. One of them was that his distaste for Calvinist notions could be traced to his childhood when (it was said) he burst into tears after his parents explained how predestination worked. (The reasons for this are unclear. Was he worried about himself or his friends? In any case his family reassured him that he, for one, was among the elect.) Christian authors sharing Mac-Donald's anti-Calvinist sympathies and his interest in literature, authors such as Lewis, added legends of their own. MacDonald's Calvinist grandmother, Lewis once wrote, "a truly terrible old woman," once "burnt his uncle's fiddle as a Satanic snare."[3] When MacDonald went to college at the University of Aberdeen, he was exposed to other Satanic snares—like so many undergraduates—including above all Romantic poets such as the Germans E. T. W. Hoffman and Novalis, English Romantics such as Samuel Taylor Coleridge, and freewheeling mystics such as Emmanuel Swedenborg, known in MacDonald's Christian circles not as an inspired visionary but as a deranged lunatic. All of these figures located religious truth less in doctrine than in intuition and imagination. The Romantics—including, as we have seen, the American thinker Ralph Waldo Emerson—set the stage for a recovery of spiritual perspectives that were independent of church authority and doctrine. Many figures interested in creating new mythologies of higher dimensions or worlds, including Edwin Abbott and C. Howard Hinton, were influenced by them.

Coleridge, for instance, spoke of the poet's imagination as the source of religious insight: It had a kind of creative and revelatory power. Coleridge, who as an adolescent also moved from orthodoxy to liberal religious views (via experimentation with alcohol, sex, opium, and poetry), eventually developed ways of talking about writing itself as a way of recapitulating God's creative activity. Borrowing this formulation, MacDonald said that imaginative writers, when morally and spiritually in harmony with God, thought God's thoughts after He did. "The imagination of man is made in the image of the imagination of God," MacDonald wrote. "Everything of man must have been of God first; and it will help much towards our understanding of the imagination and its functions in man if we first succeed in regarding aright the imagination of God, in which the imagination of man lives and moves and has its being."[4] "Indeed, a man is rather *being thought* than *thinking,* when a new thought arises in his mind," MacDonald wrote. This was the great Providential God of Calvinism through the back door, so to speak—a God who controlled everything, even one's intimate thoughts.[5] For MacDonald, this formulation meant that songs, poems, and stories could substitute for sermons and theology, and though MacDonald was evidently an engaging preacher, he chose to invite listeners into the Christian supernatural via imaginative fantasy. His ideas and his writing profoundly shaped the works of later Christian writers, including Tolkien, who also believed that the Christian writer of fairy tales and fictional work could be a co-creator of sacred narratives.[6] One of the most influential Christian mythmakers of the twentieth century, C. S. Lewis, who believed that MacDonald was better than anyone else at creating mythopoetic fantasies, said that MacDonald's fantasy *Phantastes* turned him from atheism to belief, forcing him to think seriously about the reality of invisible things.

MacDonald wrote many books, poems, and other works, including two Christian fantasy novels, *Phantastes* (1858), a novel about a young man who enters a dreamlike world, and *Lilith* (1895), which MacDonald believed was divinely inspired and which he saw as his final imaginative statement of Christian belief. Both fantasies feature dimensional doorways into otherworlds. In *Phantastes,* the protagonist Anodos ("ascent" in Greek) inherits a special key on his twenty-first birthday, a key that opens his dead father's roll-top desk. It was a key to a hidden world, for in the desk he discovered a fairy who revealed a glimpse of an alternate world. At first Anodos was skeptical. The reality of this otherworld became more plausible, however, when Anodos awoke the next day to find his room transformed into a glade near an enchanting forest. The fairy-tale adventure that followed proceeded with a dreamlike associative logic, with Anodos encountering fairy spirits and traveling to a palace in which he passed through strange corridors and doorways into other times and places. At the end of the story he became a hero by vanquishing menacing giants. At this point, however, he encountered a temple with devout congregants worshipping a wooden idol, which he promptly destroyed, to the chagrin of the multitude who pursued and killed him. Floating peacefully over this world after his noble death, Anodos then awoke in his room in the "real" world.

The surface details of the story are arbitrary in some ways, but there is an underlying logic in play, which is that the natural world and the spiritual, fairy world are linked together in a system of correspondences. Macdonald begins the book with a long epigraph from the German Romantic poet and writer Novalis that captures well the book's basic intentions.

A fairy-story is like a vision without rational connections, a harmonious whole of miraculous things and events—as, for example, a musical fantasia, the harmonic sequence of an Aeolian harp, indeed Nature itself. . . . In a genuine fairy-story, everything must be miraculous, mysterious, and interrelated, everything must be alive, each in its own way. The whole of Nature must be wondrously blended with the whole world of the Spirit.[7]

In MacDonald's fantasies he presents two worlds intermingled, our physical world and the imagined realm of Faerie, which overlays the physical world through a system of correspondences, an idea drawn not just from Novalis and the Romantics but also from Swedenborg, whose cosmology described links between heavenly worlds, nature, and human nature. Higher worlds intruded on lower ones through certain openings and fissures, including dreams, mirrors, and special doorways.

Phantastes is neither widely read nor remembered today, but it was quite remarkable in its own time, influencing how other authors developed narratives about dreams and other openings to spiritual worlds. It helped shape, for instance, Lewis Carroll's *Alice's Adventures in Wonderland* and *Through the Looking Glass.* Carroll and MacDonald shared many interests and became friends around the time of the publication of *Phantastes* (1858–1859), meeting in the waiting room of Doctor James Hunt, an expert on stuttering who helped both of them. Mark Twain met Carroll at a party at MacDonald's house, and, though MacDonald was a lively talker, Twain recalled, Carroll was "only interesting to look at, for he was the stillest and shyest full grown man I have ever met except 'Uncle Remus.'" Both MacDonald and Carroll were devoted Christians, admired the English and German Romantics, frequented the theater, and wrote imaginative fantasies with similar themes, including dream visions and fairy worlds. Both also were keenly interested in mathematics and both imported mathematical language into their dimensionally complex narratives. Carroll was a mathematics lecturer at Oxford and wrote a number of books on the subject. Though primarily a pastor and writer, MacDonald loved science and mathematics, taught mathematics at a private high school and the Ladies College in Manchester early in his career, and created protagonists who studied math, especially the works of Euclid.[8]

The years of their most intense friendship were the years just before and during Carroll's writing of *Alice's Adventures in Wonderland*, and there is no doubt that MacDonald and his *Phantastes* in particular influenced Carroll in crucial ways, as a number of scholars have pointed out. Both books have protagonists who descend underground, both make dreaming and waking central concerns, and both incorporate strange, rude creatures, haunting shadows, a room with an overflowing pool, and mysterious doorways and mirrors. Other aspects of the Alice books demonstrate the influence of MacDonald and his entire family. The white kitten in *Alice* was named after Mary MacDonald's white kitten. "Lily," the White Pawn in *Alice*, was named after George and Mary Mac-Donald's oldest daughter. MacDonald read and discussed *Alice* drafts many times with Carroll, MacDonald's children vetted the book, and both Mary and George eventually coaxed Carroll to publish it. Scholars have discovered still other shared preoccupations and literary tropes deployed by the two friends.[9]

Both writers also borrowed ideas from mathematical speculation on higher dimensions. Though "magic mirrors" appeared in fairy tales long before modern speculation about higher dimensions, when these ideas emerged they contributed in new ways to the popular fascination with magic mirrors and what lay inside them. Since the late 1820s, when the University of Leipzig mathematician August Mobius realized that a journey into the fourth dimension might turn an object into its mirror image, popular treatments of the subject, including Hinton's, discussed mirror images as evidence that a higher dimension existed. This was so because rotating any object through a higher dimension could produce a mirror image. For instance, if one draws a two-dimensional person on paper, cuts it out, lifts and rotates it, and puts it back down, one has produced a mirror image of a two-dimensional figure by rotating it in a higher (third) dimension. Might it be the case, some wondered, that rotations in a fourth dimension had caused mirror-image phenomena in nature, such as isometric molecules, the mirroring symmetry of the human body, or the mirror images of other natural objects such as snail shells?

It was for these reasons that in Germany in 1877, Karl Zollner asked the spirit medium Henry Slade to take snail shells and, by rotating them in a fourth dimension, turn them into mirror images of themselves.

(It turned out to be one higher-dimensional trick that Slade could not perform.) Hinton also was fascinated by mirror images and suspected that they were evidence for a real fourth dimension. He pointed to phenomena from stereoisomers, molecules that existed as mirror images of themselves, to human hands as indicators that nature had rotated three-dimensional things into their mirror images. It is reasonable to suspect that Carroll was familiar with many of these mathematical controversies. He also knew of Louis Pasteur's 1848 discovery of mirror-image stereoisomers and made subtle references to them, such as when Alice wondered if Looking-Glass milk would be potable. (The stereoisomers of lactose in milk exist as mirror images. By passing milk into the Looking-Glass world, would it be turned into its mirror image? Could one drink it?) In *Through the Looking Glass,* Carroll explored mirror images, symmetry, and higher-dimensional geometry in different ways that would have been familiar to his English readers.[10]

One cannot understand the fantastic spaces and places in Carroll's fiction without understanding his views on contemporary debates about mathematics, mathematical symbols, and the imagination. The Alice books speak in particular to contemporary debates about how mathematical symbols related to reality. While some mathematicians, including contemporaries of Hinton, insisted that higher dimensions were merely variables in linear algebraic equations, others entertained the possibility that these variables suggested the existence of real, higher spaces. But these questions were hard to settle. What was the relationship between symbolical algebra, with its imaginary variables and numbers, and geometry, which attempted to be more descriptive of real things? Carroll took a more conservative position on these questions and saw little reason to believe that symbolical algebra necessarily pointed to real higher dimensions. In fact several scholars have pointed out that his Alice books reveal misgivings about symbolical algebra and n-dimensional geometries. Elizabeth Throesch, for example, has argued that "the concept of the fourth dimension is, like the fantastic spaces and creatures of the Alice books, a fiction that owes its origin to the contemporary attempt to assign literal meaning to empty symbols and phrases."[11] Carroll may have been pointing to this error by having his fantastic Wonderland creatures give concrete existence to figures of speech, acts that parody the same mistakes made by people who hypostatize mathematical concepts such as the fourth dimension.

At the same time, Carroll, a deeply religious person, deacon of Christ Church, Oxford, and a member of the Society for Psychical Research, had an imaginative life that included spirits, demons, heavenly angels, and miracles. He argued that there were ways of entering other worlds, but these ways had to do with psychic states. He spoke of three—ordinary consciousness, an "Eerie" state in which one is "conscious of the presence of fairies," and a trance state in which the spirit can take leave of the body and travel to other locations on earth or in heaven. Apparently he believed in alternate worlds but associated those spaces not with mathematical dimensions but immaterial forms of consciousness.[12]

Imagined Dimensions in MacDonald's Fiction

Like his more mathematically inclined friend, MacDonald also was interested in other dimensions, looking glasses, and mathematics. In MacDonald's *Lilith,* for example, Vane, the protagonist narrator, encounters a mysterious mirror in his family estate that somehow opens into another, spiritual dimension. A young Oxford graduate who liked science and was preoccupied with correspondences between nature, metaphysical ideas and his own spiritual dreams, Vane thought he saw a ghost one day while reading in the estate's library. Looking up, he saw nothing. (Like other protagonists in fin de siècle ghost stories, he assumed it was an illusion.) One day, however, the estate's butler told him that the manor's old librarian, Mr. Raven, a reader of esoteric books, had inexplicably disappeared years ago with Vane's great-grandfather. Was the place haunted? Later Vane caught sight of "something shadowy," a spectral form that he assumed was Mr. Raven, and he followed this ghost upstairs to a room with a large mirror.[13] As he moved in front of it, the mirror's reflecting surface changed, revealing a different world, a wild, hilly country, with something small and black approaching in the foreground. A black raven hopped on the ground. Vane moved forward, stumbled over the mirror frame, and found himself in this different place, a fairyland that MacDonald called "the region of the seven dimensions."[14] This was a disorienting world crowded with bewildering sensations, not unlike Alice's Wonderland, but it soon became clear that this place would also be one of great spiritual discoveries.

When the bird began to speak, Vane discovered that it was in fact Mr. Raven, who now led Vane through this alternate world, showing him, for example, a large hawthorn tree precisely where a church stood on Vane's property in normal, three-dimensional existence. In this mirror dimension Vane could not see the church, of course; he saw only a tree and white pigeons rising up out of it, spiraling into the sky. Raven informed him that these birds were prayers on their way heavenward. Raven countered Vane's skepticism with confounding questions about identity and the meaning of human life, suggesting to Vane that not only was there more to life than Vane's self-centered ambitions but that there were layers of existence beyond his senses. "I tell you there are more worlds, and more doors to them, than you will think of in many years!" Raven exclaimed. "He spoke much about dimensions, telling me that there were many more than three, some of them concerned with powers which were indeed in us, but of which as yet we knew absolutely nothing. His words, however, I confess, took little more hold of me than the light did of the mirror, for I thought he hardly knew what he was saying."[15] But over time it became clear that Vane was embedded in a universe that was greater than expected. He had entered a parallel world of deeper realities, one that offered opportunities for him to develop his moral and religious sensibilities.

In this mirror world Vane discovered higher correspondences of earthly actions and saw Biblical and metaphysical truths played out in allegorical dramas. In this world, faithful believers experienced a purifying pre-resurrection sleep, while others who lacked faith, moral probity, or a sense of dependence on God were forced to battle skeletal zombies and struggle through various difficulties. In this realm the Biblical characters Adam and Eve battled with the arrogant, selfish Lilith, who in the end was defeated by Vane. The novel ended when Vane returned to his earthly life empowered with a kind of visionary perception by which he could see the spiritual significance of all things.

> The microcosm and macrocosm were at length atoned, at length in harmony! I lived in everything; everything entered and lived in me.

To be aware of a thing, was to know its life at once and mine, to know whence we came, and where we were at home—was to know that we are all what we are, because Another is what he is! Sense after sense, hitherto asleep, awoke in me—sense after sense indescribable, because no correspondent words, no likenesses or imaginations exist, wherewithal to describe them. Full indeed—yet ever expanding, ever making room to receive—was the conscious being where things kept entering by so many open doors![16]

Vane was now keenly attuned to openings between worlds, spiritual intuitions, and mystical incursions from another realm. Sometimes, he said at the end of the book, the solid masses of the world rippled and wavered with deeper energies, "the trees and the grass appear for a moment to shake as if about to pass away; then, lo, they have settled again into the old familiar face! At times I seem to hear whisperings around me, as if some that loved me were talking of me; but when I would distinguish the words, they cease, and all is very still. I know not whether these things rise in my brain, or enter it from without. I do not seek them; they come, and I let them go."[17]

MacDonald fashioned his open doors and mirror worlds from dimensional ideas then circulating in popular culture. Some have said MacDonald's "seven-dimensional" world came from the German Christian mystic Jacob Boehme's seven spiritual stages; others have argued that MacDonald chose the number seven because it was the sum of our three physical dimensions plus the four medieval modes of scriptural interpretation that Dante enumerated.[18] But MacDonald's imagined dimensions were not qualities, stages, or modes of interpretation; they were regions of space that Vane traversed, regions that, when Vane understood them, put the material world in new perspectives. In 1924, MacDonald's son, Greville MacDonald, shed light on his use of dimensions in *Lilith*. It was a text, Greville said, that "both binds in one and unfolds the world of concrete Beauty and the realm of abstract Truth. Necessarily also it treats of their condition in dimensions—of which there be seven in all, three concrete, as I take it, and four abstract interblending but more positively vital. The four compose an inseparable unity commonly spoken of as the much debated fourth dimension—that concept of existence which, being spiritual, is not indeed independent of the concrete, but contains and controls the concrete three dimensions in creative manifestation."[19]

Here Greville connects MacDonald's thinking to scientific speculation about the fourth dimension, which was, to be sure, pervasive in England when MacDonald was writing. (It should be noted that MacDonald and Abbott were both British clerics interested in math and science and that Abbott's *Flatland* was widely discussed in the 1880s and 1890s.) Moreover, as Jeffrey Bilbro has argued, the text of *Lilith* itself contains similarities to Abbott's narrative that could hardly be accidental. In *Lilith,* as in *Flatland,* for instance, higher-dimensional beings penetrate and see into lower-dimensional ones; higher-dimensional realities, which are associated with a thought realm, somehow manifest in simpler forms in lower worlds; and in both works there is a focus on points of intersection or openings between higher and lower worlds, including dreams in particular. In addition, the dimensional travels of the Square and Vane proceed along similar lines. Both experience confusion and disorientation when first moving through higher dimensions; both have prior scientific training that helps them understand interdimensional travel; and both are helped by learning that others also had taken transcendental journeys. In *Flatland,* the Sphere escorts the Square to a meeting of the High Council and they witness officials discussing others who "received revelations from another World"; in *Lilith,* Raven tells Vane that he first traveled to the land of seven dimensions with one of Vane's ancestors, a "Sir Upward" who studied the "relation of modes" and first deployed the mirror as a passageway into the higher realm. Moreover, as Bilbro argues, Raven's "description of Sir Upward recalls the particular mantra that A Square chants when he is back in Flatland to help him remember the direction of the third dimension: 'Upward, and yet not Northward.'"[20]

C. S. Lewis: From Agnostic to "Baptized" Imagination

Though innovative and important in their own ways, MacDonald's stories are usually seen as prologue to the life and work of Lewis, who became probably the most influential Christian writer of the twentieth century. He was a man who, like MacDonald, had to experience the death of his childhood faith before he could resurrect it in fantastic new narratives.

When Lewis was nine years old his desperate prayers failed him, and his mother died from cancer. He was sent to boarding school, beginning a journey that initially took him from conventional Anglicanism to doubt and atheism. In his teens he was confirmed in the Anglican Church, but it was only for his father, for his religious views at the time, as he revealed to a friend, were anything but Christian. "You ask me my religious views," he responded to Arthur Greeves, his best childhood friend; "you know, I think that I have no religion. There is absolutely no proof for any of them, and from a philosophical standpoint Christianity is not even the best." All religions were "man's own invention" contrived to explain the confusing facts of nature and of human life.[21] Lewis retained his skepticism and became a spiritual seeker, studying books related to mysticism, spiritualism, Theosophy, and liberal religion, including W. F. Barrett's *Psychical Research*, Frederic Myers's *Science and a Future Life*, Oliver Lodge's *Raymond, or Life and Death*, and the occult works of both the Irish poet William Butler Yeats and the mystical writer Maurice Maeterlinck. Later, after his Christian reconversion, Lewis saw these writers as dangerously engaged with malevolent spiritual forces, but at the time they satisfied a yearning for something beyond scientific materialism. His interest in these writers continued when he became an undergraduate at Oxford.[22]

Then the Great War came and Lewis enlisted, putting his academic and literary interests aside. On November 29, 1917, Lewis's nineteenth birthday, he arrived at the front lines in France's Somme Valley. His time in the trenches was shortened by a shell that exploded near him in April 1918, sending shrapnel into his left side—his wrist, leg, and ribs, with one shard penetrating his left lung. He recuperated and returned to Oxford, where he became an outstanding student and in 1919 published a book of poems under a pseudonym. The book escaped critical attention and is still mostly unnoticed, but it reveals something important about Lewis's earlier writing, the tone of which is dour in general and dismissive of religion in particular. In it Lewis tries to make sense of the war's destruction and his own loss and confusion. He bitterly attacks the idea of God, finding what solace he can in a mystical appreciation of beauty.

> Come let us curse our Master ere we die,
> For all our hopes in endless ruin lie.

The good is dead. Let us curse God most High.
Four thousand years of toil and hope and thought
Wherein man laboured upward and still wrought
New worlds and better, Thou hast made as naught.

If there was a God, he was insensitive to human needs and aspirations.
Was it not better to turn squarely to human beings for hope and joy?

Yet I will not bow down to thee nor love thee,
For looking in my own heart I can prove thee,
And know this frail, bruised being is above thee.
Our love, our hope, our thirsting for the right,
Our mercy and long seeking of the light,
Shall we change these for thy relentless might?
Laugh then and slay. Shatter all things of worth,
Heap torment still on torment for thy mirth—
Thou art not Lord while there are Men on earth.

Sometimes Lewis was angry at God for shattering the earth and "all
things of worth." At other times he was angry at God for not existing.

But over time Lewis's perspective changed. The change began before he entered the war, in 1916, when on a train platform in Leather-
head, England, he picked up a copy of MacDonald's *Phantastes,* a book
that opened doorways in his imagination. Lewis had always enjoyed
fairy tales and myths; they gave him an imaginative thrill and an exciting feeling of yearning, though as a younger person he dismissed this
feeling as mostly valueless. When Lewis read *Phantastes,* however, he
began to change his mind. A "bright shadow" rested on the travels of
Phantastes's Anodos, Lewis wrote, an illumination that lit up the story's
woods and cottages and radiated outward from there. Lewis had an experience of seeing this brightness actually come out of the book and
into the quiet room in which he read. It used to be, he wrote once, that
literary enchantments of otherworlds "left the common world momentarily a desert," but when reading *Phantastes,* he said, he perceived something else. "I saw the bright shadow coming out of the book into the
real world and resting there, transforming all common things and yet
itself unchanged. Or, more accurately, I saw the common things drawn
into the bright shadow." There was something about the way the book

created passageways between spiritual and material worlds, fairy tale and reality. "That night my imagination was, in a certain sense, baptized," Lewis wrote in a remarkable passage in *Surprised by Joy;* "the rest of me, not unnaturally, took longer. I had not the faintest notion what I had let myself in for by buying *Phantastes*."[23] In a different passage he reflected on this "baptism" of the imagination, using a metaphor drawn from the displacements of the war. It was "as if I were carried sleeping across the frontier, or as if I had died in the old country and could never remember how I came alive in the new."[24] Though he did not become a Christian until 1931, *Phantastes* opened a doorway into a new imaginative country. In time Lewis would create his own fictional doorways for skeptics and doubters.

Lewis was one of many scholars in the interwar period drawn to Christianity because of literary interests. The celebrity author Evelyn Waugh surprised England in 1930 when he announced he had converted to Catholicism. This was front-page news in one of Britain's leading newspapers, the *Daily Express,* whose columns during the succeeding week were filled with reflections on why this modern writer had turned to a premodern faith. Waugh wasn't alone. G. K. Chesterton and Graham Greene converted to Catholicism in 1922 and 1926. T. S. Eliot, whose conversion surprised almost as many as Waugh's, embraced Anglicanism in 1927. Greene, Waugh, and others criticized modern writers for losing sight of God, arguing that secular authors were less able to develop realistic, complex characters. Good stories and layered characters, they thought, depended on religious sensibilities. When Lewis converted he borrowed these ideas, arguing that Modernist writers such as George Bernard Shaw and H. G. Wells, to whom he was much indebted, seemed "a little thin"—unable, he believed, to represent in their work "the roughness and density of life."[25] Christian writers such as Lewis came to believe that theism offered a richer and more layered vision of human life, a more critical sense for its complexity and ambiguity, and a more robust hope for its eventual development in story, myth, and real life.

Lewis's development from atheism to theism and then to Christianity did not happen in one, dramatic moment; it was a slow process abetted by encounters with philosophical idealists, especially the Irish philosopher George Berkeley, the Cambridge Platonists, and the British idealist philosopher F. H. Bradley. He once planned a doctoral thesis on the seventeenth-century Cambridge Platonist Henry More, a Christian philosopher who tried to prove the existence of an immaterial substance and who speculated about the existence of a fourth (spiritual) dimension to reality. Early in Lewis's scholarly career he published books that analyzed, among other things, the influence of Plato and Neo-Platonism in Medieval and Renaissance literature. He was therefore quite familiar with the long tradition of Platonized Christianity, and as he warmed to theism he gradually embraced and reworked selected elements of this tradition.

When we examine Lewis's postconversion writings, including his fantasy novels, it is easy to see how important this tradition was as he developed a worldview that juxtaposed matter and spirit, light and shadow, higher and lower layers. In the Narnia books metaphors of light and shadow, and higher and lower worlds, structure the action, and characters sometimes even refer specifically to Plato, as, for example, at the end of the last book in the series, *The Last Battle*. After the Narnia world ends in a magical shower of falling stars, Professor Digory Kirke looks around at a strange landscape, a new, brighter, and more intensely beautiful Narnia. He explains higher and lower worlds using tropes drawn from Plato and the Bible:

> "Of course it is different; as different as a real thing is from a shadow or as waking life is from a dream." His voice stirred everyone like a trumpet as he spoke these words: but when he added under his breath "It's all in Plato, all in Plato: bless me, what do they teach them at these schools!" the older ones laughed.

Then the narrator explains the difference between the old Narnia and this new place, using language drawn unmistakably from the earlier fairy tales of Carroll, MacDonald, and others.

> You may have been in a room in which there was a window that looked out on a lovely bay of the sea or a green valley that wound away among mountains. And in the wall of that room opposite to the window there may have been a mirror. And as you turned away from the window you suddenly caught sight of that sea or that valley, all over again, in the looking glass. And the sea in the mirror,

or the valley in the mirror, were in one sense just the same as the real ones: yet at the same time they were somehow different—deeper, more wonderful, more like places in a story: in a story you have never heard but very much want to know.[26]

Why is the mirror image deeper and more wonderful than the real thing? The mirror's framed image was more like a place in a story one had never encountered, an opening to an alternate world that made one understand better the depth and layers of the familiar world. This is one example of how Lewis uses windows and mirrors to raise questions relevant to his inchoate Platonic worldview: What was the nature of our world, a place he and his friend Tolkien called "the shadowlands," and what was its relation to the unchanging reality above the shadows?

Lewis on Higher Dimensions and Spiritual Worlds

Though Lewis's interests in higher space ideas have remained underappreciated, he did in fact study Abbott's *Flatland* and Hinton's books and he used their ideas to develop views of nature as layered and multidimensional.[27] The earliest evidence we have of Lewis's encounter with higher dimensions comes from a 1922 entry in his diary—he was twenty-four—where he pondered questions related to two-, three-, and four-dimensional objects. At some point Lewis annotated and underlined copies of *Flatland* and Hinton's *New Era of Thought*. At different times he spoke of *Flatland* in particular as a modern classic—"the original manuscript of the *Iliad*," he once proclaimed, "could not be more precious."[28]

He used dimensional ideas to argue that nature was open and layered rather than closed and determined. In *On Miracles,* for instance, he used dimensional ideas to argue that nature was "perforated" and "pock-marked" rather than closed, as logical positivists and scientific materialists insisted. Like Abbott and other theists, Lewis knew that in order to persuade others about the existence of a higher, spiritual realm (not to mention miraculous incursions from that realm) he would have to advocate for a universe that was open-ended. He did this in *On Miracles* by borrowing ideas from physicists who had shown recently that subatomic particles moved in irregular ways according to laws that were probabilistic rather than deterministic. Subatomic particles appeared to have an unexpected degree of freedom. Given this fact, Lewis continued, what would happen to the older positivism that insisted that "nature has no doors, and no reality outside herself for doors to open on"? If there was a "Subnatural" world that was different, could there be other openings or layers in nature? "It is indeed from this Subnatural that all events and all 'bodies' are, as it were, fed into her. And clearly if she thus has a back door opening on the Subnatural, it is quite on the cards that she may also have a front door opening on the Supernatural—and events might be fed into her at that door too."[29] This was what miracles were: moments when God inserted something extra into nature. "The divine art of miracle is not an art of suspending the pattern to which events conform," Lewis wrote elsewhere, "but of feeding new events into that pattern."[30] Lewis also argued that physicists themselves suggested the existence of separate dimensions—"to explain even an atom Schrodinger wants seven dimensions," he wrote—not to mention the free and independent movements of human consciousness, which Arthur Eddington was just then writing about so persuasively.[31] "There may be Natures piled upon Natures," Lewis suggested, "each supernatural to the one beneath it, before we come to the abyss of pure spirit; and to be in that abyss, at the right hand of the Father, may not mean being absent from any of these Natures—may mean a yet more dynamic presence on all levels."[32]

But if Lewis used dimensional ideas to suggest that there were "Natures piled upon Natures" he also relied on dimensional notions for reasonable explanations for Christian doctrines such as the Trinity and the Resurrection. In BBC radio talks eventually collected into his *Mere Christianity,* for example, Lewis contextualized the Trinity in a broader discussion of space in which he argued that the Trinity *was a kind of higher cube.*

> On the human level one person is one being, and any two persons are two separate beings—just as, in two dimensions (say on a flat sheet of paper) one square is one figure, and any two squares are two separate figures. On the Divine level you still find personalities; but up there you find them combined in new ways which we who do not live on that level, cannot imagine. In God's dimension, so to

speak, you find a being who is three Persons while remaining one Being, just as a cube is six squares while remaining one cube. Of course, we cannot fully conceive a Being like that: just as, if we were so made that we perceived only two dimensions in space we could never properly imagine a cube. But we can get a sort of faint notion of it. And when we do, we are then, for the first time in our lives, getting some positive idea, however faint of something super-personal—something more than a person.[33]

There is much here reminiscent of Abbott, Hinton, and Claude Bragdon—a flat world, a higher world of cubes, the difficulty of visualizing higher-dimensional objects, and the notion that there was something "super-personal" at higher levels.

Lewis used higher-dimensional cubes to make sense of the Trinity in different lectures and books. In *Christian Reflections,* for example, he reminded readers that God was not a person but a single entity who, paradoxically, comprised three persons. "In that sense [Christian theology] believes Him to be something very different from a person, just as a cube, in which six squares are consistent with unity of the body, is different from a square." Residents of a lower-dimensional Flatland, however, Lewis continued, "attempting to imagine a cube, would either imagine the six squares coinciding, and thus destroy their distinctness, or else imagine them set out side by side and thus destroy the unity. Our difficulties about the Trinity are much of the same kind."[34] Three-dimensional cubes lose their wholeness and integrity when they pass through a two-dimensional mind, appearing only as shifting, flat cross-sections. In the same way, the triune Godhead looks like three separate entities when understood from our lower-dimensional perspective.

That earthly entities were combined into one thing at higher levels was a hyperspace idea that Lewis also used to insist that, as the Bible says, all of us together "die in Adam and rise in Christ." Viewing humanity from a higher angle reveals that all of us, past and present, are part of one, encompassing phenomenon. "That we can die 'in' Adam and live 'in' Christ seems to me to imply that man, as he really is, differs a good deal from man as our categories of thought and our three-dimensional imaginations represent him; that the separateness . . . which we discern between individuals, is balanced, in absolute reality, by some kind of 'inter-inanimation' of which we have no conception at all. It may be that the acts and sufferings of great archetypal individuals such as Adam and Christ are ours, not by legal fiction, metaphor, or causality, but in some much deeper fashion." We might have to admit, Lewis wrote, that each individual, "though distinct, is really present in all, or in some, others—just as we may have to admit 'action at a distance' into our conception of matter."[35] Reviewing Lewis's ideas, the Anglican theologian Norman Pittenger took offense at Lewis's deployment of a geometric theology. "I do not understand what is vulgar or offensive, in speaking of the Holy Trinity," Lewis responded to Pittenger, "to illustrate from plane and solid geometry the conception that what is self-contradictory on one level may be consistent on another. I could have understood the Doctor's being shocked if I had compared God to an unjust judge or Christ to a thief in the night; but mathematical objects seem to me as free from sordid associations as any the mind can entertain."[36]

Higher-dimensional ideas had helped Abbott reimagine how God came to a lower-dimensional earth in the Incarnation; they now helped Lewis conceptualize how Christ returned to a higher-dimensional heaven during the Resurrection and Ascension. Explaining the Resurrection at a Socratic Club meeting at Oxford in 1945, for example, he spoke in terms of spaces and dimensions. "[Jesus] apparently passed into some spatial relationship with a new universe. The senses of His new body were responsive to multidimensional space and to a time that was not unilinear." The resurrected Christ had realized a higher-dimensional body, a "new nature," that was "interlocked with the old," a body that was somehow both supernatural and natural. As such, the resurrected Christ confounded his disciples with an enigma: How could one be both body and spirit, higher and lower, at the same time? The answer, Lewis supposed, was that Christ's resurrected body pointed to a universe that was more "like a skyscraper with several floors." "God could create more systems than one," he said, reiterating points he had made in other settings, "and there might be natures piled upon natures."[37]

The same issues are in play in Lewis's explanation of Christ's Ascension to heaven, a case in which "a being still in some mode, though not our mode, corporeal, withdrew at His own will from the Nature presented by our three dimensions and five senses, not necessarily into the non-sensuous and unidimensional, but into, or through, a world or worlds of super-sense and super space." What might this process look like? Fleeting shadows? Rotating cross-sections? What might the disciples have seen? "If they say they saw a momentary movement along the vertical plane—then an indistinct mass—then nothing—who is to pronounce this improbable?"[38] It was just like the Square's visions of the Sphere's miraculous two-dimensional incarnations. But not everyone thought the rational languages of geometry and spacetime were appropriate in these contexts. Was the phenomenon of Christ merely natural? When one critic objected that Lewis had given God an "almost spatial transcendence," Lewis hit back—that indeed was the direction of his thought, he said, and he was not much worried about it.[39]

Lewis's most detailed exposition of higher-dimensional ideas came in a subtle address entitled "Transposition" given at Mansfield College, Oxford, in 1944 and later published in *The Weight of Glory and Other Addresses* (1949). In this sermon, he gave different examples of how a lower, material world could be nested in a higher, more complex order of reality. Our emotional life, he argued, for instance, was more complex and varied than our bodily sensations, which had a restricted range of operation. For instance, sadness and joy, two very different emotions, looked similar when "transposed" into the lower, less subtle realm of bodily sensations. Both of them produced tears. In the same way, emotions of fright, dread, nervousness, or joy could all produce an upset stomach. There were many examples of higher-order phenomena being expressed in lower, less complex registers. An orchestral score might be transposed into a less complex composition for solo piano; a three-dimensional cube could be rendered on paper as a two-dimensional drawing; a feeling of love could be transposed into a desire for sex. In each case the higher register is richer and more varied and subtle. Many skeptics, Lewis preached, believed that religious intuitions and experiences, which were higher-order things, were merely lower-order things— they were "merely" neurons misfiring in the brain, merely projections of psychological needs or desires. But Lewis argued that this way of understanding religion was a mistake made by people who knew only the lower register. "The brutal man never can by analysis find anything but lust in love; the Flatlander never can find anything but flat shapes in a picture; physiology never can find anything in thought except twitching of the grey matter. It is no good browbeating the critic who approaches a Transposition from below. On the evidence available to him his conclusion is the only one possible."[40] Skeptics produced perfectly reasonable explanations of higher-order religious phenomena, but they were missing something.

Lewis had a very particular way of talking about the relationship between higher and lower levels. He spoke of this relationship not as symbolic but as "sacramental." Symbols (such as words on a page) represented sounds, though they did so without actually resembling these sounds or being continuous with them. But the relationship between higher and lower transpositions was more like the relationship between a two-dimensional picture and the three-dimensional world it represented. "Pictures are part of the visible world themselves and represent it only by being part of it," Lewis argued. "Their visibility has the same source as it. The suns and lamps in pictures seem to shine only because real suns or lamps shine on them: that is, they seem to shine a great deal because they really shine a little in reflecting their archetypes." (Lewis used the same logic to call attention to the ways that human beings participate in the divine in an oft-quoted passage from *The Four Loves*—"We are mirrors whose brightness, if we are bright, is wholly derived from the sun that shines upon us.")

The point was that lower, less complex objects *point to higher objects not merely as signs of them; they do so because in the lower register "the thing signified is really in a certain mode present."* Lewis thus called the relationship between higher and lower transpositions "sacramental." The case of higher emotions and lower, embodied sensations is similar, for in this case the "very same sensation does not merely accompany, nor merely signify, diverse and opposite emotions, but becomes part of them. The emotion descends bodily, as it were, into the sensation and digests, transforms, transubstantiates it, so that the same thrill along the nerves *is* delight or *is* agony." The lower reality was drawn into the higher, and the higher reality participated in the lower.[41]

If there was a higher-dimensional world above our everyday world, how might people catch a glimpse of it? Lewis approached this issue by turning back to the example of a cube. How was it possible to understand (or see) that a two-dimensional drawing of a cube represented something that actually was quite different, a real three-dimensional object? Lewis argued that in order to know that a flat representation of a cube was really a three-dimensional cube *one needed first to know what an actual three-dimensional cube looked like.* One had to have some experience of the higher object in order to understand the full significance of its representations in the lower world. To feel the full power and significance of a landscape painting one needed to have seen and experienced a real natural landscape. When one was familiar with the higher register of things, one might understand better the phenomenon's complexity when represented in the lower register. It was the same with an orchestral piece that had been transposed and simplified for piano. "The piano version means one thing to the musician who knows the original orchestral score and another thing to the man who hears it simply as a piano piece. But the second man would be at an even greater disadvantage if he had never heard any instrument but a piano and even doubted the existence of other instruments."[42] Lewis completed his examples with a brief dialogue with a Flatlander who struggles to accept the existence of higher, three-dimensional objects.

> But when we pointed to the lines on the paper and tried to explain, say, that "This is a road," would he not reply that the shape which we were asking him to accept as a revelation of our mysterious other world was the very same shape which, on our own showing, elsewhere meant nothing but a triangle? And soon, I think, he would say, "You keep on telling me of this other world and its unimaginable shapes which you call solid. But isn't it very suspicious that all the shapes which you offer me as images or reflections of the solid ones turn out on inspection to be simply the old two-dimensional shapes of my own world as I have always known it? Is it not obvious that your vaunted other world . . . is a dream which borrows all its elements from this one?"[43]

When Flatlanders attempted to explain higher-dimensional shapes these shapes seemed merely flat shapes from a familiar lower world; when love is explained it might seem to be merely lust; when religious intuitions are explained they might appear to be only everyday intuitions or wishes. Lewis wanted people to entertain the possibility that there were higher forms of meaning and significance—and that these things could be glimpsed in our lower world, just as someone viewing a beautiful painting understood it not to be a flat mixture of colors but as something (sacramentally) connected to a larger, more beautiful world.

There was a problem, however: If people needed to be acquainted with higher realities in order to understand the significance of life in the lower world, how would people get this knowledge of higher things? How might one get a glimpse of the higher, larger, richer, and more imaginative context in which human life was embedded?

Narnian Openings and Otherworldly Portals

Lewis found answers to these questions by reflecting on his own experiences. When he had read *Phantastes,* he had experienced a joyful longing for another world of greater light, wisdom, and freedom. He pondered this feeling of longing and it became a key element in his thought. He referred to it with the German word for *yearning for* or *missing something—Sehnsucht.* (In this case, as in so many others, Lewis was indebted to Plato, who believed that souls naturally longed for the world of ideal Forms.) Lewis came to believe that everyone had this longing and that its existence pointed to the existence of an actual otherworld. "Creatures are not born with desires unless satisfaction for those desires exists. A baby feels hunger: well, there is such a thing as food. A duckling wants to swim: well, there is such a thing as water. Men feel sexual desire: well, there is such a thing as sex. If I find in myself a desire which no experience in this world can satisfy, the most probable explanation is that I was made for another world."

This yearning was deep and persistent, and it could be nourished, as it had been for Lewis, in imaginative reading. "I must keep alive in myself the desire for my true country, which I shall not find till after death; I must never let it get snowed under or turned aside; I must make it the main object of life to press on to that country and to help others to do the same."[44] Lewis set out to do this with his fantasies and fairy tales. He would create worlds that aroused and sustained the desire for that other world. "Fairy land arouses a longing [in the child] for he knows not what. It stirs and troubles him (to his lifelong enrichment) with the dim sense of something beyond his reach and, far from dulling or emptying the actual world, gives it a new dimension of depth. He does not despise real woods because he has read of enchanted woods; the reading makes all real woods a little enchanted."[45] In other words, imaginative stories were not ways of escaping reality; they were ways of training the self to see the deeper, spiritual context of the world around us. Imaginative fiction, when done properly, acquainted people with the true, higher dimensions of our lives and thus made possible an enchanted way of seeing the familiar world.

After his conversion Lewis created fictional otherworlds and doorways through which characters (and readers) could travel into them. Characters traveled to otherworlds through doorways in the sky, technologies such as the "chronoscope" in *The Dark Tower,* mysterious openings in interior walls, framed pictures, odd attic doors, pools of water, and, of course, books. In the last Narnia book, for example, *The Last Battle,* where Lewis reveals that Narnia is embedded in a higher, heavenly world—a new Narnia—the narrator explains the difference between the old Narnia and the new by talking about openings and windows. The old Narnia was like a room with a window opening to the new Narnia, a room that also had a mirror stationed on an opposite interior wall. When one saw the sea or a valley reflected in that interior mirror there was a transposition of a wider, space into a smaller, three-dimensional cubical space. Two sacramentally related worlds thus came into focus: The old world was embedded in the new, while elements of the new, marvelous Narnia invaded the old as reflections and shadows. Suggesting that windows and mirrors helped us understand "the depth and extent of our spatial environment beyond the confines of the immediate container walls we find ourselves in," the literary scholar Hilary Dannenberg has showed how Lewis used windows and mirrors to help readers experience Narnia as dimensionally complex. They made it possible to imaginatively explore and move through Lewis's fictional world; and they allowed readers to understand how Narnia's characters saw through to external horizons, surveying the world beyond their container with a magical sense of elevation and transcendence, witnessing ever-larger contexts.[46]

Lewis also used doorways and openings to ask deeper questions about fantasy and reality. "When we suppose the world of daily life to be invaded by something other, we are subjecting either our conception of daily life, or our conception of that other, or both, to a new test. We put them together to see how they will react. If it succeeds we shall come to think, and feel, and imagine more accurately, more richly, more attentively, either about the world which is invaded or about that which invades it, or about both."[47]

Alert to new experiences and armed with awe and wonder, the Pevensie children showed us what it meant to ponder the real. When, for example, Lucy first entered Narnia and had tea with Tumnus, the books on Tumnus's bookshelves, which included titles such as *Is Man a Myth?*, revealed something astonishing: that human beings like Lucy were figures in Narnian myth and fairy tale. Which world was the real world, and which world was the longed-for fantasy? This reversal of fantasy and reality took place in other Lewis stories as well. When Prince Caspian heard the earth was round he was stunned because "we have fairy tales in which there are round worlds and I always loved them. I never believed there were any real ones. But I've always wished there were and I've always longed to live in one." Why could humans get into Narnia, Caspian complained, while Narnians could not get into the human world? How exciting it must be, he thought, to live on a round object like earth—"Have you ever been to the parts where people walk upside-down?"[48] Lewis projected onto Caspian his "inconsolable longing" for a mythical world. Caspian attempted to satisfy this longing by glimpsing another world's shadows in fables, fairy tales, and, in this case, the "real" children visitors from earth. When Lewis reversed fantasy and reality in this way he invited readers to think about their own world as a shadow of some other, more real, place.

The wardrobe, of course, is Lewis's most famous dimensional doorway, one that makes possible repeated incursions of the fantastic and marvelous into everyday human life. If we agree with Dannenberg that rooms created in literature seem real when things outside of them become visible through portals, we might say that the wardrobe is what makes both earth and Narnia seem real. It is the opening that makes the contained spaces appear like real spaces. In *The Lion, the Witch and the Wardrobe*, Lucy ventured into Narnia through a wardrobe in a spare room in Professor Digory's home, and Lewis wrote in detail about the experience. Lucy stood among the hanging coats in the dark, moving slowly to the back wall, which she could not immediately find. Surprised at the wardrobe's swelling size, she continued to reach for the back wall until she felt something crunch under her feet. Were they mothballs? Reaching down, she felt something cold and soft: snow. The coats receded behind her as she collided with tree branches. It was a winter night in a snowy woodland. Then Lewis turned Lucy around, and she saw on an axis straight through two worlds. "She looked back over her shoulder, and there, between the dark tree-trunks, she could still see the open doorway of the wardrobe and even catch a glimpse of the empty room from which she had set out." On the other side nothing had changed: it was an empty room in the daytime. The visual juxtaposition of the two spaces is the first indication that reality contained open doorways that children in particular might move through.

The space of the wardrobe was a hybrid space, a borderland composed of elements that were natural and supernatural, real and fantastic. It was, therefore, to use Lewis's lexicon, a place where "ideal experiments" took place. In *The Magician's Nephew*, a prequel to *The Lion, the Witch and the Wardrobe*, we learn that the wardrobe was created from otherworldly raw materials. In that narrative, Digory Kirke (later "Professor Kirke") entered another world where Aslan had sent him to find a magic apple that conferred immortality. He was to plant this apple in Narnia, though along the way he was tempted to eat it himself or collect an additional one to deliver to his ailing mother. But Digory did as he was told, delivering the apple to Narnia and planting it. Aslan said that the tree that grew there would repel the wicked witch for centuries. From this new apple tree, Digory (now with Aslan's permission) then took an apple to heal his mother in London, and afterward he planted the core in the backyard of the home of his aunt and uncle. That tree grew and years later, after being toppled by a storm, was made into the wardrobe. So while the wardrobe was earthly furniture it also was consubstantial with the Narnian woods that Lucy entered through it. Both earthly and Narnian, the wardrobe shows how the different worlds of Lewis's *Chronicles* are sacramentally mingled together. It is no wonder, then, that in *The Lion, the Witch and the Wardrobe*, when Lucy's siblings thought she was either lying or a lunatic, Professor Digory Kirke was not surprised to hear that there was a passageway through that wardrobe into somewhere else.

The imaginary worlds of these books are not contiguous in three-dimensional space but are separate realities. Lewis's way of talking about them is not dissimilar to how he discusses levels and dimensions in *On Miracles*, "Transposition," and other lectures. In *The Magician's*

Nephew, for instance, Uncle Andrew explains how otherworlds work. "I don't mean another planet, you know; they're part of our world and you could get to them if you went far enough—but a really Other World— another Nature—another universe—somewhere you would never reach even if you travelled through the space of this universe for ever and ever—a world that could be reached only by Magic."[49] In Narnia, as on earth, there were, as Lewis said in his lectures on miracles, "Natures piled upon Natures." Perhaps there existed "Natures piled upon Natures, each supernatural to the one beneath it, before we come to the abyss of pure spirit; and to be in that abyss, at the right hand of the Father, may not mean being absent from any of these Natures—may mean a yet more dynamic presence on all levels."[50]

This is precisely the experience of the English children at the end of the last book in the Chronicles, *The Last Battle.* In *The Last Battle,* a deceptive Narnian ape named Shift convinced others that he spoke for Aslan. Many followed Shift until King Tirian and his force, which included the English children, took a stand against him. The story ended with an apocalyptic battle on a hill near a stable, which was followed by a final moment of judgment. The final judgment took place next to a "rough wooden door" with a frame but no walls that suddenly appeared on the landscape—another doorway to something else. Aslan appeared and all people living and dead gathered outside the door to be judged; those loyal to him or to Narnian morality joined him in Aslan's country, the "new" Narnia on the other side of the doorway, while others disappeared into Aslan's shadow or became regular animals. Then the world was consumed by a flood, mountains crumbled and the sun was extinguished, and Narnia froze and died. Peter closed the frozen door and locked it, and they all journeyed together "further up and further in" into the Real Narnia, which appeared brighter and more wonderful as they went—far brighter than the "shadowland" that was the old Narnia. As they went farther in and up, Real Narnia became larger and larger, eventually encompassing earth and all other worlds. This was the high point at the top of those "Natures piled upon Natures," the place that drew all other places in to form a single world of "pure spirit."[51] Here the nested worlds of the Narnian multiverse were brought into clear focus: There were Narnias within Narnias, worlds within worlds, and when one ascended through them the older, lower worlds came into focus as merely flat shadowlands.

ᖆᕧᕧᖆ

In the end, MacDonald, Lewis, and other Christian fantasists achieved something quite extraordinary: the revival of the Christian imagination in disenchanted modernity. They believed that their stories would help themselves and others recover an imaginative sense for the supernatural—and they were right. Though few have noticed or commented on this, the fact is that Lewis's fantastic Christian parables and Tolkien's Christian-inspired mythological worlds, together with the fantastic otherworlds shaped by others such as Elizabeth Nesbit, Charles Williams, and Madeleine L'Engle, have come to overshadow both theology and traditional church practice as sources of Christian thought and belief. "Theologians today exercise almost zero public influence," the Anglican theologian John Milbank has written, and yet "through the medium of children's literature and fantasy literature generally, a public theological debate of a kind continues to be conducted." A number of Christian writers, Milbank continued, have "re-presented" Christianity in a new fantastic mode, a process that has sustained the Christian vision in modernity.[52] (When one considers how widely read Lewis's fictional narratives and apologetic writings are, for instance, the point is established even more powerfully. Has there been a more influential Christian writer in the last century?) In any case, there is little doubt that these religious writers have made Christian notions plausible and appealing again by deploying them in fictional narratives about other worlds, dimensions, and levels of existence.

As popular as these new fantastic narratives have been, however, some readers have seen them as twisted and distorted by certain illusions and prejudices. Though they made fantastic, extraordinary, magical, or supernatural things seem possible again in the disenchanted West, and though of all ways of grasping basic religious truths (including studying texts and practicing prayer) this literary form of Christian self-formation was the most appealing—though all of these things were true, many readers, especially female readers, turned away from these narratives when they saw that they reinscribed older ways of thinking about women and gender, and when they perceived as a result that this literary recovery of the divine was also a recovery of narratives that denied them both a full humanity and a share in divinity. "What is disturbing in the Narnian Chronicles, as well as in the whole range of Lewis's literary corpus," Kath Filmer has written, "is the way in which ultimate good is depicted as ultimate masculinity, while evil, the corruption of good, is depicted as femininity."[53] Those who loved and were indebted to Christian fantasy writers but were affronted by these facts would respond in a way that demonstrated both dissatisfaction with earlier authors and a robust confidence that stories, when done properly, opened new doorways to a more complete life. They set out to create their own mythical narratives.

8

Madeleine L'Engle Disturbs the Universe

The fantastic fictional worlds of George MacDonald and C. S. Lewis have become sources of religious consolation and imaginative insight for millions of readers, but as this literature became an established orthodoxy, like all orthodoxies it inspired a band of critics and reformers, including women who believed that these mythopoetic stories had sidelined or maligned them. They set out to write new stories that opened up possibilities for girls and women.

Take, for instance, the life of the American writer Madeleine L'Engle, who said she learned what to believe and how to act neither from her parents, who were largely absent, nor from church, which she avoided, but from books by MacDonald, Lewis, and other Christian fantasists. Her parents had been married for two decades before her birth in 1918 in New York City, and, as she herself has written, though she was a "wanted baby," the pattern of her parents' lives "was already well established and a child was not part of that pattern."[1] On weekdays she ate dinner alone in her room, with "my feet on the desk and a book on my chest and was completely happy." Ensconced in fictional worlds, she felt the "fairy tales and fantasies which made up the mythic world . . . was for me the real world." On Sundays, when she ate with her parents, they had little to say to each other. One of her favorite writers was MacDonald, who taught her that Christian truths were most effectively rendered not in tight theological arguments but in imaginative stories. His mythical worlds comforted me, she wrote, giving me "solid ground under my feet, a place where I could stand in a world which was confusing and dangerous and unfriendly." A misfit at school and a loner at home, L'Engle had to navigate the confusing and dangerous turns of adolescence by reading about other children such as the Pevensies and studying how they lived. When she was seventeen, her father, whom she idolized, died, and MacDonald became an imagined substitute.[2] "There is something about George MacDonald that brings up an image of easy comfort, of a world where everything is going to be beautiful as long as we are loving, of a kindly God who never chastises the beloved children."[3] The triumphal power of love, and the pain of its absence, anchored her worldview and animated her stories, including *A Wrinkle in Time,* which was, tellingly, about a girl's love for an absent father. The protagonist of the story, Meg, would travel through higher dimensions to find him.

Though L'Engle used scientific concepts more than Lewis or MacDonald, her stories, like theirs, helped readers imagine enchanted openings and doorways in the world. "Any story, whether myth, fantasy, fairy tale, or science fiction," L'Engle wrote, "explores and moves beyond daily concerns to wonder. A story, instead of taking a child away from real life, prepares him to live in real life with courage and expectancy." Though, according to L'Engle, children were better at imaginatively entering into these stories, everyone could become aware that our "daily time-bound world of fact is the secondary world, and that literature, art and music . . . give us glimpses of the wider world of our whole self."[4] Fictional stories might help modern people overcome their skepticism and their wariness toward tradition, creating what L'Engle called, following Samuel Taylor Coleridge, a "willing suspension of disbelief." The children in L'Engle's stories, like the Pevensies in Lewis's Narnia, are clearly quite good at doing this. Adults could also become proficient but it required immersion in stories. As one character says in L'Engle's *A Wind in the Door,* "believing takes practice."[5]

But the lesson of modern Christian fantasy and sci-fi is not just that belief takes practice but that objects of belief have to be made believable again for new generations. This was central to the literary work of many of the authors already examined. To make older stories into appealing mythologies these stories did not merely have to reveal a world that was open to deeper meaning and significance; these stories also had to make sense of urgent contemporary questions. Part of doing this, as we have seen, involved integrating older magical and mythological narratives with modern scientific concepts. L'Engle was involved in this project as well.

This however was not the only rethinking that took place or that needed to take place. For L'Engle, part of making older mythologies believable again involved reworking how girls and women were depicted in these stories. This was one way in which she (and other women of her time) departed quite dramatically from the projects of MacDonald and Lewis. In L'Engle's work, then, dimensional doorways and openings did not just open the way to new transcendent spaces that might liberate souls from a mechanized and secular world. They also opened up new ways of thinking about the social order and new possibilities in particular for women and girls, who in L'Engle's hands became prophetic and heroic and indeed central to the modern conception of ultimate things.

A Scientific Reenchantment

L'Engle graduated from Smith College in 1941 and then moved to New York City to begin a career as a theater actor and writer. She impressed others with her intense determination and powerful inner life. Even while acting, which involves the creation of its own kind of imaginal world, L'Engle was thinking about fantastic fictional characters, stories, and worlds. She wrote her first books backstage while waiting to perform. By the early 1950s she had left the city and was living with her husband and children in Goshen, Connecticut, where she found it difficult to conform to conventional expectations. The local minister, for example, asked her if she could teach in the church's Sunday school. But by this time, her curious mind had generated doubts about both the existence of God and the wisdom of Christian doctrine. "I explained to the minister that I didn't really believe in God, but I couldn't live as though I didn't believe in him. I found life intolerable without God, so I lived as though I believed in God. I asked him, 'Is that enough for you?'" To live "as though" one believes—this was religious faith as its own type of acting. But, as she told her minister, perhaps the performance of faith was enough.

Apparently it was, for she took the position—at least for a while. In time, however, she found church spiritually deadening and was particularly confounded by the theological books that friends, trying to help, loaned her. "I tried to read German theologians. I thought, if I have to believe the way they believe, I cannot be a Christian. I found them depressing." (She added that their works did, however, "help my insomnia."[6]) What about theology made her depressed and drowsy? Too many rationalistic formulas and tidy answers, all pronounced by male theologians.

From this time forward she found herself aligned against the male-dominated, rationalistic theology of her time and the stifling role of housewife. For much of her life she found going to church "an ordeal," she confessed to a friend in 1972, summarizing her religious situation. "I got impatient, I got angry, I got frustrated. I finally took to writing poetry during the service." Part of the problem was that church doctrines were hard to believe. "It is easier for me to believe in God than in Christ," she noted in the same letter, partly because the doctrines and miracle stories were hard to grasp and believe. She sensed that some type of God existed but believed that he might not be showing himself in the churches.[7] In other letters she communicated disappointment about the churches and other religious institutions. Religion, she wrote once to a fan, had become dangerous. Dictators, demagogues, damning priests, and politicians—all had used religion and religion had used them. "Hate," L'Engle continued, "is usually masked by 'religion.'" Finding God was important, but could he be found while sitting in church pews or pursuing conventional religious paths? "A great many people go to church with regularity because it's the safest place they can go to escape God," she continued. The church was too easy, its certainties loudly proclaimed but not deep or deeply affecting; its ways of talking and listening to God were comforting but not nuanced enough; its ideas were inflexible and rooted in the past rather than nimble and relevant to our time; its god was too small, its world too closed. "I don't wear lace scarves, like your grandmother, and my communion with God is stormy."[8] She did not say it in this letter, but she did in other places—she was descended, she said, referring to ancestors who were suffragists and troublemakers, "from a long line of women who were universe disturbers."[9]

Like others formulating new, enchanted views that could be independent of church doctrines, L'Engle borrowed scientific concepts that were already disturbing the universe and our picture of it. She read Albert Einstein, Arthur Eddington, James Jeans, Edwin Abbott, and hyperspace philosophers such as C. Howard Hinton. Einstein, L'Engle said once, relocating religious inspiration and authority, was "my favorite theologian. Einstein was my entrance into the world of astrophysics and quantum mechanics; it's my theology. I was asking myself all the big questions about life and the universe and not finding the answers. Then I picked up a book of Einstein's and he said anyone who is not lost in rapture at the power of the mind behind the universe 'is as good as a burned out candle.'"[10] Scientists knew that good questions led to other good questions rather than to sealed-off systems with comforting formulas; their work led to "an open and not a closed universe."[11]

L'Engle began thinking more about God or some ultimate creative and providential force. What would it be like to believe in such a force or imagine it as real? To L'Engle, modern scientists affirmed "that there is pattern & reason in the universe," she wrote in a handwritten reflection. "What this meant to me is if there is pattern & reason in the universe then there is a power of creativity, of anti-chaos, behind this pattern & reason, & this power is responsible to his creation."[12] A caring God, a layered and vast universe, a providential meaning to life's events—these beliefs were not necessarily embraced by the scientists she read, but they were nevertheless the lessons she drew from them.[13] She came to embrace the view that her agnosticism was part of a wider problem, a lack of vision and imagination. "Jung says that we are a sick society because we have lost a valid myth to live by," she said once, summarizing her spiritual journey; "and in my small back room I was absorbing a mythic view of the universe, a universe created by a power of love far too great to be understood or explained by tenets or dogmas." It stretched my imagination "beyond literalism." "And the world widened."[14] It says something important that modern seekers such as L'Engle were being lit up not by the fires of evangelical revival but by fantastic, sometimes scientific, views of an extraordinary universe.

Agreeing with MacDonald and Lewis that ultimate questions were best understood through stories, myths, and fantasies, L'Engle in the late 1950s began writing narratives that integrated new scientific ideas and her own developing notions about spirit and divinity. In time she would come to see that her fiction was similar to the fiction of earlier Christian fantasists—that it could disclose spiritual meaning and purpose in the world.

When she wrote her classic, *A Wrinkle in Time,* it was a therapeutic way to work through her religious questions. But when the book was finally published in 1962, it was transformed into something much larger: it became a new religious mythos bringing religious insights to millions of readers, one that affirmed the universe's ultimate meaning and helped others think imaginatively about spiritual realities and other dimensions. The story follows the tribulations of an awkward teenager named Meg Murray, who lives with her scientist mother and three brothers, including Charles Wallace, a five-year-old with unique intellectual and psychic powers. (Meg's father, a government scientist, had mysteriously disappeared.) At the beginning of the story, Meg, Charles Wallace, and Meg's friend Calvin meet three older women, Mrs. Whatsit, Mrs. Who, and Mrs. Which, who reveal that they know the location of Mr. Murray and are ready to help retrieve him. These three "Mrs. Ws" turn out to have supernatural powers. They guide Meg, Charles Wallace, and Calvin to other worlds and dimensions in the universe via a process they call "tessering," until they find Mr. Murray, rescue him from an evil intelligence on the planet Camazotz, and return him to earth.

Meg's development as a character drives the plot. In order to triumph over the evil forces that have abducted her father, she has to learn to embrace her idiosyncrasies, trust herself, and accept that the ability to love another human being is a unique and potent force in the universe. Along the way, the Mrs. Ws offer Meg strategic advice and spiritual wisdom gathered from a variety of sources, including Jesus, Einstein, Euripides, and the Buddha. The mythology of Meg and her family continues in four other novels that fill out L'Engle's so-called Time Quintet. Though publishers repeatedly rejected the manuscript, when finally published by Knopf it became a stunning success, quickly making L'Engle famous. It eventually sold more than ten million copies.

A Wrinkle in Time

In L'Engle's books, alternate worlds and dimensional doorways between them function in the ways they did for Lewis: They make the spaces of these fictional worlds seem more realistic, allowing characters to explore ontological and metaphysical questions and discover the existence of a complex universe with many layers. In L'Engle's *Wrinkle in Time* (and more generally in her Time Quintet series), characters travel to different times and places, to outer spaces and inner microscopic landscapes, into Biblical stories, and even across two-dimensional flatland worlds.

L'Engle read a lot of math and science fiction, and when creating her own stories she drew on Abbott, Hinton, and other sci-fi-oriented authors. In the opening scene of *Wrinkle*, for instance, when Mrs. Whatsit first enters the Murray home at night, this odd visitor displays an uncanny knowledge of the place that is reminiscent of the Sphere's transcendent perspective on the Square's home in *Flatland*. When asked if she wanted anything to eat, Whatsit said she enjoyed Russian caviar, which prompted Charles Wallace to point out that Whatsit had just "peeked" into their closed pantry. The Russian caviar, Charles Wallace responded, was off limits, saved for their mother's birthday. (Seeing or reaching into higher-dimensional spaces was a common trope in science fiction magazines in the first half of the twentieth century, and in addition to knowing *Flatland*, L'Engle surely knew this sci-fi literature as well. For example, in Miles Breuer's "The Appendix and the Spectacles" [1928], doctors worked through a fourth dimension to probe into a man's body and remove his appendix—without making an incision. In several stories by the sci-fi writer Bob Olsen, including "The Four-Dimensional Roller-Press" [1927] and "Four Dimensional Robberies" [1928], characters used the fourth dimension to access hidden or enclosed items.) After Mrs. Whatsit saw into the closed spaces of the kitchen pantry but was denied the caviar, she settled for tuna salad. She ate her sandwich and prepared to leave, but not before suggesting that she had seen more than anyone suspected. She knew this home's other secrets, including the most disturbing one—that Mr. Murray, a physicist working on a top-secret project on interstellar travel and higher dimensions, had disappeared. On her way out, Mrs. Whatsit turned unexpectedly to

Mrs. Murray and spoke about her husband's scientific work. "By the way," she said, "there is such a thing as a *tesseract*."[15] The next morning, Meg asked her mother about Mrs. Whatsit's odd comment: What was a tesseract? Her mother changed the subject.

But Meg would soon find out about tesseracts, which in L'Engle's books become passageways between worlds. The word "tesseract," of course, was Hinton's term for a hypercube, and in many ways L'Engle continued in the tradition of Hinton enthusiasts deploying this mystical object in order to glimpse higher realities. In *Wrinkle,* Mr. Murray and other government scientists had studied tesseracts and had had some success in creating them. Mr. Murray had "tessered" through the universe, in fact, landing, unfortunately, on an evil planet where he was now imprisoned. When the Mrs. Ws began their search for Mr. Murray with Meg, Charles Wallace, and Calvin O'Keefe, they explained tessering to them as a folding or wrinkling of spacetime. Mrs. Who lifted the hem of her skirt and stretched it into a straight line. She told the children to imagine an ant traveling along the hem. It would take a long time to travel straight across, but imagine if the path itself could be folded and its two ends brought together? If this were the case, the ant could very quickly travel from one end to the other. Tessering, she said was folding the fabric of spacetime to create new, shorter paths between destinations. (See Figure 8.1.)

When Meg complained that she did not understand, Mrs. Whatsit said that Meg was thinking of space "only in three dimensions," and that tessering involved higher levels of spacetime. This led to a lengthy lesson on dimensionality that would have made Hinton proud, though L'Engle's presentation of the mathematical details was confused and erroneous at several points. One dimension could be represented with a line, two with a flat square, three with a cube, and four—well, Mrs. Whatsit said, it had "something to do with Einstein and time." (Time for L'Engle, as for others in this period, was the fourth dimension.) But it was possible to wrinkle this four-dimensional spacetime into a higher, unseen fifth dimension. In this formulation, tessering was "disturbing the universe" in a literal way: It bent and warped everything in new configurations.[16]

Responses to this dissertation on higher space were similar to responses to Hinton's writings: Some "saw" it and others did not. "I see!" Meg cried. "I got it! For just a moment I got it! I can't possibly explain it

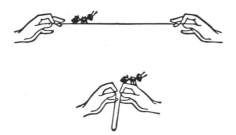

Figure 8.1   Mrs. Who explains "tessering." From Madeleine L'Engle, *Wrinkle in Time* (New York: Farrar, Straus and Giroux, 1962).

now, but there for a second I saw it!" The youngest in the group, the "genius" child who understood all intellectual things, Charles Wallace, understood the concept immediately. Calvin O'Keefe, however, was confused, admitting that he could not grasp the idea as Charles Wallace had. (After the explanation of tessering, Calvin responded in a way remarkably similar to a character in Bob Olsen's "Four Dimensional Robberies." In that short story one character complained that an explanation of the tesseract was "simple as mud." This is virtually the same reaction Calvin offered, saying the idea was as "clear as mud.")[17]

The children and the Mrs. Ws traveled to different places in search of Mr. Murray. They first tessered to the planet Uriel, where they, like the Pevensie children, landed in another world that was brilliantly illuminated. (It also was a different season, as it was in Narnia; they left during the fall and arrived in the spring.) Then they tessered again, this time veering off course into a two-dimensional world, in another moment reminiscent of the *Flatland* narrative. As they tessered into this flat world, Meg "felt a pressure she had never imagined, as though she were being completely flattened out by an enormous steam roller." She tried to breathe but "a paper doll can't gasp"; and she tried to think but her "flattened-out mind" was unable to function. Even her heart, trying to beat, made a "knifelike, sidewise movement" but had trouble expanding. The three Ws realized they had erred by taking the children into this world and quickly tessered to another planet. Dimensionally nimble, the three Ws could flatten and expand and had forgotten that earthly beings had other requirements—they had forgotten "how limiting protoplasm is." Finally they tessered to Camazotz, where Mr. Murray was imprisoned by a superior intelligence called IT, which had a kind of hypnotic hold on all of that planet's people and which threatened to entrance Meg, Charles Wallace, and Calvin. In the end, the smartest among them, Charles Wallace, fell victim to IT's hypnotic powers, while Meg remained in control because of her strong sense of individuality. She finally freed both Charles Wallace and her father by marshaling her sense of independence and ruminating on her deep emotional connection to them. Her emotions represented capacities that IT lacked, capacities that (it turned out) circumvented IT's mesmerizing grip.[18] The group tessered back to earth together.

In *Wrinkle,* tessering often led to unexpected difficulties. The Ws spoke of it as a "dematerializing," a dissolving of matter into some higher form and then a rematerializing of matter in its three-dimensional form. (When L'Engle explained this process to the Brown University geometer Thomas Banchoff, he was disappointed to find that, at least on this issue, L'Engle was using science in a magical way unfamiliar to him.)[19] All three Mrs. Ws had difficulty dematerializing and rematerializing at different points. Mrs. Which had the hardest time. She often appeared as a shimmering blur and spoke in fuzzy sentences—"Ddidd annybbodyy asskk yyou ttoo?" Mrs. Who also seemed to shimmer in a middle ground between matter and energy, at times floating above the ground and radiating a phosphorescent glow. She spoke in aphorisms or poetry borrowed from otherworldly authorities such as Shakespeare. Apparently, when one tessered, one traveled into a deeper, spiritual subspace. The Mrs. Ws were in touch with this deeper realm of truth, and the children, at least at the beginning of the story, were not. The Mrs. Ws showed them deeper truths as they tessered; they loaned them Mrs. Who's large, unusual glasses that allowed them to see through matter; they talked with aliens (such as those on the planet Ixchel, who lacked eyes) about seeing and knowing things. One of these aliens, called "Aunt Beast," paraphrased a Biblical verse on seeing and insight. "We look not at the things which are what you could call seen, but at the things which are not seen. For the things which are seen are temporal. But the things which are not seen are eternal."[20] Like other tales with alternate realities, *Wrinkle* made the universe's unseen worlds visible to readers.

Tesseracts and Other Doorways

L'Engle was not the only writer using tesseracts as doorways to other dimensions. In fact, beginning in Hinton's time, many fantasy and sci-fi writers used the tesseract as an opening to other places or times. The prolific ghost story and science fiction author Algernon Blackwood, a writer who, like L'Engle and Lewis, used fiction to develop new mythologies, used tesseracts in many stories. Blackwood created characters who shared his preoccupation with spiritual signs and portents. "My fundamental interest, I suppose," he wrote to a correspondent, "is signs and proofs of other powers that lie hidden in us all; the extension, in other words, of human faculty. So many of my stories, therefore, deal with extension of consciousness; speculative and imaginative treatment of possibilities outside our normal range of consciousness." Our consciousness can grow, Blackwood continued, echoing hyperspace philosophers, revealing "new, extra-ordinary powers etc., and the word 'supernatural' seems the best word for treating these in fiction. I believe it possible for our consciousness to change and grow, and that with this change we may become aware of a new universe."[21]

In Blackwood's "Victim of Higher Space" (1914), for instance, a Mr. Mudge studied the tesseract, memorized its configurations, and developed higher ways of seeing the underlying unity of all things. But one day he began accidentally slipping "bodily into the next world, the world of four dimensions, yet without knowing precisely how I got there, or how I could get back again."[22] It took Blackwood's hero physician, Dr. John Silence, to show Mudge how to close doors in his imagination, shut down the tesseract's portals, and remain on earth. In other stories, Blackwood combined older fairy-tale motifs, including mirrors, with newer dimensional notions, as in "The Pikestaffe Case" (1924), in which a mathematics professor studying Gauss, Minkowski, and Einstein disappeared into an antique mirror. (The story was made into a 1962 episode of the supernatural anthology TV series *Tales of Mystery*.)

Many other imaginative writers used the tesseract as a plot device, including the American horror fiction writer H. P. Lovecraft and the "dean of science fiction writers," Robert Heinlein. Heinlein, who used ideas from John Dunne, P. D. Ouspensky, and other hyperspace writers, wrote a story with a tesseract in "And He Built a Crooked House" (1941), in which a California architect built a house in the shape of an unfolded tesseract—until two earthquakes collapsed the structure, causing its windows and openings to connect to other temporal and spatial dimensions. Other writers used tesseracts to connect characters with alternate times or geographies. In Henry Kuttner and C. L. Moore's sci-fi classic "Mimsy Were the Borogroves" (1943), a scientist millions of years in the future tested his time machine by sending some of his son's toys into the past. One of the toys was a beaded wire puzzle in the shape of a tesseract. Back in the present, the American children Scott and Emma Paradine discovered one of the boxes and as they played with the toys in it their mathematical skills and mental powers developed in remarkable ways. At the end they discovered how to travel to the future and mysteriously disappeared. In William McGivern's "Doorway of Vanishing Men" (1941) an overworked store clerk transforms his store's revolving glass door into a tesseract in order to stem the tide of foot traffic past his desk. Customers walk through the doorway and disappear into the fourth dimension, until the clerk fixes the door and the missing customers reappear. Finally, in a story with notable similarities to L'Engle's *Wrinkle,* Mark Clifton's "Star, Bright" (1952), a precocious young girl studies Mobius strips, Klein bottles, and tesseracts and develops the ability to transport herself into the fourth dimension. Her astonished father exclaims—"The Moebius Strip, the Klein Bottle, the unnamed twisted cube—Einsteinian Physics. Yes, it was possible." In this story a father searches for his children; in *Wrinkle,* children search for their father. In both stories protagonists use the tesseract to travel. (Clifton's story was anthologized in a well-known book of math fiction and also aired on radio's "X minus 1" program in April 1956.)[23]

In more recent comic books, television, and films, tesseracts and "cosmic cubes" have been deployed as objects of incredible power. Stan Lee and Jack Kirby first used a "cosmic cube" not long after L'Engle published *Wrinkle,* in a 1966 issue of *Tales of Suspense* (#79). The cosmic cube was an object that could alter reality, control matter and energy, make wishes come true, transport beings into other dimensions, or even help them ascend unto godhood. Cosmic cubes were formed by creating a singularity or "grey hole," which generated enough force to open up a dimensional tunnel. Extra dimensional energies flowed into the

Figure 8.2 The American evangelist Billy Graham did not speak of tesseracts, but he did use the "5th Dimension" to talk about the spirit world. This 1964 book featured highlights from a film shown at Graham's pavilion at the 1964 World's Fair in New York City. The book and the film praised the marvelous work of scientists and pointed to new discourses that suggested realms beyond the limits of science, including amazing new discourses about higher dimensions.

rift in space and entered our familiar three-dimensional world, taking shape in a cube-shaped matrix. In Marvel films there are tesseracts that are similar to cosmic cubes. Tesseracts are featured, for example, in *Captain America: The First Avenger* and *The Avengers* and are discussed in *Iron Man 2* and *Thor: The Dark World.* The tesseract is a powerful cube that can be used as a weapon or deployed to open portals to other worlds. In *The Avengers,* for instance, scientists study a tesseract at a remote facility until one day it begins radiating energy and opens a wormhole. The wormhole allows an evil alien, Loki, to reach earth and steal the powerful tesseract. Eventually Loki uses it to open another wormhole over New York, and an alien army enters the city through it. (They are ultimately defeated, of course, by the Avengers.)

Finally, there is also the tesseract space in Christopher Nolan's film *Interstellar* (2014), which, like L'Engle's *Wrinkle*, features a girl searching for her father through a tesseract that connects them across vast distances. *Wrinkle*, Nolan once said, was "my introduction to the idea of higher dimensions, including the notion of a tesseract."[24]

Tessering and Gendered Spaces

If some used tesseracts as technologies that forged new pathways through outer space, others used them as objects that opened up new modes of liberation from the body and traditional ways of thinking about sex and gender. In fact, hyperspace thinkers going back to Hinton and Abbott talked about seeing the social order from a higher, critical point of view, and though it might be grandiose to call either of them *feminist*, there is no doubt that they recognized that contact with hyperspaces subverted inherited ways of thinking about men and women. Abbott's satirical book did not just make British ideas about gender look rigid and ridiculous, for instance; it also pronounced them deficient when considered from a transcendent perspective. Hinton, we might recall, took an experimental attitude toward sex and marriage in part because he believed that at higher levels of reality these conventional three-dimensional arrangements were superseded by a higher-dimensional oneness. For this reason, Hinton and later hyperspace writers spoke of how contact with higher spaces caused corporeal dissolution or inversion: Encountering hyperspaces disordered the human body. In Hinton's fictional "A Plane World," for instance, a harmonious heterosexual household was disturbed when a female right-oriented isosceles triangle learned how to access a higher dimension and was flipped into her mirror image—made, in other words, into a man.[25] (Hinton spoke of mirror-image isomers [stereoisomers], opposite electrical charges, and the mirror symmetry of the body as evidence that these natural phenomena had been rotated through a higher, fourth dimension.)

But Hinton was only the beginning. In science fiction from H. G. Wells to Robert Heinlein, protagonists have been anatomically reversed in higher-dimensional experiments and accidents of every variety. Bodies crashing through hyperspaces have had their internal organs reversed (Wells's "The Plattner Story"), hands stuck in dimensional contraptions have been transformed from right- to left-handed (*The 4D Man* [1959]), and even the eyesight of someone next to an infirm power plant saw things backward (Clarke, "Technical Error").[26] Still others have written about hyperspaces that changed human genitalia and sexual identity. Marcel Duchamp, who incorporated higher-dimensional notions in his art, demonstrated a long-standing interest in mirror images, gender, and sex. In several works, Duchamp experimented with the paradoxes and differences that mirror images produced, using these ideas, for example, when he deployed a rotated photographic negative of the sculpture *Female Fig Leaf* (1950) on the cover of *Le Surrealism, Meme* (1956).[27] Duchamp used the same type of mirror inversion in his *Objet-Dard* of 1951, a phallic sculpture produced by a vagina-like mold—something the French art historian and essayist Jean Clair called a representation of mirror-image genitalia. Human genitals were reversible, like right and left hands, or, more accurately, like when one turns a glove inside out, a fact to Clair that established that "the penis and vagina are a single organ, one and the same—an otherworldly organ." Our perception of them as different or opposite was merely the result of our limited three-dimensional vision.[28] Others aware of hyperspace speculations, including, for example, the American Modernist poet Hart Crane, used dimensional ideas to rethink sexual orientation. Experiencing a remarkable religious vision in a dentist's chair and trying to understand it by reading Ouspensky, Crane, buoyed with a new sense of the power of the poet's voice, developed poems that offered what one scholar has called a "queered *vision* of the world" that unsettled the lines between both matter and spirit on the one hand, and heterosexual and same-sex attraction on the other.[29]

If L'Engle was not necessarily thinking about genital inversion or homosexuality, she certainly was using the hyperspace tradition to explore ways of dissolving the body and troubling gender assumptions. When the Mrs. Ws tessered, for example, their bodies disappeared or became transparent, dematerializing into a space in between material reality and energetic spirit: Male and female bodies were destroyed in moments of hyperspatial transcendence. When Meg tessered she left behind the confusions of her teenage identity as well, abandoning prescribed roles and expectations, and growing eventually into a more complete person who did something that both her "genius" brother and her powerful physicist father could not: She defeated the forces of evil and the hypnotic alien intelligence called IT. For L'Engle, then, tessering was not just a plot device used to carry protagonists, aliens, or villains through space; it was an opening through which Meg could find a more complete, more androgynous self. When she signed copies of *Wrinkle,* L'Engle encouraged fans to make the same imaginative journey that both she and Meg had made, using a phrase that signaled new movement, liberation, and power—"Tesser with joy."[30]

Hardly Any Women

As indebted as L'Engle was to Lewis, there is no question that she also wanted to reverse the gendered logic of his fantastic mythological imagination. Regarding Lewis's views of women, L'Engle seems to have shared the view of another Lewis admirer, the British novelist and playwright Dorothy Sayers. When asked to recommend great Christian books, Sayers routinely suggested Lewis's work, with an important caveat—"I do admit," she wrote to a correspondent just after the Second World War, "that he is apt to write shocking nonsense about women and marriage."[31] Though some of Lewis's ideas about gender changed over time, in general he had an essentialist view of gender and a hierarchical understanding of male-female relations, believing, for example, that "the authority of parent over child, husband over wife, learned over simple, to have been as much a part of the original plan as the authority of man over beast."[32] It is not difficult to find evidence of these views in Lewis's nonfiction and fictional writings, and indeed many analysts have already done so. In *Mere Christianity* Lewis asserted that men were more rational and just, women more emotional. In his fiction he developed female characters who were vain, frivolous, and unafraid to use beauty to their advantage—such as Susan Pevensie, the only Pevensie child who does not get to heaven, a girl interested in nothing "but nylons and lipstick and invitations." Lewis argued for a quota on women admitted to Oxford. He was wary of wives and other women intruding on his circle of friends, complaining that "the two things that some of us most dread for our own species" were "the dominance of the female and the dominance of the collective."[33] And he argued against female ordination in the Anglican Church, insisting that because God represented ultimate masculinity, a woman could not represent him among the people of God.[34] These views were common among men of Lewis's age and class; indeed it was precisely for this reason that feminist theologians such as Mary Daly, and writers such as L'Engle, had to attack and dismantle them. As feminist theologians have been saying for half a century, in order to be serviceable again, mythologies need to be shorn of their unbelievable, misogynist elements.

In many ways, the narrative that L'Engle lays out in *Wrinkle* is a reversal of the gender logic in Lewis's Narnia series. In Narnia, as Laura Miller has pointed out, it was not just that two of the most memorable villains, the White Witch and the Lady of the Green Kirtle, were women, nor that their nefarious power over men had to do with their sex appeal, nor that female Narnian heroines were either prepubescent girls or tomboys, such as Aravis. It also was deeply problematic that Lucy, who, of course, is central to the Narnia books, models the way a girl becomes important by abandoning girly things and turning away from preoccupations with beauty, clothes, and parties. When she emerged as a genuine heroine, armed with bow and arrow at the climactic battle in *The Horse and His Boy,* another character left no doubt about how to understand what had happened. She was "as good as a man, or at any rate as good as a boy," the impulsive and pugnacious Corin, Prince of Archenland, remarked. In short, girls became good insofar as they approached Lewis's ideals of masculinity.[35]

L'Engle often commented on the importance of having a determined and victorious female protagonist in *Wrinkle* and she believed that this made the book threatening to publishers and many readers. She would correctly point out that there were few strong female characters in fantasy or science fiction at the time, genres written mostly by and for men (and boys). In science fiction in particular, girls and women prior to the 1960s were generally represented by a few stereotypes: timid victims waiting to be saved; sexually desirable but terrifying "Amazons" to be feared or vanquished; devoted wives or daughters to be protected; objectified, one-dimensional props marveling at heroic male victories or validating men as acceptably masculine. "There are plenty of images of women in science fiction," the feminist writer Joanna Russ complained in 1970. "There are hardly any women."[36]

Meg's presence in *Wrinkle* disturbed science fiction stereotypes and challenged in particular the troubling trajectory of one character whom L'Engle knew well—Narnia's Lucy Pevensie. Instead of conforming to an older standard of masculine heroism, Meg had to become *more herself* in order to destroy the enemy and save male protagonists such as Charles Wallace and Mr. Murray. Meg began as antagonistic and stubborn—she even fought at school(!)—but in the end she defeated the evil in the universe, that disembodied, rational brain, IT, by embracing the redemptive power of her idiosyncratic inner qualities and her deep love for her family. This way of reading the story was liberating for those who believed that love and intuition were "female" and that women should use these qualities to triumph over evil. Of course, this way of thinking about *Wrinkle* also reinscribed essential gender categories: Men were one thing, and women another.

A second way of reading the gender logic of *Wrinkle*, however, is that the story troubles essentialist assumptions, opening up new ways of achieving a full humanity for all people by creating characters who are more complex. At the beginning of the story L'Engle assigns Meg characteristics traditionally seen as masculine—she is aggressive, independent, and outspoken. But as the novel unfolds, Meg's development is not imagined as a *becoming feminine* as much as a process of embracing the range of qualities that compose her unique personality. It is not a story of Meg overcoming her antagonistic, stubborn individualism; it is a story in which these "faults" make possible her ultimate triumph.

When each of the Mrs. Ws offered Meg magical gifts to help her find her father, Mrs. Which offered only "her faults"—anger, impatience, and stubbornness. Combining in their own unique ways characteristics of humorous tricksters, super-scientists, and spirit guides, the Mrs. Ws show Meg how to become more fully human, which meant embracing her individualism and assertiveness while developing other capacities for intuition and emotion. In this reading of *Wrinkle,* L'Engle's book deliberately cuts against the gender logic in play in earlier (male) Christian fantasies and indeed in the male-oriented world of science fiction.

To be sure, girls who read this book were forever changed by it. Meg was astonishing, Cynthia Zarin wrote in her *New Yorker* profile of L'Engle, "because here is a girl who at that moment is stronger than her father. For some of us, it planted the seeds of the women's movement." Zarin read her copy of *Wrinkle* every year, and read it to her children, and this book, together with other L'Engle books, affected her deeply. It "influenced how I thought about religion and politics, about physics and mystery, and how I imagined what family life could be. It wasn't just me. When I was in college, I remember a friend saying to me, 'There are really two kinds of girls. Those who read Madeleine L'Engle when they were small, and those who didn't.' "[37]

Thinking about Meg as a character who claimed for women a more complete humanity appeared also to be how L'Engle thought of her heroine's journey. In different comments on gender, feminism, and fiction, L'Engle insisted that contemporary women should embrace a "both/and" sense of self that united opposites—reason and emotion, independence and vulnerability, conscious and subconscious parts of the self. "If we are healthy we are whole; if we are whole we are holy." Wholeness implied spirituality for L'Engle, of course; being whole meant embracing inner, spiritual intuitions and developing a feminist spirituality in which women could now embrace all parts of the self as redemptive—just as Meg did. "My job is to live fully as a woman, enjoying the whole of myself and my place in the universe."[38] Like others interested in feminist spirituality in the 1970s and 1980s, L'Engle understood this psychological and spiritual reorientation as laying a new foundation for social changes. It would change how we understood "what comes naturally" in our domestic life, she said, as well as women's places in society, politics, and churches.

Of course, L'Engle was not the only one expanding the definition of gender in the early 1960s. In fact while L'Engle wrote *Wrinkle*, Betty Friedan, a classmate from Smith College, was researching and writing *The Feminine Mystique*, published in 1963. (L'Engle was class of 1941; Friedan, class of 1942. As students they were both editors at the *Smith College Monthly*, a literary magazine that Friedan and several others transformed into a more political publication, to L'Engle's chagrin.)[39] In 1964, in *Ladies' Home Journal*, Friedan followed up *The Feminine Mystique* with an article that also attempted to limn a way beyond the feminine mystique, "which defined woman solely in terms of her three-dimensional sexual relation to man as wife, mother, homemaker." Women needed to claim a more complete identity as androgynous, talented, and independent. Friedan characterized this as a "breaking through" to a "fourth dimension in woman's existence"—using higher-dimensional language that pointed the way toward a space of liberation, as it did for L'Engle. Friedan, L'Engle, and many others used the fourth dimension as a new, imagined space in which girls and women would be free of limits and able to develop into more complete individuals.[40]

ᘛᘚ

L'Engle once said that her fiction represented a welling up of spiritual ideas and mythological narratives from a "superconscious" part of her inner self.[41] Her job was to listen and write these narratives down. In this formulation, her stories, along with the Christian mythologies of MacDonald, Tolkien, and Lewis, were not merely interesting pastimes, imaginative thought experiments or forms of momentary escape; they were revelatory and mythical, fictional only to casual readers who ignored their deepest truths. In many ways these stories represented something quite remarkable: They were ways of reconstituting *the religious* in the modern West.

It is certainly the case that beginning in the late nineteenth century, fiction began to compete with religious stories. For the first time, the literary imagination was embraced as something healthy, useful, and even redemptive.[42] One astute contemporary observer, the philosopher George Santayana, talked about "religion" in a way that accommodated this way of thinking about faith, fictional stories, and imagination. Religion, he said simply, was "another world to live in." "The vistas it opens and the mysteries it propounds are another world to live in; and another world to live in—whether we expect ever to pass wholly into it or no—is what we mean by having a religion."[43] Santayana captured something important in this definition, arguing not just that religion represented another imaginative world to live in but also that the nature of our participation in these imaginative worlds varied. Did religious people entirely believe in the supernatural stories or beings that they imagined? When people prayed to gods or saints, did they always *believe* in those entities—or were there elements in those prayers of wishful thinking, hopeful optimism, or playful irony? Santayana's observation that expectations varied concerning how or whether one might "pass wholly into" religious otherworlds has been shown to be true by countless ethnographers working among religious practitioners. More often than not, these practitioners are willing to admit that they see into other orders of existence only during fleeting moments, that feelings of inspiration come infrequently, and that in general they are confounded and puzzled by the presence of that otherworld's absence.

In the modern forms of artistic or literary imagining examined thus far in this book, including L'Engle's work, the same impulse to *live in or pass into* imagined otherworlds is clearly at work. And the same range of attitudes toward those otherworlds also is in play. Sometimes the impulse to live in another literary world or dimension is marked by irony and detachment; at other times it is accompanied by an intense desire to find liberation in the face of oppression; and in still other settings it is a source of comfort in the face of suffering and death. (Recall that when Jacqueline Kennedy Onassis died in 1994, her son, JFK Jr., reported that she died surrounded by friends, family, and her books.) Like MacDonald and Lewis, L'Engle had an essentially Romantic belief in a divine part of the self that could produce new, otherworldly stories and myths in which truths about human nature and the cosmos might be revealed. She made these new stories seem believable by drawing on Christian tropes and new scientific notions about the universe's many layers and dimensions. Writing about the power of fairy tales and other forms of fantastic literature, she wrote once that readers who immersed themselves in these stories inevitably became aware that our "daily time-bound world of fact is the secondary world, and that literature, art and music . . . give us glimpses of the wider world of our whole self."[44] In her books, however, L'Engle did more than merely open up a "wider world" of supernatural wonders, supernormal psychic powers, or new spiritual hopes. She also showed that journeys into these otherworlds held out redemptive possibilities for all people, including girls like Meg, who found that, in addition to traversing a wider world of layers and dimensions, she could also embrace a more complex inner life of virtually unlimited personal qualities and aspirations.

9

One Step Beyond

I f modern people used different techniques to imagine themselves within a supernatural universe—if they did so by studying, for example, their uncanny dreams, or by reading fantastic tales of interdimensional travel, or by creating art that reached into the abstract and metaphysical, or by thinking scientifically about the universe's invisible spaces—if they developed a renewed *supernatural imagination* using these tools, there were still other media that generated a longing for a wider world of supernatural beings and invisible realities.

Without a doubt, a crucial one was television. Extending in miraculous ways the power of the senses, so that human beings for the first time could see things far away; receiving energetic transmissions that moved somehow through invisible frequencies; and allowing human beings to see fictions they had previously only imagined, including stories taking place in otherworldly landscapes, the television transformed how people in the second half of the twentieth century imagined things, how they assessed what was believable, how they understood the difference between the real and imaginary. In order to understand these developments, I examine in this chapter how science-fiction television in the 1950s and 1960s depicted televisions and other electrical devices as haunted technologies that came alive with presences from other worlds. This was an important trope in early sci-fi anthology programs such as *The Outer Limits* and *The Twilight Zone,* shows that themselves marked off televisual space as a separate space with mystical meaning. In these shows ethereal alien voices and extradimensional monsters transmitted themselves via televisions, conveying messages about the afterlife, ethics, psychic phenomena, and God. In these programs, other TV shows, and even films, writers and directors deployed televisions as openings to energetic forces and spiritual worlds that existed just beyond the boundaries of things known and understood.

But television writers and directors were not the only people who believed that televisions might help us overcome the modern loss of spiritual vision. As we will see, evangelicals, spiritualists, pagans, ghost hunters, and psychics also embraced television as a transmission technology for otherworldly entities or forces. Some of these believers asked congregants to lay their hands on TVs to feel emanations of spiritual power or healing vibrations; others meditated on blurry TV screens or studied static in order to see glimpses of dead relatives ensconced in other-dimensional, heavenly afterworlds. In short, since the 1950s, TV has been a powerful receiver of mystical transmissions from spirits and other beings in higher dimensions.[1]

Do Televisions Tune in Spiritual Energies?

The transition from being a society that relied on imaginative books and magazines to one in which fictional realities were transmitted and televised was remarkably swift. Though some upper-class families owned televisions in the 1930s and 1940s, as late as 1950 only 9 percent of American families had purchased a television. By 1960 that number was close to 90 percent.[2] The transformations that the television caused went beyond changes in consumption and leisure time to encompass alterations in everyday ways of thinking and believing. Assessing the cultural changes brought about by electronic media, Vivian Sobchak has pointed to specific changes in perception catalyzed by electronic media such as radio, film, and television. After 1890 the cinema brought about new ways of imagining time, duration, and movement, to be sure; but with the rise of television the electronic environment no longer merely attempted to represent reality. The televisual broadcast environment was more diffuse and pervasive, having neither a "point of view nor a visual situation" as film and photographs had. This new electronic presence was "bound up in a centerless, network-like structure of instant stimulation and desire," Sobchak has shown. Televisions, and, later, video recordings and computers, formed an "encompassing electronic representational system whose various forms 'interface' to constitute an alternative and absolute world that uniquely incorporates the spectator/user in a spatially decentered, weakly temporalized, and quasi-disembodied state."[3] Discrete parts of information were transmitted across networks, broadcasting everywhere through an ether that had now come alive with a mysterious presence.

A sense of mystery surrounded how moving images and information were transmitted invisibly and received by television antennae. In fact when televisual technologies emerged they were understood by many as a type of psychic seeing-at-a-distance. Stefan Andriopoulos has argued that the arrival of the television in Europe in the 1930s was facilitated not just by advances in engineering and physics but also by occult beliefs and practices related to telepathy, telesight, and clairvoyance. The imaginative insight and technical knowledge that made electrical television possible, he has shown, developed in part from "occultist studies on psychic 'clairvoyance' (*Hellsehen*) and 'television' (*Fernsehen*), carried out in the same period by spiritualists who emulated the rules and procedures of science." When early electrical televisions brought wireless moving pictures into peoples' homes many wondered if this was a new way of bringing the "supernatural or marvelous in one's own living room." Televisions were like crystal balls or the magic mirrors of fairy tales. When philosophers and scientists discussed electrical television they referred to the fairy tale's magic mirror in particular—it was, Andriopoulos wrote, "a figure that, in addition to shaping the technology's cultural reception in the late 1920s, already surfaces in most of the early writings on television from the late nineteenth century." As the chemist and physicist R. E. Liesegang confirmed, "Mirrors in which we can see distant objects can be found in the fairy tales of all countries. Faust saw Helena in such a mirror. The mirrors of Amamterasu, Dschemschid, Agrippa and Nostradamus all had the same marvelous property."[4] When electrical television arrived, it was a modern magic mirror in which distant objects somehow might be seen.

Television also was often theorized as an extension of the human senses and nervous system. In an influential piece written in 1877, "Grundlinien einer Philosophie der Technik," the German philosopher Ernst Kapp developed a theory of technology that defined it as "organ projection," a formulation later taken up by scientists, engineers, and others in the late nineteenth and early twentieth centuries. Both Liesegang in his *Contributions on the Problem of Electrical Television* (1899) and Fritz Lux in his *The Electrical Televisor* (1903) imagined television in particular as a magical extension of the sense of sight. In the 1940s and 1950s, when televisions were being manufactured and sold, marketers and TV enthusiasts spoke of this new invention as a "window on the world" that made possible astonishing views of faraway places.[5] The best-known inheritor of this tradition is the Canadian media theorist Marshall McLuhan, who insisted that, regardless of content, new media profoundly shaped our sensory abilities and thus our psychological and social environments. McLuhan argued that television was an extension of our nervous system and consciousness, one that involved all the senses but was primarily a technology of touch. Television, with its blurry reception and pixilated images, required, like touch, the cooperation of many senses. He also believed that television and the computer had occult resonances. The new society these technologies would create, he argued, "will be one mythic integration, a resonating world akin to the old tribal echo chamber where magic will live again: a world of ESP. The current interest of youth in astrology, clairvoyance and the occult is no coincidence. Electric technology, you see, does not require words any more than a digital computer requires numbers. Electricity makes possible— and not in the distant future, either—an amplification of human consciousness on a world scale, without any verbalization at all."[6]

McLuhan was not the only one who noticed that new spiritual sensibilities were being fostered by television and other electronic media. Several commentators have pointed out that the rise of electronic images coincided with the reemergence of a new religious or spiritual sensibility, showing that the new symbolic environment created by television and other electronic media played an important part in shaping new religious sensibilities from the 1950s onward. Madeleine L'Engle had discussed how fantasy and sci-fi literature cultivated the ability to suspend disbelief—but were electronic media even more powerful means to such an end? Probing the contours of the information age, the sociologist Manuel Castells has argued that modern, electronic societies have generated a flowing, timeless network of information collage, one that transcends history and biology. Our electronic culture, he has said, possesses religious qualities. This new culture, "the culture of real virtuality," Castells wrote, is "where make-believe is belief in the making."[7] Pointing to other ways that electronic media have fostered mystical sensibilities, Hent de Vries has argued that special effects have become a new species of "miracle," eliciting awe and wonder and leading people to suspend (perhaps momentarily) their disbelief in another order of existence. In de Vries's words, "Mediatization and the technology it entails form the condition of possibility for all revelation."[8]

Others, like Catherine Albanese, have made similar points, arguing that media have fostered new ways of imagining the supernatural. Albanese has pointed out that new spiritual discourses of "energies," "transmissions," and "fields" suddenly emerged alongside electronic media during the 1960s. She has argued that spirit channelers, New Age shamans, and other modern believers now plausibly talk of transcendent spirits—and even experience otherworldly visions of them—because these kinds of otherworldly visions materialize everyday on television and in film.[9] Religious people themselves have been keen to borrow televisual metaphors for reimagining a world enchanted by spirits. Reminding us that modern physicists have proved that reality is not solid but closer to "thoughts" or energies, the Theosophical writer Norman Pearson, for example, wrote that the human mind was a lot like a television set. From the invisible reality behind everything there came waves "to which we give the names 'Spirit' and 'Matter.' Within the body—a living, vitalized 'receiving set'—there arises consciousness in response thereto." Like the television, our consciousness also was "a simulation, a copy . . . of the Reality of the Unmanifest."[10] Televisions also electrified the imagination with new metaphors of transmission and reception. What was it that was being received by a TV? And what *other* kinds of invisible energies pulsing through the atmosphere were picked up by new technologies or sensitive human beings?

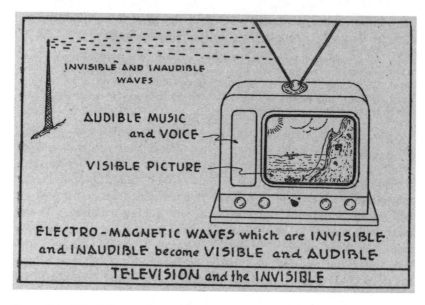

Figure 9.1 Televisions make visible mysterious forces and waves. Could spiritual energies also be tuned in? From E. Norman Pearson, *Space, Time and Self* (Adyar, India: Theosophical Publishing House, 1957), 23.

When television emerged there also was an unusual immediacy to it that caused people to ask questions about the nature of visual perception and "the real." Unlike film, broadcast television presented viewers with something that was actually taking place. As the American sociologist Leo Bogart has written, people generally were aware of how films and even books were edited, reworked, and revised, but televisual stories and events were immediate and thus seemed more real. They were happening now. Moreover, viewers reported a greater emotional connection to characters and dramas on television, in part because TVs brought these stories into the intimate spaces of their homes.[11] For these reasons, when television emerged, a new discourse began about the problem of confusion over real versus electrical spaces. Lynn Spigel has examined films from the 1930s that exploited or commented on reality confusion, but genre television in the 1950s and 1960s also pointed to this issue with characters who moved magically between television studios and "real" life, as, for example, in *The Twilight Zone*'s "World of Difference" and *Lights Out*'s "Something in the Wind."

These episodes and others like them show that writers and producers were self-reflexive about TV as a window into other forms of reality. In *Lights Out*'s "Something in the Wind," for example, a TV director who has redacted lines and cut characters from a script begins to feel guilty when characters come to life and demand their lines back. In other shows from this era, characters attempt to get into or out of electrical or televisual otherworlds or see things on TV that turn out to be psychic visions, hallucinations, or, more disturbing still, real life.[12] An anxious psychological literature accompanied these self-reflexive sci-fi narratives, analyzing why and how TV might create psychopathologies. The American activist and writer Jerry Mander rehearsed these concerns in his *Four Arguments for the Elimination of Television* (1978), which discussed cases in the scientific literature where patients felt lost in the television or controlled and confused by it. TVs created confusion about what was real. Others, like Marina Warner, have shown that media technologies created such powerful worlds that some contemporary Europeans and Americans reported in surveys that Hitler was a fictional character and that events in Tolkien's *Lord of the Rings* books, such as the Battle of Helm's Deep, actually took place.[13]

Contemporary media scholars also have noted that television raises questions about perception and reality. "It has long struck me," the philosopher and theorist Samuel Weber has argued, that "the self-evident quality of this experience of visual perception is increasingly being shaken, but also exploited, by a medium such as television."[14] Since the Enlightenment, many have trusted the visual sense above all, but the rise of the television has led to new questions about what our eyes are telling us. What is the status of things seen and heard on television? Were they real? What was the real? "As a visual medium," Jenny Slatman has pointed out, addressing this problem, "television asks us to believe in something that we have not seen with our own eyes. Thus, it obscures the apparently clear-cut distinction between faith and seeing, a distinction that has thoroughly dominated our tradition." Slatman also argued that tele-vision was structurally similar to seeing the transcendent, for everything on TV always existed in a location that was *beyond*—in other words it was always "tele" (remote) vision. "The tele-visible is the transcendent being."[15] Television creates a kind of imaginative play because it both forces viewers to doubt whether they see things truly and causes them to wonder in new ways about the possibility of seeing transcendently.

For all these reasons, when televisions arrived in American living rooms in the 1950s they were regarded with feelings of awe, sometimes ascribed mystical powers, and often accompanied by urgent questions about the nature of the electrical world that they mediated. Questions about the "liveness" and reality of the televisual world are well illustrated in discourses about haunted televisions and ghosts trapped in TV's electronic dimensions. Some families reported ghosts that materialized in TV static and could not be tuned out. In December 1953 the *New York Times* reported the case of Jerome Travers, who was watching *Ding Dong School* with his three children when a woman's face appeared on the screen and would not go away—even after the set was turned off. The only solution was to turn the TV toward the wall. Reporters, writers, and others came to view the set before the image disappeared a day later.[16]

"Ghosts on a TV screen can be a problem," one reporter wrote in 1954, referring to the well-known static ghosts in untuned TVs, "but it's a rare occasion when one drives a housewife 'crazy' and ends up in the police station." In this unusual case, it was the image of an Indianapolis housewife's dead grandfather that appeared on the screen—not a metaphorical ghost lost in static but a literal one haunting the set. After two days of trying to banish the image, Mrs. Mackey was disturbed enough to report she was "going crazy." She took the TV to the police. When the police activated the set, her grandfather reappeared, clad again in the suit he was buried in two months prior. More than five hundred people visited the police station to see the apparition before it disappeared.[17] Another illustration of contemporary anxieties about televisual presences comes from a story about a TV signal from a defunct station tuned in by several people in England and America. Rosella Rose of Milwaukee tuned in the KLEE signal twelve years after the station had been abandoned. More mysteriously still, the transmission included images of a man and woman arguing on a balcony, a station identification scene with KLEE on the screen, and then, superimposed over the KLEE, the letters "HELP," flashing on and off.[18] What was the nature of the electronic otherworld seen via televisions? Could one get trapped in them? These events pointed to ways that the American public, a public mostly ignorant about how electromagnetic waves and cathode tubes worked, wondered about the liveness of TV and its status as an occult space.

Fiction and television in the 1950s played on anxieties that the family TV could be possessed by a spirit. One of the first television broadcast shows ever made, the New York–based broadcast *The Television Ghost* (1931–1933), used fifteen-minute episodes that featured the departed spirits of murder victims who materialized onscreen to describe how they were killed. J. B. Priestley, who, as we have seen, was interested in otherworlds and dimensions, wrote a 1953 short story in which an aggrieved (and dead) Uncle Phil returned to haunt his family via the television set they purchased with insurance money collected after his death. Each time Phil's sister, Mrs. Grigson, watched the set, she noticed a figure resembling Uncle Phil. The Grigson daughter, Una, also noticed it. Gradually Uncle Phil made his presence clearer until Mrs. Grigson and Una were certain that somehow he was appearing on television programs. They told others, but Una's husband, George, thought they were merely indulging their imagination. Over time other family members encountered Uncle Phil on different shows, and eventually Uncle Phil spoke directly to his family through the set, becoming angry. With Mrs. Grigson and Una watching, Uncle Phil appeared on an afternoon "programme for women" accusing them directly—"You Grigsons haven't done so bad with that hundred and fifty quid of mine." Finally the whole family argued about the reality of Uncle Phil's image on TV. Was Uncle Phil really there or was he "being projected into the screen by their imagination"? In the final scene, with the Grigson family gathered around the set, Uncle Phil accused them of hiding his heart medicine and causing his death. (It was true in fact that many disliked Uncle Phil. It was also true that someone had put his pills up on the mantel where he could not easily reach them.) In any case, when Uncle Phil's TV ghost accused family members of putting his pills out of reach, one person hurled a stool into the screen in a final effort to destroy Uncle Phil and his postmortem life-world.[19]

The 1953 film *The Twonky* also features a TV possessed by an otherworldly intelligence. Originally a 1942 Lewis Padgett story about a haunted radio, *The Twonky* film featured a possessed Admiral sixteen-inch TV that could walk, vacuum, do dishes, play cards, and even light cigarettes. It was assisted by electrical beams that emanated from its screen. Though the TV initially was useful, its owner, a philosophy professor named Kerry West, soon discovered the machine's sinister side. The TV followed West and, deploying its electrical beams, took away his coffee, chose the music on his stereo, restricted his reading, censored his thoughts, and followed him everywhere. When West's friends and the police took action against the mysterious machine, the Twonky's electrical beams hypnotized them, neutralizing the threat. West eventually tried to escape, but the Twonky followed him into his car until, finally, a car accident destroyed it. Somehow, televisions brought mystical presences into the world.

Electronic Openings to Higher Dimensions

In the 1950s and 1960s, TV functioned as a portal to otherworldly, electronic presences and occult spaces. The awe and fascination that people felt toward TV was exploited by sci-fi, supernatural, and paranormal television shows that brought viewers to the borderlands of the known world in different episodes about alien visitors, psychic powers, the supernatural, and monsters from other dimensions.[20]

A number of these programs signaled from the beginning that they were openings to other worlds. *The Outer Limits* and *The Twilight Zone,* for instance, incorporated opening sequences that marked off televisual space as a set-apart zone of mysterious and unexpected possibilities. "There is a fifth dimension, beyond that which is known to man," *Twilight Zone* creator Rod Serling said in his voice-over, borrowing the fifth-dimensional language that was ubiquitous at the time. "It is a dimension as vast as space and as timeless as infinity. It is the middle ground between light and shadow, between science and superstition, and it lies between the pit of man's fears and the summit of his knowledge. This is the dimension of imagination. It is an area which we call the twilight zone." In later seasons this language was modified slightly, but the voice-over still described the show as a form of dimensional travel. In the third season, opening comments about traveling through dimensions were accompanied by a twisting vortex cone, suggestive of a wormhole opening into unknown dimensions. In the fifth season, the voice-over was paired with a door floating in space—"You unlock this door with

Figure 9.2   A number of anthology TV programs from the 1950s and 1960s, including *The Twilight Zone,* incorporated opening sequences that marked off televisual space as a set-apart zone of mysterious and unexpected possibilities. "There is a fifth dimension beyond that which is known to man," *The Twilight Zone* creator Rod Serling told viewers in the show's opening.

the key of imagination. Beyond it is another dimension. A dimension of sound. A dimension of sight. A dimension of mind. You are moving into a land of both shadow and substance." Here the opening sequence also incorporated a spinning clock and Einstein's famous equation "$E = mc^2$," deploying scientific tropes to build an atmosphere of credibility. Many episodes incorporated a prologue in which Serling stood on the set speaking directly to the camera, buttressing the intimacy of the show and bringing this dimensional portal directly into the home.[21]

Like *The Twilight Zone, The Outer Limits* (1963–1965) used an opening sequence to suggest that televisions could tune in to realities that lay beyond the borders of the known world. In fact, the show opened with a kind of televisual spirit-possession in which a disembodied presence—the narrator—explained that he had taken over the television. A white-on-black sine wave, a momentary flicker, and then a collapsing of the transmission into a small, white dot, as if someone had turned off the television—this was the beginning. As the white dot pulsed, the narrator began. "There is nothing wrong with your television set. Do not attempt to adjust the picture. *We* are controlling transmission. If we wish to make it louder, we will bring up the volume. If we wish to make it softer, we will tune it to a whisper. *We* will control the horizontal. *We* will control the vertical." The controlling intelligence stretched the white dot in horizontal and then vertical directions, and then demonstrated other ways that it controlled the image by rolling it (in a vertical roll) or blurring the screen. There was nothing for the viewer to do except participate in something beyond. "*You* are about to participate in a great adventure. *You* are about to experience the awe and mystery which reaches from the inner mind to the outer limits." The screen displayed shifting sine waves that expanded and collapsed, giving the impression that the "outer limits" probed in the show were distinctly electromagnetic outer spaces. In quite striking ways, the show used this opening sequence, in Jeffrey Sconce's phrase, to "partition off an avowedly occult space within television itself."[22]

This era's genre television self-consciously depicted televisions as technologies that received mysterious signals from the borders of the known world. In *Science Fiction Theater*'s "The Missing Waveband" (1956) and *The Outer Limits*' "Behold Eck!" (1964), for example, scientists built radio or television transmitters that discovered alien voices conveying breakthrough scientific knowledge or metaphysical tidings about God and the afterlife. In other episodes televisions tuned in the souls of departed loved ones, magically replayed memories of past events, or materialized disturbing pictures of the future—and, in some episodes, as in *Twilight Zone*'s "The Sixteen-Millimeter Shrine" (1959), characters entered the electronic worlds they saw onscreen. At the beginning of "The Sixteen-Millimeter Shrine," an aging film star watched her younger self in old movies via an in-home projection system. At this point there seemed to be nothing remarkable about watching a woman watching herself on film, but as the episode proceeded, viewers discovered not just the intensity of her longing for that electronic world but the astonishing fact that she somehow had the power to enter it. Serling opened the episode by remarking on the self-reflexivity of a program that featured a woman watching her electronic self: "Picture of a woman looking at a picture," he crooned. He closed the episode by musing about the power of dreams and the ability of electronic media to fulfill them. "To the wishes that come true, to the strange, mystic strength of the human animal, who can take a wishful dream and give it a dimension of its own." An aging actress had entered the screen, taking up residence in the other dimension within it. Since the 1960s there have been many other examples of TV characters entering and exiting an electrical existence that resided in a separate realm inside their televisions.[23]

But if entering other spaces or times via the television sometimes fulfilled the deepest forms of longing, it also could lead to terrifying experiences of loss and destruction. When the television in *The Twilight Zone*'s "What's in the Box?" (1964), for example, received transmissions from another time, it set in motion events that unraveled the lives of the show's protagonists.

The episode began with a married couple in New York City fighting in the kitchen. The wife, Phyllis, accused her husband, Joe, of adultery while a television repairman in an adjoining room examined a TV that tuned in only static. When Joe entered the living room hoping to watch a wrestling match, he berated the repairman for taking too long and charging too much. Joe came to regret this. With a grin, the repairman stood up, pronounced the set fixed, and told Joe there was no charge. Joe turned on the set and was surprised to receive a new channel, channel ten. He was more surprised when this channel brought into focus scenes from his past, present, and future. He first saw himself cavorting with his mistress. He then saw a replay of the fight with Phyllis in the kitchen. But what he saw next terrified him—he and Phyllis fought, he punched her, and she fell through a window. Then the televisual Joe sat in court, and was tried, convicted, and finally executed in an electric chair. Obviously disturbed, he told Phyllis to come and examine the TV. Phyllis saw only static and called a doctor, who gave Joe a sedative, recommended a psychiatrist, and told Phyllis that an "over-mechanized culture" caused these kinds of delusions. "Perhaps he's been staring at this electronic blessing, the television set, so long, that its life has become his," the doctor reasoned. "And he's reached such a state of confusion that he no longer knows whether he's watching the action or participating in it." Even the doctor had to admit, "I on occasion have found myself asking for sutures and sponges during operations performed by television surgeons." Television confused reality and fantasy. The doctor left, the couple fought again, Joe punched Phyllis, and she fell out a window to her death.[24]

This episode reminds us that from the very beginning televisions were associated with unusual powers variously termed psychic, spiritual, or paranormal. For centuries, mystical visionaries have reported remarkable powers—seeing into the future, hearing disembodied voices, or witnessing events occurring far away. When televisual technologies came along they seemed like new ways of making these mysterious powers possible. As scholars such as Stefan Andriopoulos have pointed out, early discussions about television and related technologies in the 1880–1940 period linked these technologies to occult and psychic phenomena. Andriopoulos argued in fact that television did not just materialize earlier spiritualist wishes for otherworldly powers; he argued that the imaginative speculations and religious practices of psychics and Spiritualists *made possible* the creation of electrical television.[25] From psychic telesight came electrical television. Journalists, engineers, pundits, and mystics—all of them linked earlier spiritual powers with new televisual technologies. In 1958, as people around the world grappled with television's miraculous ability to mediate sights and sounds from a distance, Pope Pius XII announced that the thirteenth-century nun Clare of Assisi would be television's patron saint. Her powers, after all, had been televisual: When too ill to attend mass, she could see and hear it on the wall of her room.

The content of genre television shows in the 1950s and 1960s shows how closely people associated television with psychic or supernatural events—a remarkable case in which the televisual medium itself became the message. *One Step Beyond* in particular based its episodes on actual reports of paranormal phenomena, a fact shared by host John Newland in episode prologues and codas. "You are about to see the rarest kind of human experience," he said at the beginning of one episode entitled "Epilogue." "You may question or challenge what follows. Nevertheless it is the personal record of someone who took that one step beyond." *One Step Beyond* featured episodes with psychic visions of future tragedy ("Night of April 14," "Emergency Only," "Earthquake"), women and children who saw or heard things that saved them from disaster ("Call from Tomorrow," "Epilogue"), and traumatic events such as war that generated psychic visions ("The Dream," "The Vision").[26] Other programs, such as *The Twilight Zone, The Outer Limits,* and Rod Serling's *The Night Gallery,* foregrounded technologies such as telephones, radios, and televisions that probed into faraway places, other planets, or heavenly landscapes. These programs were pioneers in a paranormal genre that would explode in popularity later in the twentieth and twenty-first centuries.[27]

Episodes about psychic or spiritual powers often raised questions about the desirability of belief, the problem of credulity, and the role of gender. Though the "man of reason" is a trope going back centuries, when scientists professionalized their disciplines in the nineteenth century they reinforced the binary between masculine rationality and feminine credulity, and this binary informed sci-fi literature and television. In genre TV, there was (and is) no shortage of male scientist-heroes and credulous, emotional women. In *The Twilight Zone*'s "Little Girl Lost" (1962), for example, six-year-old Bettina Miller fell through a dimensional portal in her room and was lost in the "fourth dimension." Bettina's mother sobbed and shrieked while her husband and their physicist friend Bill calmly solved the problem. Bill examined Bettina's room, moving the bed and crouching down with outstretched hands to detect energies or openings. When he got to the wall behind Bettina's bed, one of his hands slipped into a dimensional doorway and disappeared.

Bettina's parents wanted to jump through and pull her out, but Bill was cautious. "If it's what I think, it's kind of a . . . gap, opening, on another dimension. Probably the fourth dimension. It just wouldn't be laid out like our world." Bill tried to outline the contours of the opening on the wall, saying that lines in the fourth dimension were perpendicular to all lines in our dimension, and that somehow fourth-dimensional lines converged in Bettina's room. Finally, Bettina's father reached and fell through the portal into a dark, smoky landscape where he became a reflective presence on the surface of a sphere—a higher-dimensional being spread out like a Flatlander. He found Bettina, and then Bill pulled them both back through the portal. In the show's epilogue, Serling mused out loud about the location of the missing girl. Was it the fourth dimension? The fifth? Where were these mysterious spaces? We would probably never know. Elements from this episode reappear in the 1982 film *Poltergeist* and in other films and television programs.

Figure 9.3   Bill the physicist locates an opening into the fourth dimension. From *The Twilight Zone,* "Little Girl Lost."

Other programs from this era, however, critiqued the reasonable male scientist and created female characters who were more perceptive, open-minded, or ethical than men. Female characters were often more knowledgeable about the psychological, the psychic, and the spiritual—a fact that could be seen as both empowering to women who felt dominated by male experts as well as oppressive to those who saw that this formulation reinscribed older essentialist binaries. In either case, one commentator has noted that in *One Step Beyond* there were over thirty female protagonists with enhanced psychic abilities, representing a full third of the show's episodes. In many of them, women had psychic experiences that obtuse husbands and male doctors dismissed as hallucinations, hysteria, or mental illness. In "Tonight at 12:17," for instance, a woman named Laura heard a plane in distress overhead every night at 12:17 a.m. Her concerned husband summoned a male doctor, and the men agreed that it was all in her head. Laura was sedated, but she had said enough to elicit her husband's curiosity. She had mentioned the serial number of the plane, which she had somehow seen. After making a few phone calls, her husband discovered that the plane was indeed registered at a local airport. In an excess of caution, he took his wife to a hotel room where they might be safe from this upcoming flight. However, at 12:17 a.m. that night the plane crashed into their hotel room. It turned out that her visions were not just "in her head." Episodes that critique scientific men and vindicate credulous women reveal how in the postwar period Americans had begun questioning science and the problems of an engineered world of dangerous technologies.[28]

Other episodes of *One Step Beyond* underscored the arrogance and ignorance of male authority figures. In "Moment of Hate," for example, Karen Wadsworth, a female protagonist with telekinetic powers, could kill people with rage. The episode began with Karen in an emotional fit—screaming at her (male) psychiatrist until he sedated her. Later she told him that in moments of anger and rage she could (accidentally) kill people. The psychiatrist explained that her hate and the accidental deaths she had witnessed were coincidences. But the coincidences accumulate as the episode proceeds. Karen got angry at her coworker and the coworker died. She got angry at her boss and he died. The psychiatrist was unpersuaded by her stories and outbursts and at one point identified the essential psychodynamics in play—a childhood accident had created a persistent belief that she could kill. She persisted in her irrational belief, he thought, because it was a form of "ego gratification" that made her feel powerful. Near the end of the episode the psychiatrist confronted her with this information, taunting her and calling her a witch, coaxing her to wish him dead so she might be rid of her false beliefs. She tired of the struggle and turned inward, however, wishing herself dead, and she promptly died. Later the psychiatrist discussed the case with another doctor, insisting that there was no "voodoo" in play. Her cause of death was simply "undetermined." But viewers of the show knew Karen's version of reality was accurate. The overall message, however, was hardly comforting—Karen was right, but she had to kill herself to be heard.

The Twilight Zone also was preoccupied with psychic and spiritual powers that often eluded reasonable men in white lab coats. The title sequence of *The Twilight Zone* linked the show's uncanny televisual zone with the "uncharted depths of the human mind," and many episodes featured extraordinary mental powers or other supernatural phenomena.

Serling's favorite quote from Shakespeare guided him—"There are more things in heaven and earth than are dreamt of in your philosophy."[29] (Edwin Abbott happened to quote this same passage from *Hamlet* in the epigraph on the cover of the original 1884 edition of *Flatland*.) Creatures from different dimensions, aliens from otherworlds, angels and demons from after- and nether-worlds—all of them populated Serling's electric imagination and unusual stage sets. Even God and Satan made appearances. Perhaps for this reason one of his biographers called the show "implicitly spiritual," noting that episodes often dealt with supernatural phenomena, ultimate values, or metaphysical issues such as free will or fate. "Though Serling necessarily avoided direct references to religion so as to survive network censorship and sponsor scrutiny," Douglas Brode and Carol Serling have written, "*Zone* was often an implicitly spiritual show." "Numerous episodes focus on the spiritual side of Serling's heroes or the lack of this quality in his villains."[30] Many characters confront death in the way the young Robert Redford did in "Nothing in the Dark"—that is, as a "new beginning." When asked if Rod had "a fascination with the supernatural," Carol Serling, repurposing a phrase used by many figures in this book, from Coleridge to L'Engle, reported that Rod practiced a "willing suspension of disbelief. He really, really wanted to believe that aliens had landed in Arizona. And he really, really wanted to believe some of the things Duke University was doing with ESP, and so on and so forth, but he really didn't."[31]

The Outer Limits

The Outer Limits is a notable example of a program that self-consciously depicted televisions and other electronic media as ways of probing into other dimensions. In the first episode, "Galaxy Being," an engineer for a local radio station named Allen Maxwell secretly used the station's equipment to receive microwave static coming from "out there."[32] He listened obsessively to the static for clues about the "secrets of the universe." He developed a television-like technology that displayed signals he received in three dimensions and one day was shocked to find a creature materializing through the static who said he was a four-dimensional being from the Andromeda Galaxy. Allan asked for his name, and the higher-dimensional creature answered, "Number. Not the same as yours. Four-dimension number." Allan asked about "life" there and the alien said he was a "nitrogen" cycle creature, not a carbon cycle creature. Allan asked if they had death, and the alien responded in a telegraphic style: Death "is property of carbon cycle in three dimensions." There is "no death in our dimension," the creature explained; "electromagnetic waves go on to infinity." Amazed, Allan asked about his own death and the prospects of an afterlife. "Do my brainwaves go on?" he asked. "Yes." Allan also asked if this creature had a God, and the alien responded that "electromagnetic forces underlying all." Allan clarified that he was talking about an intelligent force, but the alien reaffirmed his response. "Electromagnetic force intelligent. Matter, space, time—all the same. Different names. Infinity. Infinity is God." Later, another station employee turned up the transmitter too high and the alien was thrown through Allan's equipment and into our world, where he wandered around accompanied by energetic flashes, buzzing static, and pulses of radiation. He was looking for Allan. Though panicked townspeople and local authorities gathered to kill him, the alien cautioned earthlings about ignorance and aggression and, before dematerializing forever, advised everyone to "give thought to the mysteries of the universe."

This episode reflected both the imaginative hopes Americans had for television and their unsettling anxieties about its power, reach, and "liveness." The extra-dimensional alien was brought into view using an electrical contraption that looked exactly like a television, complete with tuning knobs and dials. So we have the creation of a televisual world within the viewer's television, one that not only captured mysterious transmissions from otherworlds but also was capable (somehow) of making that received transmission real. Allan's televisual space invaded his real world. Was it possible for *our* televisual world also to invade our real world? This continued to be a live question in the episode, as boundaries between virtual and real, electrical and material, were blurred in scenes where (for example) the four-dimensional alien walked directly into the camera lens.[33] Of course, the show also illustrated ways that electrical technologies could access transcendent realms of truth; Allan Maxwell got his deepest theological questions answered via a mediated conversation with this higher-dimensional creature. And, perhaps most notably, the answers themselves associated electrical and metaphysical energies. God was (intelligent) electromagnetic force.

Figure 9.4   Allan Maxwell tunes in to a four-dimensional "galaxy being."
From *The Outer Limits,* "The Galaxy Being."

ABC wanted *The Outer Limits* to be a sci-fi show with spaceships, monsters, and special effects that might appeal to a younger audience, but the show's writers and producers had other ideas. Leslie Stevens, who created the show and helped craft many of its episodes, and Joseph Stephano, the producer for the first season and a writer of many scripts, wanted to develop an intelligent show with a sense for the fantastic, unnerving, or supernatural—elements the program would share with *The Twilight Zone.* As a result, there was disagreement about the show's content. Producers wanted simple narratives with monsters and special effects; sponsors eyed the show for controversial messages; censors complained about the violence. No one wanted what Stevens and Stephano were writing. Arguments among Stevens, Stephano, and the ABC producers were legendary. "We fought continually with the censors," Stefano said.

> I used to put things into scripts knowing they'd be taken out, just
> to save other things from cutting. Dorothy Brown (the ABC censor)
> wasn't easy to deal with at all; we'd get three and four-page memos
> from her; lists of things that had to go. The signals were all crossed.
> I'd get a call from the network heads, saying, "Let's have more mon-

sters; we love this; do more of that." . . . My ace in the hole . . . was to refuse to do the show. Then all the phones would start ringing. My objective became not to get caught and crushed between the censors and the network heads.

In order to better control the show, ABC asked for a summary statement on "what the show was about," and Stephano and Stevens together produced a manifesto. "Enlightenment, education, provocation and soul-moving are the end game of all drama," they wrote; "but to these must be added the experience of terror. It must however be 'tolerable' terror. When the play has ended, when the Control Voice has returned to the viewer the use of his TV set, that willing victim of the terror must be able to relax and know self-amusement and realize that what he feared during the telling of the story could not materialize and need not be feared should he walk out of his house and stroll a night street."[34] It is not clear that the two were as committed as ABC executives to terror that was merely fun and "tolerable." Much of the evidence supports the view that Stephano and Stevens wanted the show's emotional effects to shock and linger.

Stevens in particular saw mystical significance in the show. "Science fiction is a doorway that allows your imagination to free-wheel," he said. "Science is a carefully gridded and structured view of the mysterious, so that the rational mind has a firm grounding from which you can gaze into the inexplicable peculiarity of the universe—the fearsomely odd space-time reversals, black holes, and so on." If one took the time to learn about them, real scientific facts opened up extraordinary, mystical and unexpected realities.[35] "The line I had at the beginning of The Outer Limits, 'The awe and mystery' of the universe, something awesome and mysterious about just looking up at the sky at night," Stevens said. There was something mysterious about contemplating the edges and limits of the universe.[36]

Many Outer Limits episodes dealt directly with the known limits of the universe and its spiritual borderlands, including "Behold, Eck!" and "The Borderland." "Behold, Eck!" deserves special consideration because it featured so many elements from the Flatland tradition from Abbott to L'Engle. In this episode, Dr. Stone, a brilliant optical researcher and engineer, developed new spectacles from "meteoric quartz" that unexpectedly altered his vision and enabled him to discover a two-dimensional energetic creature trapped in our plane of existence. This creature, "Eck," had been destroying optometry offices and other buildings in a desperate effort to find lenses that would help him see clearly in this foreign world. He wanted to make his way back to the dimensional rift between worlds. Stone went to work on interdimensional eyeglasses to help, while Eck, viewing a television newscast about himself, jumped into the TV to find help, believing that it represented a more familiar two-dimensional world. This caused Eck to become luminous in a way that made him suddenly visible to normal three-dimensional humans, who pursued and attacked him. (This was another case in which the television made visible hitherto unseen dimensions.) Meanwhile Stone finished the interdimensional lens and took it to the public square where the dimensional rift was located, and Eck finally was able to return to his two-dimensional world. (Stone was not the only person to use special eyeglasses to see into other dimensions: L'Engle's Mrs. Who had special glasses that she loaned to Meg; and in William Sleator's *The Boy Who Reversed Himself* [1986], the protagonist used special spectacles to see in the fourth dimension.)

By the 1960s, there was nothing unusual about an alien slipping into or out of different dimensions. In comic books and sci-fi narratives, not to mention televisual and filmic reproductions of them, other dimensions harbored invading supervillains, hostile aliens, monsters, or evil, mirror-image twins. Understanding or traveling through extra dimensions sometimes conferred extra powers, but they also could distort or endanger human beings. Sometimes scientists experimenting with higher-dimensional technologies turned themselves into monsters, as was the case in the 1959 film *The 4D Man*. At other times, characters who understood the physics of higher dimensions could travel to alien times or places, as in the film *The Time Machine* (1960) or, more famously, in L'Engle's *Wrinkle in Time* (1962). In these and in still other cases, such as the children's television program *Land of the Lost* (1974–1976), manipulating or gaining passage through dimensional doorways structured the plot. In *Land of the Lost* the Marshall family was swept down a waterfall and through a dimensional portal; they spent the rest of the show trying to reopen the portal and get back to present-day earth.

Another *Outer Limits* episode that discussed the universe's limits and higher dimensions was "The Borderland," which aired on December 16, 1963. "The mind of man has always longed to know what lies beyond the world we live in," the opening Control Voice began. "Explorers have ventured into the deeps and the heights. Of these explorers some are scientists, some are mystics." The opening scene assembled a group of scientists and mystics around a séance table in the dining room of Dwight Hartley, an eccentric British millionaire who wanted to contact the spirit of his dead son. Hartley had hired a well-known psychic, Mrs. Palmer. Also at the table were the scientists Ian and Eva Fraser and a Dr. Russell. In the middle of the ritual Ian Fraser turned on the lights, exposing Palmer as a fraud. Hartley would never have to waste money on séance superstitions again. But as it turned out, Fraser had other ideas for Hartley's money. He told Hartley about a new research project on an electronic "doorway into the fourth dimension." Fraser and his coworkers already had opened this doorway "a crack," accidentally mirror-reversing one of Fraser's hands, but they needed money to create a greater magnetic field. Hartley said he would fund the project if Fraser promised to try to find his son Dion on the other side of this experimental fourth-dimensional doorway.

The experimental doorway was a cubical structure bound by edges made of power coils and a metallic top and bottom, which made it look like something in-between a boxy hypercube and an oversized television. When a test rat exploded in the device, some doubt about its safety emerged. But white-coated Ian Fraser pressed onward, and once the device was functional again he transported himself through the machine's shimmering ion field to a remarkable otherworldly space. It was another moment of seeing through static to an electronic beyond. (The ion field effect required a tremendous amount of time, involving several people taking apart the film frame by frame and adding frames of shimmering light. When Stevens was presented with a bill for $14,000 for this special effect, witnesses recalled that he turned away and wept.)

While in this otherworldly space, Fraser reported what he was seeing. He witnessed an overlapping landscape "superimposed" somehow on reality—"I can't tell if it's another planet," he cried through the ion rain, "or another time." A rocky desert landscape briefly materialized.[37] (Visually, the scene is remarkable, though it is not the first or last time that extra-dimensional otherworlds are depicted via special effects.)[38] Fraser cried out for Hartley's son Dion three times, as promised. But at this point everything fell apart. There was a momentary power loss, and Fraser began to panic, calling out for his wife—Eva! At this point, Eva moved toward the machine, reached through the ion field, clutched Ian's hand, and refused to let go. Ultimately she hauled him out. During a later experiment, the bereaved millionaire Hartley snuck onto the device's charged platform, called out to his son, and zipped into an electronic otherworld, never to return. In the end, the episode made one thing clear: Electronic technologies, rather than séances or other superstitious practices, provided real openings to worlds beyond our own.

In "The Borderland," as in other dimensional dramas, love enables contact across worlds. Hartley's love for his son sent him through the static field and into that other world forever. Love motivated Eva to reach through the ion curtain and into Ian's dimension until she finally pulled him out. After Eva saved Ian, the closing narration pointed explicitly to the power of love—"There are worlds beyond and worlds within which the explorer must explore, but there is one power which seems to transcend space and time, life and death. It is a deeply human power which holds us safe and together when all other forces combine to tear us apart—we call it the power of love." The same theme is also at the heart of L'Engle's *Wrinkle,* for it is Meg's love that motivates her to cross dimensions, find her father, and do something no one else can do—free Charles Wallace and her father from the mind control of IT. With Charles Wallace entranced by IT, Meg ruminates on her emotional connection to him, and he wakes up: the triumph of love over rationality.

These narratives are not the only ones in which love penetrates dimensional boundaries. A 2014 film about interdimensional contact, Christopher Nolan's *Interstellar,* develops themes fashioned by Hinton, Abbott, and L'Engle in a story of another daughter trying to find her father across the many dimensions of spacetime. Love is the link that makes interdimensional communication possible. In a much-discussed monologue in the film, Dr. Amelia Brand (Anne Hathaway) talks about love as a universal force akin to gravity. "Love isn't something we invented. It's observable, powerful, it has to mean something. . . . Love is the one thing we're capable of perceiving that transcends dimensions of time and space." It is an intelligent force, guiding Brand and other characters in the film and allowing the male lead, Coop (Matthew Mc-Conaughey), to communicate with his daughter, Murph, at a critical moment from within a "tesseract" in space. (In Nolan's earlier film *Inception,* love for his children is also what drives Dom Cobb to move through dream layers and come home.)[39] Inside the tesseract, Coop sees reality "from above," like the Square in *Flatland,* looking into Murph's room through her bookshelves (see Figure 9.5). In the film *Poltergeist,* as well, the child Carol Ann is lost in a spirit world until a spirit medium, Tangina, tells Carol Ann's mother that she must guide Carol Ann and that she "can do absolutely nothing without your faith in this world and your love for the children." John Peters, in his erudite *Speaking into the Air,* identifies the same theme across a larger arc of time, arguing that people have long understood love as something that communicates across boundaries, including the boundary between living and dead. Over the centuries, many have noted Diotina of Mantinea's words to Socrates, uttered long before the creation of science fiction or electrical otherworlds—"Love bridges the chasm."[40]

Stevens was particularly proud of his "Borderland" episode and believed that the other-dimensional probing he did in this and other *Outer Limits* episodes expanded the human imagination. Above all, he said, he was interested in consciousness-expanding ideas. "Leslie has a fantastic facility of ideas," Stephano said once of his friend. "I couldn't begin to write the *Outer Limits* that he wrote. . . . He goes off on scientific flights of fancy that simply lose me as an audience, and he's more interested in what he's writing about than the characters he creates." When Stevens had to prune an episode, he chose dialogue that developed characters rather than special effects that pointed to mind-blowing otherworldly realms. ABC did not like the undeveloped characters, the production costs, or the fact that many episodes lacked monsters. "I broke the rules a few times, rather badly," Stevens recalled, "and got called for it. . . . They wanted me to get back over into my corner and give them something—killer bees, plants with spores, anything!"

Stevens was after something different, however: science fiction that would have a psychological and metaphysical impact. The characters in "The Borderland," Stevens insisted, "go inside-out, into a new realm. There was no LSD at that time, no expanding of consciousness. I wanted

Figure 9.5 In the film *Interstellar,* Coop (Matthew McConaughey) looks into other times and places from inside a tesseract in outer space. He is able to see into the past and into his daughter's room from behind her bookshelves. Attempting to communicate, he pounds against the shelves but is only able to dislodge a few books. The books that fall to the floor in his daughter's room include Abbott's *Flatland* and L'Engle's *Wrinkle in Time.*

to get what was later called the psychedelic look, to blow everyone's mind."[41] "At the inception of *The Outer Limits* there was a feeling of scratching the surface of something really important," he said once. "There was a *feel* to the first ten weeks on the air. It almost could have broken through to another level of consciousness."[42]

A New Electrical/Spiritual Society

Stevens was serious about helping usher in what he called an "electronic social transformation," and in 1969 he published a book that discussed new, multisense media (principally television) and the social and spiritual transformations these media were creating. They were responsible for wholescale changes afoot in culture and the era's obvious restlessness. Stevens's *EST: The Steersman's Handbook* was recommended as "essential" by the *Whole Earth Catalogue* and reproduced for a mass market in 1971 by Bantam Books.[43] In it, Stevens argued that the new synesthetic media world was breaking down traditional, linear and hierarchical ways of thinking, including traditional religions, though spiritual quests persisted. Questions once answered by priests were now handled by "steersmen," individuals who are able to understand and guide others through modernity's new technological changes. A sense of change and upheaval was key to the book, as was a belief that science and electronic technologies offered new pathways into the miraculous. Stevens was obviously influenced by McLuhan, who said in 1969 that "mysticism is just tomorrow's science dreamed today." Believing that "vibrational frequencies, planes of existence, astral levels; all that was once the domain of the occult" would become "important fields of exploration," Stevens argued that science, technology, and new media would open up doors to metaphysical discovery. Science now showed that nature was not uniform and unbroken, that there were cracks, gaps, and overlapping spaces. Stevens saw science, technology, and media as ways of probing those multiple spaces. "Multiple presence, multiple consciousness, the annihilation of time and space; such prospects of the far future merge into the miraculous."[44]

Stevens's views were part of the zeitgeist in the 1960s and 1970s. Many others linked the new electronic society, alternate dimensions, and new modes of consciousness and saw a new era on the horizon. In 1966 the band the Byrds produced a psychedelic rock album entitled *Fifth Dimension*, with lyrics about spaceflight, alien intelligence, Relativity, and, many believed, psychedelic drug use. One of the writers of the track "5D (Fifth Dimension)" believed that if it were played on the radio extraterrestrials might hear the song and make contact. A well-known manual for psychedelic drug use, *The Psychedelic Experience* (1964), spoke of such experience as a "fifth vision" that transcended known spacetime dimensions, an experience that was similar to the energetic, virtual worlds projected by televisions. "We are little more than flickers on a multidimensional television screen," the authors wrote. There's a point in the psychedelic experience, Timothy Leary and his coauthors averred, where the drug tripper "realizes that all sensation and perception are based on wave vibrations, and that 'he is involved in a cosmic television show which has no more substantiality than the images on his TV picture tube.' "[45] Others in the 1960s used dimensional language to talk about altered states. Terence McKenna, speaking to a crowd of physicists and philosophers at the Esalen Institute in Big Sur, California, spoke of mushrooms as openings to other dimensions, saying that "right here," "one quanta away," there was "a universe of active intelligence that is transhuman, hyperdimensional and extremely alien."[46] In McKenna's essay "New Maps of Hyperspace," he conflated higher dimensions and a heavenly world, saying, in a way reminiscent of earlier hyperspace philosophers like Abbott and Hinton, that we were hyperspatial objects that cast shadows into matter. Like Hinton's tesseract, God was a "hyperobject."[47] The "electrical" and televisual were media metaphors for the vivid, intersubjective states achieved by Leary on the East Coast and Kesey and the "Merry Pranksters" on the West.[48]

Marshall McLuhan, though, was best known for arguing that media technologies extended the range of our senses and consciousness, and Stevens was undoubtedly drawing on McLuhan's notions when he insisted that new electronic technologies were reshaping the modern mind. In a 1969 *Playboy* interview with McLuhan, this "high priest of popcult and metaphysician of media" talked about the power of the television to reshape consciousness.

> The upsurge in drug taking is intimately related to the impact of the electric media. Look at the metaphor for getting high: turning on. One turns on his consciousness through drugs just as he opens up all his senses to a total depth involvement by turning on the TV dial. Drug taking is stimulated by today's pervasive environment of instant information, with its feedback mechanism of the inner trip. The inner trip is not the sole prerogative of the LSD traveler; it's the universal experience of TV watchers. LSD is a way of miming the invisible electronic world; it releases a person from acquired verbal and visual habits and reactions, and gives the potential of instant and total involvement, both all-at-onceness and all-at-oneness, which are the basic needs of people translated by electric extensions of their central nervous systems out of the old rational, sequential value system. The attraction to hallucinogenic drugs is a means of achieving empathy with our penetrating electric environment, an environment that in itself is a drugless inner trip.[49]

The significant matter here is that McLuhan claimed that the *televisual culture inspired the drug culture*. Hallucinogenic drugs were merely ways that people attempted to re-create the televisual experience and its synesthetic qualities. Since McLuhan, many others have argued that television created a new modern sensibility. Convinced that the material world was merely a reflection of some deeper transmission, the sci-fi writer Philip Dick for instance believed that electronic media were changing human subjectivity. Dick said these media were returning modern people to a kind of animism.[50]

The change that these thinkers discerned represented a dramatic shift from an "obsolete mechanical world" to a living electronic community united and alive in new ways. McLuhan, for one, developed a utopian vision of the technological future. "Our whole cultural habitat, which we once viewed as a mere container of people, is being transformed by these media and by space satellites into a living organism, itself contained within a new macrocosm or connubium of a supraterrestrial nature. The day of the individualist, of privacy, of fragmented or 'applied' knowledge, of 'points of view' and specialist goals is being replaced by the over-all awareness of a mosaic world in which space and time are overcome by television, jets and computers—a simultaneous, 'all-at-once' world in which everything resonates with everything else as in a total electrical field." Televisions and computers, McLuhan continued, might lead us to a "technologically engendered state of universal understanding and unity, a state of absorption in the logos that could knit mankind into one family and create a perpetuity of collective harmony and peace." This breathtaking vision drew from the apocalyptic sense of change in the late 1960s.

> Psychic communal integration, made possible at last by the electronic media, could create the universality of consciousness foreseen by Dante when he predicted that men would continue as no more than broken fragments until they were unified into an inclusive consciousness. In a Christian sense, this is merely a new interpretation of the mystical body of Christ; and Christ, after all, is the ultimate extension of man.

This was more than McLuhan's *Playboy* interviewer had bargained for, and he interrupted—but was not this vision more mystical than technological? "Yes," McLuhan agreed, "as mystical as the most advanced theories of modern nuclear physics. Mysticism is just tomorrow's science dreamed today."[51]

The Holy Spirit via Haunted TV

Completely documenting how televisions helped people reimagine spiritual worlds and doorways into them would involve more space than I have here. But a brief and superficial tour of the "televisual imaginary" is necessary to provide some context for the quite remarkable transformations that this new technology inspired. To be sure, it was not just sci-fi television and film producers who were intrigued by electronic technologies as a doorway into the beyond. Psychics, neopagans, chaos magicians, spiritual seekers, modern-day spiritualists, and Christian evangelicals all used televisions to see into an unknown beyond and make that transcendent space more believable. TVs made it possible again to imagine heavenly and otherworldly things.

The American Pentecostal televangelist Oral Roberts, who developed a vast television viewership by the late 1950s, is a good place to start. In 1955 he introduced a motion picture camera into his faith healing tent services and began transmitting healing energies to millions. This meant not just that many people were able for the first time to witness Pentecostal healing practices; more importantly, it meant that a great number were able to *experience spiritual healing through their televisions*. Roberts understood the power of television and its liveness and intimacy as a communication medium, and he developed "TV prayer" practices directed at the viewing audience. He asked viewers to "believe with me," he gesticulated and pointed into the camera, and he reached up and pressed his "right hand of discernment" onto a glass plate in front of the camera. Through this act he delivered the presence of the Spirit into both the private realm of the American living room and the intimate spaces of the believer's heart. "This cinematic effect produced a sensation of sacred presence for the television audience," Andrew Blanton has concluded, "as if the hand of the healer itself was actually pressing against the screen." For the viewer all that remained was to place one's own hand on the TV screen, creating a moment of electronic touch that completed the spiritual circuit. "In a televisual age, the two

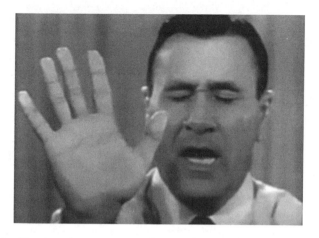

Figure 9.6   The American Pentecostal televangelist Oral Roberts uses his "right hand of discernment" to send the (electromagnetic) spirit through the television camera.

hands-at-prayer realize new tactile and experiential possibilities through the mediation of mechanical eyes, translucent screens, and special effects."[52] The Dallas televangelist Robert Tilton also invited viewers to touch their TV screens; and he said it would even work during reruns.[53]

Roberts was a pioneer in using televisions to imagine (and foster belief in) spiritual transmission, but at the heart of his ministry was a logic easily grasped by other evangelicals. The TV transmitted and received invisible forces and therefore suggested both the existence of invisible forces and ways to husband and marshal them. The TV became both proof of an invisible spirit and a medium that incarnated it. Scholars have shown how Christians around the globe embraced this logic. In an article that examined how Ghanaian charismatic/Pentecostal practices were mediated technologically, for example, Marleen de Witte pointed to different ways that invisible spiritual powers were imagined and transmitted through new technologies. Some preachers called on listeners to place their hands on radios or televisions to create points of transmission. Others, such as the Pentecostal minister Agyin Asare, asked viewers to place their hands on his televised hands during prayer meetings. "Testimonies abound in Ghana of people having received the touch of the Holy Spirit through a media broadcast or tape recording."[54] Moreover, as Birgit Meyer has argued, Ghanaian producers of religious video and film regarded their work as using technology to make invisible spiritual forces plain to the naked eye: televisions as technologies that make visible the invisible.[55]

Other observers have seen televangelists urge viewers to put a glass of water or oil on top of the TV as a receptacle for the Holy Spirit. This oil or water later could be used to heal or succor. Studying media and religion in Kinshasa, in the Democratic Republic of the Congo, Katrien Pype argued that people in this part of Africa saw visual representations not as mere signs but as images that came freighted with real magical power. TV pastors in Africa often invited viewers to participate in prayers by touching the screen, some of them insisting that one's hands *must* touch the screen in order for the spirit to do its work. Some have analogized televisions, phones, and the Internet to traditional African spiritual technologies. These western technologies, Pype wrote, "are often jokingly called 'the witchcraft of the white man' . . . and are contrasted with 'the witchcraft of the Africans.'" In other contexts around the world, televisions are regarded as objects that can transmit the spirit or be supernaturally possessed.[56]

But it would be mistaken to think that televisions have been deployed only by evangelicals. To be sure, neopagans, psychics, Spiritualists, and an assortment of spiritual seekers have turned to televisions instead of older media such as crystal balls or reflective ("scrying") pools to facilitate reflection, trance, and inner vision. Some using televisions in these ways stare at the featureless, reflective surfaces of deactivated TVs, a process that apparently clears the mind. Others treat televisions as objects that transmit spiritual energies alongside electromagnetic ones. In Christopher Penczak's *City Magick* (2002), for instance, the technopagan Penczak recommended a computer or a TV as the centerpiece of a home altar, arguing that these devices could send and receive magical signals. Penczak included instructions for "TV scrying," a practice in which believers stare at static until entering a trance state. "I have found the TV to be a medium for magick traveling over distance, much like a photograph or voodoo doll used in traditional magick." While many consider watching TV a passive activity, among technopagans it can become an active process of transmitting or receiving. "When I see a tragedy [on TV], my immediate response is to help. . . . At other times my reasonable response is magick," Penczak wrote. "When sending healing energy to a war-torn area or disaster zone, I go right up to the TV and send my intent through the image to the actual people and place needing it. . . . Transform your TV from a tool of dis-information and hypnotism to a global healing device."[57] Other pagans and spiritual seekers, locating televisions and computers at the center of our new, networked identity, have said that televisions connect them to "the world's mixing board."[58]

Televisual technologies have taken on mystical significance for many others who believe it is possible to tune in to an afterlife. Those involved in the electronic voice phenomenon (EVP) and the instrumental transcommunication (ITC) movements believe that electronic devices such as video recorders, tape recorders, telephones, and televisions can pick up visual or auditory signals from the dead. With roots in early twentieth-century Spiritualism and spirit photography, these movements appropriate recording technologies to capture the voices and images of departed spirits. In the 1940s and 1950s there were scattered attempts to tune and record voices of the dead, and in the 1950s two men in particular, Latvian-born Konstantin Raudive and the Swede Friedrich Jürgenson, initiated the modern movement. In 1959, Jürgenson was recording bird songs and discovered other mysterious sounds on his tape recordings. When the Swedish painter and opera singer later played the tapes, he heard the voices of his dead father and mother. This was the beginning of Jürgenson's interest, which continued until his death in 1987—and beyond, according to some. On the day of his funeral, Jürgenson appeared on a television set tuned to a vacant channel.[59] The black and white image was captured by a Polaroid camera and can still be viewed on the World ITC website.[60]

But Jürgenson was not the only one haunting TV static since the 1970s. Many European and American psychics and paranormal researchers have seen dead family members on TV. Hanna Buschbeck, a paranormal researcher who died in 1984, appeared smiling and youthful on the video equipment of the ITC researchers Maggy and Jules Harsch-Fischbach.[61] Other ITC researchers have tuned in images of loved ones and famous personalities, including the Austrian actress Romy Schneider, the American singer John Denver, and the Hollywood filmmaker Hal Roach.[62] ITC aficionados have experimented with different technologies in efforts to materialize other-dimensional "spirit faces" on their TVs.

Figure 9.7   The German psychic Klaus Schreiber was the first to use a video feedback system in which he pointed cameras directly at video display screens. This Polaroid of his black-and-white television captured the image of his dead brother-in-law, who appeared suddenly one day in the static.

The German psychic Klaus Schreiber was the first to use a video feedback system in which experimenters pointed video cameras directly at display monitors. This created a feedback loop and a visual effect called the Droste effect, which is when a picture appears within itself. (The effect makes a pattern of recursive mirrors within mirrors, "magic mirrors" that lead outward into their own recursive infinity.) Investigators replaying video recordings of these kinds of infinite loops have reported the appearance of single-frame images of relatives and other dead people.[63] And if ITC researchers have seen departed spirits on television, others have argued that they have glimpsed television or film personalities in near-death or out-of-body experiences. Describing one out-of-body experience, Robert Monroe, the radio broadcaster and author of *Journeys Out of the Body* (1971), said that in heaven he encountered, among other things, W. C. Fields in character.[64]

In another recursive loop, experiences of seeing dead people through the static have been dramatized in fictional television programs and films. Films that incorporate recorded spirit voices or images include *The Changeling* (1980), *Videodrome* (1983), *Poltergeist* (1982), *The Sixth Sense* (1999), *White Noise* (2005), and *White Noise: The Light* (2007). Producers of fictional television, TV talk shows, reality TV, and ghost-hunting programs also have been keenly interested in electronic voices and images from the afterlife. The list of television programs that feature such voices and images is extensive.[65]

∽∽∽

If nineteenth-century scientists and other authorities attempted to discipline and expunge religious ways of thinking, the twentieth-century technologies that these scientists created, technologies such as the television, generated powerful new ways of imagining spiritual transmissions and exchanges. Televisions shaped new ways of seeing the spirit by materializing energetic transmissions on screens in that most intimate and personal of environments, the home. As we have seen, the earliest televisions installed in American living rooms were regarded as objects of mystical importance, as openings to things that were marvelous, uncanny, or supernatural. Early television programming, including early genre TV, reflected the public's curiosity about these new techno-wonders and stimulated hope that electronic technologies might satisfy buried or suppressed feelings of spiritual longing. Televisions recharged the spiritual imagination in different ways—by receiving invisible transmissions that could be thought of as either spiritual or "like" spiritual forces; by proving that there were invisible forces and that these forces could be efficacious, transmitted, and received; and by creating visual narratives that depicted new electronic technologies as not merely material things but agents of extraordinary, psychic, or supernatural realities.

Conclusion

The Astonishing Afterlife of the Square

N ot all good stories have good endings. It is quite remarkable, for instance, that Edwin Abbott's *Flatland,* his imaginative gospel of higher dimensions, ended not with a hopeful statement of new possibilities, not with a moment of redemption or resurrection as in the older, Biblical gospel, but with a depressing scene of futility and despair. At the end of *Flatland,* the heroic Square, who had journeyed to higher space and boldly proclaimed its reality to others, had been arrested, his views censured, his body imprisoned within a two-dimensional cell. He was considered too subversive, too dangerous, to be set free. No trial, no formal sentence, and no release date, apparently, were even contemplated.

Destitute of friends and disciples; visited only occasionally by his brother, who, though "one of the best Squares" and an eye-witness to one of the Sphere's manifestations, did not believe the Square's story; and susceptible, after seven years of imprisonment, to fits of self-doubt during which he wondered if he had a "diseased imagination," the Square sat alone in his cell, penning a narrative of higher-dimensional experiences that he could hardly recall.[1] As far as I can see, the Square wrote, "the millennial Revelation has been made to me for nothing." If the reality of that higher world he glimpsed was going to become widely known, it was difficult to see how. The conventionality of contemporary British society was too entrenched. And even more disturbing was a fact about human nature that *Flatland* made clear over and over again: that people in general were not interested in pursuing or finding truth—the real truth, that is. They were not interested in finding the kind of truth that, rather than confirming one's preexisting tastes and prejudices instead rose above them, sometimes even challenging and critiquing them.

But in a development that surely would have astonished both the Square and Edwin Abbott, writers and thinkers in the twentieth and twenty-first centuries rescued *Flatland's* disgraced hero, transforming him into a scientific authority, spiritual guide, and cultural icon. There were many imaginative sequels to Abbott's *Flatland* and even more books, television programs, and films that retold, referred to, or modified this classic story. Scientists writing books for general audiences used the Square to introduce readers to the idea of higher dimensions; sci-fi and fantasy writers referred to *Flatland* to make their fantastic otherworlds seem plausible; and spiritual seekers pointed to the Square's adventures as somehow making more credible extraordinary spiritual visons, parapsychological powers, or other apparently supernatural realities.

Mapping out these developments and the trajectories of other higher-dimensional speculations since the 1970s is the nearly impossible task attempted in this Conclusion. No era was more preoccupied with *Flatland*-like meditations on the universe's invisible dimensions; no era produced anything close to the number of scientific reflections, sci-fi stories, and spiritual intuitions about hidden levels, spiritual afterworlds, and material (or spiritual) multiverses. Reasons for this new efflorescence of otherworldly creativity vary but they certainly include the explosion of extradimensional scientific theories and the successful popularization of these ideas. Readers have certainly been eager for new scientific and science fictional ideas—and, quite remarkably, they have even incorporated these ideas into new, hybrid belief systems and worldviews. Perhaps the most important reason, however, for this outburst of extra-dimensional speculation is a more persistent aspiration, one shared by those seeking new scientific knowledge and novel spiritual notions, to reach beyond the limits of present knowledge and wisdom. Here I examine this persistent aspiration and its many manifestations in new settings that mix as never before ambitious scientific speculation, fantastic science fiction, and novel forms of spiritual seeking.

Flatland Sequels

There have been many writers who have developed *Flatland*-inspired sequels and sci-fi stories that have incorporated narrative elements or characters from Abbott's classic. Some of these writers regarded their imagined worlds as pure fiction; others, possibly channeling George MacDonald and C. S. Lewis on mythopoesis, saw their literary work as suggesting new poetic or metaphysical facts about the universe. In the former category are writers who borrowed from *Flatland* to develop fanciful narratives or think through the geometry or physics of other dimensions. Hinton back in 1907 wrote *An Episode of Flatland*—a book that Abbott recommended to readers. Norman Juster in 1963 published *The Dot and the Line: A Romance in Lower Mathematics,* and Dionys Burger wrote a sequel to *Flatland* entitled *Sphereland* (1965).[2] Several animated film adaptations also have been made—*Flatland* (1965); *Flatland* (2007); *Flatland: The Movie* (2007), with Martin Sheen as "Arthur Square"; and *Flatland 2: Sphereland* (2012). Scientists such as Carl Sagan and Stephen Hawking have retold the Square's story to introduce the idea that the universe might have higher dimensions, as Sagan did, for example, in his television series *Cosmos* (1980).

Other writers have cared more, and written more, about what we might call the Square's spiritual or philosophical preoccupations. One of them was the American mathematician and prolific science writer Martin Gardner, who shared with Abbott and C. Howard Hinton a disdain for both simplistic religious dogmas and the closed-world materialism of many contemporary scientists. Though converting early in life to Protestant fundamentalism, it was not long before he turned away from this form of faith, pronouncing it "very ugly" and entirely unbelievable for a thoughtful adult. And yet he retained the view that nourishing a spiritual faith and attempting to pray led human beings to greater happiness. Gardner explored different positions on spirituality and science in many articles that ranged from popular science reporting to imaginative fiction. In the latter category was "An Adventure in Hyperspace at the Church of the Fourth Dimension" (1962), in which he described discovering a London church shaped like a vertically oriented, unfolded hypercube. This was a fictional adventure, but Gardner made it as realistic as possible. Inside the church he listened to a sermon by a minister named Arthur Slade—Henry Slade's great-nephew—on higher space and conversed with Slade about higher dimensions and the hyperfaith of people such as Plato, Hinton, Abbott, William James, and a number of Christian theologians. Slade was able to show Gardner that his great uncle's higher-dimensional feats were mere magic; but he also clearly believed that, as he said, our universe was just "the three-dimensional 'surface' of a vast, four-dimensional sea."[3] We were merely two-dimensional Flatlanders, he said, shadows flittering on the wall of Plato's cave.

In a number of publications, including his regular "Mathematical Games" column in *Scientific American,* which ran from 1956 to 1981, and in several books that addressed the fourth dimension, Gardner wrote about hypercubes, fictional flatworlds, mirror symmetry in nature, the Kaluza-Klein five-dimensional theory, and mystics who tried to see into higher realms. He championed the imaginative power and real excitement that came from speculating about invisible, higher spaces.

During Gardner's lifetime, the audience for these kinds of reflections, for scientifically informed thinking about higher spaces, spiritual or otherwise, was growing. In the late 1970s, the mathematician Alexander K. Dewdney began thinking in detail about how a two-dimensional world might work—how its science might develop and what its technology might look like. The sci-fi narrative that resulted, *The Planiverse* (1984), told the story of computer science students who designed a virtual two-dimensional world. This virtual world accidentally came in contact with a real two-dimensional creature named Yendred, a perceptive explorer journeying through his world and willing to talk about it. (The book was so believable that "it surprised and worried" me, Dewdney recalled, "that so many people believed the tale was factual."[4]) Yendred answered questions about his world's geography, politics, biology, and built environment, communicating this information to Dewdney and his students by thinking thoughts that were rendered in text on a classroom computer screen. Yendred was traveling throughout his flat world, looking for a sage named Drabk who was said to have knowledge of "the beyond" as well as mystical powers that included the ability to leave the two-dimensional planiverse and "glide along beside it." Yendred discovered that Drabk lived near the square shrine of an old, prophetic figure named Amada who had once united many tribes. At the end of the book, Yendred reached the Shrine of Amada on the planiverse's high plateau, found Drabk, and learned that there was a Presence that was beyond thought and words. Yendred asked where this Presence was. "It beside you is. Closer than your body," Drabk explained, Yoda-like. Drabk concluded his sermon with a thought straight out of the Qur'an: the Presence was "Closer than your blood." Drabk then pointed in a direction outside of the planiverse, his arm disappearing momentarily.[5]

Like *Flatland's* Square, Yendred sought a way of imaginatively probing into something beyond conventional realities—he was on a quest, Dewdney once said of his protagonist, "for the third dimension, or, at least, a spiritual version of it."[6] The search for something spiritual was Dewdney's as well. Calling himself a Platonist and insisting that there was a higher world of mathematical and absolute realities,[7] Dewdney spoke of this book as a "Sufi story," a narrative of a long, difficult search for spiritual knowledge that ended with the protagonist joining a spiritual order and learning from a spiritual master. (As one commentator has pointed out, the word "Yendred" itself incorporated mystical yearning and awe—"yen" and "dread"—but was also Dewdney's name backward with the "w" changed to an "r".)

Active first in a Christi Sufi order and then in the Algerian Alawi order, Dewdney built Islamic tropes and images into his narrative and drew on his own experiences as he fashioned Yendred's adventures. Dewdney based Yendred's Ardean language on Maltese Arabic, because, he said, "it is subject to both Arabic/Islamic and Western/Christian influences"; he spoke of the prophet Amada (Ahmad/Muhammad)[8] as one who, like Muhammad, united tribes; and he described the Shrine of Amada as a kind of two-dimensional Ka'aba, the large, black stone shrine in Mecca. (Here was another mystical square that stretched into higher dimensions.) The sage Drabk, who appeared to have miraculous three-dimensional powers, was obviously a Sufi saint—"Drabk," Dewdney himself admitted, was "a thinly disguised reworking of my own teacher's name"—and many of Drabk's teachings were indebted to Muslim theological notions, including, for instance, the idea that the Presence beyond "was closer than your jugular vein" (Qur'an 50:16).[9]

Perhaps the best-known writer to extend the Abbott/Hinton hyperspace tradition, however, is the American mathematician and sci-fi author Rudy Rucker. He uses dimensional mathematics in novels, nonfiction works, and short stories, including the afterlife fantasy *White Light* (1980), a book about sex with hyperdimensional aliens called *The Sex Sphere* (1983), short stories that deploy Hinton's cubical reflections and Abbott's Flatlanders in new adventures, and a popular book on the mathematics and metaphysics of a fourth (spatial) dimension. Rucker, who has won two Philip K. Dick awards for his sci-fi novels and who helped found the cyberpunk literary movement, began his career with a Ph.D. in mathematics. A great-great-great-grandson of the German philosopher G. W. F. Hegel, Rucker inherited something of Hegel's metaphysical ambitions and idealist worldview, but he built his own metaphysics using higher dimensions, a process that began when he read *Flatland* in high school. In college he reread the book but its importance became clear only when he was a graduate student in mathematics at Rutgers. On one night in particular, while smoking pot and listening to Frank Zappa, Rucker began a sequel about the Square that developed the *Flatland* narrative with new cartoon panels and additional storylines. He showed his many drawings to his friends—one of whom wondered if Rucker's career goal was "to write, like, Tubeland?"— and to his baffled father who worried he was preoccupied with the imaginative life of a two-dimensional square. He asked, in the way of many tuition-paying parents, "Where are you going with this?"[10]

Rucker became a professor of mathematics first at the State University of New York at Geneseo and then at other colleges in Europe and America, retiring in 2004 as a computer science professor from San Jose State University in California. But his real passion was speculative nonfiction and science fiction, which he wrote in order both to think imaginatively about math and metaphysics and to develop a sense of awe and wonder toward the universe.[11] In several nonfiction and fictional works, Rucker revisited the Square's life, retold the story of *Flatland,* and added further adventures. In *Geometry, Relativity and the Fourth Dimension,* for instance, the Sphere lifted the Square out of jail and helped him (and Rucker) convince others that higher dimensions in fact did exist. In Rucker's more upbeat narrative, Flatlanders were finally persuaded of this new truth, going so far as to bestow upon the Square a professorship at Flatland University. (Was there a higher honor in 2D or even 3D existence?)

The Square's adventures continued in Rucker's *The Fourth Dimension* (1984), a book that introduced the fourth (spatial) dimension with drawings, mathematical puzzles, philosophical asides, and excerpts from Rucker's science fiction. In this book, the Square blundered by initiating a secret affair with a married woman named Una. When confronted by Una's aggrieved husband, the situation deteriorated. But in a final scene the Sphere, intervening again at the crucial moment, reminded the Square that his life was merely a shadowy fragment within a larger life, a mere dream of some creative Author, and that all personal problems might be resolved by seeing things from a higher realm of real love and repentance.[12] The resolution was Hintonian. The Square learned, just as Hinton had, that vexing questions about love and marriage might be resolved through higher-dimensional vision.

Though Gardner and Dewdney used higher-dimensional fiction to imagine not just unusual physical spaces but also unconventional spiritual realities, Rucker went a step further and wrote explicitly about the spiritual power of these kinds of sci-fi works. "There's still a lot of room of all kinds inside science fiction," Rucker once said. "If you just need to have an arbitrary door to another world, then let's do it. I mean, there's been so many surprises in the history of science, why would we think we couldn't still have something really surprising happen?" Science fiction opened imaginative doorways to other ways of thinking and believing.

> Science fiction is one possible tool for trying to explore the greater reality. It's a good tool because it tries to start from fresh, bringing in all sorts of new scientific concepts. And it has an irreverent open quality to it. We can forget, at least temporarily, about being serious and religious, we can just play, and ask questions like whether there might be many Gods, what it would be like in their homeland, how many dimensions of space and time they have, and so on. It's a relief sometimes not to strive for spiritual growth and simply to speculate. In the end, as the speculations become part of your worldview, they will have a spiritual meaning.

Convinced that "it would be preposterously self-centered to believe that humans are in a position to understand everything about the

Cosmos," and sensing, moreover, that "there is some other order to reality than what we ordinarily perceive," Rucker has said that meditation, prayer, and imaginative writing are ways of getting closer to higher orders of existence. "If you pray or meditate, you can sometimes have an experience of being in touch with a higher order of being, whom we might as well call God. Sometimes I have a sensation, for instance, that individual humans are part of a single great spacetime body, that each of us is a kind of 'eye' that God uses to look at things with, and that people are like eyestalks on the Mystical Body of Humanity, if you will."[13] These are not the visions and inspirations of the conventionally devout, but rather something new—they are hybrid spiritual thoughts that playfully combine religious ideas about God(s), mathematical notions about higher dimensions, and sci-fi narratives about eyestalks, aliens, and other forms of life.

There is one final person who, though he has not written a *Flatland* sequel, has probably done more than anyone else to revive the Square's story and explore its imaginative power. A mathematics professor for forty-seven years at Brown University (where he is now emeritus), Thomas Banchoff first encountered the idea of higher dimensions when reading *Captain Marvel* and *Strange Adventures* comics. Those works featured futuristic scientists who studied "the seventh, eighth and ninth dimensions" and witnessed mysterious blobs suddenly appear, grow larger, and then disappear—obviously fourth-dimensional objects passing through our lower plane of existence. By the age of sixteen, the Catholic Banchoff had also read *Flatland* and was formulating tentative higher-dimensional theories of Catholic doctrines, including the Trinity, which he would communicate with genuine enthusiasm "to any teacher or classmate who would listen."[14]

He continued to try to understand Catholic doctrines and the problem of how properly to talk about higher, spiritual things using limited, human concepts, writing an undergraduate paper at Notre Dame on these topics. "Most of what I worried about when I was a boy was connected to words, because words used to describe theological mysteries did not mean the same thing when they talked about God as they did when they talked about human beings." For instance, he said, "heaven is a state and a place, according to the words of the Bible," but it was not the kind of state or place we were accustomed to talking about. How would we wrestle with this? "How do we express the ineffable in words? The theologian and the mathematician share the same problem: the dimensional analogy is an attempt on the part of mathematicians to explain situations in which our words no longer mean the same thing." The Square, Banchoff continued, confronted the same problem.[15]

If as a boy Banchoff approached these problems with theological curiosity, as a man he examined them with scientific rigor. (It is fair to add, however, that even as a man he never lost his youthful sense of excitement for the subject.) He went on to a remarkable career not just as an expert on the geometry and topology of higher-dimensional objects, but also as someone who wrote extensively about Abbott's life, produced (with a colleague) an exhaustively annotated version of *Flatland,* and publicly promoted the scientific study of higher spatial dimensions. His work influenced artists, writers, and sci-fi television and film producers—people such as Madeleine L'Engle, Salvador Dalí, and the filmmaker George Lucas. He first caught the attention of the national media in a 1975 *Washington Post* article that featured his hypercube models, which he had constructed in both folded cardboard and computer-generated versions. "We want to be able to visualize objects which are just beyond our comprehension," Banchoff said, displaying his models. (The *Post* reporter wondered if Banchoff's work was less science than it was metaphysical speculation on Plato's world of ideal forms.) The article discussed Banchoff's research, how to understand lower-dimensional cross-sections and shadows of higher-dimensional objects, and how higher-dimensional objects had been used in fiction such as Abbott's *Flatland* and in art such as Salvador Dalí's *Corpus Hypercubus* (1954). (See Figure C.1.) When Banchoff shared with the *Post* reporter a few higher-dimensional religious reflections it must have seemed natural in an era of alternative metaphysics and New Age spirituality. "Could Christ's miracles have been done in the fourth dimension?" Banchoff wondered. Could his incarnation and his crucifixion be better understood using higher mathematics?[16]

The *Washington Post* article was only the beginning for Banchoff. He subsequently published many articles in academic journals, and his work was featured in *Newsweek,* the *Christian Science Monitor,* and *Scientific American.* His research attracted the attention of many artists, writers, and general readers. Dalí, for example, read this *Washington Post*

Figure C.1   Salvador Dalí, *Corpus Hypercubus* (1954). Like other twentieth-century artists Dalí knew something about higher spatial dimensions. Here he uses a three-dimensional representation of a hypercube to suspend a crucified Christ in between two worlds, 3D and 4D, lower and higher, earthly and heavenly.

article, contacted Banchoff, and initiated a series of conversations about mathematics, art, science, and higher dimensions. At their first meeting at Dalí's New York hotel, Banchoff brought his cardboard hypercube model and showed Dalí how it worked. In heavily accented English, Dalí said to Banchoff, "I may have this." With an imperious personal style, Dalí could be hard to refuse. Banchoff noted, wryly, "It was not exactly a question."[17]

Scientific Theories of Higher Dimensions

If the mathematical investigations of scholars such as Banchoff and the fantastic fictions of writers such as Rucker generated enthusiasm for higher-dimensional imaginings, these developments were not primarily responsible for the stunning rise in popularity of higher-dimensional discourses in the twentieth and twenty-first centuries. That accomplishment was the work of a cadre of mathematical physicists who developed different higher-dimensional theories beginning in the 1970s and discussed them in bestselling books, popular television documentaries, and PBS science specials. Though the number of physicists working on such things as string theory or multiverse theory is not large compared to the total number of academic physicists, their influence on the public's imagination has been outsized. As a result, since the 1970s discourses about the universe have become speculative and fantastic, otherworldly and multidimensional, in ways few could have anticipated.

Mathematical physicists who have developed extra-dimensional theories have done so in order to solve what is perhaps the greatest problem in modern physics—the strange incompatibility between the laws of General Relativity, which describe the behavior of the very large, and the laws of quantum mechanics, which describe the behavior of the very small. Both sets of laws have been shown to be true, but they also cannot be combined. Why would the universe be governed by not one but two sets of incompatible laws? Attempts to develop a single, encompassing framework that might unify nature's laws began in the early decades of the twentieth century, when three European researchers—Gunnar Nordstrom, Theodor Kaluza, and Oskar Klein—developed five-dimensional mathematical systems with more "room" to accommodate all forces and objects in the universe, big and small. At first these ideas drew attention; but these theories presented a number of their own difficulties and some physicists believed that positing extra dimensions was unnecessary and extravagant.[18] These problems together with the fact that physicists were busy developing consensus around quantum mechanics meant that higher-dimensional models were laid aside for decades.

Then, in the 1970s and 1980s, a group of mathematical physicists turned attention again to the incompatibility between General Relativity and quantum mechanics and the possibility that a solution might be found in higher-dimensional mathematics. Developing new approaches, these thinkers devised "string" theories that attempted to unify all of nature's laws and forces in a single set of equations. As these equations were created and refined, the hoped-for unification came into focus as a possibility, but there was a catch. For everything to work, the universe needed to have—*uh, em*—ten dimensions. String theories reconceived the most basic elements of nature as tiny, one-dimensional, vibrating strings that moved in a many-dimensional world. Several versions of string theory emerged, until in 1995 the next theory to develop, M theory, tried to reconcile the different string theories into a single eleven-dimensional framework. (The theory's creator, Edward Witten at Princeton, said that the "M" stood for "magic," "mystery," or "membrane"; detractors suggested another option—"murky.")[19] Since then, string theories have expanded in different directions. Witten and others have discussed the role of higher-dimensional objects such as membranes (or "branes"), and some have argued that our universe is merely the "surface" of one membrane lying next to many others within a cosmic "bulk." Though physicists working out these theories are convinced that they are generating important discoveries and perhaps even progressing toward a final unification of nature's laws, support for their elaborate mathematical systems can be lukewarm at best among physicist colleagues working in other subfields.

Tiny strings vibrating in extra dimensions, a universe that exists on the surface of a lower-dimensional brane—these are remarkable theories but they are not the only ones to posit the existence of extra-dimensional spaces or worlds. Since the 1980s, physicists have developed other multiverse models and theories. Inflationary multiverse theories hold that different rates of cosmic inflation produce countless new branching "bubble" universes in an ever-expanding, massive cosmic bulk. Cyclic multiverse theories argue that the cosmic bulk's many braneworlds collide in cyclical patterns, causing "big bangs" over and over. Quilted multiverse theories point out that if our universe goes beyond the observable universe to infinity, it must also contain an infinite number of far-distant areas that are identical to our own. Mathematical multiverse theories argue that because physical reality *is* mathematics, different mathematical structures also have physical existence in other realms with distinct natural laws. Holographic theories developed by black hole cosmologists speculate that our universe is merely one world spread out within the interior of a huge black hole. In some of these theories, including the holographic and brane multiverse theories, our universe comes into focus as a real Flatland, a mere lower-dimensional layer of a higher-dimensional whole.

A final theory, responding to a different set of questions and fostering a very different world-picture, comes from a way of interpreting objects in the quantum world of the very small. These objects do not look or behave in familiar ways. Scientists represent them by using a mathematical equation, Schrödinger's wave equation, which describes not what or where they are but instead the probability that they will appear in a certain place upon observation. Prior to observation, these objects exist in forms that some have called "unpicturable," but which we can think of as something like fuzzy, spread-out waves of possibilities. When scientists observe or measure them they take on more definite shape as either particle or wavelike entities. The conventional interpretation of this, the Copenhagen interpretation, says that the wavefunction that represents the object before it is observed collapses upon observation, and the fuzzy, indeterminate quantum state of the object is transformed into something located in time and space. But this interpretation presents difficulties. The biggest one is trying to understand how an object defined as a spread-out set of possibilities might be transformed into a more well-defined entity via observation. Many have wondered about this problem and criticized the Copenhagen interpretation's idea of wavefunction collapse as arbitrary, ad hoc, or mathematically inconsistent.

Several alternatives to the Copenhagen interpretation have attempted to deal with these problems, including Hugh Everett's Many Worlds

Interpretation (MWI), which avoids the arbitrary collapsing of the wavefunction but substitutes in its place something that may be even harder to believe—that all of the infinite possibilities contained in the probability wavefunction continue to exist in imperceptible, parallel worlds. The many possibilities of the wavefunction do not go away; it is simply that we notice in our world only certain outcomes and events, and these events seem to be "what happened." According to the MWI, all other possibilities continue to exist in infinitely branching other-worlds that we cannot perceive.

The MWI can be difficult to accept. Physicists have complained that the theory is speculative, that it opens up more difficulties than it resolves, and that it is unnecessarily complex, introducing an infinite number of unobservable universes and therefore violating scientific preferences for simpler, falsifiable models. (As the sci-fi writer Philip K. Dick once said, the MWI was "hardly an economical or orderly way for God to handle things."[20]) But the theory also has scientific supporters, including those who believe that it offers the most mathematically consistent theory even if its implications are hard to understand for real life. "When I think about the Everett interpretation in everyday life, I do not believe it," Juan Malcedena, a theoretical physicist at the Institute for Advanced Study in Princeton, said in 2006. "But when I think about it in quantum mechanics, it is the most reasonable thing to believe."[21] It might sound like fantastic science fiction, but it might also be true.

Some theories, such as the MWI, do indeed raise questions about the relationship between higher-dimensional science and imaginative science fiction. The July 2007 issue of *Nature* raises these questions explicitly, discussing how science both "inspires and feeds on" fables and stories. (See Figure C.2.) Certainly Abbott's *Flatland* has had this kind of imaginative power. "Physicists hone their intuition," the Columbia University physicist Brian Greene once said, about "extra dimensions by contemplating what life would be like if we lived in an imaginary *lower*-dimensional universe—following the lead of Edwin Abbott's enchanting 1884 classic popularization *Flatland*." Greene argued here that physicists have used narratives such as *Flatland to think about* problems in the field, and there is certainly evidence for this.[22]

But more commonly physicists use such stories not to create science but to explain it to the public. In Sagan's *Cosmos* series, for example,

Figure C.2　"Many Worlds" fiction and facts on the cover of *Nature*'s July 2007 issue, which marked the fiftieth anniversary of the publication of Hugh Everett's original Many Worlds Interpretation. This issue combined articles on the science of MWI with others discussing the literary uses of this theory. That scientific ideas could be both speculative and valid and that science somehow "feeds on" fables and stories were surprising statements in a science journal, reflecting perhaps a new openness to the cultural context of scientific discovery. From *Nature* 448:7149 (July 5, 2007).

he used Abbott's *Flatland* to introduce the idea that our three-dimensional universe could be bent in a fourth dimension and be therefore "finite but unbounded," much like the two-dimensional surface of the earth. Others have used *Flatland*-style analogical reasoning to make it seem more plausible that our universe might be the flat shadow of something higher—that, as the physicist Paul Davies wrote once in a book on string theory, our spacetime might be "enfolded in a universe of five (or even more) dimensions."[23] Still others have deployed *Flatland* to make more comprehensible the characteristics of higher-dimensional spaces, the reasons we cannot perceive them, and the nature of multiverse models in which human beings, like Abbott's Flatlanders, live on only one surface in a many-layered cosmos.[24]

If scientific ways of thinking and speaking are related to science fiction in these ways, might scientific thinking also function for some scientists and certainly many nonscientists in ways that one might call "spiritual"? In other words, might scientific ideas probe imaginatively into supernatural territory or something very close to it or provide a kind of spiritual freedom, existential comfort, or religious awe and wonder?

For example, Hugh Everett, the atheist creator of the MWI believed that the branching otherworlds of his theory "guaranteed him immortality." Everett argued that his self "is bound at each branching to follow whatever path does not lead to death—and so on ad infinitum." Can we call this kind of speculation "spiritual" even though Everett's afterworld was (in a weird way) within the physical cosmos?[25] Other scientists have imagined the existence of a beyond space that is both the source of all earthly life and its final destination. Some have speculated that a higher, more intelligent life form created our world as a simulation, holograph, or projection.[26] (The Stanford physicist Andrei Linde, sounding very *Men in Black,* once ad-libbed, "Probably God is just a physicist hacker who baked our universe in his own laboratory!"[27]) The physicist Michio Kaku, noting that these parallel universe scenarios were "once viewed with suspicion by scientists as being the province of mystics, charlatans, and cranks," has posed the possibility that one day a "dimensional lifeboat" might allow us to escape our dying sun and unlivable earth and transport to another (physical) location. We might in this way save our civilization from extinction.[28] And the Stanford string theorist Lawrence Krauss, a self-described "anti-theist," has also mused about the higher-dimensional boundaries of our universe, wondering "if material or information from these extra dimensions can 'leak' into our own world"—asking furthermore what it might mean if "the source of our own existence lies across that invisible boundary."[29] If we think of religion or spirituality as an attempt to overcome the secular limits of nature or history, are not these speculations spiritual in some way?[30]

Higher-Dimensional Powers on Earth and in Heaven

Entertaining the possibility that scientific theories might point toward the spiritual or even discussing the philosophical implications of scientific ideas—these generally are not activities that physicists pursue in professional journals, meetings, or conferences. Most physicists, after all, spend their time solving practical problems in industrial settings or laboratories. But once one ventures beyond these professional environments, where disciplinary norms inhibit freewheeling speculation, discourses about physics, philosophy, and metaphysics open up considerably. In popular science books and television documentaries, new discoveries are explained and their meanings are discussed and negotiated. Philosophical and metaphysical questions come into play. And audience interest and buy-in are important considerations.[31] Different types of scientists, on a spectrum from the cautiously metaphysical to the speculative and visionary, have become involved, including religious physicists such as Stephen Barr or John Polkinghorne, philosophically oriented physicists such as Paul Davies or Michio Kaku, and scientists who have transformed themselves into full-time mystics and spiritual teachers, people such as Amit Goswami and Fred Alan Wolf. For all of these thinkers, as well as for many philosophers, theologians, and other observers, new discoveries in physics have implications for big questions concerning free will, human immortality, mystical experience, and the meaning of a many-dimensional world.

On the visionary and speculative end of the scale is one physicist-turned-countercultural-mystic who has helped develop a new spiritual worldview out of ideas in modern physics. (This new worldview sometimes goes by the name of "quantum mysticism.") Fred Alan Wolf received his Ph.D. in theoretical physics at UCLA in 1963 and was an academic

Figure C.3 A popular spiritual writer and speaker, Fred Alan Wolf writes books about spirituality, consciousness, and quantum physics. He sometimes appears as his superhero alter ego "Dr. Quantum" in YouTube videos and New Age films such as *What the Bleep Do We Know?* Here he visits an animated Flatland to show that their world, like ours, is embedded in a dimensionally complex cosmos.

physicist until a 1971 sabbatical trip to India and Kathmandu, where in a Buddhist temple he had a mystical experience in which he felt himself merging into everything around him—the meditating monks, the temple architecture, even a fly that buzzed around his foot. This altered state of consciousness made him wonder if all things were connected at a deep level.[32] Wolf left his academic position at San Diego State University in 1974 to seek answers to this and other metaphysical questions, joining forces with a few other hippie physicists in San Francisco who wanted to use quantum mechanics to explain ESP, psychokinesis, occult phenomena, and spirit communication. Wolf and others in this "Fundamental Fysiks Group" were disgusted that mainstream physics had turned its back on important philosophical questions. He came to believe, for instance, that quantum entanglement, a phenomenon in which particles separated in space are mysteriously linked, helped make sense of his mystical experience: At a higher-dimensional level, even things separated by vast spaces are somehow interconnected. Wolf made this point in various writings and in an animated online video in which he floated over a two-dimensional Flatland, inserted his finger into it, and,

Sphere-like, introduced himself and his world to astonished onlookers. Like Abbott's *Flatland,* this sequence tried to make more plausible the idea of layered, higher worlds.

Wolf and other scientifically trained mystics have argued that the existence of higher dimensions makes possible extraordinary and unexplained extrasensory abilities that enable some to see across vast distances, predict the future, telepathically send or receive thoughts, or even travel out of the body. Might it be possible that our consciousness has a slight extension into an invisible direction, an extension that enables us to sense things in these unexpected ways?

Wolf's friend and fellow hippie physicist, Elizabeth Rauscher, for example, developed cosmological models in which the universe had additional temporal and spatial dimensions, models that made it possible that lengthy spatial distances actually could be probed through shortcuts into higher layers. Rauscher thought higher-dimensional models of the universe might explain both unusual mental abilities and the strange ("nonlocal") behavior of entangled particles. Several other physicists with mystical inclinations, including Bernard Carr, who was at one time a Ph.D. student of Stephen Hawking, have developed models in which physical objects and mental ones are simply lower-dimensional cross-sections of a single higher-dimensional space. In Carr's model, nonphysical percepts that are precognitive or telepathic are transmitted between subjects through a higher-dimensional fabric that he calls the Universal Structure, which, he has also noted, is similar in outline to the multidimensional cosmic bulk discussed by contemporary physicists.[33]

Parapsychological researchers have also borrowed dimensional language in order to talk about unexplained mental powers. With associates at the Stanford Research Institute (SRI) and funding from the federal government, the parapsychological researcher Russell Targ, for example, studied what he and others at the SRI called "remote viewing"—receiving mental images of shielded or remote events or objects. These researchers, who at one point found themselves featured on the front page of the *Wall Street Journal* and in the NOVA documentary *A Case of ESP,* surmised that psychic events were in some sense "an interaction of our awareness with nonlocal, hyperdimensional space-time in which we live."[34] These kinds of hyperspace speculations have taken place within a much wider, and persistently growing, subculture that celebrates the parapsychological, psychic, and supernatural. In the earlier decades of the twentieth century this subculture was small and marginal, nourished in Spiritualist circles, psychical research societies, and among fans of supernatural fiction. But today this impulse has moved closer to the center of modern religious and spiritual pursuits in the West. One need only think of the many supernatural horror films, the parapsychological powers of characters in fantasy books and films, the astonishing ghost-hunting documentaries and reality TV shows, the super/psi powers of comic-book heroes, the stupendous special-effect miracles on electronic screens big and small—all of these point to the cultural power of parapsychological wonders and the higher-dimensional discourses that make them possible. I am not alone in pointing to the pervasiveness of this new pop culture, especially powerful in electronic media, and the ways that it has reenchanted modern western culture.[35]

But perhaps the most striking example of the power of this pop culture of higher dimensions is how people today talk of death and the afterlife as "higher dimensional." Today dying is not something that deposits the soul in an afterlife heaven or hell; it is something that sends the self somehow to "another dimension." From sci-fi characters to professional theologians and participants in the new "afterlife movement," people now often talk in this new way about death and dying. Given that virtually no one (in fiction or reality) used these terms even fifty years ago, this change in terminology is quite remarkable.

Examples of this are not difficult to find. In sci-fi television and film, for example, including films such as *Poltergeist* (1982) and *White Noise* (2005), and in comic books, the afterlife is glossed as a higher dimension or plane of reality. Comic-book heroes, superheroes, and other protagonists enter heavenly, dimensional otherworlds—with names such as "Fifth Dimension," "Dream Dimension," and "Astral Realm"—in order to retrieve dead characters, to reunite heavenly souls with their hollow earthly bodies, to acquire divine or supernatural powers, or to learn about the mysteries of existence.[36] When the Fantastic Four foment plans to retrieve their fallen comrade Ben (aka "The Thing"), for example, their discussion about afterlife worlds and other kinds of alternative dimensions shows how the pop cultural imagination has mixed higher dimensions and heaven. Sue, the Invisible Woman, has misgivings about bringing their friend back. "I don't know what to say. You keep talking about heaven like it was just another Negative Zone. I don't want to debate theology. . . . But any afterlife there may be is a sacred kingdom to billions of people. It's not the 'Afterverse.' It's a domain of spiritual faith. How do you know it even exists?"[37] Was this afterverse an extra space that could be technologically probed or an impenetrable spiritual world perceived by faith?

In other comics and in a lot of science fiction, including one notable episode of *Buffy the Vampire Slayer*,[38] there is the same kind of playful experimentation with categories such as heaven, afterworld, multiverse, and extra dimensions. Moreover, this experimentation goes beyond fiction—for if comics and sci-fi deploy scientific language to talk of heaven not as an afterlife but as an "afterverse," a number of popular science books (such as Paul Davies's book on string theory) use comic-book language to talk of higher dimensions as fantastic "superspaces." Fiction borrows the language of science; popular science borrows the language of fiction—and, sometimes, even of faith.

The same type of conceptual slippage between heavenly afterlives and higher dimensions has found its way into the works of religious writers as well. Is heaven a wholly other, nonphysical place or a more immanent type of transcendence suggested by higher-dimensional theory? Some contemporary Christian pastors and theologians speak now of heaven as an extra-dimensional space. "Some believe that there is nothing beyond earth and the stars," while others believe in a "literal heaven and hell," the evangelist Daniel Duval has written. But these conceptions were simplistic. The key to a new Christian understanding of heaven was recalling that both the Bible—in 2 Corinthians 12:2–4, for example—and modern physics posited the existence of different levels and dimensions. Why should Christians refuse to put both discourses together when they might shed light on each other? Gesturing to the variety of dimensional ideas in string and M theories, Duval developed a tentative ten-dimensional layout for heaven. (See Figure C.4.)

Other believers, such as the South Korean Pentecostal megachurch pastor David Yonggi Cho and the founder of the Happy Science religion, Ryuho Okawa, have argued that one's earthly piety and virtue determine how high one's spirit travels upward through these higher, heavenly dimensions. When these ways of talking about upward spirit

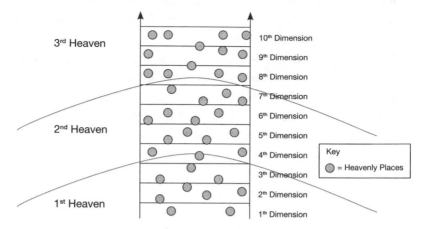

Figure C.4 Daniel Duval offers a tentative organization of the afterlife that incorporates 2 Corinthians's three heavens with the dimensional language used in string theory. From Daniel Duval, *Higher Dimensions, Parallel Dimensions, and the Spirit Realm* (2016).

travel and heavenly dimensions elicit skepticism from critics, pastors can simply refer back to Abbott's text. Such skeptics, the American megachurch pastor Rob Bell once complained, are simply trapped in their own closed-minded, lower-dimensional Flatland.[39]

Discourses about the afterlife as a higher-dimensional reality go far beyond Christian pastors and churches, however. One setting in which the language of higher dimensions has become ubiquitous is in the many clinical studies, journalistic accounts, and personal memoirs of out-of-body and near-death experiences, a growing literature that has stimulated a new "afterlife movement" reshaping the modern western spiritual landscape. Throughout history, dying or gravely ill people have reported glimpsing heavenly, afterlife worlds, but the psychiatrist Raymond Moody, in his *Life after Life* (1975), was the first to collect testimonies from different people and introduce these experiences to the modern reading public. Moody identified distinctive characteristics and stages in these experiences—including the feeling of leaving (and often rising above) one's body, traveling through a tunnel, encountering dead relatives and sometimes religious teachers, and seeing a bright light. In

Life after Life and later books, Moody collected near-death experiences (NDEs), identified their characteristics, called for additional study, and insisted with unflagging earnestness that "on the basis of what my patients have told me," these people "did get a glimpse of the beyond."[40]

When glimpsing the beyond, Moody's subjects also sometimes saw worlds with strange, dimensionally complex geometries. "As I was going through this [death experience], I kept thinking, 'Well, when I was taking geometry, they always told me there were only three dimensions,'" one subject in *Life after Life* recalled, "and I always just accepted that. But they were wrong. There are more."[41] Relatives and friends of the dying also sometimes saw such things. Moody himself said that when his mother died family members experienced a change in the geometry in the room that was difficult to describe. Another near-death patient reported that her square room "shifted." Others who sat beside dying relatives described space opening into an "alternate reality." One man who "had a shared death experience at the bedside of his mother offered a confusing description of a room that 'collapsed and expanded at the same time. It was as though I was witnessing an alternative geometry.'" Another witness said it was like experiencing Disneyland because "it made me realize that most of the stuff that happens in the world happens behind the scenes and that all we see is the surface."[42] Seeing the surface of something deep, or the shadows of something bright, or three-dimensional reflections of complex higher geometries, or a Disneyland-like stage projected outward from something more real—these were ways that Moody's subjects developed a new, more plausible, and more scientific vocabulary for heavenly spaces.

Moody's work was merely a beginning. Emergency room doctors, journalists, psychologists, and bestselling writers have recently published accounts that speak of NDEs as a kind of movement into higher dimensions. Many associated with the International Association for Near-Death Studies (IANDS), for example, have discussed out-of-body and near-death experiences in terms forged by Hinton, Abbott, and other hyperspace philosophers. "The unusual modes and characteristics of spatial and temporal perception" in NDEs, Jean-Pierre Jourdan, the director of research for IANDS, has written, "reveals a 'hidden' logic for which I propose a model where the point of perception would be in an extra dimension." In this essay, this physician and near-death researcher identified several ways that NDE experiencers had abilities that might be predicted if they had gone into a higher dimension as the Square did in *Flatland*. They had remarkable powers of panoptical perception, seeing all sides of things at once. "I was able to see the sofa and my body simultaneously from all directions. I saw my body through the sofa, I could see the top of my head and in the same time I saw my left and right sides and the sofa from below and from above, and all the room like that, I was everywhere at the same time!"[43] Details of NDEs reported to Jourdan suggested that these experiences of altered consciousness might be *empirical evidence* for the reality of additional higher dimensions.[44] The idea here was that if NDE experiencers were having perceptions while brain-dead or seeing things that could not normally be seen, such nonphysical perceptions would be evidence that consciousness could occupy some kind of heavenly, extra-dimensional space.[45] In his bestseller *Proof of Heaven*, the neurosurgeon Eben Alexander used similar words to talk about his NDE, insisting that he became "conscious in another dimension" from which he could look down on our three-dimensional space and "access any time or place in our world."[46]

∾∾∾∾

Not everyone living in the nineteenth- or twentieth-century West experienced a sense of disorientation or disenchantment, but those who did often searched for ways of fashioning new philosophical and religious perspectives out of the cultural rubble created when science, technology, and secular society changed life forever. Many used books like *Flatland* to help them navigate these changes. *Flatland* and hyperspace meditations such as Hinton's have helped many modern people develop new angles of vision on inherited ways of thinking about race, social order, the technological future, artificial intelligence, the power of fiction, and, of course, the existence of a transcendent space or level to reality. This story is much larger than the narrative I have presented here.[47]

But perhaps *Flatland*'s most remarkable legacy points us back to one of Abbott's cherished ambitions—to develop a perspective on the world that could be both reasonable and imaginative, scientific and spiritual, at the same time. To be sure, *Flatland*'s ongoing cultural power derives mostly from its ways of using mathematics to suggest the existence of something beyond our familiar world. Like other higher-dimensional reflections, it illustrates well the modern impulse to develop enchanted scientific perspectives, an impulse that today seems stronger than ever. "The human imagination has been inspired for centuries by the possibility of a higher dimension," Deepak Chopra wrote in 2014, channeling contemporary spiritual aspirations. There were "surprising resemblances," he thought, between religious heavens and scientific hyperspaces, between the "realm of God or the gods" or of "higher states of consciousness" and the fantastic superspaces posited by physicists. To him, science had made possible a new kind of religious imagination. "What is haunting about the juxtaposition of superstring theory and theology is that both describe the unseen as ultimately responsible for our being. Maybe superstrings are real but arise wholly from natural forces; maybe they are real and were made by God; maybe the idea will be discarded. At any rate, hundreds of advanced physicists now believe that invisible planes of existence are everywhere around us, maybe by the dozens. Is it so hard, in that context, to believe there is one real but invisible plane of the spirit?"[48] In other words, given the extraordinary facts of contemporary science, was it so difficult to believe in the extraordinary realities imagined by contemporary religion? The same point has been made many times in more general terms: The hidden dimensions of science give us reason to buttress spiritual faith in unseen things.[49]

To build what we might call one's spiritual imagination in this way, to shape it on a scaffolding of complex mathematical formulas, or nature's beautiful laws, or speculation about the cosmos's invisible dimensions—this move has been made by many of the Europeans and Americans examined in this book, people who wished either to replace entirely their childhood faiths or make them scientific and believable. Scientific concepts and assumptions did indeed challenge older ways of thinking and believing, and in some cases religious traditions were left behind forever. There is no doubt that traditional religious congregations and practices have recently suffered setbacks and declines. But the last 150 years also has been a time of remarkable creativity, one characterized by a new kind of spiritual imagination that is only today coming into focus. The despairing depression of C. Howard Hinton, the crisis of faith of Edwin Abbott, the loss of imagination felt by Max Weber, C. S. Lewis, and Madeleine L'Engle, and even the imprisonment of body and soul endured by fictional protagonists such as Abbott's Square hero—all of these were merely initial stages in a much longer narrative, which is still being written today, about religious reform, change, and spiritual revival. This ongoing narrative shows that scientific ideas have not just generated doubt and skepticism but have also buttressed enchanted views of a universe that is open, surprisingly complex, and perhaps even layered with fantastic dimensions that exist just beyond the borders of what we can see and know.

NOTES

Introduction

1. For a sample of these surveys, see http://www.pewresearch.org/daily-number
   /goblins-and-ghosts-and-things-that-go-bump-in-the-night/; http://www
   .pewforum.org/2009/12/09/many-americans-mix-multiple-faiths/;
   http://www.gallup.com/poll/11770/eternal-destinations-americans-believe
   -heaven-hell.aspx; http://religionnews.com/2014/08/05/the-great-decline
   -61-years-of-religion-religiosity-in-one-graph-2013-hits-a-new-low/;
   http://www.pewresearch.org/fact-tank/2016/12/01/if-the-u-s-had-100
   -people-charting-americans-religious-beliefs-and-practices/; http://news
   .gallup.com/poll/193271/americans-believe-god.aspx?g_source
   =RELIGION&g_medium=topic&g_campaign=tiles.
2. Christopher White, *Unsettled Minds: Psychology and the American Search for Spiritual Assurance* (Berkeley: University of California Press, 2009).
3. Herbert Croly, "American Protestant Churches during the War," *New Republic* 30 (March 29, 1922), 143.
4. These matters are discussed in more detail in Christopher White, "Seeing Things: Science, the Fourth Dimension and Modern Enchantment," *American Historical Review* 119:5 (December 2014), 1466–1491. On the contested histories of geology, biology, and evolution, see, for example, C. C. Gillispie, *Genesis and Geology: A Study in the Relations of Scientific Thought, Natural Theology, and Social Opinion in Great Britain, 1790–1850* (Cambridge, Mass.:

Harvard University Press, 1951); James Secord, *Victorian Sensation: The Extraordinary Publication, Reception, and Secret Authorship of Vestiges of the Natural History of Creation* (Chicago: University of Chicago Press, 2000); James Secord, *Controversy in Victorian Geology: The Cambrian-Silurian Dispute* (Princeton, N.J.: Princeton University Press, 1986); Frank Turner, *Between Science and Religion: The Reaction to Scientific Naturalism in Late Victorian England* (New Haven, Conn.: Yale University Press 1974); James Moore, *The Post-Darwinian Controversies: A Study of the Protestant Struggles to Come to Terms with Darwin in Great Britain and America 1870–1900* (Cambridge: Cambridge University Press, 1979); Peter Bowler, *Monkey Trials and Gorilla Sermons: Evolution and Christianity from Darwin to Intelligent Design* (Cambridge, Mass.: Harvard University Press., 2007); James Turner, *Without God, without Creed: The Origins of Unbelief in America* (Baltimore: Johns Hopkins University Press, 1985); and Jon Roberts, *Darwinism and the Divine in America: Protestant Intellectuals and Organic Evolution, 1859–1900* (Madison: University of Wisconsin Press, 1988). Several historians identify positivism as a central issue in the scientific attack on religion, though no one does this as thoroughly as Charles Cashdollar in his *Transformation of Theology, 1830–1890: Positivism and Protestant Thought in Britain and America* (Princeton, N.J.: Princeton University Press, 1989).

5. Strauss is quoted in Karl Heim, *God Transcendent: Foundation for a Christian Metaphysic*, trans. Edgar Primrose Dickie (London: Nisbet and Co., 1935), 31.

6. Paul Carter, "Science and the Death of God," *American Scholar* 42:3 (Summer 1973), 410. Carter's full quote was "The growing body of impersonal factual knowledge plus the insensate discipline of the machine increasingly gave industrial man a worldview in which intangible reality had no place." James Turner, studying the history of agnosticism, put it this way: "The lust for empirical proof proved, in the end, nothing less than disastrous for belief." Turner, *Without God, without Creed*, 189.

7. See Max Weber, *From Max Weber: Essays in Sociology* (London: Routledge, 2009), 139.

8. Quoted in A. Pais, "Einstein and the Quantum Theory," *Reviews of Modern Physics* 51 (1979), 907.

9. Alfred North Whitehead, *Science and the Modern World* (New York: Free Press, 1967; orig. 1925), 188–190.

10. David Kaiser, *How the Hippies Saved Physics: Science, Counterculture and the Quantum Revival* (New York: Norton, 2011), 244.

11. It is worth acknowledging that the idea that there are other worlds or realms within our world is a common one in cultures and religions around the world. Many religions discuss metaphysical realms where ancestors, angels, or gods dwell; and many philosophers in history have spoken about

the possibility of life on other planetary worlds. Some of this history is summarized in Priyamvada Natarjan, *Mapping the Heavens: The Radical Scientific Ideas That Reveal the Cosmos* (New Haven, Conn.: Yale University Press, 2016), 202–210.

12. Sequels include *The Dot and the Line* by Norton Juster (1963), *Sphereland* by Dionys Burger (1965), *The Incredible Umbrella* by Marvin Kaye (1980), *The Planiverse* by A. K. Dewdney (1984), *Flatterland: Like Flatland Only More So* by Ian Stewart (2001), and *Spaceland* by Rudy Rucker (2002). Hinton himself developed his own *Flatland* sequel called *An Episode on Flatland: Or How a Plain Folk Discovered the Third Dimension* (1907), which Abbott recommended to others. *Flatland*-inspired films include an animated short film called *Flatland* (1965), a feature film based on the novella called *Flatland* (2007) and another, more recent animated film called *Flatland: The Movie* (2007), with voiceovers by Martin Sheen, Kristen Bell, and Tony Hale. There also was a sequel to this last film called *Flatland 2: Sphereland* (2012).

13. C. S. Lewis used the concept in different places, most notably in C. S. Lewis, *The Weight of Glory and Other Addresses* (New York: Macmillan, 1949), 16–29; *Miracles: A Preliminary Study* (New York: Macmillan, 1947), 19–25, 103, 133–160; and *God in the Dock: Essays on Theology and Ethics* (Grand Rapids, Mich.: Eerdmans, 1970), 177–188. The contemporary American evangelical author and preacher Rob Bell used the flatland concept to make a heavenly world more believable in his "Everything Is Spiritual" lecture tour, which can be found online. See "Atheists: Trapped in Flatland?," http://www.youtube.com/watch?v=9JmMTobaM68.

14. Wassily Kandinsky, *Concerning the Spiritual in Art* (New York: Wittenborn, Schultz, 1947), 21–27.

15. In this book I use "spiritual" as basically synonymous with "nonphysical" or "supernatural." Other scholars have done excellent work on the genealogy of "spiritual" or "spirituality," examining how these categories took shape vis-à-vis other parts of culture that we call "religion" or the "secular." Leigh Schmidt and John Modern have examined the ascent of "spirituality" to its exalted place in contemporary society by discussing how American Protestants used the term (and related categories such as "mysticism") to develop more rational, scientific, individualistic, and secular forms of religiousness. I see their approaches as essentially complementary to mine. For more on how "spirituality" resulted from pressures exerted on religion by science and secular society, see Leigh Schmidt, *Restless Souls: The Making of American Spirituality* (New York: HarperCollins, 2005); John Modern, *Secularism in Antebellum America* (Chicago: University of Chicago Press, 2011); and Courtney Bender and Omar McRoberts, "Mapping a Field: Why and How to Study Spirituality," *SSRC Working Papers* (October 2012).

16. See Franz Boaz, "Introduction," in James Teit, *Traditions of the Thompson River Indians of British Columbia* (Boston: Houghton Mifflin, 1898), 18.

1. Edwin Abbott's Otherworldly Visions

1. Elizabeth Hurth, *Between Faith and Unbelief: American Transcendentalists and the Challenge of Atheism* (Leiden: Brill, 2007), 53.
2. Edwin A. Abbott to J. E. B. Mayor, February 20, 1895, Trinity College Archives, Cambridge University.
3. Quoted in Owen Chadwick, *The Victorian Church, Part II: 1860–1901* (New York: Oxford University Press, 1970), 65.
4. Abbott, *Through Nature to Christ, or, The Ascent of Worship through Illusion to the Truth* (London: Macmillan, 1877), 3.
5. The book is sometimes discussed as "science fiction" or "math fiction" but it is different from these genres in certain ways. Elliot Gilbert called it "part science fiction adventure, part Socratic dialogue"; Ray Bradbury called it "fiction based on science." The subtitle of the work uses the nineteenth-century term for fiction, "romance," calling itself a "Romance of Many Dimensions." Elliot Gilbert, "'Upward, Not Northward': *Flatland* and the Quest for the New," *English Literature in Transition, 1880–1920* 34:4 (1991), 392. Ray Bradbury's introduction is appended to Edwin Abbott, *Flatland: A Romance of Many Dimensions* (San Francisco: Arion Press, 1980). I am indebted to Thomas Banchoff for information about the number of translations.
6. Edwin A. Abbott, *Flatland: An Edition with Notes and Commentary by William Lindgren and Thomas Banchoff* (Cambridge: Cambridge University Press, 2010), 176.
7. Ibid., 138, 140.
8. The language is taken from Plato, *Republic* 7.515d–516b; Abbott borrows a lot from Plato. See Abbott, *Flatland*, 170, 174, 202–203.
9. Abbott, *Flatland*, 208, 212–214, 216.
10. For Banchoff and Lindgren's note on this, see Abbott, *Flatland*, 9.
11. Abbott said for instance that he assumed that "every educated person believes" in the common occurrence of visions of departed souls. Edwin Abbott, "Revelation by Visions and Voices," self-published pamphlet, Edwin Abbott Papers, St. John's College Library, Cambridge University, 26 (hereafter cited as EAP).
12. Fearing an outcry from the orthodox, fewer invitations to speak at places like Oxford, and even the loss of his job as headmaster at the City of London School, he "struck out," he said to Macmillan, "almost all the 'Dreams' and 'Visions' portions of the text." Edwin A. Abbott to Macmillan, January 23, 1877, Macmillan Archive, British Library, London.

13. Quoted in Abbott, *Flatland,* 225.

14. Edwin Abbott, *The Spirit on the Waters: The Evolution of the Divine from the Human* (London: Macmillan, 1897), 32. See also Abbott, *Flatland,* 226.

15. Kant was here arguing that there were only three dimensions to reality, but as Hud Hudson has written, he also anticipated in this passage "debates on the possibility of higher dimensions, on their plenitude, occupants, variability" and "on their relation to God's nature (or—stripped of theological overtones—on their role in cosmology)." See Hud Hudson, *The Metaphysics of Hyperspace* (Oxford: Oxford University Press, 2005), 20.

16. Quoted in Michael Heidelberger, *Nature from Within: Gustav Theodor Fechner and His Psychophysical Worldview* (Pittsburgh: University of Pittsburgh Press, 2004), 20–22.

17. Ibid., 26; G. Stanley Hall, *Founders of Modern Psychology* (New York: Appleton and Co., 1912), 127; for details on these episodes see Alexandra Hui, *The Psychophysical Ear: Musical Instruments, Experimental Sounds* (Cambridge, Mass.: MIT Press, 2013),

18. James is quoted in Richardson, *The Heart of William James* (Cambridge, Mass.: Harvard University Press, 2010), 282.

19. Gustav Fechner, "Space Has Four Dimensions," in Fechner, *Kleine Schriften von Dr Mises* (Leipzig: Breitkopf und Hartel, 1875), 261. (Translated into English by John Benjamin.)

20. Ibid., 254.

21. These ideas are from a lecture that Helmholtz gave in 1870 entitled "On the Origin and Significance of Geometrical Axioms." This lecture was reprinted in different places, including in Hermann von Helmholtz, *Popular Lectures on Scientific Subjects,* 2nd series (New York: Longman, Green and Co., 1893; reprint 1908), 34–37. He presented similar ideas in two essays in the British journal *Mind* in 1876 and 1878.

22. Edwin A. Abbott, *The Kernel and the Husk: Letters on Spiritual Christianity* (London: Macmillan, 1886), 100.

23. Ibid., 102, 106–107; Abbott, *Spirit on the Waters,* 117.

24. Charles Darwin, *On the Origin of Species* (New York: Collier and Son, 1909; orig. 1859), 213.

25. Helmholtz was writing about the eye's errors before *Origin* but Darwin did not know of his work when he published the first edition of *Origin.* However in a later edition of *Origin* that has become the standard version he inserted a paragraph in which he used Helmholtz's arguments about the eye. See Darwin, *Origin,* 214.

26. Gillian Beer, "'Authentic Tidings of Invisible Things': Vision and the Invisible in the Later Nineteenth Century," in *Vision in Context: Historical and Contemporary Perspectives on Sight,* ed. Teresa Brennan and Martin Jay (New York: Routledge, 1996), 90.

27. Abbott, *Kernel and the Husk,* 100, 248, 273, 306–307.

28. Ibid., 185, 104, 107–109, 199.

29. Ibid., 19.

30. Abbott, *Flatland,* 56.

31. Ibid., 142, 150, 174–176, 190, 194.

32. Edwin A. Abbott, *Apologia: An Explanation and Defense* (London: A. and C. Black, 1907), xii, 66.

33. Abbott, "Revelation by Visions and Voices," EAP, 26.

34. Abbott, *Through Nature to Christ,* front matter; Abbott, *Apologia,* 66–67.

35. Abbott, "Revelation by Visions and Voices," 26–27; Abbott, *Flatland,* 8–9.

36. Abbott to Macmillan, January 23, 1877, Macmillan Papers, British Library.

37. Abbott, *Spirit on the Waters,* 117.

38. Abbott, "Revelation by Visions and Voices," 11–14.

39. "Additional Note on Seeing (ὁράω) the Father," handwritten manuscript, EAP.

40. He wrote more on these issues in manuscript notes labeled "Truth through falsehood. A paper, on miracles and illusions, read by Abbott at the Monthly Church Conference, 4 March 1880" in EAP.

41. Abbott, *Apologia,* 69, 71–72, 82.

42. Abbott, *Kernel and the Husk,* vi–viii.

43. Abbott, *Apologia,* 14, 83.

2. The Man Who Saw the Fourth Dimension

1. Hinton's letters to his father are from Ellice Hopkins, ed., *Life and Letters of James Hinton* (London: Kegan, Paul, Trench, 1883), 251, 253, 335–336; the last quotation is from Charles Howard Hinton, *A New Era of Thought* (London: Swan Sonnenschein & Co., 1888), 10–12.

2. This tradition came under strain during the second half of the century, when new debates about the foundations of mathematics generated disagreement about whether mathematics was merely an internally consistent logical discourse or a privileged access point to truths above the senses. See Jeremy Gray, *Plato's Ghost: The Modernist Transformation of Mathematics* (Princeton, N.J.: Princeton University Press, 2008); and Joan Richards, *Mathematical Visions: The Pursuit of Geometry in Victorian England* (New York: Academic Press, 1988), 108–111.

3. These are James Hinton's words, as he summarizes his son's earlier letter to him. See Hopkins, *Life and Letters of James Hinton,* 251.

4. See Rudy Rucker's introduction to Charles Howard Hinton, *Speculations on the Fourth Dimension: Selected Writings of Charles H. Hinton,* ed. Rudy Rucker (New York: Dover, 1980), vi.

5. Hinton, *New Era*, 33. For more on his cube learning techniques, see Charles H. Hinton, *Scientific Romances (First Series)* (London: Swan Sonnenschein, 1886), 206–208.

6. Hinton, *Scientific Romances (First Series)*, 208–210.

7. Hinton's project was similar to efforts of contemporaries striving for a kind of scientific certainty built on what Lorraine Daston has called "aperspectival objectivity": He was trying to fashion a scientific perspective free of subjective preferences, whims, desires, feelings, and idiosyncrasies. Lorraine Daston, "Objectivity and the Escape from Perspective," *Social Studies of Science* 22:4 (1992), 599–609.

8. C. Howard Hinton, *Casting Out the Self* (London: Swan Sonnenschein, 1886), 215.

9. Hinton may have derived the word "tesseract" from "tessarines," which was a word used in the nineteenth century for bicomplex numbers.

10. Charles Hinton, "Higher Space Perception" lecture notes, from series 1, box 6, Gelett Burgess Papers, Bancroft Library, University of California, Berkeley (hereafter cited as GBP).

11. "One has the feeling sometimes of being on the edge—as if all this materialistic hypothesis after all wasn't absolute reality, as if it were mental representation too." Charles H. Hinton to Gelett Burgess, June 1903, GBP.

12. Daston documents scientific fears of the imagination in Daston, "Fear and Loathing of the Imagination," *Deadelus* 127:1 (Winter 1998), 74. For the same fears of irrationality, religious credulity, and the imagination among social scientists, see Christopher White, *Unsettled Minds: Psychology and the American Search for Spiritual Assurance, 1830–1940* (Berkeley: University of California Press, 2009), 158–195.

13. Marvin H. Ballard, "The Life and Thought of Charles Howard Hinton" (master's thesis, Virginia Polytechnic Institute, 1980), 31.

14. See Hinton, *Education of the Imagination* (London: Swan Sonnenschein & Co., 1888), 6–19.

15. Yaffa C. Draznin, *"My Other Self": The Letters of Olive Schreiner and Havelock Ellis, 1884–1920* (New York: Peter Lang, 1992), 54–55.

16. Ellis quoted in Mrs. Havelock Ellis, *James Hinton: A Sketch* (London: Stanley Paul & Co.), xii; see also Olive Schreiner's letters to Havelock Ellis in Draznin, *"My Other Self"*; Phyllis Grosskurth, Havelock Ellis, and Seth Koven, *Slumming: Sexual and Social Politics in Victorian London* (Princeton, N.J.: Princeton University Press, 2006), 16–17.

17. Ellis, *James Hinton: A Sketch*, 191.

18. Havelock Ellis to Olive Schreiner, December 23, 1884, from Draznin, *"My Other Self,"* 275–276.

19. For details, see Mark Blacklock, "The Fairyland of Geometry: A Cultural History of Higher Space, 1853–1907," accessed 12/10/10 at https://higherspace.wordpress.com/.

20. Havelock Ellis to Olive Schreiner, April 12, 1885, from Draznin, *"My Other Self,"* 337.

21. For details, see Mark Blacklock, "The Fairyland of Geometry," http://higherspace.wordpress.com/.

22. See Draznin, *"My Other Self,"* 361 and 423, and Blacklock, "Fairyland of Geometry."

23. All are quoted in Blacklock, "Fairyland of Geometry."

24. Edwin Bird Johnson, *Dictionary of the University of Minnesota* (Minneapolis, Minn.: n.p., 1908), 104.

25. C. Howard Hinton to William Swann Sonnenschein, February 22, 1887, quoted in Blacklock, "Fairyland of Geometry"; the last quotation is from a set of Hinton's lecture notes entitled "Higher Space Perceptions," which are in a collection of Hinton papers contained in GBP.

26. Charles H. Hinton, *Scientific Romances (Second Series)* (London: George Allen & Unwin, 1898), 14–19.

27. Hinton's son Sebastian, who settled in Illinois and became a lawyer, went on to develop and sell the idea, the first "jungle gym," and was awarded a U.S. patent for it on March 25, 1924. Sheila Duran, "'J' Is for Jungle Gym," Winnetka Historical Society, http://winnetkahistory.org/gazette/j-is-for -jungle-gym/. In Japan Hinton thought the Buddhist monks he had met had imaginative skills that allowed them to see into other dimensions, and he spoke approvingly about Buddhist forms of meditation and visualization. "Either one of two things must be true—that four-dimensional conceptions give a wonderful power of representing the thought of the East, or that the thinkers of the East must have been looking at and regarding four-dimensional existence," he wrote. C. Howard Hinton, *The Fourth Dimension* (London: George Allen and Co., 1912; orig. 1904), 28. See also C. H. Hinton to Gelett Burgess, June 1903, GBP.

28. Review of *The Fourth Dimension,* by Charles H. Hinton, *Nature* 70 (July 21, 1904), 268.

29. Bertrand Russell, review of *The Fourth Dimension,* by Charles H. Hinton, *Mind* 13 (October 1904), 573–574. "Conscientious bigamist" is from Russell, *Foundations of Logic, 1903–1905* (London: Routledge, 1994), 578.

30. On Maxwell and Clifford, see Alfred M. Bork, "The Fourth Dimension in Nineteenth-Century Physics," *Isis* 55:3 (September 1964), 326–338, here 328–330, 334. The Santayana quote is from Paul Halpern and Michael Labossiere, "Mind Out of Time: Identity, Perception and the Fourth Dimension in H. P. Lovecraft's 'The Shadow Out of Time' and 'The Dreams in the Witch House,'" *Extrapolation* 50:3 (2009), 520.

31. T. Proctor Hall, "The Possibility of a Realization of Four-Fold Space," *Science* 19 (May 1892), 272–274; responses included Edmund Sanford, "The Possibility of a Realization of Four-Fold Space," *Science* 19 (June 10, 1892), 332; and C. Staniland Wake, "The Notion of Four-Fold Space," *Science* 19 (June 10, 1892), 331–332.

32. Reviewing Hinton's *The Fourth Dimension,* the *New York Times* acknowledged that Hinton's presentation "to non-mathematical readers in untechnical language is a task that might well cause dismay to the bravest," pointing out that Hinton "has gone at it courageously and with no little skill and ingenuity." The cube apparatus was helpful, but it required patience. "Anybody who is unable to understand the fourth dimension after a scrutiny of this kindergarten apparatus," the *Times* concluded, "is probably hopelessly condemned to three." Review of *The Fourth Dimension,* by Charles H. Hinton, *New York Times,* June 25 1904. Other reviews touched on similar themes. "This book is a powerful mental gymnastic," a writer for the *Literary World* said about Hinton's *Scientific Romances.* "Mr. Hinton brings us panting, but delighted, to at least a momentary faith in the Fourth Dimension, and upon the eye there opens a vista of interesting problems. It exhibits a boldness of speculation and a power of conceiving and expressing even the inconceivable, which rouses one's faculties like a tonic" (quoted on the back pages of Hinton, *Scientific Romances, Second Series*).

33. Richards, *Mathematical Visions,* 74; W. H. Stromberg, "Helmholtz and Zollner: Nineteenth–Century Empiricism, Spiritism and the Theory of Space Perception," *Journal of the History of the Behavioral Sciences* 25:4 (1989), 371–383.

34. See Jonathan Smith, *Fact and Feeling: Baconian Science and the Nineteenth-Century Literary Imagination* (Madison: University of Wisconsin Press, 1994), 180–209; Richards, *Mathematical Visions,* 61–114; Stromberg, "Helmholtz and Zoellner," 371–373; and Bork, "Fourth Dimension in Nineteenth-Century Physics." A 1911 bibliography of geometry papers, for example, estimated that up until that time there had been eighteen hundred papers written on multidimensional geometry and related subjects. See Duncan M. Y. Sommerville, *A Bibliography of Non-Euclidean Geometry* (London: Harrison & Sons, 1911), 263–310.

35. G. Stanley Hall, *Founders of Modern Psychology* (New York: Appleton, 1912), 266–268.

36. For historical perspectives on the religious imagination and post-Enlightenment ways of disciplining and controlling it, see Leigh Schmidt, *Hearing Things: Religion, Illusion and the American Enlightenment* (Cambridge, Mass.: Harvard University Press, 2000); Ann Taves, *Fits, Trances and Visions: Experiencing Religion and Explaining Experience from Wesley to James* (Princeton, N.J.: Princeton University Press, 1999); Andrew Heinze,

Jews and the American Soul: Human Nature in the Twentieth Century (Princeton, N.J.: Princeton University Press, 2004); and White, *Unsettled Minds.*

37. Arthur Crathorne, "The Fourth Dimension the Playground of Mathematics," in *The Fourth Dimension Simply Explained,* ed. Henry Manning (New York: Munn and Co., 1910), 154–162, here 161.

38. See Manning, *Fourth Dimension Simply Explained,* 30, 83. Another mathematician objecting to popular appropriations of the fourth dimension was Hermann Schubert, "The Fourth Dimension: Mathematical and Spiritualistic," *Monist* 3 (April 1, 1893), 402–449.

39. Manning, *Fourth Dimension Simply Explained,* 8–10.

40. W. T. Stead, "Throught; or, On the Eve of the Fourth Dimension," *Review of Reviews* 7 (1893), 426–432, here 427; E. H. Neville, *The Fourth Dimension* (Cambridge: Cambridge University Press, 1921), 2.

41. Simon Newcomb, "The Fairyland of Geometry," *Harper's Magazine* (January 1902), 252.

42. "Picturesque Personalities," *Johns Hopkins Alumni Magazine* 15:1 (November 1926), 153.

43. "Picturesque Personalities," 152–154.

44. Edwin Slosson, "That Elusive Fourth Dimension," *Independent* (December 27, 1919), 274–275.

45. "An Oxford Undergraduate's Suicide," *Jackson's Oxford Journal* (April 28, 1900), 8.

46. Francis Galton, *Inquiries into Human Faculty and Its Development,* 2nd ed. (London: J. M. Dent, 1892; orig. 1883), 68.

47. See Charles H. Hinton to William James, October 30, 1896, and Charles H. Hinton to William James, August 12, 1898, William James Papers, Houghton Library, Harvard University (hereafter cited as WJP). For one student's notes on James's Philosophy 4 class and how he covered Hinton, see the Philosophy 4 notebook of W. E. B. Du Bois, online at the University of Massachusetts Amherst Special Collections.

48. C. Howard Hinton to William James, October 8, 1892, WJP.

49. C. Howard Hinton to William James, October 19, 1895, WJP.

50. Pieter Ouspensky, *Tertium Organum: The Third Canon of Thought* (New York: Knopf, 1922), 111.

51. J. J. Sylvester, "Presidential Address to Section 'A' of the British Association," in H. F. Baker, ed., *The Collected Mathematical Papers of James Joseph Sylvester,* 4 vols. (Cambridge: Cambridge University Press, 1904–1912), 2:654. For context, see Karen Hunger Parshall, *James Joseph Sylvester: Jewish Mathematician in a Victorian World* (Baltimore: Johns Hopkins University Press, 2006), 203–206; and Smith, *Fact and Feeling,* 181–182.

52. In Sylvester's time it was not known if non-Euclidean geometries corresponded with reality in any way, though in the early twentieth century Al-

bert Einstein showed that space was indeed non-Euclidean. For the controversies over geometry and truth, see Jeremy Gray, *Worlds Out of Nothing: A Course in the History of Geometry in the 19th Century* (London: Springer Science, 2007), 314–323; Jeremy Gray, "Geometry—Formalisms and Intuitions," in *The Symbolic Universe: Geometry and Physics, 1890–1930,* ed. Jeremy Gray (Oxford: Oxford University Press, 1999), 58–83; and Andrew Warwick, *Masters of Theory: Cambridge and the Rise of Mathematical Physics* (Chicago: University of Chicago Press, 2003), 462–469.

53. Sylvester, "Presidential Address," 655.

54. Ibid., 659. For context, see Parshall, *James Joseph Sylvester,* 201–206. Though he was an atheist, John Tyndall, speaking a year after Sylvester's talk, gave an address, "On the Scientific Use of the Imagination," that also argued that the imagination was essential if scientists wanted to continue to uncover hidden aspects of the physical universe. See Gilian Beer, *Open Fields: Science in Cultural Encounter* (Oxford: Oxford University Press, 1996), 262–271.

55. Richards, *Mathematical Visions,* 107.

56. Sylvester, "A Plea for the Mathematician," *Nature* (January 6, 1870), 237–239, here 238.

57. The discovery of new, non-Euclidean geometries led to confusion about the relationship between geometrical spaces and reality. See Gray, *Plato's Ghost,* 100, 347; Gray, "Geometry—Formalisms and Intuitions," 69–81; and Richards, *Mathematical Visions,* 94–95.

58. Sylvester, "Plea," 238.

59. Quoted in Richards, *Mathematical Visions,* 138.

60. Bork, "Fourth Dimension in Nineteenth-Century Physics," 329. For Simon Newcomb, see "Picturesque Personalities of Johns Hopkins," *Johns Hopkins Alumni Magazine* 45:1 (November 1926), 153–156. A Columbia University mathematician, David Smith, also fits in this category. In his presidential address to the Mathematical Association of America in 1921, he suggested that mathematical reasoning, including reasoning by analogy to higher dimensions, made the existence of the soul and immortality more likely. David Eugene Smith, "Religio Mathematici," *American Mathematical Monthly* 28:10 (October 1921), 339–349. Also see "The 'Fourth Dimension' as a Refuge from Materialism," *Literary Digest* 12:3 (November 16, 1895), 74–75.

61. Balfour Stewart and Peter Tait, *The Unseen Universe, or Physical Speculations on a Future State* (New York: Macmillan, 1875), 156–164. Tait's friend James Clerk Maxwell also was a deeply religious person. In 1879, while dying from cancer, he wrote a poem that included the following lines. "My soul's an amphicheiral* knot // Upon a liquid vortex wrought // By Intellect in the Unseen residing, // While thou dost like a convict sit // With marlin-spike untwisting it // Only to find my knottiness abiding, // Since all the

tools for my untying // In four-dimensioned space are lying // Where playful fancy intersperces, // Whole avenues of universes" (*a knot that can be twisted into its mirror image). From Daniel S. Silver, "The Last Poem of James Clerk Maxwell," *Notices of the American Mathematical Society* 55:10 (November 2008), 1266–1270.

62. Smith, "Religio Mathematici," 339–349.

63. Quoted in Richards, *Mathematical Visions,* 113. Speaking of his childhood Anglicanism, Clifford wrote, "We have parted from it since with such searching trouble as only cradle-faiths can cause. We have seen the spring sun shine out of an empty heaven to light up a soulless earth; we have felt with utter loneliness that the Great Companion is dead. Our children, it may be hoped, will know that sorrow only by the reflex light of a won-dering compassion." W. K. Clifford, *Lectures and Essays, by the Late William Kingdon Clifford* (London: Macmillan and Co., 1886), 389.

64. Edward Kasner and James Newman, *Mathematics and the Imagination* (New York: Simon & Schuster, 1940), 131.

65. Cassius Keyser, "Mathematical Emancipations, the Passing of the Point and the Number Three: Dimensionality and Hyperspace," *Monist* 16:1 (January 1906), 65–83, here 82–83; Cassius Keyser, *Mathematical Philosophy: A Study of Fate and Freedom* (New York: E. P. Dutton, 1922), 341.

66. Walter B. Pitkin, "A Logical Aspect of the Theories of Hyperspaces," *Monist* 17:1 (January 1907), 114–125, here 121; Cassius J. Keyser, "Mitigating the Tragedy of Our Modern Culture," *American Scholar* 3:2 (Spring 1934), 180–192; Cassius Keyser, "The Spiritual Significance of Mathematics," *Religious Education* 6:5 (December 1911), 374–384.

67. C. Howard Hinton to William James, n.d., WJP.

68. From Charles H. Hinton, "Travels of an Idea," unpublished typescript in GBP, 65–66.

69. Arnold wrote this poem, "The Grande Chartreuse," around 1850. It was first published in *Fraser's Magazine for Town and Country* 51:304 (April 1855), 437–440.

70. Linda Henderson, *The Fourth Dimension and Non-Euclidean Geometry in Modern Art* (Princeton, N.J.: Princeton University Press, 1983), xix. For Hinton's influence on writers in the early twentieth century, see Elizabeth Throesch, "Nonsense in the Fourth Dimension of Literature: Hyperspace Philosophy, the 'New' Mathematics, and the *Alice* Books," in *Alice beyond Wonderland: Essays for the Twenty-First Century,* ed. Cristopher Hollingsworth (Iowa City: University of Iowa Press, 2009), 37–52; Mark Blacklock, "The Higher Spaces of the Late Nineteenth-Century Novel," *19: Interdisciplinary Studies in the Long Nineteenth Century* 17 (2013), 1–19; Willard Bohn, "Writing the Fourth Dimension," *Comparative Critical Studies* 4:1 (2007), 121–138; Elmar Schenkel, "Ghostly Geometry: The Fourth Dimension in Literature," in

Magic, Science, Technology and Literature, ed. Jarmila Mildorf, Hans Ulrich Seeber, and Martin Windisch (Berlin: Lit, 2006), 179–190; Rudy Rucker, *The Fourth Dimension: Toward a Geometry of Higher Reality* (Boston: Houghton Mifflin, 1984); and Nancy Bentley, "The Fourth Dimension: Kinlessness and African-American Narrative," *Critical Inquiry* 35:2 (Winter 2009), 270–292.

3. New Heaven, New Earth

1. G. H. Bryan, "The Popular Fallacy of 'the' Fourth Dimension," *Cornhill Magazine* 37 (1914), 647–652.
2. Mary Hinton to William James, December 2 1907, William James Papers, Houghton Library, Harvard University.
3. Quoted in Alex Owen, *The Place of Enchantment: British Occultism and the Culture of the Modern* (Chicago: University of Chicago Press, 2004), 23.
4. Quoted in Umar F. Abd-Allah, *A Muslim in Victorian America: The Life of Alexander Russell Webb* (Oxford: Oxford University Press, 2006), 69.
5. H. G. Wells, *The Wonderful Visit* (New York: E. P. Dutton, 1914; orig. 1895), 25–26.
6. K. G. Valente, "'A Finite Universe'? Riemannian Geometry and the Modernist Theology of Ernest William Barnes," *British Journal for the History of Science* 38:2 (June 2005), 197–217; K. G. Valente, "Transgression and Transcendence: Flatland as a Response to 'A New Philosophy,'" *Nineteenth-Century Contexts: An Interdisciplinary Journal* 26:1 (2004), 61–77; Gabriel Motzkin, "Science, Secularization and Desecularization at the Turn of the Twentieth Century," *Science in Context* 15:1 (2002), 165–175; Harry W. Paul, *The Edge of Contingency: French Catholic Reactions to Scientific Change from Darwin to Duhem* (Gainesville: University Presses of Florida,1979), 169; Joseph Dauben, "Georg Cantor and Pope Leo XIII: Mathematics, Theology, and the Infinite," *Journal of the History of Ideas* 38:1 (1977), 85–108; and Peter Bowler, *Reconciling Science and Religion: The Debate in Early Twentieth-Century Britain* (Chicago: University of Chicago Press, 2001), 110–114.
7. W. F. Tyler, *The Dimensional Idea as an Aid to Religion* (New York: R. F. Fenno, 1907), 57–58, 65.
8. See, for example, Valente, "'A Finite Universe'?" 212; W. Whately-Smith, *A Theory of the Mechanism of Survival: The Fourth Dimension and Its Applications* (London: Kegan, Paul, Trench, 1920); and Anon. (An Officer in the Grand Fleet), *The Fourth Dimension: Essays in the Realm of Unconventional Thought* (London: C. W. Daniel, 1919).
9. Robert C. Williams, *Artists in Revolution* (Bloomington: Indiana University Press, 1977), 103; Gary Lachman, *Jung the Mystic: The Esoteric Dimensions of Carl Jung's Life and Teachings* (New York: Penguin, 2010), 49.

10. Srdjan Smajic, *Ghost Seers, Detectives and Spiritualists: Theories of Vision in Victorian Literature and Science* (Cambridge: Cambridge University Press, 2010), 178.

11. K. G. Valente, "Who Will Explain the Explanation: The Ambivalent Reception of Higher Dimensional Space in the British Spiritualist Press, 1875–1900," *Victorian Periodicals Review* 41:2 (Summer 2008), 131; Corinna Treital, *A Science for the Soul: Occultism and the Genesis of the German Modern* (Baltimore, Md.: Johns Hopkins University Press, 2004), 15, 10.

12. Valente, "Who Will Explain the Explanation," 134; Montrose Moses, "Vale Owen, Spiritualist Rector, Pictures Life in World Beyond," *New York Times*, February 4, 1923.

13. Johan Van Manen, *Some Occult Experiences* (Madras: Theosophical Publishing House, 1913), 58–62, 97. Hinton's four-dimensional wheel is in Hinton, *The Fourth Dimension* (London: George Allen and Co., 1912; orig. 1904), 61, 71–73. Among the many examples of Spiritualist appropriation of the fourth dimension is John Page Hopps, *A Scientific Basis of Belief in a Future Life* (London: Williams and Norgate, 1881). For context see Richard Noakes, "Natural Causes? Spiritualism, Science and the Supernatural in Mid-Victorian Britain," in *The Victorian Supernatural*, ed. N. Bown, C. Burdett, and P. Thurschwell (Cambridge: Cambridge University Press, 2004), 23–42.

14. Rudolf Steiner, *The Fourth Dimension: Sacred Geometry, Alchemy and Mathematics* (Great Barrington, Mass.: Anthroposophic Press, 2000), 19. Yeats is quoted in Catherine E. Paul and Margaret Mills Harper, eds., *The Collected Works of W. B. Yeats Volume XIII: A Vision* (New York: Scribner, 2008), 142.

15. For many of these details I am indebted to Gregory John Tillet, *Charles Webster Leadbeater, 1854–1934*, http://www.leadbeater.org/.

16. Charles Leadbeater, *Clairvoyance* (London: Theosophical Publishing Society, 1903), 38–39.

17. Charles Leadbeater, *The Astral Plane, Its Scenery, Inhabitants and Phenomena* (London: Theosophical Publishing Society, 1895), 9, 42.

18. Mabel Shine, *Little Journeys into the Invisible: A Woman's Actual Experiences in the Fourth Dimension* (Richmond, Va.: Allshine, 1911), 4–5, 8.

19. Ibid., 10, 12, 71.

20. Charles Brodie Patterson, *A New Heaven and a New Earth* (New York: Thomas Y. Crowell, 1909), 140, 114, 136, 12.

21. This literature includes Martin Jay, *Downcast Eyes: The Denigration of Vision in Twentieth-Century French Thought* (Berkeley: University of California Press, 1993); Jonathan Crary, *Techniques of the Observer: On Vision and Modernity in the Nineteenth Century* (Cambridge, Mass.: Harvard University Press, 1990); Teresa Brennan and Martin Jay, eds., *Vision in Context: Historical and Contemporary Perspectives on Sight* (London: Psychology Press, 1996); David Michael Levin, ed., *Modernity and the Hegemony of Illusion* (Berkeley: University of California Press, 1993); and Barbara Maria Stafford, *Artful Science:*

Enlightenment Entertainment and the Eclipse of Visual Education (Cambridge, Mass.: Harvard University Press,1994).

22. Iwan Morus, "Seeing and Believing Science," *Isis* 97 (2006), 101–110. On magical and scientific exhibitionism and educating the eyes about illusion during the Enlightenment and after, see Robert Darnton, *Mesmerism and the End of the Enlightenment in France* (Cambridge, Mass.: Harvard University Press, 1968); Grete de Francesco, *The Power of the Charlatan,* trans. Miriam Beard (New Haven, Conn.: Yale University Press,1939); Richard D. Altick, *The Shows of London* (Cambridge, Mass.: Harvard University Press,1978); James W. Cook Jr., "From the Age of Reason to the Age of Barnum: The Great Automaton Chess Player and the Emergence of Victorian Cultural Illusionism," *Winterthur Portfolio* 30 (Winter 1995), 231–257; Martin Willis, *Vision, Science and Literature, 1870–1920: Ocular Horizons* (London: Pickering & Chatto, 2011); and Isobel Armstrong, *Victorian Glassworlds: Glass Culture and the Imagination, 1830–1880* (Oxford: Oxford University Press, 2008).

23. Claude Bragdon, *Four Dimensional Vistas* (New York: A. A. Knopf, 1923), 17. See also Jonathan Massey, *Crystal and Arabesque: Claude Bragdon, Ornament and Modern Architecture* (Pittsburgh: University of Pittsburgh Press, 2009), 160–161.

24. For more on how science cultivated a sense of wonder, see Fred Nadis, *Wonder Shows: Performing Magic, Science and Religion in America* (New Brunswick, N.J.: Rutgers University Press, 2005). On the ways that science stimulated a quest for the invisible, see Catherine Maxwell, *Second Sight: The Visionary Imagination in Late Victorian Literature* (Manchester: Manchester University Press, 2008); and Gillian Beer, "'Authentic Tidings of Invisible Things': Vision and the Invisible in the Late Nineteenth Century," in Brennan and Jay, eds., *Vision in Context.*

25. Richard Maurice Bucke, *Cosmic Consciousness: A Study in the Evolution of the Human Mind* (Philadelphia: Innes and Sons, 1905), 2, 55; for context, see Linda Henderson, "Mysticism, Romanticism and the Fourth Dimension," in *The Spiritual in Art: Abstract Painting 1890–1985,* ed. Maurice Tuchman (New York: Abbeville Press, 1986), 224.

26. He was a curate under F. D. Maurice at the end of the 1860s and into the early 1870s but felt suffocated by the ministry and thus departed. See Tom Swan, *Edward Carpenter: The Man and His Message* (London: Arthur Fifield, 1905), 4.

27. Edward Carpenter, *From Adam's Peak to Elephanta: Sketches in Ceylon and India* (London: S. Sonnenschein, 1892), 154–156, 160–161; see also Henderson, "Mysticism, Romanticism and the Fourth Dimension," 223.

28. Gary Lachman, *In Search of P. D. Ouspensky: The Genius in the Shadow of Gurdjieff* (Wheaton, Ill.: Quest Books, 2004), 49–58.

29. P. D. Ouspensky, *Tertium Organum: The Third Canon of Thought: A Key to the Enigmas of the World,* 2nd ed. (New York: Knopf, 1922), 79, 115, emphasis in

the original. I am also indebted in this section and others to Linda Henderson's discussion of the cultural power of the fourth dimension in Linda Henderson, *The Fourth Dimension and Non-Euclidean Geometry* (Cambridge, Mass.: MIT Press, 2013), especially chapter 5.

30. Claude Bragdon, *A Primer of Higher Space (The Fourth Dimension)* (Rochester, N.Y.: Manas Press, 1913), 59. For Blavatsky's views on the meaning of squares and other shapes, see Ann Davis, *The Logic of Ecstasy: Canadian Mystical Painting, 1920–1940* (Toronto: University of Toronto Press, 1992), 101.

31. Bragdon, *Primer of Higher Space,* 76–77; Massey, *Crystal and Arabesque,* 138.

32. Quoted in Mark Blacklock, "On the Eve of the Fourth Dimension: Utopian Higher Space," in *Utopian Spaces of Modernism: Literature and Culture, 1885–1945,* ed. R. Gregory and B. Kohlmann (London: Palgrave Macmillan, 2012), 45.

33. Tillet, *Charles Webster Leadbeater,* chapter 12. Appendix 1 has Leadbeater's entire evolutionary system; Blacklock, "On the Eve of the Fourth Dimension," 43.

34. See, for example, Paul Ivey's account of one Theosophical community in California in *Radiance from Halcyon: A Utopian Experiment in Religion and Science* (Minneapolis: University of Minnesota Press, 2013).

35. Gauri Viswanathan, "The Ordinary Business of Occultism," *Critical Inquiry* 27:1 (Autumn 2000), 1–20.

36. Joseph Conrad and Ford Madox Ford, *The Inheritors: An Extravagant Story* (Liverpool: Liverpool University Press, 1999), 9, 12.

37. Quoted in Elliot Gilbert, "'Upward, Not Northward': *Flatland* and the Quest for the New," *English Literature in Transition, 1880–1920* 34:4 (1991), 397.

38. Thomas Banchoff, "The Fourth Dimension and the Theology of Edwin Abbott Abbott," https://acmsonline.org/home2/wp-content/uploads/2016/05/Banchoff-The-4th-dimention.pdf; Edwin A. Abbott, *Flatland: An Edition with Notes and Commentary by William Lindgren and Thomas Banchoff* (Cambridge: Cambridge University Press, 2010) 252, 262.

39. Abbott, *Flatland,* 176.

40. Joy Dixon, *Divine Feminine: Theosophy and Feminism in England* (Baltimore, Md.: Johns Hopkins University Press, 2003), 179, 202–203.

41. All from Martha Patterson, *Beyond the Gibson Girl: Reimagining the American New Woman, 1895–1915* (Urbana-Champaign: University of Illinois Press, 2005), 125–126, 133, 138–139.

42. Grace Thompson Seton, *A Woman Tenderfoot in Egypt* (New York: Dodd, Mead and Co., 1923), 8, 209–218.

43. Notes from Du Bois's Philosophy 4 Notebook, W. E. B. Du Bois Papers, University of Massachusetts, Amherst, http://credo.library.umass.edu/view/full/mums312-b230-i008.

44. Du Bois's fragmentary "A Vacation Unique" is reprinted in Shamoon Zamir, *Dark Voices: W. E. B. Du Bois and American Thought, 1888–1903* (Chicago: University of Chicago Press, 1995), 221, 223, 218. Zamir argues that

Du Bois here drew on Abbott's *Flatland,* but in Du Bois's story he mentioned a "Mr. Fields" of Flatland. Mr. Field is a character briefly mentioned in Hinton's *An Episode of Flatland,* which was published in 1907. Perhaps Du Bois drew on both Abbott and Hinton, or conflated them. Or he may have drafted and revised portions of his "Vacation Unique" at different times.

45. Zamir, *Dark Voices,* 222, 48–51. Du Bois's narrative here was part of a wider impulse among African American writers to develop counterfactual narratives with "impossible" or fantastic geographies and imaginal social spaces that stood apart from the hierarchies of Jim Crow America. See Nancy Bentley, "The Fourth Dimension: Kinlessness and African American Narrative," *Critical Inquiry* 35:2 (Winter 2009), 270–292. The phrase "impossible geography" also is from Bentley.

46. See Nicole Waligora-Davis, *Sanctuary: African Americans and Empire* (Oxford: Oxford University Press, 2011), 24–27.

47. Stephen Finley et al., eds., *Esotericism in African American Thought* (Leiden: Brill, 2015), 105–107.

48. Ibid., 107, 111–112; Jean Toomer and Frederik Rusch, *A Jean Toomer Reader: Selected Unpublished Writings* (Oxford: Oxford University Press, 1993), 31–35. See also Cynthia Kerman and Richard Eldridge, *The Lives of Jean Toomer: A Hunger for Wholeness* (Baton Rouge: Louisiana State University Press, 1989), 114.

49. Schomburg is quoted in Mitch Horowitz, *Occult America: White House Seances, Ouija Circles, Masons and the Secret Mystic History of our Nation* (New York: Bantam, 2010), 143–145. See also Robert T. Browne, *The Mystery of Space: A Study of the Hyperspace Movement in the Light of the Evolution of New Psychic Faculties and an Inquiry into the Genesis and Essential Nature of Space* (New York: E. P. Dutton, 1919), 251, 252, 336.

50. Horowitz, *Occult America,* 145.

51. W. Sherwin Simmons, "Kasimir Malevich's 'Black Square': The Transformed Self Part Three: The Icon Unmasked," *Arts Magazine* 53 (December 1978), 128, 132–133.

52. Roland Boer, "God in the World," *Heythrop Journal* (2015), 1, 5–6.

53. Williams, *Artists in Revolution,* 125.

4. Cathedrals without Walls

1. Walter Lippmann, *Drift and Mastery: An Attempt to Diagnose the Current Unrest* (Madison: University of Wisconsin Press, 1985; orig. 1914), 111–112.

2. Claude Bragdon, *More Lives Than One* (New York: Knopf, 1938), 129.

3. Abba Goddard, *The Trojan Sketch Book* (Troy, N.Y.: Young and Hartt, 1846), 131–133.

4. Unpublished manuscript by Henry Bragdon entitled "Upstate Heritage," from Bragdon Family Papers, Department of Rare Books, Special Collections and Preservation, University of Rochester Libraries (hereafter cited as BFP).

5. Bethel Church Constitution, BFP.

6. See Joan Shelley Rubin, "Cosmopolitan Ideals, Local Loyalties, and Print Culture: The Career of George Chandler Bragdon in Upstate New York," in *Print Culture Histories beyond the Metropolis,* ed. James J. Connolly, Patrick Collier, Frank Felsenstein, Kenneth R. Hall, and Robert G. Hall (Toronto: University of Toronto Press, 2016), 150–180; and Eugenia Ellis and Andrea Reithmayr, *Claude Bragdon and the Beautiful Necessity* (Rochester, N.Y.: Rochester Institute of Technology Press, 2010), 22.

7. George Bragdon, *Undergrowth* (Oswego, N.Y.: R. J. Oliphant, 1895), 100.

8. Claude Bragdon, "How and Why I Became a Theosophist," *Theosophist* (November 1935), 120; Bragdon, *More Lives Than One,* 282–284.

9. Claude Bragdon, *The New Image* (New York: Knopf, 1928), 151–152.

10. Ralph Waldo Emerson, *The Conduct of Life* (Boston: Ticknor and Fields, 1860), 42.

11. Claude Bragdon, *The Beautiful Necessity: Seven Essays on Theosophy and Architecture* (Rochester, N.Y.: Manas Press, 1910), 76, 14.

12. Claude Bragdon to Katherine Bragdon, February 24, 1907, BFP.

13. Claude Bragdon, "Learning to Think in Terms of Spaces," *The Forum* 52:2 (August 1914), 202.

14. Henry W. Clune, "Seen and Heard: Aid to Scholarship," *Rochester Democrat and Chronicle,* December 14, 1962.

15. Fritz Trautman to Chandler Bragdon, December 3, 1963, BFP.

16. Linda Henderson has done the detective work involved in suggesting links between Bragdon and many others. See Henderson *The Fourth Dimension and Non-Euclidean Geometry in Modern Art* (Cambridge, Mass.: MIT Press, 2013); Henderson, "The Image and Imagination of the Fourth Dimension in Twentieth-Century Art and Culture," *Configurations* 17:1 (Winter 2009), 131–160, and Henderson, "Francis Picabia, Radiometers and X-Rays in 1913," *Art Bulletin* 71:1 (March 1989), 114–123.

17. Claude Bragdon, *A Primer of Higher Space (The Fourth Dimension)* (Rochester, N.Y.: Manas Press, 1913), plates 18 and 19.

18. Paul Emmons, "On Turning the Corner to the Fourth Dimension: Claude Bragdon's Isometric Perspective," in Ellis and Reithmayr, *Claude Bragdon and the Beautiful Necessity,* 60.

19. Kenneth M. Swezey, "What Can't He Do? The Story of Claude Bragdon, Who Finds in Quietness of Spirit the Secret of Marvelous and Manifold Activities," *Psychology* (November 1929), 26.

20. Quoted in Robert Crunden, *Body and Soul: The Making of American Modernism* (New York: Basic Books, 2000), 382.

21. Bragdon, *The Beautiful Necessity: Seven Essays on Theosophy and Architecture* (Rochester, N.Y.: Manas Press, 1910), 13.

22. Quoted in Jonathan Massey, *Crystal and Arabesque: Claude Bragdon, Ornament and Modern Architecture* (Pittsburgh, Pa.: University of Pittsburgh Press, 2009), 181–182, 14.

23. Lewis Mumford, *Roots of Contemporary American Architecture* (New York: Dover, 1972), 422.

24. Bragdon, *More Lives Than One*, 165.

25. Henry W. Clune, "Seen and Heard: Man of Many Parts," *Rochester Democrat and Chronicle*, July 13, 1963.

26. Bragdon, *Projective Ornament* (Rochester, N.Y.: Manas Press, 1915), 5.

27. Quoted in Massey, *Crystal and Arabesque*, 101.

28. For this description I am indebted to Massey, *Crystal and Arabesque*, 106, 114.

29. Bragdon, *New Image*, 93–94.

30. Claude Bragdon, "The New Mysticism," *Reader Magazine* 4:2 (July 1904), 189–190. On Berlage and Theosophical influences on Modernist architecture, see Iain Boyd Whyte, ed., *Modernism and the Spirit of the City* (London: Routledge, 2013), 7–9; and Harry Francis Mallgrave, *Modern Architectural Theory: A Historical Survey, 1673–1968* (Cambridge: Cambridge University Press, 2009), 218–219.

31. Adolf Loos, quoted in Elissa Auther and Adam Lerner, eds., *West of Center: Art and the Counterculture Experiment in America, 1965–1977* (Minneapolis: University of Minnesota Press, 2012), 89.

32. Bragdon, *More Lives Than One*, 166–168.

33. Bragdon, *Projective Ornament*, 33.

34. Quoted in Massey, *Crystal and Arabesque*, 145.

35. Bragdon, *Projective Ornament*, 77.

36. Claude Bragdon to Fritz Trautman, October 10, 1916, BFP.

37. The onset of the war and America's entry into it also made it hard to get work as an architect.

38. Bragdon to Eugenie Macaulay Bragdon, June 2, 1913, BFP.

39. In Massey, *Crystal and Arabesque*, 186, 198.

40. Bragdon, *More Lives Than One*, 72.

41. In Massey, *Crystal and Arabesque*, 185.

42. No author, "Harry Barnhart, the Billy Sunday of Music," *Current Opinion* 62:6 (June 1917), 403.

43. All from Thomas Stoner, "'The New Gospel of Music': Arthur Farwell's Vision of Democratic Music in America," *American Music* 9:2 (Summer 1991), 188–190.

44. Claude Bragdon, quoted in Massey, *Crystal and Arabesque*, 188.

45. In ibid., 189.

46. Lewis Mumford, *Sketches from Life: The Autobiography of Lewis Mumford: The Early Years* (Boston: Beacon, 1982), 120, 129.

47. See Massey, *Crystal and Arabesque,* 151.

48. In ibid., 191, 197, 143.

49. All in ibid., 203–205.

50. From Paul Gallico, "Only in New York," *New York Sunday News* (1931), from the clippings of Claude Bragdon, BFP. See also Bragdon, *More Lives Than One,* 112–114.

51. Geoffrey Hellman, "Profiles: Lights, Please!" *New Yorker* (January 31, 1931), 24.

52. Ibid.

53. The "liturgical revival" is covered in James White, *Protestant Worship and Church Architecture: Theological and Historical Considerations* (Oxford: Oxford University Press, 1964); and in David Bains's work, including his "Conduits of Faith: Reinhold Niebuhr's Liturgical Thought," *Church History* 73 (March 2004), 168–194.

54. Martha Candler, *Drama in Religious Service* (New York: Century Company, 1922). See also Tisa Wenger, "The Practice of Dance for the Future of Christianity: 'Eurythmic Worship' in New York's Roaring Twenties," in Laurie Maffly-Kipp et al., *Practicing Protestants: Histories of Christian Life in America, 1630–1965* (Baltimore, Md.: Johns Hopkins University Press), 222–249.

55. "Church Helps New Theater," *Rochester Democrat and Chronicle,* January 17, 1934.

56. Quoted in Massey, *Crystal and Arabesque,* 250, 254.

57. Susan Tenneriello, "The Divine Spaces of Metaphysical Spectacle: Ruth St. Denis and Denishawn Dance Theatre at Lewisohn Stadium, the Esoteric Model in American Performance," *Performance Research* 13:3 (2008), 130.

58. Geddeth Smith, *Walter Hampden: Dean of the American Theater* (Madison, Wis.: Fairleigh Dickinson University Press, 2008), 137.

59. Ibid., 230.

60. See the online World's Fair exhibition, http://exhibitions.nypl.org/biblion /worldsfair/node/340.

61. Christiana Cogdell, "The Futurama Recontextualized: Norman Bel Geddes's Eugenic 'World of Tomorrow,'" *American Quarterly* 52:2 (June 2000), 214, 220, 223.

62. Ibid., 224–225.

63. In Leigh Schmidt, *Restless Souls: The Making of American Spirituality* (San Francisco: Harper, 2005), 164.

64. Linda Henderson has documented the cultural power of higher dimensions in art and culture in her exhaustively researched *Fourth Dimension and Non-Euclidean Geometry in Modern Art.*

5. Max Weber and the Art of an Invisible Geometry

1. Alfred Werner, "Max Weber: Hasidic Painter," *Jewish News,* September 23, 1960.

2. Linda Henderson, "The Image and Imagination of the Fourth Dimension," *Configurations* 17:1 (Winter 2009), 131–160, here 136–137.

3. Linda Henderson, *The Fourth Dimension and Non-Euclidean Geometry in Modern Art* (Princeton, N.J.: Princeton University Press, 1983), xix. See also Robert Williams, *Artists in Revolution: Portraits of the Russian Avant-garde, 1905–1925* (Bloomington: Indiana University Press, 1977), 109.

4. Wassily Kandinsky, *Concerning the Spiritual in Art* (New York: Wittenborn, Schultz, 1947; orig., 1912), 21–27.

5. Max Weber, *Cubist Poems* (London: Elkin Mathews, 1914), 15.

6. In fact this is a ubiquitous trope in the memoirs of Jewish Modernist artists. When aniconic attitudes were present in the older generation they were often motivated by religious zeal or a desire to uphold (what was thought of as) traditional values in the face of modern challenges. In spite of this aniconic viewpoint, however, there was in fact a long tradition of Jewish art and visual culture. I am indebted to my colleague Marc Epstein for his ideas on this subject and on related topics. Alfred Werner, "Ghetto Graduates," *American Art Journal* 5:2 (November 1973), 73.

7. Carol Gruber, "The Reminiscences of Max Weber," an interview with Max Weber, January 20, 1958, Oral History Research Office, Columbia University, 34.

8. Percy North and Alfred Stieglitz, "Turmoil at 291," *Archives of American Art Journal* 30:1 (1990), 81.

9. Gruber, "Reminiscences of Max Weber," 73–74.

10. Lloyd Goodrich, "Max Weber Retrospective Exhibition," Whitney Museum of American Art (1949), 11, http://www.philamuseum.org/exhibitions /312.html?page=2; Holger Cahill, *Max Weber* (New York: Downtown Gallery, 1930), 11–12.

11. No author, "Max Weber at the Photo-Secession," *Craftsman* 19:6 (March 1911), 643.

12. Gruber, "Reminiscences of Max Weber," 40, 195.

13. From an autobiographical typescript called "Escape from Reality," Gelett Burgess Papers, Bancroft Library, University of California, Berkeley (hereafter cited as GBP). Some details here also are from Joseph Backus, *Gelett Burgess behind the Scenes* (San Francisco: Book Club of California, 1968), 10–12.

14. "Image Breakers: Dr. Cogswell's Stature Overturned under Shadow of Night by a Silent Gang of Hoodlum Miscreants," *San Francisco Call* (January 3, 1894), 8.

15. Rollin Hartt, "The Funniest Man That Ever Lived," *Macon Telegraph* (1919), clipping from GBP.

16. H. C. Norris, "Everybody Is Jumping over the Moon," *Public Ledger,* from Burgess notebooks, GBP; Claude Bragdon, "The Purple Cow Period," *Bookman* 69 (July 1929), 476.

17. Charles H. Hinton to Gelett Burgess, June 1903, GBP; Charles H. Hinton to Gelett Burgess, June 7, 1903, GBP; and Charles H. Hinton to Gelett Burgess, September 1 (no year), GBP.

18. From an unpublished typescript by Burgess, "The Fourth Dimension," GBP.

19. Burgess, "Escape from Reality." Hinton and Burgess both complained about Spiritualists and superstitious Christians holding religious beliefs without evidence or proof.

20. Charles H. Hinton to Gelett Burgess, September 18 (no year), GBP.

21. S. J. Woolf, "Still No Purple Cow," *New York Times,* January 26, 1941.

22. Gelett Burgess, "The Wild Men of Paris," *Architectural Record* 27:5 (May 1910), 401–403, 405.

23. John Lane, "The Sources of Max Weber's Cubism," *Art Journal* 35:3 (1976), 234.

24. Burgess, "Wild Men of Paris," 403.

25. Percy North, *Max Weber: The Cubist Decade, 1910–1920* (Atlanta, Ga.: High Museum of Art, 1991), 23–24; Lane, "Sources of Max Weber's Cubism," 233–234.

26. Lane, "Sources of Max Weber's Cubism," 234.

27. Quoted in Percy North, "Bringing Cubism to America: Max Weber and Pablo Picasso," *American Art* 14:3 (Autumn 2000), 73.

28. Mark Antliff and Scott Klein, *Vorticism: New Perspectives* (Oxford: Oxford University Press, 2013), 169–170.

29. Miscellaneous handwritten notes by Weber, Max Weber Papers, Archives of American Art, Smithsonian Institution (hereafter cited as MWP).

30. Max Weber, "The Fourth Dimension from a Plastic Point of View," *Camera Work* 31 (July 1910), 25. See also Henderson's extensive discussion of the importance of this article and Weber's dimensional ideas in Henderson, *Fourth Dimension and Non-Euclidean Geometry in Modern Art* (2013), 291–298.

31. Weber, *Cubist Poems,* 11.

32. North, *Max Weber,* 34.

33. From a two-page typescript essay on art from 1912, MWP.

34. Max Weber to Mabel Dodge Luhan, January 22, 1913, MWP.

35. Claude Bragdon, *Four Dimensional Vistas* (New York: Knopf, 1923), 17. See also Jonathan Massey, *Crystal and Arabesque: Claude Bragdon, Ornament and Modern Architecture* (Pittsburgh: University of Pittsburgh Press, 2009), 160–161. For more on how science cultivated a sense of wonder, see Fred Nadis, *Wonder Shows: Performing Magic, Science and Religion in America* (New Brunswick, N.J.: Rutgers University Press, 2005). On the ways that science stimulated a quest for the invisible, see Catherine Maxwell, *Second Sight: The Visionary Imagination in Late Victorian Literature* (Manchester: Manchester University Press, 2008); and Gillian Beer, "'Authentic Tidings of Invisible Things':

Vision and the Invisible in the Late Nineteenth Century," in *Vision in Context: Historical and Contemporary Perspectives,* ed. Teresa Brennan and Martin Jay (New York: Routledge, 1996).

36. Mabel Dodge Luhan, *Movers and Shakers* (Albuquerque: University of New Mexico Press, 1936), 39.

37. Weber, *Essays on Art* (New York: William Edwin Rudge, 1916), 12–15, 37.

38. Max Weber to Jake Heyman, May 25, 1903, MWP.

39. Weber, *Essays on Art,* 40.

40. Mark Cheetham, *The Rhetoric of Purity: Essentialist Theory and the Advent of Abstract Painting* (Cambridge: Cambridge University Press, 1991), 4, 93.

41. Lawrence Rinder, ed., *Knowledge of Higher Worlds: Rudolf Steiner's Blackboard Drawings* (Berkeley, Calif.: Berkeley Art Museum and Film Archive, 1997), 38.

42. American Artists Group, *Max Weber* (New York: American Artists Group, 1945).

43. Roger Lipsey, *An Art of Our Own: The Spiritual in Twentieth-Century Art* (Boston: Shambhala, 1997), 37.

44. Tom Gibbons, "Cubism and 'The Fourth Dimension' in the Context of the Late Nineteenth-Century and Early Twentieth-Century Revival of Occult Idealism," *Journal of the Warburg and Courtauld Institutes* 44 (1981), 143. See also Henderson, *Fourth Dimension and Non-Euclidean Geometry in Modern Art* (2013), chapter 2; Sixten Ringbom, "Art in 'The Epoch of the Great Spiritual': Occult Elements in the Early Theory of Abstract Painting," *Journal of the Warburg and Courtauld Institutes* 29 (1966), 386–418. How these ideas came to Weber we do not know exactly, though he could have read Leadbeater's earlier works, such as *The Astral Plane* (1895), *Clairvoyance* (1899), and *The Other Side of Death* (1903), or Hinton or Bragdon before moving to France in 1905.

45. Miscellaneous handwritten notes by Weber, MWP.

46. Weber, *Essays on Art,* 19–20.

47. Ibid., 20–21; Max Weber to Henry Hurwitz, January 7, 1935, MWP.

48. Quoted in Gibbons, "Cubism and 'The Fourth Dimension,'" 141.

49. Weber, miscellaneous writings, MWP.

50. Max Weber to Louise Nevelson, October 7, 1950, Louise Nevelson Papers, Archives of American Art, Smithsonian Institution.

51. In fact, Weber may have been drawing from James's widely read *Varieties of Religious Experience* (1902). Weber sometimes uses James's word "overplus" when talking about the vital emotion that comes from the primitive.

52. Matthew Baigell, "Max Weber's Jewish Paintings," *American Jewish History* 88:3 (September 2000), 352.

53. Max Weber, "A Note on 'Talmudists,'" *Menorah Journal* 23 (April–June 1935), 100.

54. Quoted in Henderson, *Fourth Dimension and Non-Euclidean Geometry in Modern Art* (2013), 304.

55. Max Weber, lecture notes, MWP.

56. No author, "Maker of Curious Pictures in Town: Weber Modestly Unburdens His Soul and Discusses Rivals," *Baltimore Evening News,* 1915, from Weber's collection of news clippings, MWP.

57. See, for example, Robert Alter, *Necessary Angels: Tradition and Modernity in Kafka, Benjamin and Scholem* (Cambridge, Mass.: Harvard University Press, 1991), 102–107.

6. The Spacetime of Dreams

1. John G. Bennett, *Witness: The Autobiography of John G. Bennett* (London: Turnstone, 1974), 1–2.

2. Ibid., 2.

3. Ibid., 3.

4. Ibid., 4.

5. John G. Bennett, *The Crisis in Human Affairs* (New York: Hermitage House, 1951), xv. For Bennett's way of thinking about time later in life, see J. B. Priestley, *Man and Time* (London: Aldus, 1964), 272–273.

6. George Kernodle, "Time-Frightened Playwrights," *American Scholar* 18:4 (Fall 1949), 446; J. B. Priestley, *Thoughts in the Wilderness* (London: Heinemann, 1957), 44; J. B. Priestley, *Midnight on the Desert, Being an Excursion into Autobiography during a Winter in America, 1935–36* (New York: Harper and Brothers, 1937), 244. For context on this era's preoccupation with time, see J. W. N. Sullivan, "What and Where Are We? Reflections on Man's Place in the Universe," *Harper's Monthly Magazine* 175 (June–November 1937), 20–26; Tim Armstrong, *Modernism: A Cultural History* (London: Polity, 2005), 1–18; Clive Barker, "The Ghosts of War: Stage Ghosts and Time Slips as a Response to War," in *British Theatre between the Wars, 1918–1939,* ed. Clive Barker and Maggie Gale (Cambridge: Cambridge University Press, 2000), 215–243; and Jesse Matz, "J. B. Priestley in the Theater of Time," *Modernism/Modernity* 19:2 (2012), 321–342.

7. Priestley, *Man and Time,* 244; J. W. Dunne, *An Experiment with Time,* 2nd ed. (London: A & C Black, 1929; orig. 1927), 1.

8. Dunne, *Experiment,* 32–33.

9. Ibid., 34–38.

10. Dunne says actually that when he read the newspaper he misread the headline as saying there were four thousand killed—not forty thousand. It was later that he looked again at the headline and saw that he had misread it. Dunne makes the point that his dream sequences showed him not just elements of the disaster itself but also the future moment when he opened the newspaper and read the story.

11. Dunne, *Experiment*, 50–52.

12. Ibid., 54, emphasis in the original.

13. Robert Graves and Alan Hodge, *The Long Week-End: A Social History of Great Britain 1918–1939* (New York: W. W. Norton, 1963), 97. Dunne's detailed instructions for how to reflect on and record dreams are in *Experiment*, 64–65.

14. It is not unreasonable to see Dunne's flying experiments as attempts to move in a higher dimension. If Hinton liberated his boys from two-dimensional living by training them to *climb up and down* on his "jungle gym," Dunne developed an even more powerful way of moving in the third, up-and-down, dimension. For the first time in history, airplanes made it possible to move off the surface of the (mostly) flat surface of our planet and into the atmosphere of a higher space. In his writings, Dunne used words like "higher order," a "higher dimension," and "going up" to describe how conscious observers rose above simpler time-worlds. See *Experiment*, 156–168.

15. Ibid., 93, 99–112. A scientist who remained something of an open-minded spiritual seeker, Arthur Eddington wrote to Dunne in 1928 that he agreed with him about Serialism. "My own feeling is that the 'becoming' is really there in the physical world, but is not formulated in the description of it in classical physics (and is, in fact, useless to a scheme of laws which is fully deterministic)." This was a powerful endorsement from a scientific celebrity, and Dunne reproduced Eddington's comments in the front matter of his second edition. Ibid., viii.

16. See, for example, H. Levy, "Time and Perception," *Nature* 119 (June 11, 1927), 847–848; A. S. Russell, "Do Dreams Come True?" *Discovery* 10:113 (May 1929), 168–170; A. S. Russell, "Mr. Dunne's Serial Universe," *Discovery* 16:182 (February 1935), 51–54.

17. For these complaints and others, see Charles Hartshorne, "The Reality of the Past, the Unreality of the Future," *Hibbert Journal* 37 (January 1939), 246–257; C. D. Broad, "Mr. Dunne's Theory of Time in 'An Experiment with Time,'" *Philosophy* 10:38 (April 1935), 168–185; C. E. M. Joad, "Time and Prophecy," *Spectator Literary Supplement* 138:5154 (April 9, 1927), 651; Maurice Cornforth, *New Statesman and Nation* 8:200 (December 22, 1934), 941–942; and Grover Smith Jr., "Time Alive: J. W. Dunne and J. B. Priestley," *South Atlantic Quarterly* 56:2 (April 1957), 224–233.

18. F. C. S. Schiller, review of *An Experiment with Time*, *Hibbert Journal* 26 (October 1, 1927), 188–190; see also Ernest Nagel, review of *An Experiment with Time*, *Journal of Philosophy* 24 (1927), 690–692; C. T. Krishnama Chari, "An Epistemological Approach to the Special Theory of Relativity," *Mind* 46:182 (April 1937), 159–179; and the chapter on Dunne in M. F. Cleugh, *Time and Its Importance in Modern Thought* (London: Methuen and Co., 1937).

19. Sullivan, "What and Where Are We?," 26.

20. J. W. Dunne to H. G. Wells, January 3, 1904, H. G. Wells Papers, University of Illinois.

21. Katy Price, *Loving Faster Than Light: Romance and Readers in Einstein's Universe* (Chicago: University of Chicago Press, 2012), 191.

22. J. W. Dunne, *Intrusions?* (London: Faber and Faber, 1955), 119.

23. Ibid., 79, 143–144.

24. Victoria Stewart, "J. W. Dunne and Literary Culture in the 1930s and 1940s," *Literature and History* 17:2 (2008), 63.

25. Ibid., 71–72.

26. C. S. Lewis, *The Dark Tower and Other Stories* (New York: Houghton Mifflin, 2002), 22. In a chance encounter at a pub in 1959, the American Daniel Morris remembered Lewis talking extensively about Dunne's theories, our life in time, and our abilities to transcend time. "He went into Dunne a good bit (that is, J. W. Dunne: *An Experiment in Time,* published in 1925) and he doesn't see (neither do I) why Dunne had to postulate an infinity of times at right angles to one another. Two times would cover the whole thing. Granted, that leaves a mystery as to what makes the thing run, but Dunne simply puts that off at infinity. And thence to previsions, and to extrasensory perception, and predestination. . . . In the course of our talk about Dunne, and such, he said it was a shame we couldn't control the rate of flow of time. As it was, the clock was rapidly moving on towards half past seven, and the end of this delightful talk he was having with me." From David Graham, *We Remember C. S. Lewis: Essays and Memoirs* (Nashville, Tenn.: Broadman and Holman, 2001), 112–113.

27. Edward Wagenknecht, in his *Six Novels of the Supernatural* (New York: Viking, 1944), also points to Dunne's influence in interwar fiction, saying that his ideas were "in the air." Dunne's theory "haunts the imagination of the modern writer and apparently appeals to something vital in the spirit of the age" (3). Wagenknecht mentions Balderston's *Berkeley Square* as an important play that uses Relativity to show that time was relative and that future and present could be mixed (777). Other novels that experimented with time and dimensions in this period included, for example, Forrest Reid's *Uncle Stephen,* Esther Meynell's *Time's Door,* Maxwell Anderson's *The Star Wagon,* Sheila Kaye-Smith's *Ember Lane,* Elizabeth Goudge's *The Middle Window,* Alison Uttley's *A Traveler in Time,* Nevil Shute's *An Old Captivity,* Eleanor Smith's *Lovers' Meeting,* and Warwick Deeping's *The Man Who Went Back* (777).

28. Quoted in Verlyn Flieger, *A Question of Time: J. R. R. Tolkien's Road to Faerie* (Kent, Ohio: Kent State University Press, 1997), 8, 3.

29. Tolkien is quoted in Michael D. C. Drout, ed., *J. R. R. Tolkien Encyclopedia: Scholarship and Critical Assessment* (New York: Routledge, 2006), 649–650.

30. Quoted in Flieger, *Question of Time,* 136. See also Drout, *Encyclopedia,* 649.

31. Tolkien felt connected to the past by at least one recurrent dream that he called his "Atlantis haunting," a dream in which he is overwhelmed by a primordial wave of water. "This legend or myth or dim memory of some ancient history has always troubled me. In sleep I had the dreadful dream of the ineluctable Wave, either coming out of the quiet sea, or coming towering in over the green islands. It still occurs occasionally, though now exorcised by writing about it. It always ends by surrender, and I awake gasping out of deep water." In his books, his characters' dreams also function as doorways into different times. "In dreams strange powers of the mind may be unlocked" (from Flieger, *Question of Time,* 75–78).

32. In *God the Invisible King* (1917), Wells saw on the horizon a "renascent religion" crystallizing "out of the intellectual, social, and spiritual confusions of this time," a religion that was taking shape in himself and in many others around the globe. It amounted to "a profound belief in a personal and intimate God," a God who was not remote and infinite but close and finite, working with human beings against evil, a God of another dimension who existed above our three-dimensional world. Modern sciences even suggested this God's existence. "Our modern psychology is alive to the possibility of Being that has no extension in space at all, even as our speculative geometry can entertain the possibility of dimensions—fourth, fifth, nth dimensions—outside the three-dimensional universe of our experience. And God being non-spatial is not thereby banished to an infinite remoteness, but brought nearer to us; He is everywhere immediately at hand, even as a fourth dimension would be everywhere immediately at hand." "Mr. Wells Describes 'Renascent Religion,'" *New York Times,* May 13, 1917. Also, in different novels Wells used the fourth-dimension concept to allow characters to travel across vast spaces ("Remarkable Case of Davidson's Eyes"), transform left-handed objects into right-handed ones ("The Plattner Story"), travel through time (*The Time Traveler*), allow characters to become invisible (*The Invisible Man*), or locate the dwelling-place of God and his angels (*The Wonderful Visit*).

33. H. G. Wells, "New Light on Mental Life: Mr. J. W. Dunne's Experiments with Dreaming," in H. G. Wells, *The Way the World Is Going: Guesses and Forecasts of the Years Ahead* (London, <AU: publisher?>1928), 210.

34. H. G. Wells, *The Last Books of H. G. Wells* (Rhinebeck, N.Y.: Monkfish, 1996), 7; H. G. Wells, *The Shape of Things to Come: The Ultimate Revolution* (London: Hutchinson & Co., 1935), 15.

35. David C. Smith, *H. G. Wells: Desperately Mortal* (New Haven, Conn.: Yale University Press, 1986), 34–35.

36. Willis B. Glover, "The Religious Orientation of H. G. Wells: A Case Study in Scientific Humanism," *Harvard Theological Review* 65:1 (January 1972), 124.

37. Smith, *H. G. Wells*, 33–34.

38. Jesse Matz, "J. B. Priestley in the Theater of Time," *Modernism/Modernity* 19:2 (2012), 334.

39. J. B. Priestley, *Margin Released: A Writer's Reminiscences and Reflections* (New York: Harpers, 1962), 108–109.

40. Melba Cuddy-Keane, *Virginia Woolf, the Intellectual, and the Public Sphere* (Cambridge: Cambridge University Press, 2003), 29–31.

41. Quoted in Matz, "J. B. Priestley," 324; Priestley, *Midnight on the Desert*, 245.

42. J. B. Priestley, *Rain upon Godshill: A Further Chapter of Biography* (London: William Heinemann, 1939), 117.

43. Quoted in the Rudy Vallee Show Sound Recording, January 6, 1938, NBC Radio Collection, Motion Picture, Broadcasting and Recorded Sound Division, Library of Congress, Washington DC

44. Priestley, *Man and Time*, 250.

45. Quoted in Matz, "J. B. Priestley," 335.

46. Priestley, *Midnight on the Desert*, 304.

47. Ibid., 306–308.

48. Ibid., 74–76.

49. Ibid., 107–109.

50. All from Matz, "J. B. Priestley," 328.

51. J. B. Priestley to Claude Bragdon, January 12, 1938, Bragdon Family Papers, University of Rochester Special Collections.

52. Priestley, *Man and Time*, 244–245.

53. Rudy Vallee Show Sound Recording, January 6, 1938.

54. Priestley, *Man and Time*, 117.

55. Dunne, *Intrusions?*, 86, 90, 111.

56. See Laura Marcus, *Dreams of Modernity: Psychoanalysis, Literature, Cinema* (Cambridge: Cambridge University Press, 2014), especially chapters 9 and 10. See also Natalya Lusty and Helen Groth, *Dreams and Modernity: A Cultural History* (London: Routledge, 2013).

57. Priestley, *Man and Time*, 187.

58. Ibid., 250.

59. Ibid., 198; J. W. Dunne, *An Experiment with Time,* 3rd ed. (New York: Macmillan, 1949), 240 and footnote on p. 247.

7. Mirrors, Doorways, and Otherworldly Openings

1. Luke Ferretter, *The Glyph and the Gramophone: D. H. Lawrence's Religion* (London: Bloomsbury, 2013), 2. See also S. Freer, *Modern Mythopoeia: The Twilight of the Gods* (London: Palgrave Macmillan, 2015).

2. In Tolkien's metaphysical notion of "Mythopoeia," as Michael Saler has characterized it, "all myths were, at some level, real, with Christianity ex-

pressing the highest truth as well as being incarnate within history." All quotes from Michael Saler, *As If: Modern Enchantment and the Literary Prehistory of Virtual Reality* (Oxford: Oxford University Press, 2012), 66, 160, 163.

3. C. S. Lewis, *George MacDonald: An Anthology* (New York: Macmillan, 1947), 12.

4. George MacDonald, "The Imagination: Its Function and Culture," in *A Dish of Orts: Chiefly Papers on the Imagination, and on Shakespeare* (London: Sampson Low, Marston & Co., 1895), 3.

5. Quoted in Rolland Hein, *Christian Mythmakers* (Stevens Point, Wis.: Cornerstone, 1998), 151–152.

6. MacDonald, "Imagination," 3.

7. George MacDonald, *Phantastes: A Faerie Romance for Men and Women* (London: Smith, Elder and Co., 1858), epigraph. Translated from the German here: http://instituteofphilosophy.org/c-s-lewis/lewis-and-macdonalds-phantastes/.

8. R. B. Shaberman, "George MacDonald and Lewis Carroll," *North Wind* 1 (1982), 11–12. See also David Neuhouser, "C. S. Lewis, George MacDonald and Mathematics," *Wingfold* 15 (Summer 1996), 1, http://library.taylor.edu/cslewis/mathematics.shtml.

9. J. MacIntyre, "Phantastes into Alice," *Newsletter of the Victorian Studies Association of Western Canada* 3:2 (1977), 6–7; Shaberman, "George MacDonald," 17, 21–22.

10. Joanna Shawn Brigid O'Leary, "Where 'Things Go the Other Way': The Stereochemistry of Lewis Carroll's Looking-Glass World," *Victorian Network* 2:1 (Summer 2010), 70–72; Elizabeth Throesch, "Nonsense in the Fourth Dimension of Literature: Hyperspace Philosophy, the 'New' Mathematics, and the *Alice* Books," in *Alice beyond Wonderland: Essays for the Twenty-First Century*, ed. Cristopher Hollingsworth (Iowa City: University of Iowa Press, 2009), 38.

11. Throesch, "Nonsense in the Fourth Dimension of Literature," 38, 41.

12. Marina Warner, *Phantasmagoria: Spirit Visions, Metaphors and Media into the Twenty-First Century* (Oxford: Oxford University Press, 2008), 52.

13. George MacDonald, *Lilith: A Romance* (London: Chatto and Windus, 1896), 8.

14. Ibid., 25.

15. Ibid., 52–54.

16. Ibid., 337–338.

17. Ibid., 350.

18. Jeffrey Bilbro, "'Yet More Spacious Space': Higher-Dimensional Imagination from *Flatland* to *Lilith*," *North Wind* 28 (2009), 2.

19. Quoted in ibid., 3.

20. Ibid., 7–8.

21. Quoted in P. H. Brazier, *C. S. Lewis—The Work of Christ Revealed* (Eugene, Ore.: Wipf and Stock, 2012), 198

22. C. S. Lewis, *Surprised by Joy: The Shape of My Early Life* (New York: Harcourt Brace, 1955), 174.

23. Ibid., 180–181. See also Cynthia Marshall, *Essays on C. S. Lewis and George MacDonald: Truth, Fiction and the Power of the Imagination* (Lewiston, N.Y.: Edwin Mellen Press, 1991), 105–107.

24. Lewis, *Surprised*, 169–170.

25. Alister McGrath, *C. S. Lewis, a Life: Eccentric Genius, Reluctant Prophet* (Carol Stream, Ill.: Tyndale House, 2013), 134.

26. C. S. Lewis, *The Last Battle* (New York: Harper, 1984; orig. 1956), 192, 195–196.

27. P. H. Brazier, "C. S. Lewis: A Doctrine of Transposition," *Heythrop Journal* 50:4 (2009), 671. Surprisingly, Brazier doesn't connect Lewis's address to dimensional thinking or *Flatland*.

28. C. S. Lewis, *Of Other Worlds: Essays and Stories* (New York: Houghton Mifflin, 2002), 96. Lewis said that *Flatland* was a classic in a 1937 *Times Literary Supplement Review* of *The Hobbit*. See George Beahm, *The Essential J. R. R. Tolkien Sourcebook* (Franklin Lakes, N.J.: Career Press, 2004), 22.

29. C. S. Lewis, *Miracles: A Preliminary Study* (New York: Macmillan, 1947), 24–25, 34–35, 124.

30. C. S. Lewis, *God in the Dock: Essays on Theology and Ethics* (Grand Rapids, Mich.: Eerdmans, 1970), 178.

31. Lewis, *God in the Dock*, 35.

32. Ibid.

33. C. S. Lewis, *Mere Christianity* (New York: Macmillan, 1960), 126.

34. Quoted in David L. Neuhouser, "Higher Dimensions in the Writings of C. S. Lewis," 8, https://library.taylor.edu/dotAsset/9bfa4539-cbf0-409f-bcfc-3752a902bff1.pdf.

35. C. S. Lewis, *The Problem of Pain* (New York: HarperCollins, 2001; orig. 1940), 83–84.

36. Lewis, *God in the Dock*, 182.

37. From Neuhouser, "Higher Dimensions," 9.

38. Ibid.

39. Lewis, *God in the Dock*, 181.

40. C. S. Lewis, "Transposition," in C. S. Lewis, *The Weight of Glory and Other Addresses* (New York: Macmillan, 1949), 25.

41. Ibid., 23, 24, 27. The passage from *The Four Loves* is Lewis, *The Four Loves* (New York: Houghton Mifflin, 1991; orig. 1960), 131.

42. Lewis, "Transposition," 22.

43. Ibid., 23.

44. Quoted in William G. Johnson and Marcia K. Houtman, "Platonic Shadows in C. S. Lewis' Narnia Chronicles," *MFS Modern Fiction Studies* 32:1 (Spring 1986), 81–83.

45. C. S. Lewis, *On Stories: And Other Essays on Literature* (New York: Harcourt Brace, 1982), 38.

46. Hilary P. Dannenberg, "Windows, Doorways and Portals in Narrative Fiction and Media," in *Magical Objects: Things and Beyond,* ed. Elmar Schenkel and Stefan Welz (Berlin: Galda and Wilch, 2007), 182.

47. Lewis, *On Stories,* 23.

48. C. S. Lewis, *The Voyage of the Dawn Treader* (New York: Harper Trophy, 1994; orig. 1952), 231.

49. Quoted in Hilary Dannenberg, "Doorways to Anywhere vs. Repetitive Hierarchy: The Multiple-World Structure of C. S. Lewis's Narnian Universe," *Inklings-Jahrbuch* 16 (1998), 142.

50. Lewis, *God in the Dock,* 35.

51. Lewis, *Last Battle,* 159.

52. John Milbank, "Fictioning Things: Gift and Narrative," *Religion & Literature* 37:3 (Autumn 2005), 1–2.

53. Kath Filmer, *The Fiction of C. S. Lewis: Mask and Mirror* (New York: Palgrave Macmillan, 1993), 110. Even J. K. Rowling has complained, telling one interviewer for *Time*—"There comes a point where Susan, who was the older girl, is lost to Narnia because she becomes interested in lipstick. She's become irreligious basically because she found sex. I have a big problem with that." Lev Grossman, "J. K. Rowling: Hogwarts and All," *Time,* July 17, 2005.

8. Madeleine L'Engle Disturbs the Universe

1. Quoted in Donald R. Hettinga, *Presenting Madeleine L'Engle* (Woodbridge, Conn.: Twayne, 1989), 2.

2. MacDonald, L'Engle said once, using a curious phrase, "overlapped" with her father, by which she might have meant that MacDonald's influence began during her father's life and extended after his death when she was seventeen.

3. All from a L'Engle typescript about George MacDonald entitled "George MacDonald: Nourishment for a Private World," Madeleine L'Engle Papers, Wheaton College (hereafter cited as MLP).

4. Madeleine L'Engle, "Childlike Wonder and the Truths of Science Fiction," *Children's Literature* 10 (1982), 105, 110.

5. Madeleine L'Engle, *A Wind in the Door* (New York: Macmillan, 2010; orig. 1973), 153.

6. "Allegorical Fantasy: Mortal Dealings with Cosmic Questions," *Christianity Today* (June 8, 1979), accessed online January 6, 2016.

7. L'Engle to Ed [no last name given on the letter], August 26, 1972, MLP.

8. Madeleine L'Engle to Ron Irwin, November 21, 1976, MLP.

9. Quoted in Marek Oziewicz, *One Earth, One People: The Mythopoeic Fantasy Series of Ursula K. Le Guin, Lloyd Alexander, Madeleine L'Engle, Orson Scott Card* (Jefferson, N.C.: McFarland, 2008), 171.

10. Shel Horowitz, "Madeleine L'Engle: Faith during Adversity," http://www.frugalfun.com/l%27engle.html.

11. *Madeleine L'Engle: Stargazer* (1990) (documentary film); the quote is at 20:40.

12. Handwritten journaling, MLP.

13. Linda Chisholm, "Interview with Madeleine L'Engle Franklin in the Cathedral Library, St. John the Divine, New York, NY," April 15, 1976, MLP.

14. L'Engle typescript about George MacDonald entitled "George MacDonald: Nourishment for a Private World," MLP.

15. Madeleine L'Engle, *A Wrinkle in Time* (New York: Farrar, Straus and Giroux, 2007), 27.

16. Ibid., 87–88.

17. Ibid., 89, 70.

18. Ibid., 90, 92.

19. Leonard Marcus, *Listening for Madeleine: A Portrait of Madeleine L'Engle in Many Voices* (New York: Macmillan, 2012), 138.

20. L'Engle, *Wrinkle,* 215, 205.

21. Quoted in M. Grant Kellermeyer, *Algernon Blackwood's "The Willows" and Other Tales of Terror* (Fort Wayne, Ind.: Oldstyle Tales, 2014), 10.

22. Algernon Blackwood, "A Victim of Higher Space," in Algernon Blackwood, *Day and Night Stories* (London: Cassell, 1917), 318.

23. Mark Clifton, "Star, Bright," in *The Mathematical Magpie,* ed. Clifton Fadiman (New York: Simon and Schuster, 1962), 87.

24. Jon J. Eilenberg, "9 Easter Eggs from the Bookshelf in *Interstellar,*" *Wired Magazine,* November 17, 2014.

25. Deanna K. Kreisal, "The Discreet Charm of Abstraction: Hyperspace Worlds and Victorian Geometry," *Victorian Studies* 56:3 (Spring 2014), 405–407.

26. H. G. Wells, "The Plattner Story," in H. G. Wells, *The Plattner Story and Others* (London: Methuen & Co., 1897), 2–28; Jack H. Harris, *The 4D Man* (film), directed by Irvin Yeaworth, Universal-International (1959); Arthur C. Clarke, "Technical Error," in Arthur C. Clarke, *Reach for Tomorrow* (New York: Ballantine, 1956), 48–66.

27. Thomas Singer, "In the Manner of Duchamp, 1942–47: The Years of the 'Mirrorical Return,'" *Art Bulletin* 86:2 (June 2004), 362–363. See also Linda Henderson, *The Fourth Dimension and Non-Euclidean Geometry in Modern Art* (Princeton, N.J.: Princeton University Press 1983), 251–256.

28. Ana Teixeira Pinto, "Enantiomorphs in Hyperspace: Living and Dying on the Fourth Dimension," *e-flux journal* 72 (April 2016), 8.

29. Niall Munro, *Hart Crane's Queer Modernist Aesthetic* (New York: Palgrave Macmillan, 2015), 139.

30. Traveling through other dimensions in works by Robert Heinlein and many other sci-fi writers was often a psychological process. L. Ron Hubbard's first science fiction story, for example, "The Dangerous Dimension" (1938), concerned a professor who came up with an "Equation C" about other dimensions. When one merely looked at this equation, one gained the ability to teleport. (Unfortunately, the teleportation happened whether or not characters actually wished to go, and the professor had to find a way to control this process. In the end, he did: an "Equation D.")

31. In George Marsden, *C. S. Lewis's Mere Christianity: A Biography* (Princeton, N.J.: Princeton University Press, 2016), 150.

32. Quoted in Carolyn Curtis and Mary Pomroy Key, eds., *Women and C. S. Lewis: What His Life and Literature Reveal for Today's Culture* (Oxford: Lion Books, 2015), 150.

33. Laura Miller, *The Magician's Book: A Skeptic's Adventures in Narnia* (New York: Little, Brown, 2008), 129, 133–134, 139–140.

34. See C. S. Lewis, "Priestesses in the Church?," in C. S. Lewis, *God in the Dock: Essays on Theology and Ethics* (Grand Rapids, Mich.: Eerdmans, 1970).

35. C. S. Lewis, *The Horse and His Boy* (Grand Rapids, Mich.: Zondervan, 1994), 182.

36. From the *Encyclopedia of Science Fiction,* "Women in SF," accessed February 2, 2017, at http://www.sf-encyclopedia.com/entry/women_in_sf.

37. Cynthia Zarin, "The Storyteller: Fact, Fiction and the Books of Madeleine L'Engle," *The New Yorker* (April 12, 2004), http://www.newyorker.com/magazine/2004/04/12/the-storyteller-cynthia-zarin.

38. Madeleine L'Engle, "Shake the Universe," *Ms.* 16:1–2 (July/August 1987), 182.

39. Leonard Marcus, *Listening for Madeleine: A Portrait of Madeleine L'Engle in Many Voices* (New York: Macmillan, 2012), 8–9, 18–19.

40. Betty Friedan, "Woman: The Fourth Dimension," *Ladies Home Journal* 81:5 (June 1964), 48–49.

41. Rolland Hein, *Christian Mythmakers* (Stevens Point, Wis.: Cornerstone, 1998), 257.

42. Michael Saler examines this development in his *As If: Modern Enchantment and the Literary Prehistory of Virtual Reality* (Oxford: Oxford University Press, 2012), introduction and chapters 1 and 2.

43. George Santayana, *The Life of Reason, or the Phases of Human Progress: Reason in Religion* (New York: Charles Scribner's Sons, 1921), 6.

44. L'Engle, "Childlike Wonder," 110.

9. One Step Beyond

1. In this chapter I am indebted to Jeffrey Sconce for his analysis of how sci-fi television has been haunted by "electronic presences." See Jeffrey Sconce,

Haunted Media: Electronic Presence from Telegraphy to Television (Durham, N.C.: Duke University Press, 2000).

2. Lynn Spigel, *Make Room for TV: Television and the Family Ideal in Postwar America* (Chicago: University of Chicago Press, 1992), 30–32.

3. Vivian Sobchak, "The Scene of the Screen: Envisioning Cinematic and Electronic 'Presence,'" in *Materialities of Communication,* ed. Hans Ulrich Gumbrecht and K. Ludwig Pfeiffer (Stanford, Calif.: Stanford University Press, 1994), 100, 104.

4. Quoted in Stefan Andriopoulos, "Psychic Television," *Critical Inquiry* 31:3 (Spring 2005), 632. Other quotations are from pages 620 and 622.

5. This "window on the world" tradition also spoke of how TVs brought hitherto public spaces and the natural world into the private world of the home. See Spigel, *Make Room for TV,* 9–10, 102–105.

6. From "The *Playboy* Interview: Marshall McLuhan," *Playboy Magazine* (March 1969), http://www.nextnature.net/2009/12/the-playboy-interview -marshall-mcluhan/.

7. Quoted in Hent de Vries and Samuel Weber, eds., *Religion and Media* (Stanford, Calif.: Stanford University Press, 2001), 13.

8. Ibid., 23, 28.

9. "My argument is a simple one. It is in some—and considerable—measure because of the ubiquitousness of electromagnetically derived images in our society that individuals can turn easily to shamanic spirituality." Catherine Albanese, "From New Thought to New Vision: The Shamanic Paradigm in Contemporary Spirituality," in *Communication and Change in American Religious History,* ed. Leonard Sweet (Grand Rapids, Mich.: Eerdmans, 1993), 353–354.

10. E. Norman Pearson, *Space, Time and Self* (Adyar, India: Theosophical Publishing House, 1957), 22.

11. Leo Bogart, *The Age of the Television: A Study of Viewing Habits and the Impact of Television on American Life* (New York: F. Ungar, 1956), 28, 30–31.

12. See, for example, the *Tales of Tomorrow* episode "The Window"; *One Step Beyond*'s "The Open Window"; and *Twilight Zone*'s "16 Millimeter," "Showdown with Rance McGrew," and "World of Difference."

13. Jerry Mander, *Four Arguments for the Elimination of Television* (New York: HarperCollins, 1978), 86–87, 108–112; Marina Warner, *Phantasmagoria: Spirit Visions, Metaphors and Media into the Twenty-First Century* (Oxford: Oxford University Press, 2008), 335.

14. de Vries and Weber, *Religion and Media,* 94.

15. Jenny Slatman, "Tele-Vision: Between Blind Trust and Perceptual Faith," in de Vries and Weber, *Religion and Media,* 216, 221.

16. See Sconce, *Haunted Media,* 1–2.

17. From ibid., 124.

18. Jeffrey Sconce, "The Outer Limits of Oblivion," in *The Revolution Wasn't Televised: Sixties Television and Social Conflict,* ed. Lynn Spigel and Michael Curtin (New York: Routledge, 1997), 28–29.

19. J. B. Priestley, "Uncle Phil on T.V.," *Lilliput* 32:5 (April–May 1953), 71, 74, 80.

20. Shows analyzed here include *Tales of Tomorrow* (1951–1953), *Science Fiction Theater* (1955–1957), *One Step Beyond* (1959–1961), *The Twilight Zone* (1959–1964), *Way Out* (1961), *The Outer Limits* (1963–1965), *Rod Serling's Night Gallery* (1970–1973), *The Sixth Sense* (1972), and *The Next Step Beyond* (1978).

21. Peter Wolfe, *In the Zone: The Twilight World of Rod Serling* (Bowling Green, Ohio: Bowling Green State University Press, 1997), 17–20.

22. Sconce, *Haunted Media,* 133.

23. There are many such examples. In a 1994 episode of *Are you Afraid of the Dark* entitled "Tale of the Crimson Clown," a clown doll is shown reaching out of a television when trying to attack a misbehaving child; ITV's modern-day adaptation of *A Christmas Carol 2000* had Eddie Scrooge's father climb out of the TV to talk to him; in *Nightmare on Elm Street 3: Dream Warriors,* Freddy Krueger kills a character after suddenly popping out of the television; in *Freddy's Dead: The Final Nightmare,* Spencer is pulled into a video game; in *Shocker,* an electrocuted serial killer travels through electrical lines into television sets; in the film *The Ring* (2002), the ghost of a recently killed character materializes on a TV screen, crawls out of the TV, and kills someone else; and so on. See also http://tvtropes.org/pmwiki /pmwiki.php/Main/TrappedInTVLand and http://tvtropes.org/pmwiki /pmwiki.php/Main/RefugeeFromTVLand.

24. *The Twilight Zone,* "What's in the Box?" (1964).

25. Andriopoulos, "Psychic Television," 622.

26. For many ideas here I am indebted to John Kenneth Muir, *An Analytical Guide to Television's "One Step Beyond"* (Jefferson, N.C.: McFarland, 2001), 273–279.

27. Later shows in this genre include *The Sixth Sense* (1972), *Beyond Reality* (1991–1993), *The X-Files* (1993–2002), *Millennium* (1996–1999), and many others.

28. Muir, *Analytical Guide,* 273–274.

29. Douglas Brode and Carol Serling, *Rod Serling and the Twilight Zone: The 50th Anniversary Tribute* (Fort Lee, N.J.: Barricade Books, 2009), xxvi.

30. Ibid., 43.

31. Quoted in Stewart Stanyard, *Dimensions behind the Twilight Zone: A Backstage Tribute to Television's Groundbreaking Series* (Toronto: ECW Press, 2007), 135.

32. This pilot episode was originally called "Please Stand By," but the Cuban Missile Crisis in October 1962 had just occurred, and producers were afraid of flashing "Please Stand By" across the TV screen.

33. See, for example, the scenes at 31:35 and 39:40.

34. David J. Schow, "Revisiting *The Outer Limits*," *Epi-Log Magazine* (1992), 7, 12.

35. David J. Schow and Jeffrey Frentzen, *The Outer Limits: The Official Companion* (New York: Ace Science Fiction Books, 1986), 59.

36. Frank Garcia, "Outer Limits," *Cinefantastique* (August 1998), 52.

37. Schow and Frentzen, *Outer Limits,* 61, 63.

38. Televisual and filmic representations of higher-dimensional heavens include the electronic static barrier in *White Noise;* the cloudy visual effects in *The Twilight Zone*'s "Game of Pool"; the televisual afterworld with fourth-dimensional lines in "Little Girl Lost"; the gridded threshold into the other life in *Poltergeist*; and many others

39. For more, see http://www.tor.com/blogs/2014/11/love-in-sci-fi-interstellar -speech.

40. In John D. Peters, *Speaking into the Air: A History of the Idea of Communication* (Chicago: University of Chicago Press, 1999), 189.

41. Schow and Frentzen, *Outer Limits,* 61–63.

42. Schow, "Revisiting *The Outer Limits*," 19.

43. Schow and Frentzen, *Outer Limits,* 360.

44. Leslie Clark Stevens, *EST: The Steersman's Handbook* (New York: Bantam, 1971), 16, 19, 141, 147.

45. Timothy Leary, Ralph Metzner, and Richard Alpert, "The Psychedelic Experience" (pamphlet), 4, 23, 24, 26.

46. Quoted in Jeffrey Kripal, *Esalen: America and the Religion of No Religion* (Chicago: University of Chicago Press, 2007), 372–373.

47. Terence McKenna, "New Maps of Hyperspace," *Magical Blend Magazine* 22 (April 1989); reprinted in Terence McKenna, *The Archaic Revival: Speculations on Psychedelic Mushrooms, the Amazon, Virtual Reality, UFOs, Evolution, Shamanism, the Rebirth of the Goddess, and the End of History* (San Francisco: HarperSanFrancisco,1991), 90–103.

48. Erik Davis, *Techgnosis: Myth, Magic and Mysticism in the Age of Information* (New York: Harmony Books, 1998), 178–199.

49. From "*Playboy* Interview: Marshall McLuhan."

50. Davis, *Techgnosis,* 223.

51. From "*Playboy* Interview: Marshall McLuhan."

52. From Andrew Blanton, "TV Prayer," http://forums.ssrc.org/ndsp/2013/04 /10/tv-prayer/. See also Andrew Blanton, *Hittin' the Prayer Bones: Materiality of Spirit in the Pentecostal South* (Chapel Hill: University of North Carolina Press, 2015).

53. Sconce, *Haunted Media,* 174.

54. Marleen de Witte, "The Electric Touch Machine Miracle Scam: Body, Technology and the (Dis)Authentication of the Pentecostal Supernatural," in *Dues in Machina: Religion, Technology and the Things in Between,* ed. Jeremy Stolow (New York: Fordham University Press, 2013), 73–74.

55. Birgit Meyer, "Religious Sensations: Why Media, Aesthetics and Power Matter in the Study of Contemporary Religion," in *Religion: Beyond a Concept,* ed. Hent de Vries (New York: Fordham University Press, 2008), 710–711.

56. Katrien Pype, *The Making of the Pentecostal Melodrama: Religion, Media and Gender in Kinshasa* (New York: Berghahn, 2012), 146–148.

57. Quoted in Emily Edwards, *Metaphysical Media: The Occult Experience in Popular Culture* (Carbondale: Southern Illinois University Press, 2005), 24–26. See also http://www.tanahoy.com/psychic-development/scrying/.

58. Genesis P. Orridge, *Esoterrorist: Selected Essays, 1980–1988,* http://325.nostate.net/wp-content/uploads/2016/01/Genesis-P-Orridge-Esoterrorist.pdf.

59. Imants Baruss, "Failure to Replicate Electronic Voice Phenomenon," *Journal of Scientific Exploration* 15:3 (2001), 359.

60. See the website for the World ITC Association, http://www.worlditc.org/.

61. "Hanna Buschbeck: A Vision from Beyond?," http://www.strangerdimensions.com/2014/04/07/hanna-buschbeck-vision-beyond/.

62. See http://www.worlditc.org/.

63. Ernst Senkowski, "Instrumental Transcommunication—A Review," http://www.worlditc.org/f_07_senkowski_itc_review.htm.

64. Robert Monroe, *Ultimate Journey,* (New York: Broadway Books, 2000), 48–50. I'm indebted to Rick Jarow for this reference.

65. See, for example, Wikipedia's entry for "electronic voice phenomenon," https://en.wikipedia.org/wiki/Electronic_voice_phenomenon#TV_and_radio.

Conclusion

1. Edwin A. Abbott, *Flatland: An Edition with Notes and Commentary by William Lindgren and Thomas Banchoff* (Cambridge: Cambridge University Press, 2010), 216–218.

2. Other stories borrowing from *Flatland* include Ian Stewart's *Flatterland* (2001), Marvin Kaye's *The Incredible Umbrella* (1978), and many works by the cyberpunk author Rudy Rucker.

3. Martin Gardner, *The Colossal Book of Mathematics* (New York: W. W. Norton, 2001), 151.

4. A. K. Dewdney, *The Planiverse: Computer Contact with a Two-Dimensional World* (New York: Copernicus, 2001), xi.

5. Ibid., 203, 208.

6. A. K. Dewdney, "The Planiverse Project: Then and Now," *Mathematical Intelligencer* 22:1 (2000), 48.

7. "REAL mathematics exists in and of itself, shrouded by its own beauty, giving itself only to the ardent suitor. I was a platonist. I still am." See http://www.csd.uwo.ca/~akd/PERSONAL/Math_and_CS.html.

8. Some Islamic traditions consider "Ahmad" another name of Muhammad, given at his birth; many Muslims consider the name to be the more esoteric name of Muhammad and crucial to understanding the real meaning of his prophetic role and destiny.

9. P. J. Stewart, "Allegory through the Computing Glass: Sufism in 'The Planiverse' by A. K. Dewdney," *The Sufi* 9 (Spring 1991), 3, 7, 9.

10. Rudy Rucker, "All the Interviews" (updated November 4, 2013), 91, http://www.rudyrucker.com/pdf/interviewsposted.pdf.

11. His speculative nonfiction books, including *Geometry, Relativity and the Fourth Dimension* (New York: Dover, 1977), *Infinity and the Mind: The Science and Philosophy of the Infinite* (Princeton, N.J.: Princeton University Press, 2005; orig. 1982), and *The Fourth Dimension: A Guided Tour of the Higher Universes* (New York: Houghton Mifflin, 1985), use cartoons, puzzles, and thought experiments to ponder the philosophical implications of scientific concepts.

12. Rucker, *Fourth Dimension*, 202–203. "The *Fourth Dimension* is probably my all-time best-seller, maybe a quarter million of them out there. Over the years, scores of people have written me to tell me that this book changed their lives." From Rudy Rucker, *Rudy's Blog*, " 'Endless Road Trip.' '4th D.' Author's POV," http://www.rudyrucker.com/blog/2014/09/05/endless-road-trip-4th-dimension-authors-pov/. Rucker borrows and extends the *Flatland* narrative in still other ways. In his 1983 collection of short stories, *The Fifty-Seventh Franz Kafka,* there are several narratives that incorporate Abbott's *Flatland* story, including "Message Found in a Copy of *Flatland*," in which a man visiting London finds an odd story written in the margins of a first-edition copy of *Flatland*. The handwritten story was written by a mathematics professor who had visited London and, in a Pakistani restaurant on the site of Abbott's old City of London School, had jumped through an opening—an Einstein-Rosen bridge—into a real Flatland, where, regretfully, he was trapped forever.

13. Rucker, "All the Interviews," 22–23, 171. On prayer, Rucker once said, "It's been my experience that, for whatever reason, asking for help seems to work. I get the help right away, not for things like winning a lottery, but for things like staying sober, being kinder, and feeling less uptight. Maybe there really isn't a God, maybe asking for help just sets off some neurochemical process in my head. Whatever; for me it works." Rucker, "All the Interviews," 45.

14. Thomas Banchoff, "Salvador Dalí and the Fourth Dimension," http://archive.bridgesmathart.org/2014/bridges2014-1.pdf.

15. Thomas Banchoff, "The Fourth Dimension and the Theology of Edwin Abbott Abbott," https://acmsonline.org/home2/wp-content/uploads/2016/05/Banchoff-The-4th-dimention.pdf.

16. Tom Zito, "Visual Images and Shadows from the Fourth Dimension," *Washington Post,* January 22, 1975.

17. Banchoff, "Salvador Dalí and the Fourth Dimension," 5.

18. Brian Greene, *Fabric of the Cosmos: Space, Time and the Texture of Reality* (New York: Knopf, 2004), 366. See also Michio Kaku, *Hyperspace: A Scientific Odyssey through Parallel Universes, Time Warps and the 10th Dimension* (New York: Anchor Books, 1995), 107.

19. Paul Halpern, *Edge of the Universe: A Voyage to the Cosmic Horizon and Beyond* (New York: Wiley, 2012), 103.

20. Philip K. Dick, *The Exegesis of Philip K. Dick* (Boston: Houghton Mifflin, 2011), 73.

21. Peter Byrne, *The Many Worlds of Hugh Everett III: Multiple Universes, Mutual Assured Destruction, and the Meltdown of a Nuclear Family* (Oxford: Oxford University Press, 2010), 388.

22. Brian Greene, *The Elegant Universe: Superstrings, Hidden Dimensions and the Quest for the Ultimate Reality* (New York: W. W. Norton, 2003), 192. For example, one group of physicists, which includes Steven Carlip at the University of California at Davis, uses two-dimensional models to think about how gravity works, hoping to get closer to a theory of quantum gravity and thus a unified theory of nature's forces. By examining gravity in a less complex, two-dimensional setting, Carlip sees progress on the horizon. "The idea of dropping down a dimension has a distinguished history," Carlip wrote, referring to Abbott's book. *Flatland* "triggered a surge of interest in geometry in diverse dimensions and remains popular today among mathematicians and physicists." "Quantum gravity in *Flatland* . . . has already taught us valuable lessons about time, observables and topology that are carrying over to real 3-D gravity. The model has surprised us with its richness: the unexpectedly important role of topology, its remarkable black holes, its strange holographic properties. Perhaps soon we will fully understand what it is like to be a square living in a flat world." *Flatland,* Carlip also remarked, had inspired physicists studying higher-dimensional objects, materials such as graphene, and black holes. In many ways, Carlip's work embodies a fascinating reversal: Instead of science fiction borrowing from science, his science borrows from science fiction. See Greene, *Elegant Universe,* 192; and Steven Carlip, "Quantum Gravity in Flatland," *Scientific American* 306:4 (April 1, 2012), https://www.scientificamerican.com/article/quantum-gravity-in-flatland/

23. Paul Davies, *Superforce: The Search for a Grand Unified Theory of Nature* (New York: Simon and Schuster, 1985), 154.

24. The Institute for Advanced Study physicist Nima Arkani-Hamed, for example, hoping to make his brane theories more understandable to *Scientific American* readers, speculated that our universe existed on the surface

of one membrane, and that other membrane universes, invisible to us, could exist just a millimeter away. Like others, Arkani-Hamed believes that gravity, an unusually weak force, might leak or travel between membranes. "We may live in a strange Flatland, a membrane universe where quantum gravity is just around the corner." Nima Arkani-Hamed, Savas Dimopoulos, and Georgi Dvali, "The Universe's Unseen Dimensions," *Scientific American* (August 2000), 69.

25. Eugene B. Shikhovtsev, *Biographical Sketch of Hugh Everett III* (2003), http://space.mit.edu/home/tegmark/everett/. The possibility of a Many Worlds immortality intrigued a number of theoretical physicists for a while, but recently some of them, including Max Tegmark at MIT, have shown that while the theory might, for example, make a suicidal game of Russian roulette more survivable, the idea that MWI leads to immortality is probably wrongheaded. Russian roulette offered a binary outcome—after pulling the trigger, one was either dead or alive—and in a Many Worlds setting, there were always unharmed copies of the self in otherworlds that could continue living. But in most cases dying was not a binary event, involving instead processes such as aging that comprised a "whole continuum of states of progressively decreasing self-awareness." Quotes here are from Max Tegmark, "Quantum Immortality," http://space.mit.edu/home/tegmark/crazy.html.

26. Max Tegmark, "Max's Multiverse FAQ: Frequently Asked Questions," http://space.mit.edu/home/tegmark/crazy.html.

27. Zeeya Merali, *A Big Bang in a Little Room: The Quest to Create New Universes* (New York: Basic Books, 2017),196.

28. Michio Kaku, *Parallel Worlds: A Journey through Creation, Higher Dimensions, and the Future of the Cosmos* (New York: Doubleday, 2005), 16.

29. Lawrence Krauss, *Hiding in the Mirror: The Quest for Alternate Realities, from Plato to String Theory* (New York: Penguin, 2005), 225. Kaku, in "Math Is the Mind of God," also once identified the activity of the many-dimensional strings in string theory with God—"The mind of God we believe is cosmic music, the music of strings resonating through 11 dimensional hyperspace." See http://bigthink.com/dr-kakus-universe/math-is-the-mind-of -god?utm_source=feedburner&utm_medium=feed&utm_campaign =Feed%3A+bigthink%2Fblogs%2Fdr-kakus-universe+%28Dr.+Kaku%27s+ Universe%29.

30. Paul Davies, for example, has called for "a natural rather than a supernatural God." See John Polkinghorne, *Faith, Science and Understanding* (New Haven, Conn.: Yale University Press, 2000), 192. Others talking about new, scientific forms of enchantment and enchanted popular cultures, including the role of parapsychology in all of this, include David J. Hess and Egil Asprem. See David Hess, *Science in the New Age: The Paranormal, Its De-*

fenders and Debunkers, and American Culture (Madison: University of Wisconsin Press, 1993); Egil Asprem, "Psychic Enchantments of the Educated Classes," in *Contemporary Esotericism,* ed. Egil Asprem and Kennet Granholm (Durham, U.K.: Acumen, 2014), 330–350; and Egil Asprem, "Parapsychology: Naturalizing the Supernatural, Re-Enchanting Science," in *Handbook of Religion and the Authority of Science,* ed. James Lewis and Olav Hammer (Leiden: Brill, 2011), 633–670.

31. For my thinking about science's meanings in popular science I am indebted to a number of sources, including Katherine Pandora, "Popular Science in National and Transnational Perspective: Suggestions from the American Context," *Isis* 100:2 (June 2009), 346–358; Andreas Daum, "Varieties of Popular Science and the Transformations of Public Knowledge: Some Historical Reflections," *Isis* 100:2 (June 2009), 319–332; Jonathan Topham, review of *Understanding Popular Science* by Peter Broks, *British Journal for the History of Science* 41:4 (December 2008), 617–619; Marcel Lafollette, "Popularization of Science," in *The Oxford Encyclopedia of the History of American Science, Medicine and Technology,* vol. 2, ed. Hugh Richard Slotten (Oxford: Oxford University Press, 2014), 267–282; and Peter Bowler, *Science for All: The Popularization of Science in Early Twentieth-Century Britain* (Chicago: University of Chicago Press, 2009).

32. Fred Alan Wolf, *The Eagle's Quest: A Physicist Finds Scientific Truth at the Heart of the Shamanic World* (New York: Simon and Schuster, 1991), 36–37.

33. Bernard Carr, "Hyperspatial Models of Matter and Mind," in *Beyond Physicalism: Toward Reconciliation of Science and Spirituality,* ed. Edward Kelly, Adam Crabtree, and Paul Marshall (London: Rowman and Littlefield, 2015), 238–256.

34. Quoted in Jeffrey Kripal, *Esalen: American and the Religion of No Religion* (Chicago: University of Chicago Press, 2007), 343; see also David Kaiser, *How the Hippies Saved Physics: Science, Counterculture and the Quantum Revival* (New York: W. W. Norton, 2011), 94.

35. See Christopher Partridge, *The Re-Enchantment of the West: Alternative Spiritualities, Sacralization, Popular Culture and Occulture,* 2 vols. (London: T&T Clark, 2004–2005); Hess, *Science in the New Age;* and Asprem, "Parapsychology."

36. A. David Lewis, *American Comics, Literary Theory and Religion: The Superhero Afterlife* (New York: Palgrave Macmillan, 2014), 56–59, 91–94; see also Scott Beatty, *The DC Comics Encyclopedia: The Definitive Guide to the Characters of the DC Universe* (New York: DK Publishing, 2008).

37. Lewis, *American Comics,* 91.

38. The multidimensional, magical world of the sci-fi television series *Buffy the Vampire Slayer* (1997–2003) illustrates the same development in a slightly different way. Often ranked as one of the best sci-fi programs of all time, *Buffy the Vampire Slayer* features a reluctant heroine who protects human

beings from vampires until a traumatic moment at the end of season five when she sacrifices herself by leaping into a dimensional portal. Resurrected in season six, Buffy has the chance to recall the joyful peace of that enigmatic otherworld she had passed through. "Time didn't mean anything. Nothing had form. But I was still me, you know? And I was warm, and I was loved, and I was finished. Complete. I don't understand about theology or dimensions, or any of it, really, but I think I was in heaven." That she is not sure whether the appropriate discourse involves theological heavens or scientific dimensions, religious or scientific spaces, is precisely the point I want to make—the two have joined together in hybrid discourses that modern people use to reflect on the world's meaning and what lies beyond it. From *Buffy the Vampire Slayer*, season 6, episode 3, "After Life," https://en.wikiquote.org/wiki/Buffy_the_Vampire_Slayer/Season_6.

39. Daniel Duval, *Higher Dimensions, Parallel Dimensions, and the Spirit Realm* (Book Baby, 2016), Google Books version; Rob Bell, "Atheists Trapped in Flatland? There's More," https://www.youtube.com/watch?v=9JmMTobaM68.

40. From an interview on Jeffrey Mishlove's *Thinking Allowed* PBS television series. "Life After Life: Understanding Near-Death Experience with Raymond Moody," accessed online at http://www.williamjames.com/transcripts/moody.htm

41. Raymond Moody, *Life after Life* (New York: Bantam, 1975), 16.

42. Raymond Moody and Paul Perry, *Paranormal: My Life in Pursuit of the Afterlife* (New York: HarperOne, 2012), 240.

43. Jean-Pierre Jourdan, "Near Death Experiences and the 5th Dimensional Spatio-Temporal Perspective," *Journal of Cosmology* 14 (2011), http://journalofcosmology.com/Consciousness152.html.

44. See also J. Smythies, "Space, Time and Consciousness," *Journal of Consciousness Studies* 10:3 (2003) 47–56; J. Smythies, "Brain and Consciousness: The Ghost in the Machines," *Journal of Scientific Exploration* 23:1 (2009), 37–50; T. Droulez, "Conscience, espace, réalité: Implications d'une critique du réalisme perceptuel direct," *Cahiers Philosophiques de Strasbourg* 28 (2010); Bernard Carr, "Worlds Apart?" *Proceedings of the Society for Psychical Research* 59 (2008), 1–96.

45. See the *Atlantic* article on NDEs and hopes for proof of an extra-dimensional afterlife—Gideon Lichfield, "The Science of Near-Death Experiences," *Atlantic* (April 2015), https://www.theatlantic.com/magazine/archive/2015/04/the-science-of-near-death-experiences/386231/

46. Eben Alexander, *Proof of Heaven: A Neurosurgeon's Journey into the Afterlife* (New York: Simon and Schuster, 2012), 49.

47. *Flatland* and other hyperspace stories continue to inspire different reflections. Nick Sousanis, for example, rethinks how we see and understand the world around us in a comic-book style philosophical meditation that

retells *Flatland* and draws on its themes. See Sousanis, *Unflattening* (Cambridge, Mass.: Harvard University Press, 2016). Amanda Montanez's "Everyone's a Little Shapist," *Scientific American* (May 5, 2016), uses *Flatland* to understand race, prejudice, and social groups; Steve Tomasula develops a new narrative about the Square in a hybrid image-text novel about ways of representing and technologically modifying the body in *VAS: An Opera in Flatland* (Chicago: University of Chicago Press, 2002); the American artist Shahid Al-Bilali argues that "African-American art is the fourth dimensional experience," a space in-between cultures as well as in-between the physical and the spiritual. "The Fourth Dimension is the connection, the bridge of the physical world into the spiritual world, a new culture created by the African American experience." See "Shahid Al-Bilali: A Mirror for My Children," https://fac.umass.edu/Online/default.asp?BOparam::WScontent::loadArticle::permalink=ShahidAl&BOparam::WScontent::loadArticle::context_id=.

48. Deepak Chopra, "The Fourth Dimension Is Real, but Who Owns It?," http://www.huffingtonpost.com/deepak-chopra/the-fourth-dimension-is-r_b_5499775.html.

49. "The Unseen Dimensions That May Govern Existence," http://www.beliefnet.com/News/Science-Religion/2001/12/The-Unseen-Dimensions-That-May-Govern-Existence.aspx.

ACKNOWLEDGMENTS

I am grateful to many friends, colleagues, and family members who helped make this book possible. Friends and colleagues in different fields read and commented on chapters or portions of the book, and their feedback was crucial in helping me avoid errors and shape the book's overall narrative. They include Harald Atmanspacher, Thomas Banchoff, Courtney Bender, Colin Duggan, Marc Epstein, Andrew Fiss, William Germano, David Hall, Linda Henderson, Naomi Janowitz, Jonathon Kahn, James Kloppenberg, William Lindgren, Jose Perillan, Andrea Reithmayr, Joan Rubin, Philip Scepanski, and Michael Walsh. I am especially grateful to David Hall, Naomi Janowitz, and Harvard University Press's outside readers for carefully reading the entire manuscript and offering many helpful criticisms and comments. A number of dedicated research assistants at Vassar College—Brett Anker, Kristiana Bowman, Toscane Clarey, Katherine Durr, Natalie Hine, Alyssa Maldonado, Connor Martini, Rachel Schorr, and Lydia Wood—also assisted in many ways. Vassar College has generously supported research travel and sabbatical time and I am very grateful to both Dean Jon Chenette and President Catherine Bond Hill.

For less formal but nevertheless crucial feedback, conversation, and leads concerning the many directions I take in the book, I also am indebted to Thomas Banchoff, Marc Epstein, Linda Henderson, Rick Jarow, Jonathon Kahn, James Kloppenberg, Jeffrey Kripal, Don Kunkel, Lynn Lidonicci, Andrea Reithmyer, Rudy Rucker, Leigh Schmidt, and Michael Walsh. I am also grateful for the unflagging enthusiasm and savvy advice of my editor at Harvard University Press, Kathleen McDermott.

While collecting information for this book I relied on many libraries and archives in the United States and the United Kingdom. I want to thank archivists and reference librarians from the following libraries: Andover-Harvard Theological Library; the Archives of American Art, Smithsonian Institution; the Bancroft Library at the University of California, Berkeley; the Beinecke Rare Book and Manuscript Library, Yale University; the Boston Public Library; the British Library; Houghton Library, Harvard University; King's College Archive, Cambridge University; the Motion Picture, Broadcasting and Recorded Sound Division, Library of Congress; the Henry S. Olcott Memorial Library; Manuscripts Division of the Department of Rare Books and Special Collections, Princeton University Library; Special Collections, the Senate House Library, University of London; Sterling Memorial Library Special Collections; St. John's College Special Collections, Cambridge; the Theosophical Library of America Archives; Special Collections, Trinity College, Cambridge; Special Collections at the University of Bradford; University College of London's Special Collections; Rare Book and Manuscript Library at the University of Illinois; Special Collections and University Archives, University of Massachusetts at Amherst; the Department of Rare Books, Special Collections and Preservation at University of Rochester; Vassar College Libraries; and Wheaton College Archives and Special Collections.

I am quite sure that I would not have completed this book without the support of my parents, in-laws, and other family and close friends, including our many friends in the Bahá'í community. They have lifted us up in so many ways. My children offered patience, good cheer, and helpful diversions at every step along the way. They grasped intuitively what the book was about and offered assurance at several key points that the book was going to be "very cool." To Tracy I owe an unpayable debt. Collaborator, sounding-board, energetic booster, believer-in-me, partner in many dimensions of a life together, she made it all possible. I dedicate the book to her.

∽∾∽∾∽

Portions of Chapters 2 and 3 were first published in Christopher White, "Seeing Things: Science, the Fourth Dimension and Modern Enchantment," *American Historical Review* 119:5 (December 2014), 1466–1491. I thank Oxford University Press for permission to include this text in my book.

CREDITS

Figure 1.1. Illustration by Edwin A. Abbott. *Flatland: A Romance of Many Dimensions. With Illustrations by the Author*, A Square (London: Seeley & Co., 1884), 71.

Figure 1.2. Illustration by Edwin A. Abbott. *Flatland: A Romance of Many Dimensions. With Illustrations by the Author*, A Square (London: Seeley & Co., 1884), 23.

Figure 2.1. Cube diagram. C. Howard Hinton, *The Fourth Dimension* (London: George Allen and Co., Ltd., 1912; orig. 1904), 265.

Figure 3.1. Sketch of a fourth-dimensional globe. Johan Van Manen, *Some Occult Experiences* (Adyar, Madras, India: Theosophical Publishing House, 1913), 59.

Figure 3.2. "'Philosophic Calm' 'A' the Individual and 'B' the Personal Consciousness." Claude Bragdon, *A Primer of Higher Space (The Fourth Dimension)* (Rochester, N.Y.: The Manas Press, 1913), 68.

Figure 3.3. "The New Jerusalem." Claude Bragdon, *Man the Square* lecture drawing, ca. 1912. Bragdon Family Papers. Courtesy of the Department of Rare Books, Special Collections and Preservation, University of Rochester River Campus Libraries.

Figure 3.4. Kazimir Malevich laying in state, Leningrad, 1935. Photographer unknown. Archive of the State Russian Museum, St. Petersburg.

Figure 4.1. "The Projections made by a Cube in Traversing a Plane." Claude Bragdon, *A Primer of Higher Space (The Fourth Dimension)* (Rochester, N.Y.: The Manas Press, 1913), Plate 30.

Figure 4.2. "Man as seen by Clairvoyant (4-Dimensional Vision) and by Ordinary Human sight." Claude Bragdon, *A Primer of Higher Space (The Fourth Dimension)* (Rochester, N.Y.: The Manas Press, 1913), Plate 19.

Figure 4.3. Postcard, New York Central Station, Rochester, N.Y. Bragdon Family Papers. Courtesy of the Department of Rare Books, Special Collections and Preservation, University of Rochester River Campus Libraries.

Figure 4.4. Corresponding Developments and Projections of a Cube and of a Tesseract in Lower Spaces." Claude Bragdon, *A Primer of Higher Space (The Fourth Dimension)* (Rochester, N.Y.: The Manas Press, 1913), Plate 4.

Figure 4.5. "Regular Polyhedriods of Four Dimensional Space in Plane Projection, Correlatives of Three Platonic Solids." Claude Bragdon, *The Frozen Fountain: Being Essays on Architecture and the Art of Design in Space* (New York: Alfred A. Knopf, 1932), 59. Quotation in caption from Irving Pond, *The Autobiography of Irving K. Pond: The Sons of Mary and Elihu* (Oak Park, Ill.: Hyoogen Press, 2009), 301.

Figure 4.6. The Song and Light stage, Central Park, 1916. Photographer unknown. Bragdon Family Papers. Courtesy of the Department of Rare Books, Special Collections and Preservation, University of Rochester River Campus Libraries.

Figure 4.7. Claude Bragdon, projective ornament panel, Central Park, 1916. Photographer unknown, Central Park, 1916. Bragdon Family Papers. Courtesy of the Department of Rare Books, Special Collections and Preservation, University of Rochester River Campus Libraries.

Figure 5.1. "The Nonsense School." Frontispiece, Gelett Burgess, *The Burgess Nonsense Book: Being a Complete Collection of the Humorous Masterpieces of Gelett Burgess* (New York: Frederick A. Stokes Company, 1901), 4.

Figure 5.2. Max Weber, *Woman in Tents* (1913). Collection of Bill Marklyn. Reprinted by permission of the Estate of Max Weber. Reproduction courtesy of A. J. Kollar Fine Paintings, LLC.

Figure 5.3. Max Weber, *Interior of the Fourth Dimension* (1913). National Gallery of Art, Washington, D.C. Gift of Natalie Davis Spingarn in memory of Linda R. Miller and in Honor of the 50th Anniversary of the National Gallery of Art, 1990.78.1. Reprinted by permission of the Estate of Max Weber. Reproduction licensed via NGA Images.

Figure 5.4. Max Weber, *Invocation* (1919). National Gallery of Art, Washington, D.C. Gift of Jack and Margrit Vanderryn, 1997.128.14. Reprinted by permission of the Estate of Max Weber. Reproduction licensed via NGA Images.

Figure 5.5. Max Weber, *The Talmudists* (1934). The Jewish Museum, New York. Gift of Mrs. Nathan Miller, JM 51-48. Photo by John Parnell. Reprinted by permission of the Estate of Max Weber. Reproduction licensed via The Jewish Museum / Art Resource, NY.

Figure 6.1. Illustration from "Flight Pioneers" portrait series in *Flight* 88, No. 36, Vol. II (London: IPC Transport Press Ltd., September 3, 1910), 705. Quotation in caption from J. B. Priestley, *Man and Time* (London: Aldus, 1964), 244.

Figure 6.2. J. B. Priestley, Jean Forbes-Robertson, and J. W. Dunne, London (1937). Photographer unknown. Reproduction courtesy of J. B. Priestley Archive, Special Collections, University of Bradford, Bradford, U.K., PRI 21 / 4 / 38.

Figure 6.3. J. B. Priestley at his home in Stratford-on-Avon, ca. 1963. Photographer unknown. J. B. Priestley, *Man and Time* (London: Aldus Books Ltd., 1964), 191.

Figure 8.1. Mrs. Who explains "tessering." Madeleine L'Engle, *Wrinkle in Time* (New York: Farrar, Straus and Giroux, 1962).

Figure 8.2. Cover, Billy Graham, *Billy Graham Presents Man in the 5th Dimension: Pictorial highlights of the Todd-AO and Technicolor® motion picture shown at the New York World's Fair 1964–1965* (Minneapolis: World Wide Publications, 1964).

Figure 9.1. "Television and the Invisible." E. Norman Pearson, *Space, Time and Self* (Adyar, Madras, India: Theosophical Publishing House, 1957), 23.

Figure 9.2. Rod Serling, promotional photomontage for *The Twilight Zone* (1959–1964), CBS Television Network.

Figure 9.3. Robert Sampson (as Chris Miller), Sarah Marshall (as Ruth Miller), and Charles Aidman (as Bill) in *The Twilight Zone*, "Little Girl Lost," Season 3, Episode 26 (CBS Television / Cayuga Productions, Inc., March 16, 1962).

Figure 9.4. Cliff Robertson (as Allan Maxwell) in *The Outer Limits*, "The Galaxy Being," Season 1, Episode 1 (ABC Television, Daystar Productions / Villa Di Stefano / United Artists Television, September 16, 1963).

Figure 9.5. Matthew McConaughey (as Cooper) in *Interstellar* (Paramount Pictures / Warner Bros. Pictures in Association with Legendary Entertainment, Syncopy / Lynda Obst Productions, 2014).

Figure 9.6. Oral Roberts, *Million Soul Crusade*, Spokane, Washington, 1959. Oral Roberts Evangelistic Association, Tulsa, Oklahoma.

Figure 9.7. ITC image capture by Klaus Schreiber of brother-in-law, Heinrich Boden, ca. 1985. Rainer Holbe, *Bilder aus dem Reich der Toten: Die Paranormalen Experimente des Klaus Schreiber* (Munich: Droemer Knaur, 1987).

Figure C.1. Salvador Dalí, *Crucifixion (Corpus Hypercubus)* (1954). The Metropolitan Museum of Art, New York. Gift of The Chester Dale Collection, 1955. © 2017 Artists Rights Society (ARS), New York.

Figure C.2. Cover, *Nature*, Vol. 448, No. 7149 (July 5, 2007). © 2007 Nature Publishing Group, Macmillan Publishers Limited / Springer Nature.

Figure C.3. "Dr. Quantum Visits Flatland." Title screen from a promotional clip for *What the Bleep!?: Down the Rabbit Hole, 10th Anniversary Edition* (Beyond Words / Lord of the Wind Films, 2014).

Figure C.4. Diagram. Daniel Duval, *Higher Dimensions, Parallel Dimensions, and the Spirit Realm* (Richardson, TX: BRIDE Publications, 2016), Figure 1.

INDEX

Artists, 10; Duchamp, 241; Malevich, 98–100; use of math and geometry, 139; "The Wild Men of Paris" (Burgess), 144, 149. *See also* Bragdon; Cubists; Weber, Max (artist); *individual artists*

Artists, modern, 141, 151, 160. *See also* Weber, Max (artist)

Asare, Agyin, 279

Ascension, 216–217

"Astral," 157

Astral Plane, The (Leadbeater), 78–79

Banchoff, Thomas, 236, 292–295

Barnhart, Harry, 124, 129, 130

Bel Geddes, Norman, 135–137

Bell, Rob, 9, 306

Bennett, John G., 169–172, 176

Besant, Annie, 89

Bilbro, Jeffrey, 208

Blacks, 92, 93–95

Blackwood, Algernon, 237

Blake, William, 23, 36

Blanton, Andrew, 278

Blavatsky, Helena, 78, 95, 96, 134

Boas, Franz, 14

Boer War, 174

Bogart, Leo, 254

Bohr, Niels, 2, 6

Born, Max, 6

Bragdon, Claude, 10, 86–88, 102–138, 139, 187, 189, 215; architecture of, 114–119; artistic ability, 108; background, 103–105; on Burgess, 146; critique of capitalism, 117; decoration of, 116–117; disillusionment of, 105–106; ideals of, 123–124; influence of, 131–133, 137–138, 140, 157; influences on, 105, 106; isometric perspective, 113; on Ouspensky, 96; *Projective Ornament*, 119; relocation of religiousness, 137; Song and Light movement, 124–131; as stage designer, 133–135; in theater, 133–135; view of First World War, 129–130; views of feminine, 137; views on church, 132–133; writings of, 109, 111

Bragdon, Eliza Salisbury, 104

Bragdon, George L., 104, 105

Braque, Georges, 149, 151

Breuer, Miles, 233

Bricoleur, 14

British Association for the Advancement of Science, 63

British society, 142; in *Flatland*, 19; gender in, 240; inability to change, 286; revolt against, 70–71. *See also* Change, social; Gender; Marriage; Sex/sexuality; Women

British Society for Psychical Research, 60, 61

Brode, Douglas, 266

Brooke, Stopford, 17

Browne, Robert T., 96–98

Buchan, John, 182

Buck, Richard Maurice, 83

Buffy the Vampire Slayer, 305

Burge, Dionys, 287

Burgess, Gelett, 108, 144–150; friendship with C. Howard Hinton, 146–149

Burned-Over District, 102

Byrds, the, 275

Calvinism, 199–200

Candler, Howard, 46

Candler, Martha, 132

Capitalism, Bragdon's critique of, 117

Capra, Fritjof, 7–8

Carpenter, Edward, 62, 70, 83–84

Carr, Bernard, 303

Carroll, Lewis, 202, 203, 204, 212

Castells, Manuel, 253

Cathedral without walls, 128

Catholicism, 211, 292

Cayley, Arthur, 64

Certainty, 43, 45

Cézanne, Paul, 139–140, 142, 143

Change, social, 70–71, 101–102, 122, 123, 124–131, 250–251, 274–278

Cheetham, Mark, 156

Chesterton, G. K., 211

Chopra, Deepak, 309

Christianity: appeal to writers, 211; attempts to reinforce doctrines, 71–72; challenges to foundations of, 71; Dunne and, 179–181; illusion in, 32–33; L'Engle's views on, 229–231; modernity's incompatibility with, 73; use of supernatural narratives to buttress, 197–199; use of television, 278–280. *See also* Dimensions, higher; God; Religion; Theology

Christians, Modernist, 71

Churches, Bragdon's influence on, 131–133

Clair, Jean, 241

Clare of Assisi, 262

Clifford, William K., 38, 53, 54, 65

Clifton, Mark, 238

Cobb, Elisabeth, 51

Coburn, Alvin, 151

Cogswell, Henry, 145

Coleridge, Samuel Taylor, 200, 228

Colonialization, reverse, 90

Comic books, 238, 292, 304

Community singing movement, 124–125. *See also* Song and Light movement

Conrad, Joseph, 89, 90

Consciousness: evolution of, 83, 91; reality and, 6–7

Consciousness, cosmic, 83–86

Consciousness, fourth-dimensional, 80

Consciousness, sleeping, 176, 177. *See also* Dunne, John

Consciousness, waking, 177. *See also* Dunne, John

Contemplation, Weber on, 156

Copenhagen interpretation, 297

Cosmic consciousness, 83–86

Cosmos, 298, 300

Crane, Hart, 241–242

Crary, Jonathan, 81

Crathorne, Arthur, 55–56

Croly, Herbert, 2

Crookes, William, 74, 78

Crystal Palace, 136

Crystals, 151

Cubes, 79, 87–88, 99–100, 139, 218–219; Hinton's, 43–46, 52; Trinity as, 214–216

Cubes, cosmic, 238, 240

Cubes, fourth-dimensional, 45–46. *See also* Tesseracts

Cubists, 140–144, 149–160, 163. *See also* Weber, Max (artist)

Culture, American, 130–131

Dalí, Salvador, 293, 295

Daly, Mary, 243

Dance, 134–135

Dannenberg, Hilary, 221

Darwin, Charles, 31–32, 35, 83, 91

Davies, Paul, 300

Day view, 26

Dead, contacting, 281–283

Death, 304

Decoration, 116–117, 118–123, 137

Democracy, 129–130

Desires, 220

De Vries, Hent, 253

Dewdney, Alexander K., 288–289

De Witte, Marleen, 279

Dick, Philip, 277, 298

Dignity, human, 178

Dimensions, higher: as afterlife space, 304–308; in art, 109, 152–155, 294; brief history of, 8–14; causing mental illness, 59–61; in church settings, 131–133; concept of, 3–4; as explanation for near-death experiences, 171, 306–308; as explanation for predictive dream

Dimensions, higher (*continued*)
experiences, 175–180; Fechner on, 24–28; in fiction, 181–186, 188–190, 198–199, 201–208, 210–213, 220–225, 233–234, 237–238, 240, 287–292, 298–300, 304–305; in *Flatland*, 18–24, 34–40; as hallucination, 59–62; Helmholtz on, 28–29; Hinton's ideas on, 45–46, 49–55, 61–62, 67, 146–149; Kant on, 24; mathematical speculation on, 45, 53–59, 62–67, 203; pop culture of, 304–305; religious uses of, 71–81, 84–89, 107–108, 109–114, 148–149, 154–159, 180–181, 184–196, 203–208, 212–221, 231–233, 281–283, 287–289, 291–295, 300–310; scientific theories of, 295–301, 303; scientists avoiding, 58–59; in Song and Light, 124–129; as space beyond physical reality, 3–4, 304–308; television's electronic, 256–283; in the theater, 133–135; as way to rethink race, 93–98; as way to rethink sex and gender, 89–93, 240–248; in works of C. S. Lewis, 212–226; in *Wrinkle in Time*, 233–236. *See also* Fourth dimension
Dimensions, unseen, 24
Disbelief, suspension of, 253, 266
Disenchantment, 5
Dissociative states, 176
Divine intrusions, 180–181, 192
Doorways, 221–222, 228, 229, 233; in television shows, 271–272; tesseracts as, 237–238, 240–242. *See also* Portals
Doubt, 13, 41. *See also* Skepticism
Dreams: culture of, 193; Dunne's, 174–176; in *Flatland*, 19; of future, 182; recording, 11, 175, 176, 185, 187; time and, 193–194; Wells and, 185
Dreams, predictive, 11, 174–175, 178, 184, 194, 196

Drugs, psychedelic, 275–277
Du Bois, W. E. B., 11, 93–95
Duchamp, Marcel, 138, 241
Dunne, John, 11, 172–182, 197; appeal of, 178–179, 180; Christianity and, 179–181; criticisms of, 178; divine intrusions, 180–181, 192; dreams of, 174–176; *An Experiment with Time*, 175–176, 178, 179, 182, 183, 184, 187; influence of, 181–186, 187, 237; legacy of, 186; redemptive theory of time, 193; religion and, 180–181, 191–193; in Second Boer War, 174; *The Serial Universe*, 176, 179; speaks to the London cast of *Time and the Conways*, 189–190; Universal Mind, 180–181
Dunne Dreams, 178, 183
Duval, Daniel, 305

Eddington, Arthur, 2, 176, 180, 187, 231
Education, of women, 91
Einstein, Albert, 5, 6, 7, 176, 180, 187, 231
Electronic voice phenomenon (EVP), 281
Eliade, Mircea, 187
Eliot, T. S., 211
Ellis, Havelock, 48, 49
Emerson, Ralph Waldo, 105, 106, 107, 137, 142, 151, 152, 200
Emmons, Paul, 113
Empire, 89
Empiricism, 5, 192–193
Enantiomorphs, 91
EST: The Steersman Handbook (Stevens), 274–275
Ethics, 47–48
Ethnocentrism, 89
Everett, Hugh, 297, 300
Evolution, 83; spiritual, 83–89
Evolutionary consciousness, 83, 91
Extramarital relationships, Hinton's, 48
Eye: connection with religion, 31; ocularcentrism, 81; susceptibility to mistakes, 81. *See also* Vision

Fairy tales, power of, 247–248
Fantastic Four, 304
Farwell, Arthur, 125, 128–129
Fechner, Gustav, 24, 26, 28, 31
Feminine Mystique, The (Friedan), 246
Femininity, 226
Feminism, 91
Feminist spirituality, 245
Fiction, 181–186. *See also* Narratives, Christian; Narratives, supernatural
Fifth Dimension (Byrds), 275
Filmer, Kath, 226
Films, 270; afterlife in, 304; featuring recorded spirit voices / images, 282; *Flatland* adaptations, 287; *Interstellar*, 272; *Poltergeist*, 273; tesseracts in, 240
Finley, Stephen, 96
Finney, Charles G., 104
First World War. *See* Great War
Flatland (Abbott), 8–9, 14, 39–40, 158, 216, 217, 219, 273, 285–287, 306, 310; annotated version of, 293; end of, 285–286; epigraph, 36, 266; film adaptations of, 287; gender in, 19, 90–91, 240; influence of, 13, 18, 208, 213, 233, 286–292, 298, 300; legacy of, 308–309; miracles in, 37; narrative, 18–24; overall point of, 23–24; sequels to, 287–292; social and racial hierarchies in, 95; vision in, 33; visions in, 19. *See also* Abbott, Edwin A.
Florence, Maud, 48–51, 67
Forakis, Peter, 138
Ford, Ford Madox, 89, 90
Fourth dimension: as hallucination, 59–62; mathematical ideas on, 45, 53–59, 62–67; mental illness and, 59–62; ways to think about, 85
Fox, George, 23, 36, 37
Fox sisters, 104
Freedom, 178
Freedom, human, 179, 182

Friedan, Betty, 246
Frontier, 101, 102
Frothingham, Octavius, 71
Fuller, R. Buckminster, 137
Futurama, 136
Future, 11, 175, 182, 183. *See also* Time

Galton, Francis, 60
Gardner, Martin, 287–288
Gauguin, Paul, 156
Gauss, Carl Friedrich, 54, 63
Gender, 226; in art, 241; in Bel Geddes's Crystal Palace, 136–137; depictions of on television, 263–265; Duchamp and, 241; in fiction and science fiction, 89–93, 240–242; in *Flatland*, 19, 90–91, 240; Hinton and, 240–241; L'Engle and, 228–230, 242–248; in Lewis's works, 242–245; rethinking, 89–93, 240–248; tesseracts and, 242. *See also* Marriage; Sex / sexuality; Social order; Women
Genital inversion, 241
Geometric theology, 216
Geometry: Abbott's use of, 18; artists' use of, 139; certainty and, 43; in *Flatland*, 20; relation with absolute truth, 64; Weber on, 151–152. *See also* Mathematics
Ghana, 279–280
Ghosts, 60, 256
Gibbons, Tom, 158
Girls: depictions of, 229, 244–245; divinity and, 12. *See also* Gender; Women
God: belief in, 1–2; housing problem for, 5. *See also* Christianity; Religion; Theology
Goops, 144–150
Graham, Billy, 239
Graham, Martha, 135
Gravity, 177

Japan, 51
Jeans, James, 231
Jefferies, Richard, 89
Johnston, Mary, 91–92
Jourdan, Jean-Pierre, 307
Journaling, 176
Judaism: in art, 141; Weber's relation to, 159–164. *See also* Religion
Jung, Carl, 73, 184, 187, 231
Jungle gyms, 53
Jürgenson, Friedrich, 281
Juster, Norman, 287

Kaku, Michio, 300
Kandinsky, Wassily, 141, 157
Kant, Immanuel, 24, 54
Kapp, Ernst, 252
Kasner, Edward, 65
Kernodle, George, 171
Keyser, Cassius J., 66
Kirby, Jack, 238
Knowledge: aspiration to reach beyond, 286–287; in *Flatland*, 21; science's challenge to, 4–5
Knowledge, spiritual, 32–33
Krauss, Lawrence, 300–301
Kuttner, Henry, 238

Land of the Lost, 270
Lane, John R., 151
Lanterns, 127–129
Larmor, Joseph, 171
Lawrence, D. H., 197–198
Laws, natural, 15–16
Leadbeater, Charles, 78–79, 88–89, 95, 157–158
Leary, Timothy, 275
Lee, Stan, 238
L'Engle, Madeleine, 9, 225, 227–248, 310; gender and, 228–229, 242–248; and impulse to live in otherworlds, 247–248; influence of, 240, 245; influences on, 228, 231, 233, 242, 293; on suspension of disbelief, 253;

use of science, 231, 236; use of tesseracts, 242; views on Christianity, 229–231; *A Wind in the Door*, 228; *A Wrinkle in Time*, 12, 228, 232–236, 238, 240, 242, 244, 270, 272
Lenin, Vladimir, 99
Lewis, C. S., 9, 11, 198, 208–225, 228, 310; *Christian Reflections*, 215; *The Dark Tower*, 183; depiction of girls, 244; on Dunne dreams, 183; in Great War, 209; influence of, 208; influences on, 196, 201, 210–211, 212, 213, 220; interest in other dimensions, 213–220; on MacDonald, 200; *Mere Christianity*, 214, 243; *On Miracles*, 213–214; Narnia chronicles, 220–225, 243; spiritual journey, 209–212; *That Hideous Strength*, 183; views of women, 242–243; *The Weight of Glory and Other Addresses*, 217
Liesegang, R. E., 251, 252
Life after Life (Moody), 306–307
Life of Jesus (Strauss), 16, 32
Light of Asia, The (Arnold), 134–135
Linde, Andrei, 300
Lippmann, Walter, 102
Lipsey, Roger, 158
Literary imagination, 246–247
Longing, 220
Loos, Adolf, 118
Love, 272–273, 291
Lovecraft, H. P., 237
Luhan, Mabel Dodge, 155–156
Lux, Fritz, 252
Lyell, Charles, 15

MacDonald, George, 198, 225; background, 199–203; influence of, 196, 201, 202, 203, 210, 212, 220, 228; influences on, 208; interest in other dimensions, 205–207; *Lilith*, 205–207; *Phantastes*, 196, 201–202, 203

Nationalism, 130
Natural, belief in, 1–2
Nature, 115; complexity of, 5–6; as reflection of divine, 106; Romantics' view of, 25; spiritual in, 137
Nature (journal), 64
NDEs (near-death experiences), 307–308
N-dimensional geometries, 24
Near-death experiences (NDEs), 307–308
Neoplatonism, 156–157, 212
Neville, E. H., 57
Newcomb, Simon, 57–58, 65
Newland, John, 262
Newman, James R., 65
New Thought, 79, 80
New York Central Railroad Station, 115–117
Night view, 26
Nolan, Christopher, 240, 272–273
North, Percy, 151

Observer 1, 176
Observer 2, 176, 177, 184
Occult, revival of, 77
Ocularcentrism, modernity associated with, 81
Olsen, Bob, 233, 235
Onassis, Jacqueline Kennedy, 247
One Step Beyond, 262–263, 264–265
Openings, 221–222, 228, 229
Optical delusions, 35, 36
Optical illusions, 25
Origin of Species (Darwin), 31–32, 35, 91
Ornamentation, 116–117, 118–123, 137
Otherworlds, 233; longing for, 247–248, 249; Many Worlds Interpretation (MWI), 297–298, 300; seen via television, 256; television depictions of, 271–272
Ouspensky, Pieter, 62, 84–86, 95–96, 187, 237, 241

Outer Limits, The, 258, 259–260, 266–274
Over-soul, 107

Pagans, 280–281
Pageantry movement, 132
Paley, William, 31
Parapsychological researchers, 303
Particles, elementary, 6
Past, 11. *See also* Time
Pasteur, Louis, 204
Patterson, Charles Brodie, 80–81, 88
Paul, Saint, 38
Pearson, Norman, 253
Penczak, Christopher, 280–281
Peters, John, 273
Philosophers, 178
Physicists, 7–8, 295–303
Physicists, hippie, 7, 301–303
Physics, 7–8, 213–214
Picasso, Pablo, 149–150, 152, 158–159, 160
Pittenger, Norman, 216
Place, Bennett's sense of, 169–172
Planck, Max, 6
Planiverse, The (Dewdney), 288–289
Plato, 151, 152, 156, 212, 220
Platonists, 211–212, 289
Poltergeist (film), 273
Polyhedroids, 119, 120
Portals, 258; in television shows, 270; in *Twilight Zone*, 258–266
Pratt Institute, 143–144
Preiswerk, Samuel, 73
Priestley, J. B., 11, 172, 186–196, 197, 257; *The Good Companion*, 186; letters on unusual time experiences, 194–196; *Man and Time*, 189; and redemptive theory of time, 193; on time, 186; *Time and the Conways*, 188–191; Time Plays, 188–191
Progressive era, 123, 124, 129
Proof of Heaven (Alexander), 308
Psychedelic Experience, The (Leary), 275–276

Psychic events, 303
Psychic visions, 262–263
Puritans, 144–145
Pype, Katrien, 280

Quantum mechanics, 6, 7, 179, 295–298
Quantum mysticism, 301

Race, 11, 89, 92, 93–98, 129, 160–162, 354n47; Browne on dimensions and, 96–98; Du Bois on dimensions and, 93–95; modern art, the "primitive," and, 160–162; Theosophical ideas on, 95–96; Toomer on dimensions and, 95–96
Racism, higher dimensions as refuge from, 96
Railroads, 116
Raudive, Konstantin, 281
Rauscher, Elizabeth, 303
Raynal, Maurice, 160
Reagent, 178
Reality: consciousness and, 6–7; relation to symbols, 204; television and, 254–256
Reality confusion, 254–255, 262
Reform, 101, 123, 124, 132
Relativity, 5, 6, 11, 171, 176–177, 179, 295–298
Religion: decline in, 1–2, 13, 14; Dunne and, 180–181, 192; empiricism and, 192–193; eye's connection with, 31; Lewis's spiritual journey, 209–212; and literary imagination, 246–247; relation with science, 4; *Twilight Zone* and, 266. *See also* Christianity; God; Judaism; Theology
Religious universalism, 72–73
Resurrection, 37–38, 216
Rhine, J. B., 179, 193
Rhine, Louisa, 193
Riemann, Bernhard, 24, 54

Roberts, Oral, 278–279
Romantics, 36, 200, 247
Romantics, German, 25
Rose, Rosella, 256
Rowland, Henry, 58
Rucker, Rudy, 290–292
Russ, Joanna, 244
Russak, Marie, 115
Russell, Bertrand, 53, 65
Russia, 98–100

Sagan, Carl, 287, 298
San Francisco Call (newspaper), 145
Sanity, fourth dimension and, 59–62
Santayana, George, 54, 246
Sayers, Dorothy, 242
Schermerhorn, Catherine, 103–104
Schiller, F. C. S., 178
Schofield, Alfred, 72
Schomburg, Arthur A., 97
Schreiber, Klaus, 282
Science: challenge to knowledge, 4–5; explaining, 298, 300; L'Engle's use of, 231, 236; relation with religious views, 1–13; repurposed in popular culture, 4; role in imaginative life, 2; spiritual assurance in, 73–74; theories of higher dimensions, 295–301. *See also* Technology
Science (journal), 54, 57
Science fiction: gender in, 241; spiritual power of, 291
Science Fiction Theater, 260
Scientific American (journal), 56, 57
Sconce, Jeffrey, 260
Screens, 127–129
Second Boer War, 174
Seeing, 155; in Abbott's *Flatland*, 29–38; Darwin on, 31–32; Helmholtz on, 32. *See also* Hinton, C. Howard; Vision
Seeing, spiritual, 37, 29–38, 75–82
Seeley, John, 17
Seers, Abbott on, 36–37

Supernatural (*continued*)
23–24, 32–39; artists on the
supernatural or spiritual, 156–159;
Dunne's conception of, 179–181,
191–194; Lewis's conception of,
113–120; in Narnia books, 222–224;
in pop culture, 304–305; Rod
Serling's interest in, 266; supernatural fiction, 197–214, 220–226,
237; supernatural imagination on
television, 251–254, 258–266, 268,
278–283; supernatural seeing in
Abbott, 32–40
Supernatural, scientific, 4, 192,
300–301, 352n 30
Superstitions, 55
Swedenborg, Emmanuel, 200, 202
Sylvester, J. J., 54, 63–64
Symbols, 204, 218

Tagesansicht, 26
Tait, Peter, 65
Targ, Russell, 303
Tart, Charles, 137
Technologies, visual, 82
Technology: and communication
across dimensions, 75; to see into
invisible, 155; spiritual assurance in,
73–74
Telescopes, 155
Television, 249–283; associated with
mysterious powers, 262; *Buffy the
Vampire Slayer*, 305; contacting dead
and, 281–283; depictions of women
on, 263–265; doorways and,
271–272; drug culture and, 275–277;
as extension of senses, 252; ghosts
in, 256; *Land of the Lost*, 270; new
spiritual sensibilities fostered by,
252–253; new ways of imagining
supernatural, 253; *One Step Beyond*,
262–263, 264–265; *The Outer Limits*,
259, 266–274; patron saint, 262; as
portal, 258–275; possessed, 257–258;

reality and, 254–256; reality
confusion and, 262; seeing otherworlds via, 256; sense of mystery
surrounding, 251–252; spiritual
energies in, 250–258; spiritual
transmission and, 278–282; and
suspension of disbelief, 253;
transformations caused by,
250–251, 274–278; *The Twilight Zone*,
258–266; visual perception and, 254
Television Ghost, The, 257
Tennyson, Alfred, 35
Tesseracts, 12, 45–46, 119, 234–242;
gender and, 242; in *Interstellar*, 273;
L'Engle's use of, 242
Theater, 133–135
Theology: challenged by science, 4–5;
mathematics and, 42–43. *See also*
Christianity; God; Religion
Theology, geometric, 216
Theosophical Society, 78, 104
Theosophy, 78, 91, 95, 97, 111, 115,
118, 133, 134, 157–158, 253
Thompson, J. J., 171
Thring, Edward, 50
Throesch, Elizabeth, 204
Tilton, Robert, 279
Time, 11; Bennett's sense of, 169–172;
dreams and, 193–194; Priestley on,
186; problem of, 172; redemptive
theory of, 193; Relativity, 176–177;
spacetime, 177; transcendence of,
179. *See also* Dunne, John
Tolkien, J. R. R., 11, 183–184, 198, 199,
201, 213, 225, 255
Toomer, Jean, 95–96
Tradition, 141, 159, 164–167
Transcendentalism, 118
Transcendental Physics (Slade), 74
Transpositions, 218
Trautman, Fritz, 108–109
Travers, Jerome, 256
Trinity, 214–216, 292
Truth, 64, 286

Women (*continued*)
  Hinton's views on, 91; Lewis's
  views of, 242–244; linked to
  higher-dimensional thinking, 90;
  marriage and, 47; in mythology,
  229; rethinking roles of, 90–93;
  spirituality of, 136; as villains,
  243. *See also* Gender; L'Engle;
  Sex/sexuality
Wordsworth, William, 36
World's Fair, 135–137
Worldview, 5. *See also* Change, social
World War I. *See* Great War
Wright, Fanny, 131

Wrinkle in Time, A (L'Engle), 12, 228,
  232–236, 238, 240, 242, 244, 270,
  272

X-rays, 82, 155

Yeats, George, 77
Yeats, W. B., 77
Yokohama, Japan, 51

Zamir, Shamoon, 95
Zarin, Cynthia, 245
Zollner, Johann Karl Friedrich, 74–75,
  158, 203